A Theology of the Living Church

A

THEOLOGY

OF THE

LIVING CHURCH

By L. HAROLD DeWOLF

HARPER & BROTHERS   PUBLISHERS   NEW YORK

Library of Congress catalog card number: 53–5989

To
MADELEINE

CONTENTS

PART ONE PRESUPPOSITIONS OF A
CHRISTIAN THEOLOGY

FIRST SECTION: Theological Knowledge

SECOND SECTION: Theism

PART FOUR MAN

PART SIX THE KINGDOM AND THE CHURCH

ACKNOWLEDGMENTS

THE reader of these pages will see that I am indebted to a numerous company. It would be impossible to name them all. I shall have to limit myself to a few persons who have had most directly to do with the actual preparation of this volume.

Several students in my classes have made useful criticisms of various chapters and Miss Clarice Bowman, especially, gave me valuable suggestions. My revered teacher and predecessor, Dean Emeritus Albert C. Knudson, has been especially loyal and helpful throughout the writing and painstakingly commented on the whole work. Miss Dean Hosken also read the entire manuscript and made more than a score of discerning criticisms, nearly all of which elicited revisions in form of statement and one a significant addition in substance.

I am also grateful to the three men who especially encouraged me to undertake and persevere in this work—Dean Walter G. Muelder, and Professors Edgar S. Brightman and Nels F. S. Ferré. They are not responsible for my failure to accomplish all for which they must have hoped.

Dr. Jannette E. Newhall has given invaluable assistance in the Library of Boston University School of Theology. Miss Dorothy Lord has made available important secretarial assistance.

Most of all I am indebted to my wife, who, despite her many responsibilities in home and community, typed all these thousands of words and helped with innumerable details. To her the book is dedicated.

I am grateful to Henry Holt and Company for permission to quote from *John Calvin: The Man and His Ethics* by Georgia Harkness and to Earl B. Marlatt for permission to quote from his hymn, "Are Ye Able."

The scriptural quotations in this publication are, with some indicated exceptions, from the *Revised Standard Version of the Bible*, copyrighted 1952 by the Division of Christian Education, National Council of Churches, and are used by permission, which is gratefully acknowledged.

L. Harold DeWolf

Newtonville, Massachusetts
February 20, 1953

MEMORIAL NOTE

After the type was set for this volume I received word that Edgar Sheffield Brightman had gone from earth. The publishers have kindly permitted me to add this note.

As my teacher, major adviser in doctoral studies, faculty colleague and unfailing friend, Professor Brightman did more for me than words can express.

In him the philosopher's candid search for truth and the Christian's obedient faith in God were one. In death as in life he has brought a clearer vision of the Heavenly City to both Athens and Jerusalem.

L. HAROLD DeWOLF

PART ONE

PRESUPPOSITIONS
OF A CHRISTIAN THEOLOGY

CHAPTER 1

The Task of Theology

IN the midst of the world's tyranny, oppression and fear a wonderful story once began and spread like wildfire from village to village and from nation to nation. Those who told it called it "the good news" and they were so full of its wonder and gladness that even the sternest commands and harshest punishments of emperors could not stop the telling of it. So revolutionary was their message and its power that guardians of the old order said to one another, "They are turning the world upside down." So they were. By the influence of their faith slaves were freed, cruel oppressors were brought down from their thrones, the poor were assisted, the ill were healed, little children were made to laugh and sing as never before and the timid were enabled to face death with triumphant serenity and even with fierce joy.

One striking result of all this great new power in the world was that those who experienced it in their lives invariably banded themselves together in loyal, intimate fellowship. So strong were the ties which the believers of the story felt for one another that their comradeship broke over all the barriers of age, sex, class and nation. They formed a single body, sensitive in every part to the weakness and strength, the sorrow and joy of every other. "The church" they called it, while even their cynical persecutors exclaimed in wonder, "See how these Christians love one another!"

Even after the passage of many centuries, today millions of human beings, both learned and ignorant, rich and poor, put their trust in the ancient story. To these people, who call themselves Christians, the story and the life of the church which has risen from the faith in that story give the clue to solving both the deepest problems of the philosophers and the most stubborn practical difficulties of men and nations.

The theoretical questions and the problems of conduct take new forms in every age. Hence in every age the meaning of the Christian faith must be re-examined in relation to the changing thought and experience of mankind. Such a task of interpretation and testing has been performed wherever men have loved truth and have taken the Christian faith seriously enough to think it worth examining. This work includes both the theoretical task of systematic statement, critical evaluation and rational defense and the practical task of translating the meanings of the faith into personal and corporate commitment and appropriate action. The theoretical work is Systematic Theology.

Systematic Theology is the critical discipline devoted to discovering, expounding and defending the more important truths implied in the experience of the Christian community.

This definition differs considerably from many which have been stated in other works on this subject. Some explanation and defense should be offered.

A. A CRITICAL TASK

Especially would many writers object to speaking of theology as critical. The traditional definitions often describe it as a "science," [1] but do not mean to suggest by this that its content is subject to independent critical judgment. The content has been widely regarded as given "once and for all" in ancient revelation, or as having developed in the life of the church in such a way that it would now be presumptuous or impious for the theologian to propose changes in its doctrinal substance. Therefore, it is supposed, the theologian's task is to expound, systematize and defend [2] the traditional doctrine, but not to add, subtract nor criticize.

Even the thinkers who have exercised a large measure of critical originality and have not hesitated to reject ancient doctrines when new evidence showed them to be untenable, have nevertheless shown a marked reluctance to avow a critical purpose in defining their subject. Thus, such vigorous and independent thinkers as William Adams Brown and Albert C. Knudson define Christian theology in terms hardly suggesting such critical treatment as they actually give to the subject.[3]

Actually all theology is critical, whether avowedly and rationally so or not. This is attested by the wide disagreement among theologians, even among the Roman Catholic writers and among the most conservative Protestants, by their denunciations of opposing views and by the historical origination of doctrines in theological writings, even of such conservative defenders of tradition as Augustine, Aquinas, Luther, Calvin and Karl Barth. Each writer uses some set of standards for judgment. These standards differ greatly and often they are hidden, but they are invariably present. No theologian accepts every doctrine

[1] So Thomas Aquinas, many times in Part I of the *Summa Theologica.* Cf. A. H. Strong, and William B. Pope.

[2] Karl Barth is one who insists that it must not be defended. All his polemical writings are a kind of defense, nevertheless. See his *Credo,* pp. 185–86.

[3] See Brown, *Christian Theology in Outline,* pp. 3, 4, and Knudson, *The Doctrine of God,* p. 19. In this and many other instances, additional bibliographical data concerning books cited in footnotes will be found in the Bibliography at the end of this volume.

which has been taught as revealed. Much has been added to the body of Christian teaching by the original thought of theological writers.

Theology is critical. There are distinct advantages in stating this fact in the definition and keeping it steadily in mind throughout the investigation.

By this means our study can be prevented from being confused with a mere description of traditions without regard to their truth. History of doctrine is an important discipline but taken alone it is not of much help to the person seeking a system of truth by which to live. The history of Christian thought sets forth ideas far too promiscuous and mutually contradictory to qualify for indiscriminate acceptance.

Again, by openly professing the critical nature of theology its students may do something to bring to it more respect from people who are not accustomed to believing everything they hear. Much of theological writing shows little sustained, orderly effort to distinguish between truth and falsehood. Hence it does not commend itself to thoughtful minds sincerely eager to find truth and avoid error. It therefore behooves the theological writer who intends to "test everything; hold fast what is good," [4] to say so clearly from the beginning of his work.

Finally, a critical intention candidly avowed at the start may be expected to promote clarity of purpose and directness of approach. These are values not to be despised. Surely truth is more likely to be discovered and effectively taught when sought with clear purpose and set forth with candid directness than when treated with obscurity and pious evasion.

B. THE DISCIPLINE OF THEOLOGY

Theology has often been known as a science and even as "queen of the sciences." [5] This is quite proper if the meaning is not misunderstood. The writer has no scruples against it. However, in the formal definition, to avoid the narrowing connotation which modern usage has often attached to the word "science," theology has been called a "critical discipline," instead. The necessity of its being critical has been briefly set forth. It must be emphasized also that it is a discipline.

A curious notion of our proudly scientific age is that in the most important matters "one man's opinion is as good as another's." Yet this age has produced appalling evidence that some views of men and nations lead to almost incredible chaos and desolation. Some opinions are not so good as others. Indeed, some are monstrously false. In matters of ethics, metaphysics and theology, as well as in matters of chemistry and biology, only that man who pays the price of learning

[4] I Thess. 5:21. For quotations from the English Bible the Revised Standard Version of 1946 and 1952 will be used except as otherwise noted.

[5] Cf. the able argument for the treatment of theology as a science in Alan Richardson, *Christian Apologetics.*

the relevant data, mastering the needed critical procedures and persisting in the loyal quest of truth earns the right to have his opinions seriously regarded.

Theology has the reputation of being difficult. In part this reputation is a result of bad writing by some theologians. On the other hand, it must not be expected that a critical study of weighty problems which have most occupied many great minds, ancient and modern, can be effectively pursued without the paying of a price. The effort required is, in the main, of three kinds.

First, there is the intellectual effort of learning a wide range of relevant facts, following with sympathetic understanding some of the various, opposing interpretations of the facts, patiently evaluating the worth of these arguments and drawing appropriate conclusions.

Second, there is the moral and spiritual task of living the kind of life in which the relevant data are to be found. The data of religion can be no more effectively evaluated without entering into the disciplines of prayer and self-denial than the evidences of astronomy can be properly evaluated without giving attention to the instruments, charts and tables by which celestial observations and computations are made and recorded. Christian theology, well expounded, should be reasonably *intelligible* to an educated and diligent student who is not a Christian. But many of its evidences are not likely to seem *convincing* to him unless some Christian who witnesses to their truth has become for him an authority in such matters. Even then the evidence will take on new significance when he commits himself to "the Way" and shares the experience of the Christian community.

There are really minimal and maximal requirements in this matter. At the least, the student must disarm himself of hostility and defensive prejudice so that his mind will be open. Religious ideas, like other ideas having to do with deeply personal experiences and relationships, must be entertained with at least tentative sympathy in order to be understood. It seems fair to ask of every reader a self-disciplined exercise of this receptive and imaginative open-mindedness. It is not fair to expect a person not committed to the Christian faith to make an all-embracing, momentous and decisive commitment to it without reason. But it can be added that those who have, by an open-minded reception and evaluation of the evidence, found reason to meet the maximum requirements of faith and have given themselves in unstinted devotion, have discovered then a wealth of evidence previously unknown to them.

Finally, this pursuit requires the discipline of dispassionate objectivity in which prejudices are discounted and the love of truth overmatches every opposing motive. If any believer is afraid to subject his belief to this kind of single-minded truth-seeking, his fear betrays the fact that he has already ceased to accept it as true. What he calls his belief is his desire or his public profession, but it is no longer his belief when he dares not to search with all his powers for the fullest truth concerning it. This is why Tennyson was right in saying,

> There lives more faith in honest doubt,
> Believe me, than in half the creeds.[6]

C. THE SCOPE OF CHRISTIAN THEOLOGY

All specialized studies, if pressed persistently enough, bring the student into some consideration of problems and data lying outside their distinctive fields. Thus the serious botanist, astronomer and physicist all find themselves confronting problems in chemistry, mathematics and logic and no thorough sociologist can avoid questions of psychology, economics and ethics. But this fact of the overlapping and interpenetration of the various subjects does not make botany identical with chemistry nor sociology with economics. To this general rule, theology is no exception.

Christian systematic theology unavoidably and properly is in mutual interdependence with various other disciplines. But the distinctive, central area of its specialization is the experience of the Christian community. To be sure, much experience of Christians is like the experience of everyone else, just as many characteristics of living plants are like those of all other physical objects. But just as the botanist concentrates his attention on those problems and data of living plants which are peculiarly characteristic of them, so the Christian theologian devotes his thought primarily to the problems and data which are peculiarly relevant to the Christian community.

His data embrace the Bible, the history of Christianity—including external events, recorded personal experiences and past theological writings—and the present religious experience of himself and others. His problems are those which most concern the Christian community. He will not be disturbed when he finds these problems leading him into areas shared with philosophy, psychology, sociology and physics, nor will he fail to employ important relevant data from the other disciplines. On the other hand, he will make his best contribution to the whole field of knowledge as well as to his chosen area if he persistently concentrates attention on the problems and experiences belonging peculiarly to his special province.

From what has been said it will be obvious that systematic theology is most immediately dependent on the following related disciplines: Biblical studies, church history, history of doctrine, psychology of religion and sociology of religion. No less intimate is its relation to philosophy of religion. Philosophy of religion is a critical search for truth in all the religions of the world. It deals

[6] *In Memoriam,* 96:3.

especially with problems and data which occur in all religions, or at least in several. Systematic theology is a more specialized study of that particular religion known as Christianity. Each of these two studies is of great aid to the other.

One part of the definition may seem particularly vague, namely, the phrase "the experience of the Christian community." [7] A really precise explanation of the Christian community would necessarily presuppose a great amount of theological labor already done. Not the easiest problem of our subject will be the refining of that very concept near the end of the present volume. However, it can be pointed out that in the definition it is used very broadly. It is an ecumenical or catholic concept. It refers not merely to "good" or "orthodox" Christians, much less to members of some particular denomination, Catholic or Protestant. Until such time as good reason for limitation may appear, it includes the experience of all persons who are bound together with other persons in the profession of a religious faith which they or others call Christian. This does not mean that all who are called Christians are so, much less that the experiences of all professed Christians are of equal theological value. It is only insisted that the distinction between true and false Christians or between more and less significant experiences, will need to come forth as a *result* of critical study, not as a *presupposition* to it.

Finally, something must be said about the meaning of the word "implied." In the definition, reference is made to "the more important truths implied in the experience of the Christian community." It might be supposed that all the beliefs and practices of Christians were to be taken at face value as premises from which conclusions might be drawn. This would, of course, constitute a denial of the intention to make this study critical. In the history of the church and of theology many doctrines have been tried out theoretically and practically. This testing has produced much evidence against many of them as well as data of a more favorable character. The negative implications will be relevant to our study as well as the positive evidences. People called Christians have given many horrible examples of beliefs and practices which ought not to be embraced, as well as other examples of ennobling truth in thought and life. We should profit by both kinds of experience.

D. The Problem of Method

The method to be relied upon for the gaining of truth is an important problem for the systematic theologian. Particularly, the relations between reason, revelation and faith must undergo careful study. These relations will occupy our attention in the next three chapters.

[7] Cf. Charles C. Morrison's statement that the theology of the early church "was the church's explanation of its own existence." *What Is Christianity?* (New York: Harper & Brothers, 1940), p. 179.

CHAPTER 2

Reason and Certainty

A. THE DEMAND FOR CERTAINTY

WHENEVER any religious doctrine is presented, some hearer is bound to raise the question whether the doctrine is known certainly to be true. Even little children, under Christian instruction, often ask their teachers, "Are you sure that is so?" or "How do you know?" Such questions are asked with renewed intensity after young people are taught critical methods of distinguishing truth from error in the natural sciences, history and other studies. Again in hours of sorrow or at times of such moral decision as requires of religious faith an ultimate determining role, the questions occur with new emphasis. Sometimes they are asked of a minister or priest, often of an intimate friend and yet oftener in the private stillness of the heart. But silently or in words, from people young and old the urgent questions rise, "How can we be sure?" "Is there any way that I can *know*?"

Sometimes the priest answers such queries with the command to say a few "Our Fathers" and "Hail Marys," adding the good-natured assurance that "Everything will be all right." Or the minister solemnly warns against the sin of doubt and commands belief on authority of the Bible and on pain of divine punishment. Some such pastors would be surprised to learn with what sadness their confessants and questioners have reported these events to their college teachers and how wistfully they have sought for evidence. They have been asking not for commands but for knowledge whether there was any real authority behind the commands, not for terms of forgiveness—though freely admitting that forgiveness was needed—but for evidence that there existed in very truth a God from whom forgiveness might be sought. The plea of such questioners is not for autosuggestion or any kind of emotional assurance. It is plainly and simply a plea for truth and the evidences by which it may be known as truth. Is it not the business of clergymen and, indeed, of all intelligent Christians, to know how to answer such queries? And does not this task demand the examination by careful reasoning of the great doctrines and problems of the Christian faith?

But a major difficulty confronts us at once. Is human reason capable of attaining such certainty as the doubters seek? Before this question can be answered, or even clearly understood, we must consider what reason is and what are its resources.

B. THE MEANING OF REASON

Broadly conceived, reason is any mental activity self-directed for the purpose of attaining truth. When the question is raised whether human reason can attain certainty in religious matters the problem does not always concern merely some particular kind of intellectual activity. It is being asked frequently whether there is any process by which human thinkers can discover truth about matters of religion and know that truth with certainty. But in order to answer, it is necessary to observe some of the particular methods by which proof is achieved or attempted.

Sometimes reason is defined narrowly in terms of a specific procedure, and as a condition of belief proof of a particular kind is demanded. For example, a doubter may require a rationalistic demonstration like the proofs of geometry. Again he may demand the immediate testimony of his own senses and regard belief in anything not capable of being seen or touched as unreasonable credulity. Or perhaps it is the experimental method of the natural sciences on which exclusive reliance is placed. In any event the powers of human thought to find and recognize the truth with certainty cannot be evaluated in general abstraction, but only in terms of the specific methods which men can employ. Fortunately, the various methods have been criticized so thoroughly by others that the present treatment can be brief.

1. *Rationalistic or "Geometrical" Method*

When Descartes observed how general was the agreement of mathematicians and how steady the progress of their science and when he contrasted the disagreement and repetition of ancient theories among the philosophers, he concluded that what philosophy lacked was a sufficiently clear and sure method. He tried to provide a way of constructing philosophical proof as sure as mathematical demonstrations and similar in principle. He would doubt all that could be doubted and upon the foundation of his indubitable proposition, "I think, therefore I am," he would rear his system of knowledge.

Unfortunately for his method, much was being assumed by Descartes besides his proposition, "I think." Indeed he admitted this, saying,

I did not therefore deny that it was necessary to know what thought, existence. and certitude are, and the truth that, in order to think it is necessary to be, and the like; but, because these are the most simple notions, and such as of themselves afford the knowledge of nothing existing, I did not judge it proper there to enumerate them.[1]

He assumed that these ideas were inborn and "that such are not to be reckoned among the cognitions acquired by study,"[2] a highly questionable assumption. Moreover, it is hardly reasonable to suppose that knowledge about existing realities can best be gained by a method which deliberately discards all testimony of the senses and all the evidences of inner experience. As Immanuel Kant showed, analytical knowledge of abstractions could be so gained, but not knowledge of existing reality. Much earlier, Thomas Aquinas had briefly but effectively criticized and rejected the one serious theological effort to use the abstract analytical method of mathematics in support of a Christian belief, namely, Anselm's ontological argument.[3] If a human mind is to know existing reality, some existing data, that is, some actual experiences, must be employed as evidence. Otherwise there is no way of knowing that a transition has been made from the cognition of purely fictitious objects to cognition of real, existing beings.

To be sure, like Augustine, Descartes could have found good evidence, in experience, that he doubted and therefore existed.[4] But he rejected experienced perceptions as unreliable and so he sought to build on the necessities of sheer rational indubitability. He thus fatally narrowed the avowed base of his philosophy and removed it from contact with existence. He only seemed to succeed in overcoming this handicap by adding many unproved postulates presumed to be innate, by the illicit leaps of his subsequent deductions, and by quickly bringing back perceptual experience, its reliability "proved" by these questionable abstract procedures.

Similarly Spinoza's "geometrical method" only seems to succeed in establishing knowledge of existence by a method of pure rational deduction. Actually the essentials of his system are implicitly assumed with no proof whatever, in his "definitions" and "axioms."[5]

A knowledge of any reality, whether material or spiritual, could only be gained, if at all, by some method which employed evidence given to the thinking self by reality, in experience—whether experience of itself or of other being.

[1] *The Principles of Philosophy*, I.x.
[2] *Ibid.*
[3] *Summa Theologica*, I, Ques. 2, Art. 1, Reply Obj. 2.
[4] Cf. Augustine, *On the Trinity*, XV.12.21.
[5] E.g., see his *Ethics*, Definition 3 and Axiom 3.

2. Sense Perception

The prominence of sense perceptions in the development of our knowledge and the feeling of assurance which we usually have concerning objects seen or handled give rise naturally to the demand for sensory evidence in every field. Many a modern doubter says with Thomas,

Unless I see in his hands the print of the nails, and place my finger in the mark of the nails, and place my hand in his side, I will not believe.[6]

If the voice of the dead is not heard to speak and if God is not seen with the physical eyes they will regard the existence of God and the immortality of man as unproved.

Yet no man consistently exacts such a test in other areas of his belief. Who requires the sensory proof of counting objects, before granting that $1,000^2 = 1,000,000$? Does the doubter doubt that doubting occurs? Doubting is not seen, touched, heard, smelled nor tasted. To be sure, the positivist may say that he knows none of these things but only the sensory qualities of which he is immediately conscious. Yet every word that he utters is an emphatic assertion of his belief that his own mind exists, that he thinks thoughts worth expressing, that other minds also exist, that through written or spoken words ideas can be communicated, and many other affirmations. If he insists that such practical belief is not "knowledge," it must be replied that every statement he makes concerning any subject, even regarding the limitations of knowledge, is nevertheless asserting a judgment with at least as great conviction as that attached to his acknowledged affirmations. If he chooses to reserve the word "knowledge" for some other kind of cognition, very well. But he should not be surprised if his philosophizing about that "knowledge" is thereafter regarded by most men as a game quite detached from the serious business of life. The faith which he affirms by taking the trouble to talk and write is more significant than the skeptical propositions he more weakly affirms in a theory by which he does not propose to live.

Sense perception would seem to be a highly important means of contact with the realm of being which is not the knower himself. We have found evidence that it is not very helpful if taken alone. It requires organization and criticism in order to be useful.

3. Experimental Method

So great have been the accomplishments of the sciences by use of the experimental method, that this method has naturally been put forward by some as the one way in which truth is to be assured.

[6] Jn. 20:25.

In the rigorous mode of employment through which its greatest successes have been won, the experimental method seems hardly applicable to the problems about which the theologian is most concerned. For as employed in the natural sciences the method requires the isolation of a single change from all others and the observance of precisely measured results. Such a method works well when the question concerns the effect of penicillin on a bacillus or of a great nearby mass on a ray of light. It may even be used with somewhat modified rigor to determine the average effects of specific rewards and punishments on the learning of primary children. But how will it be employed to determine whether there is a purpose controlling the entire world process? By actual trial one may roughly determine the effect of a discipline of prayer on the lives of individuals, but the controls can hardly make possible, in this instance, such isolation of the one factor—discipline of prayer—as to constitute the test a genuine example of experimental method in the scientific sense. "Experimental religion" may be a magnificent adventure, but it is not experimental science. And even if we could determine precisely what were the effects of prayer, isolated from all other factors, what experiment would prove the truth or falsehood of the belief that the conscious self goes on after the death of the body?

4. Pragmatic Method

Somewhat analogous to experiment but less rigid in form is the dependence on practical consequences. There are many kinds of pragmatic theories and methods.[7] This is not the place either to make an exact classification of them or to criticize them in detail. A few general observations will suffice to direct us to a more inclusive conception of reason.

Few would seriously question that if one is dealing with problems about right conduct the evaluation of consequences is important. The difference in moral intent and value between offering to a man who has done me harm an open hand of friendship and pulling the trigger of a loaded pistol pointed at him is due to the difference in probably predictable consequences. It is not so evident that the difference in the truth of rival solutions of problems in non-Euclidean geometry is due to differences in consequences. To be sure, a conclusion is often called a "consequence" but here the word is used to mean logical implication and not result of causation. Sometimes the test of consequences is described in such broad terms that it becomes almost, if not quite synonymous with the criterion of coherence,[8] about to be described.

In any event we seem hardly entitled to assume in advance that any proposition or course of action, commitment to which brings consequences of some

---

[7] See A. O. Lovejoy, "The Thirteen Pragmatisms," *Jour. Phil.*, Vol. 5.
[8] Cf. John Dewey, *Logic: A System of Inquiry*, p. 13.

prescribed kind, will always be true or right. Nor does any good reason appear why considerations other than consequences should be ruled out in advance of examination.

5. *Comprehensive Coherence*

One of the commonest meanings of reason and also one of the most highly commended in philosophical circles is the process of examining an idea or object in the widest possible context of thought and experience. He who uses the reason of comprehensive coherence will accept as most probably true that proposed solution of a problem which is, on the whole, supported by the greatest net weight of evidence from all quarters. It is assumed that the truth is not actually contradicted by experience nor by other truth and that we can have evidence of the truth of an idea only through its significant relation to some experience.

Thus we believe it is not true that all horses are white, because some experiences contradict such an idea. Again, we have no reason to accept the proposition that a planet 14,500 miles in diameter revolves around the star Sirius. There are no experiences which contradict the idea that such a planet exists but there are no experiences to which it is sufficiently related to give it significant support. Experience does uphold the proposition that most random ideas unsupported by any evidence are false, and only a credulous fool would try to believe every proposition which is not flatly contradicted by experience. On the other hand, we believe that all mammals require oxygen if they are to live, for we have no experiences of mammals living without oxygen, much experience of mammals breathing oxygen and a vast structure of systematized information and theory about physiology, chemistry, pathology and other subjects, all positively related to the belief that oxygen is required to maintain the life of every mammal.

The reason of comprehensive coherence seems the most adequate rational instrument for discerning truth. Its superiority to more abstract and limited procedures is especially evident in dealing with the problems which are of chief concern in religion. Religion has to do with a man's relation to the whole of existence. To deny a hearing to any kind of data, by a prior limitation of method, when dealing with religious problems, would therefore be at the risk of losing truth. For the kind of data excluded might bring evidence from some aspect of the great totality of being especially significant or even decisive for a problem concerning the whole. For example, if the student of theology is concerned with the question whether God cares for him and the student decides in advance to leave out of consideration the materials in the New Testament, he is making a decision which as a lover of truth he has no right to make. How seriously he ought to regard the statements of the New Testament he is hardly in a position to know until he has given careful consideration to them.[9]

But however favorably a theologian may regard the method of comprehensive coherence as compared with other forms of rational inquiry, he has yet to raise the question whether a complete and purely rational certainty can be gained by means of such a method. Can man, even by the most careful consideration of the widest possible circle of evidence, *prove beyond all rational doubt* any doctrine essential to Christian faith? Intimately related to this question is a broader one. Can any doctrine, religious or otherwise, which has to do with the real world, be proved with such absolute rational certainty? Obviously, if no belief concerning existence can be proved with absolute certainty the sensible man will scarcely look for this kind of proof in theology.

C. Dependence of Reason on Experience

If we are to know anything about existence, we must build our knowledge upon the data which existence thrusts into our experience. Without the support of experience, we can construct all kinds of elaborate images. But we have no reason to think that such dreams represent anything which exists outside our imaginations. Evidence of existence arises only from the impact of existence upon human consciousness. We cannot reason effectively about reality without considering the data of experience.

But here the seeker after certainty runs into difficulty. Our reasoned construction of knowledge is dependent upon the data. Yet the data are far from infallible. We see bent sticks in the water when the sticks are not bent—at least as they appear to be. We hear ringing sounds when the cause is no ringing but a drug in our blood streams. We are the victims of optical illusions, mirages of the desert, hallucinations and dreams. Even when our sensory powers are working under highly favorable conditions we see and feel solid, space-filling materials where the careful arguments of the scientists indicate there is a condition a thousand times nearer to a vacuum than to a plenum. Yet the scientist, too, is dependent on the data of those same senses which he has proved to be capable of error. How much further may our errors go than we have yet discerned?[10]

In the realm of subjective impressions our data are even more notoriously

[9] For a further comparison of comprehensive coherence with other rational methods in theology see my book, *The Religious Revolt against Reason*, pp. 187–203. Cf. also E. S. Brightman, *A Philosophy of Religion* and *Immortality in Post-Kantian Idealism*. For a defense of coherence and appeal to it by a conservative theologian, see Edward John Carnell, *An Introduction to Christian Apologetics*.

[10] The scientific formulas for discounting the "margin of error" do not answer this question, for they have to do only with the adventitious, variable errors, not the universal ones to which the human type of sensory equipment may equally subject us all at all times.

fallible than are the perceptions of our physical senses. Only a man who was both infinitely credulous and insanely capable of entertaining grotesquely contrary ideas in one mad confusion could accept at face value all the sincere reports of messages from "the spirit world," journeys into supernatural realms beyond space and time, and revelations of every fantastic being known or unknown to mythology. Reason depends on experience. Yet experience often misleads us.

We can, to be sure, correct some experience by other experience. This is part of the task and method of science and every critical quest of truth. But here another barrier presents itself. Often the most recently observed data correct our theories based on earlier experience. But how do we know that data yet to be observed—or never to be observed—by men are not of a kind to contradict our most carefully constructed knowledge?

The data experienced by any individual, and even those observed by the whole human race are limited. Vast areas of space and time are unexplored by human perception. Many kinds of reality are beyond the range of our senses. By means of instruments we have learned of oscillations occurring at a wide variety of frequencies in space—ultraviolet, radio, X rays and many others which can be neither seen nor heard by our senses. For many centuries men never suspected the existence of these realities. Until recent years who ever thought that the world contained such things as electrons? What other realities beyond the range of our senses remain yet undiscovered?

It must be noted that the most coherent available explanation may become untenable when new observations are taken into account. Who knows how much of the knowledge which now seems secure may be disproved by future extensions and refinements of our observations? What corrections of our present errors may we never be able to make because of inherent limitations of our human perceptual powers? Can we have certainty of knowledge in such a situation as ours?

D. Dependence on Unproved Postulates

Besides needing data of experience, reason also depends upon certain assumptions or postulates which no appeal to the data can establish and which reason cannot prove without assuming them while proof is attempted. We must assume the principle of consistency itself. If genuinely contradictory ideas can be true at once, then no argument for or against any conclusion whatever has the slightest force. Before we can learn much about existing reality we must also assume the validity of such basic categories of perception and thought as time, causality and quantity; likewise the essential integrity of our reasoning powers and their freedom to weigh evidence. Other postulates must also be assumed, as Lewis Carroll so delightfully shows in his humorous logical essay entitled "What the Tortoise Said to Achilles." [11]

Often our thought is radically influenced by other, gratuitous assumptions hidden even from ourselves. We approach every serious problem which involves important values, with certain predilections of emotional bias. We can and must, by sharing our thought with others and by ever-renewed personal discipline, control and discount such bias to the greatest possible degree. Yet in this process we often lean over backwards and fall into errors opposite those to which we were first inclined. Although we need not be free from strong emotional inclination in order to gain a high degree of methodological objectivity—as a physician need not be indifferent to his patient's condition in order to make an objective diagnosis—we can never be sure of having gained even that disciplined intellectual balance required for sound judgment.

E. ATTRACTIVENESS OF COMPLETE SKEPTICISM

As the ancient skeptic Carneades argued, we seem to be confronted with a tragic impossibility of proving anything whatsoever. For we must base every proof on premises already held. If we attempt to prove the premises we must proceed from other assumed premises. Eventually we shall be driven back upon premises which are assumed without proof. If we seek a way out by basing an argument on data of experience we are stopped by the discovery that only interpreted data can be so used and interpretations may be mistaken.

This ancient argument for complete skepticism has been repeated, with variations, by many philosophers. Yet no philosopher has been able to stop with complete skepticism. Thus the ancient Carneades followed his skeptical proofs with a doctrine of probabilities by which one may live in the absence of certainty. Similarly George Santayana, after arguing persuasively for the proposition that nothing can be known, advocated "animal faith." [12]

F. IMPOSSIBILITY OF SKEPTICISM

The reason why no philosopher has embraced and taught a complete skepticism is that it is impossible to do so. To believe that nothing can be known is to believe that even the meaning, to say nothing of the truth, of this belief cannot be known—an obviously self-contradictory absurdity. If that initial difficulty could be overcome there would still be no point in teaching the skeptical doctrine. To teach it would be to assert that the instructor knew some purpose for doing so and knew that a person existed to whom it could be taught, but such

---

[11] See Lewis Carroll, *Logical Nonsense*, pp. 501–4. See also W. J. Rees, "What Achilles Said to the Tortoise." *Mind*, 1951, pp. 241–46.

[12] See his *Skepticism and Animal Faith*.

knowledge would contradict the doctrine itself. If all these difficulties could somehow be hurdled, the skeptic would still teach an opposite view by every practical decision he made—whether to eat or starve, live or die. For every practical decision is an assertion of knowledge that there is value in what is decided, an assertion more emphatic than any theoretical statement as such.

G. Conclusions

The following conclusions now seem in order:

First, absolute, proved certainty on any problem concerning reality is not attainable. (This conclusion and those that follow are not exceptions to this rule but the evidence does seem to commend them to us.)

Second, complete skepticism is an absurdity which it is impossible to maintain in practice.

Third, it is therefore unreasonable to demand absolute proof before believing. This does not mean that there is no need for any proof at all. The demand for evidence is legitimate and necessary. It does not mean that one idea is as good as another. Some ideas are much more coherent within themselves and in relation to the data than are others. It does not mean that belief ought to be a sheer act of arbitrary will or a desperate existential gamble in absolute darkness. It does mean that absolute rational certainty about the real world is a will-o'-the-wisp which is never attained. In pursuing it many men and women give up the light of such evidence as they could have on life's great concerns.

CHAPTER 3

Reason and Revelation

WE HAVE seen that a belief about reality can be given only relative grounding by reasoned argument. But in matters which concern the whole meaning of our lives on earth and questions of our eternal destiny we long for certainty. It may be supposed that in this predicament an absolutely authoritative divine revelation comes to our rescue; that the certainty which human reason cannot provide is given by God's own declaration. This suggested solution of our problem must be examined.

We propose to ask just now, not whether a divine revelation has actually occurred, nor what claimed revelations are in truth actual revelations. These questions will come later. At present we are concerned with asking simply what would be the relations between revelation and human reason if any revelation had been given or should at any time occur.

By revelation is here meant any activity of God by which truth is disclosed to human persons.

It seems obvious that the predicament in which we find ourselves because of the uncertainty of human reason will not be escaped by our receiving a revelation if the process of receiving and appropriating the truth of any revelation must itself be dependent upon our reason. Yet it would appear that this is precisely the case.

A. REASON REQUIRED TO RECEIVE REVELATION

A revelation must be made to a rational being. Even a thinker who accepts so authoritarian a view of the Scriptures as Thomas Aquinas insists that "sacred doctrine also makes use of human reason." [1] Nonrational brutes and stones do not receive revelations. Without reason even the most obvious and direct meaning of a divine self-disclosure could not be apprehended. If God wished to reveal truth to a stone He would have first to endow the stone with a reasoning mind. [2]

Mere sensations as such are meaningless. The most dazzling light from the

[1] *Summa Theologica*, I, Ques. 1, Art. 8.
[2] Cf. Henry C. Sheldon, *System of Christian Doctrine*, pp. 76–77.

heavens or the clearest trumpet call of an angel would constitute no revelation until a rational being had perceived it and related it to some other perception, cause or value. If man had his senses but no power of reason he could learn nothing even from a cloud of heavenly witnesses descending upon him.

Moreover, without using the rational principle of consistency a man would gain nothing in knowledge nor in practical guidance even if some true proposition were to be miraculously planted in his soul. For if he were content with inconsistency he could, though the love of God be disclosed to him, still believe that God was hate or that no God existed. What if such ideas did contradict the miraculously given doctrine? If contradictions were to be freely entertained then the objection would come to nothing. An increase of knowledge is possible only when it is assumed that every A is A and that A is therefore not non-A.

B. Reason Needed to Decide When Revelation Has Occurred

No sane person tries to accept as authoritative revelation from God all writings which are self-declared to be such. *The Koran, The Bhagavad Gita, The Book of Mormon* and the incoherent letter I have just received from an ignorant and badly distracted woman cannot all be authoritative statements of the truth straight from the throne of God. Yet each claims to be that. Not all self-proclaimed "revelations" can be true, for writings self-described as "revelations" contradict one another. How shall I know which one to believe? This problem has been confronted by every man who has believed in special revelations from God and who has been acquainted with a number of contrary books which were regarded as such.

Few Christian writers have surpassed Tatian of the second century, in their condemnation of reason as a guide in religion. Yet Tatian reports that he turned from the pagan scriptures of the Romans and Greeks and from the secret disclosures of the Mysteries because he *reasoned* that books and ideas which were so evil in many of their teachings and their effects on their devotees could not be of God, while the superior qualities of the Bible commended it to his belief.[3]

John Calvin recognizes the necessity of such rational discrimination by including in his *Institutes* a chapter entitled "Rational Proofs to Establish the Belief of the Scripture."[4]

Even when the Bible is described to the truth seeker as an absolute authority which will put an end to all error and to all doubt, the seeker still has no way of avoiding the necessity to examine the question whether the Bible ought to be accepted as such an authority. When men carefully employ their best reason-

[3] Tatian, *Address to the Greeks*, 29.
[4] I.8.

ing powers in this examination they may still arrive at false conclusions. This is shown by the fact that careful inquirers do sometimes reach contrary conclusions concerning the Bible and they cannot, therefore, all be right. But apart from rational criticism every insane utterance which claimed revelational authority would have as good chances of winning adherents as would the Bible.

C. Reason Required to Interpret and Apply Revealed Truth

Even if a man has received a divinely revealed message, and has recognized it as such, carefully distinguishing it from "revelations" falsely so-called, he is still not done with his dependence upon his own reasoning powers. For reason will still be required to interpret the revelation and discover its implications which bear upon his ever-changing situations.

We are not given separate, specific revelations to guide our decisions infallibly in all the vicissitudes of life. Even if we have learned with perfect assurance that God is love and requires us to live by love, the application of this knowledge to all the varied circumstances of economic and political strife or even to the problems which occur in the rearing of our own children is often far from obvious. Of course if a man cares nothing for the rational principle of consistency such matters may not concern him. He can profess to be filled with God's love and still live in the same fashion as men who are avowedly motivated by hate. But it is hard to see what then has been the significance of the professed "acceptance" of the revelation. On the other hand, if revelation is to serve as a guide of life, its implications must be drawn. This is a task for reason, however fallible and uncertain that may be.

D. Reason Required for Transmission of Revealed Truth to Others

In addition to all the forms of dependence upon human reason which we have observed, the man to whom a divine revelation had been made would have yet to employ reason in the sharing of the revealed truth with other persons.

If the truth were to be shared it would have, first of all, to be put into words or some other symbols capable of conveying it. It would also be necessary to tell something about the way in which the revelation had occurred, in order to show how the recipient knew it to be authoritative. Now to make accurate statements of important truth and to describe significant and unusual events are exacting tasks of reason. Further rational powers are likely to be needed to defend the authenticity of these disclosures in the face of doubts and opposition.

But the writer or speaker who seeks to share the revealed truth with other persons must depend also upon *their* rational efforts. His testimony will not be understood unless his readers or hearers make the effort to understand, applying their rational powers to the task. His witness to the authenticity of the divine disclosures will be of no avail if no one takes the trouble to examine with discriminating mind the credentials of authority which he presents. And the truth he brings will not redeem any man unless that man interprets the meaning of that message as it applies to *him* in his own particular context of personal history and social involvement.

E. Our Resulting Predicament

We have seen that with or without the aid of divine revelation a human being must depend, at many points, on the powers of human reason if he is to know the truth, apply it to life and share it. But earlier we observed that human reason is uncertain and notoriously subject to error.

If we were concerned merely with practically inconsequential problems about the diameter of a distant star or the swimming speed of a sea urchin we might regret our uncertainty but we could easily bear with it. However, in dealing with the chief theological problems, the questions of central prominence in the experience of the Christian community, we are concerned with the issues upon which turns the whole destiny of ourselves and the entire human race. Here our uncertainty has a deep and tragic significance which must at times come home to the thoughtful individual with overwhelming weight.[5] How is this tragic predicament to be met? To answer we must consider the relations of reason and faith.

[5] Cf. N. Berdiaev, *The Divine and the Human*, pp. 2–3. This tragic disparity between our yearning for certainty in the supreme issues of life and the failure of our reason to provide it is one of the principal roots of the existentialist movement in philosophy and theology. It is especially emphasized in S. Kierkegaard, *Concluding Unscientific Postscript*. For a systematic criticism of the resulting tendency to disparage reason as judge of truth in theology, see my book, *The Religious Revolt against Reason*.

CHAPTER 4

Reason and Faith

HUMAN reason cannot attain absolute certainty. Yet our reason must be depended upon. Even if revelation is given and taught, our reason must serve as recipient, interpreter and agent of transmission. How, then, is a man ever to reach a decision on the vital issues of life? It is at this point that we must examine the role of faith in religious knowledge.

A. THE DEFINITION OF FAITH

In the broadest sense, faith is a commitment of the will to an object not indisputably proved worthy of such commitment. Thus a person may have faith in a friend, meaning that the will is committed to a high estimate of his integrity and to a firm loyalty toward him, even though there is no compelling proof that he does now and always will merit such confidence. Similarly, a citizen may have faith in the government under which he lives, giving to it wholehearted support, even though he observes some perilous trends in its affairs and there is no certain demonstration that its policies will successfully attain its objectives nor that its officials will discharge their full responsibilities.

In a narrower sense faith means a cognitive or intellectual faith. It is that kind of faith with which we are primarily concerned when we speak of the role of faith in religious *knowledge*. Cognitive faith is commitment of the will in support of a judgment (assertion, belief, the meaning of a proposition) not indisputably proved to be true.

Cognitive faith, it will be seen, is one kind of faith in the broad sense. Just as one can commit his will to an emotional attitude or a course of action, so one can likewise will an affirmation of belief. Indeed, faith in the broad sense always implies a cognitive faith, whether the believer is aware of it or not. When I have confidence in a friend or government I affirm by my attitude and action my assent to an implied proposition which might be stated in such a way as this: My friend (or government) is worthy of confidence and support. Indeed, cognitive faith cannot in any other way be so emphatically asserted as by a person's basing his whole life upon his affirmation of a belief. There is no other way of saying "I believe in God" so emphatically and convincingly as by living a life of prayer, reverence and the doing of what I understand to be God's will. On the other hand, if I say, "Lord, Lord," but do not obey His will, I profess atheism with my life so that neither God nor man should be expected to listen to the profession of my lips.[1]

B. The Possibility of Faith

It may be objected that while a religious teacher can say, "Have faith," actually it is impossible when proof is incomplete.

The facts indicate that the contrary is true. Human beings of all kinds and descriptions do have faith without the prerequisite of proved certainty. Even men rigorously trained in the sciences evince this power on many occasions. For such men, like their untrained fellows, are sometimes swindled by dishonest salesmen and by attractive but selfish and unscrupulous women.

A world-famous scientist recently addressed an assembly of theological students. In his introductory remarks he said that he and the young ministers were at opposite poles. For while they were taught, he said (mistakenly), to believe until faith was disproved, he accepted the opposite method of science, that is the doubting of everything not absolutely proved. Moreover, since nothing had been absolutely proved he was required to doubt everything. He went to great lengths to show that this doubt was so thoroughgoing as to leave him with no steadfast belief on any subject. Yet when it was pointed out by a student that the doubting scientist seemed to have absolute faith in the superior value of what he called the method of doubt, he not only admitted that this was true but said he did not know how to defend this faith.

The reader can doubtless add many other examples of his own, showing that men can have faith, commendable or not, in ideas which they have not proved to be true beyond all possibility of doubt.

C. The Necessity of Faith

Not only is faith possible: it is inevitable.

It would seem clear that nothing can be proved beyond all possibility of doubt. But a man does inevitably commit himself to belief in some judgments. He can choose within limits *what* he will believe and how consistently he will maintain his belief. He cannot choose *whether* he will believe or no. The very fact that he is a person making choices in time will see to that. For time passes whether he wills that it should or not and he cannot avoid choosing to use it in some ways rather than in others.

If a man says that he believes nothing or if, in his unbelief, he keeps silence,

[1] Cf. Mt. 7:21.

he will nevertheless choose to eat and otherwise maintain his life or he will choose not to do so. Either choice will require a vigorous commitment of will. By such commitment he will be saying in the most emphatic manner, "I believe that life is worth maintaining," or "I believe life is of so little worth as not to justify its continuance." If he chooses to die he will be making a commitment of will as absolute as can be made within the bounds of our mortal life. If he chooses to live he will yet have to choose *how* to live. As he does so in his actual practice he will be affirming one judgment after another with all the emphasis of practical decision.

D. THE OBLIGATION OF RATIONAL FAITH

Man *can* have faith in the unproved or incompletely proved. Man *must* have faith in some ideas and objectives. Now it must be added that man *ought* to have faith in more reasonable alternatives rather than in less reasonable ones.[2]

To believe what is recognized as contrary to the total evidence is willingly to yield faith to probable falsehood rather than probable truth. But to believe what one thinks to be probably false is obviously to be at war with oneself, if, indeed, it is to believe at all and not merely to make a pretense of faith when faith is not a reality. To believe while avoiding inquiry regarding the evidence is to believe irresponsibly and recklessly.

Such irrational faith is like the passion of a young man who falls in love with a girl and does not wish to learn of any evidence regarding her worthiness to be loved by him. Often in such a case a young man will even avoid asking his beloved certain questions because he is afraid her answers might confirm his suppressed doubts and fears. In this way he acknowledges the illusionary character of his love. He wills to believe in her, makes a brave show of believing in her and may violently denounce anyone who expresses doubt concerning her. Yet he himself does not really believe but only wills to believe in order to open the way for his desire.

If a man is not seeking to know the truth nor to affirm the truth by his belief, then his statements of "belief" are obviously not really assertions of faith, but rather words uttered for the sake of their effects. On the other hand, if he is seeking to know and affirm the truth, then he cannot avoid the necessity of inquiring which of the various claims of expert authority, divine revelation or immediate intuition which confront him are really valid. He will have to depend on reason in the performance of this task. When he has begun it so that some evidence has become known to him, then if he is taking belief seriously, as an attempted affirmation of *truth* and not a mere expression of desire or a

---

[2] By reasonable is here meant conforming to the requirements of comprehensive or open coherence as explained in ch. 2.

social convenience, he will be obliged to believe in accordance with the evidence until more evidence may have shifted the weight of his judgment. It cannot be too strongly emphasized that no kind of evidence should be omitted from consideration. There is no possibility, then, of setting reason on one side and the evidence of revelation or faith on the other. It is unreasonable to bar from consideration any evidence which revelation or the experience of faith may have to offer.

So often faith has been described as contrary to reason or as some way of knowledge completely different from the way of reason that some readers may suppose this whole idea of a faith which is in accord with reason to be a new notion introduced by the present author or by some other recent theologian. Actually it is very old, indeed. More than seventeen hundred years ago the great Christian teacher, Clement of Alexandria, wrote as follows:

Everything that is contrary to right reason is sin. . . . If, then, disobedience in reference to reason is the generating cause of sin, how shall we escape the conclusion, that obedience to reason—the Word—which we call faith, will of necessity be the efficacious cause of duty? For virtue itself is a state of the soul rendered harmonious by reason in respect to the whole life.[3]

It is worth noting that Clement conceived of reason as bringing harmony into the soul "in respect to the whole life," which certainly suggests, at least, a conception of reason as comprehensive coherence.

Indeed, before Clement of Alexandria and before such Greek Apologists of the second century as Justin Martyr, who taught similarly that faith should be committed in accordance with the evidence as judged by reason,[4] such doctrine was taught in the Bible itself.

"Come now, let us reason together, says the LORD." [5] The prophets denounced idolatry for its unreasoning stupidity,[6] as well as appealing continually to history and personal experience for evidence of the truth of their constructive message. Jesus reasoned by analogy,[7] by a fortiori argument[8] and from pragmatic evidence.[9] Many times he appealed to the evidence of experience to correct mistaken ideas of God or of human duty.[10] Paul began his great Epistle to the Romans with an account of the universally observable evidences of God and of the moral law [11] and described the very root of sin and unbelief as a

[3] *Instructor*, I.13. Cf. Justin Martyr, *First Apology*, 68.
[4] Cf. Justin, *Dialogue with Trypho*, 2.
[5] Is. 1:18.
[6] E.g., Is. 44:9–20.
[7] E.g., Mt. 5:43–45; 6:30; Lk. 15.
[8] E.g., Mt. 7:11; Lk. 13:15–17.
[9] E.g., Mt. 7:15–20; Lk. 7:20–23; 13:6–9.
[10] E.g., Lk. 13:1–5.
[11] Rom. 1:18–2:16.

rejecting of the God whose power and divinity were "clearly perceived in the things that have been made," so that men "became futile in their thinking, and their senseless minds were darkened." [12] In city after city Paul argued [13] the superior merits of the Christian gospel. When he called upon the brethren to commit their bodies as living sacrifices to God he added, "which is your reasonable service." [14] Again, in I Peter, all believers are exhorted, "Always be prepared to make a defense to any one who calls you to account for the hope that is in you." [15]

E. The Obligation of Strong Faith

It may be supposed that since absolutely certain rational proof is not forthcoming and we must yield faith in conformity with the greater rational probability, it would therefore be most proper to make the assertion of faith as weak and tentative as possible. Shall life itself be thrown wholeheartedly into support of a doctrine and a way of existence which we cannot absolutely prove to be true?

To this question it must be replied that reason itself favors a decisively committed, wholehearted faith, rather than a life of tentative, weak vacillation. For the surest way of seeing to it that life will not be counted on the side of truth—whatever the truth may be—is to be as noncommittal as possible.

All great achievements, for good or ill, are made by men of great faith. The pioneers and pathfinders of the world are typified by Abraham, who "by faith . . . went out, not knowing where he was to go." [16] Columbus persisted in sailing forward where charts could no longer guide him, and so every discoverer has backed his reasoned theory with a courage in striking contrast to the theoretical indecisiveness of the evidence available in advance. Similar is the course of the scientists, whose faith may well be typified by the Curies. It will be recalled that they persisted in their experimental investigations for many years of the most burdensome and costly toil before finding any reward for their labors. All the great warriors and statesmen who have altered the course of world history have been men whose intensity of zeal and perseverance of effort have far outrun the certainty of the evidence that any of their major objectives were either desirable or attainable. In the local community, too,

---

[12] Rom. 1:20–21.

[13] Note the frequent recurrence of the Greek word διαλέγομαι (dispute, reason with) in the account of Paul's missionary work in The Acts.

[14] Rom. 12:1, AV. The Greek word which is translated here as "reasonable" is λογική, the etymological equivalent of our word "logical."

[15] I Pet. 3:15. As in Rom. 12:1 the Greek seems more emphatically rational in connotation than the English of the Revised Standard Version. Note especially the words ἀπολογίαν and λόγον.

[16] Heb. 11:8.

anywhere in the world, the chief accomplishments are attained by men whose wills are decisive though rational evidence is not.

If the life of the individual is to have any meaning to himself, to human society or to God that meaning must appear in decision. A life without decision on the major issues is a cipher. To be noncommittal is to be meaningless. If a life is devoted vigorously and consistently to the service of causes or of ideas which are false but have been thought true, at least there is some chance that the devotee or his acquaintances may learn something more of truth by observing the outcome. But from halfhearted equivocation little of truth or value is to be learned by anyone, just as little is learned from any scientific experiment if it is never quite clear what hypothesis is being tested.

It is no wonder that in Revelation 3:15-16 the Spirit of God is reported as saying to the Laodicean church,

I know your works; you are neither cold nor hot. Would that you were cold or hot! So, because you are lukewarm, and neither cold nor hot, I will spew you out of my mouth.

F. FAITH AND TOLERANCE

If there is to be such wholehearted commitment to belief as even the possibility of counting for truth requires, does that imply intolerance?

Decisive commitment to *some* doctrines would seem to lead by an inexorable logic to intolerant attitudes and action. If a man believes in the superior right and worth of his own race or nation and believes further in the necessity or obligation to assert the superiority by armed might, the ruthlessly cruel intolerance of a Fascist or a Nazi seems inevitable. Similarly, the Roman Catholic belief that the papacy is the one infallible throne of saving truth in the world, that any weakening of the papal rule or deviation from papal teaching is a strengthening of deadly error and mortal sin and that it is not only proper but obligatory that political and military power be employed to protect and strengthen the papal rule throughout the world, leads inevitably to as much intolerant oppression as the Vatican and its allies have power to enforce.

But in these instances it is not the strength or decisiveness of commitment which is responsible for the intolerance. It is the substance of the belief to which the commitment is made. If the ideas which a man's faith affirms include the idea that intolerant support of his beliefs is good, then his faith will naturally lead to intolerance. But no such system of ideas is to be commended in this volume. The doctrine which is to be defended here may be expected to have radically different consequences.

Every decisive commitment is truly hostile to one attitude which sometimes goes by the name of tolerance. For a person cannot be wholeheartedly devoted to an affirmation and at the same time maintain an attitude of indifference to the corresponding denial. But such indifference is not tolerance in the desirable sense of the word. Indeed, so long as a man is really indifferent concerning an issue he has no reason to preen himself on his "tolerance" toward various views concerning it. For him the problem of tolerance has not arisen. The question of real tolerance appears only when he finds that views are being expressed which he thinks to be false and dangerous to values he holds dear. This can be seen in the fact that many people are altogether willing to allow any views and practices concerning religion to flourish in their communities without protest but quickly demand police action or even resort to mob violence if anyone begins to promote radical economic or political ideas. Such persons have not yet learned what it is to be truly tolerant. What they call religious tolerance is only religious indifference.

On the other hand, a man shows a kind of faith and a kind of tolerance worth emulating when he willingly makes any sacrifice, even to the laying down of his life for a testimony of faith, but refuses to use any weapons inconsistent with personal respect and love in its promotion. Many a Christian has exemplified such faith, thus emulating his Master, who was willing to suffer humiliation, torture and death to bring men into the kingdom but disarmed Peter when he drew a sword for its defense.[17] Acting in such a spirit a man can respect the sincerity, intelligence and personal rights of those who differ even while he uses every possible means of reason and love to bare the mistakes of which he thinks them guilty and to promote the truth. He is bound to do so if he thinks reason and love to be central in the purpose of God Himself and the most potent instruments for realization of that purpose among men.

G. Faith and Openmindedness

A more difficult problem concerns the relation between the wholehearted commitment of faith and the willingness to give real consideration to new evidence. The necessity of a thoroughgoing faith has been stressed. But continuing hospitality of mind to new evidence seems also to be of great importance.

If minds had been finally closed at the level of polytheistic idolatry or even of Jewish legalism the incomparable treasures of the gospel would never have been appropriated. With good reason Luke praised the eager, searching minds of the Jews in Beroea.[18] But Christians have learned much truth of inestimably great value since the days of Luke and Paul. To have closed the minds of the people upon the gospel as then understood would have been to deprive the

[17] The writings and life of John Woolman, devoted missionary to the North American Indians and first successful advocate of the abolition of slavery, offer many clear enunciations and examples of this principle.

[18] Acts 17:11.

world of the great new insights of Augustine, Thomas Aquinas, Luther, Calvin and many other architects of the church's thought. Likewise, there would then have been no Christian movement for universal education, nor the elevation of womanhood, nor the abolition of slavery, no Christian art, no Christian effort to establish democratic government, nor found a political structure for international peace.[19]

Someone may object that the mind should be closed to everything contrary to the Christian faith while still exploring further the meanings of that faith. But in practice no such distinction can be carried through. Nearly every new interpretation or expression of the Christian faith has been regarded on its first appearance as a betrayal of the faith. Aquinas, Luther and George Fox alike were attacked as enemies of the sacred truth by the devotees of the closed mind. Only a habitual hospitality of mind will insure the consideration of new light from heaven when that light breaks forth.

But how can such a spirit be maintained if a person has committed his life at all costs to Christ? This will be in truth psychologically impossible if the believer regards the gospel as an irrational doctrine to be held in spite of preponderant contrary evidence. For such a person faith will imply an attitude of emotional resistance to evidence opposed to any of his own views which he regards as vital elements of Christianity. But if his faith be in accord with his reason, as it should be, then he will not shrink from evidence. He will welcome any evidence from any quarter since he regards faith as truth and is confident, therefore, that all evidence, when rightly understood, will but enrich his understanding of it in all its relations.

In short, when a man closes his mind to safeguard his faith, he is by this very act declaring his doubt, declaring that what he calls his absolute, unconditioned faith is actually far from absolute. His faith is, in fact, so insecure that he is afraid of what some new ray of light might disclose concerning it.

The confident believer is willing to make great sacrifices for his belief, even laying down his life rather than be false to it. But he does not seek to protect it from thought any more than from practical expression in the arena of life. He would not want to believe in falsehood. It is because he is assured of its truth that he is willing to sacrifice for it. For this same reason he is willing to examine its meaning in every new theoretical or practical relationship.

A closed mind is a sign of hidden doubt. The same man who is afraid to examine his belief in new relationships of thought is likely also to fear its bold application to those economic and personal affairs in which most of his

[19] For a fine historical survey of Christian influence in the entire peace movement, as well as much other valuable material, see Albert C. Knudson, *The Philosophy of War and Peace.*

daily concerns are to be found. He both closes his mind to evidence and refuses to stake the values of his common life upon his faith because he harbors a suppressed fear that it is actually not adequate.

He whose belief is secure does not feel the need of protecting it from the tests either of practical application or of thought. A true faith is least in peril when willingly subjected to every peril.

CHAPTER 5

Evidences for Theism

THE faith of the Christian church assumes the belief in a God who has created man and the world and who cares for man. Such a belief is not argued in the Christian story itself, since those who originally told and heard the story were alike believers in such a God. This belief is, therefore, a presupposition of the Christian faith rather than a doctrine distinctive of the Christian faith itself. Originally it was a part of the rich heritage from Judaism. But wherever Christianity has been preached among men who did not already believe in a personal Supreme Being it has been necessary for Christians to tell why such a belief might be presumed. Indeed, even within the New Testament when the gospel is proclaimed to pagans rather than Jews or when its relation to paganism is being discussed, the superior rational claims of belief in one spiritual God are stressed.[1]

It must be borne in mind that in speaking of the evidences for theism we are not endeavoring to establish the full meaning of the Christian's faith in God, but only the rational plausibility of some theistic belief in such an age as ours.

A. Some Fallacious Arguments

Some arguments which are commonly used to establish the belief in God will actually not stand critical examination. To lean on such flimsy evidence is to bring the belief itself into disrepute. It seems well at the outset of this study, therefore, to speak briefly concerning the most frequently encountered fallacious arguments and to warn against their employment.

1. *The Claim that All People Believe in God*

From many pulpits and in many church school classrooms has issued the pronouncement that God must exist, since all human beings in all times and places have believed in Him. This argument, even when given the impressive title, *a consensu gentium*, will not stand critical examination.

---

[1] E.g., see Acts 17:16-30 and Rom. 1:18-22.

The fact is that many human beings do not believe in God. It is not necessary to go to a country where religion is officially condemned as "unscientific" and "reactionary" to find many persons who deny both by word and practice the belief in God.

Even if it were true that all human beings believed in God, as it is not, that might still be poor evidence. Whether the agreement of men is or is not of evidential value depends on the ground of the agreement. For many centuries there was doubtless universal agreement among all men who thought about the matter at all that the earth was relatively flat. Yet they were mistaken.

2. The Attractiveness of Belief

Many believers say that they believe in God simply because it is so pleasant or comforting that they would not want to believe otherwise, whatever the evidence might be. Undoubtedly there are many of the beliefs or practices of men which are founded on mere desire. It is evident, however, that such a basis is a flimsy foundation.

It is doubtless pleasant and comforting to believe that there is nowhere any hate nor hunger in the world. The facts deny such a pleasant dream. We shall have to look further if we are to find sound, reasonable evidences of theism.

3. Anselm's Ontological Argument

The great medieval theologian Anselm believed that he had found an absolutely certain rational demonstration of God's existence. Many people have supported his claim and despite its rejection by Thomas Aquinas, the Roman Catholic Church has given approval to Anselm's argument.

Anselm begins [2] by defining God as the most perfect being conceivable. He insists that this is only a preliminary definition to enable the reader to understand what it is he is talking about when he discusses the question whether God exists. His question then is: Does the most perfect being conceivable exist? To this question he replies that the most perfect being conceivable must exist, for otherwise there would be conceivable a more perfect being who had all the perfections of the nonexisting one, but, in addition, perfect existence.

Unfortunately for Anselm and his loyal defenders, the ontological argument proves only that the most perfect being conceivable must be conceived as existing, not that such a being does actually exist. Thomas Aquinas, Immanuel Kant and many others have pointed out the fallacy.[3]

In addition to the three arguments just discussed, many others have been

[2] In *Proslogium*, 2.

[3] There have been several recent efforts by Protestant thinkers to restate and validate the ontological argument. One of the most persuasive of these attempts is made by Roger Hazelton in his thoughtful book, *On Proving God*.

introduced by the frivolous or ignorant and seem hardly worth the time required for explicit criticism. Besides, our primary concern is with the evidences which are sound and helpful. There are, of course, many ways in which these may be organized and presented. I make no pretense of exhausting the possibilities in the classification here introduced.

B. Evidence from the Objectivity of Abstract Truth

There are many truths of logic and mathematics which were undiscovered by men for many thousands of years and were then brought to light. Indeed, some of these have only appeared in human thought within the present century. Yet, when one of these propositions has been discovered, both the man who has formulated it and other thinkers who have received it recognize that this discovery was not the creation of a new truth, but in actual fact a discovery of something already true. The proposition that the square on the hypotenuse of a right triangle is equal to the sum of the squares on the sides adjacent to the right angle did not become true when Pythagoras or one of his disciples formulated this theorem. It was already true, and the Pythagoreans only discovered that it was so.

These abstract truths were not only true before their discovery by men; they resist any effort at alteration with an absolute inflexibility surpassing the resistance of any material objects whatsoever. Trees and rocks and stars are everywhere and always subject to change. But the truths of geometry, so long as they are veritable truths and not merely partial opinions, are subject to no change whatsoever. Even though a universally representative parliament of mankind were to vote unanimously to change the Pythagorean Theorem or the ratio of the circumference to the diameter of a circle the truth about these matters would continue to be exactly what it has always been. *Men can be mistaken about such truths but they cannot change them.*

How are we to think of the being of such truths in their timeless independence of human opinions? They are nowhere perfectly represented by material substances and cannot be coherently conceived as having any being apart from their being thought. Yet, clearly, they do have being apart from the thought of man. They must then be timelessly thought in a Mind not human, but a Mind after which human thought at its best is patterned. If there is veritably a God who has made us then we can readily understand why our own minds are forever kept in restless searching, progressively satisfied only as we discover what is already in the thought of our Maker.[4]

---

[4] Cf. Augustine, *On True Religion*, 21; *On Free Will*, II.9; *On the Trinity*, XIV.21; *Confessions*, I.1.

The principal alternative to the belief in God, as a solution of the problem we have raised, is the notion of Plato that the eternal truths simply are, quite apart from mind or any other existing being. This theory would require a man to believe that truth can have being quite independent of thought and of material existence. It is not clear what is meant by any such form of being. Idea and truth occurring in the thought of a mind are familiar experiences. An idea apart from any thinking mind seems about as intelligible as the grin of a Cheshire cat apart from the cat. Many modern philosophers have chosen to by-pass this problem altogether. But to evade a problem is not to solve it. Until a better solution shows itself the reasonable man will support the view which is most intelligibly related to the data which experience provides. The belief in a Supreme Mind undergirding our own existence seems best to commend itself as the solution of the problem of abstract truths.[5]

C. Evidence from Causal Law

The material world which we know both through common observation and the discoveries of the sciences is, on the whole, a remarkably systematic order. Every advance in the natural sciences has given further evidence of the ordered causal relations among the phenomena of nature. There was a time when some Christians and their critics alike supposed that the advance of science was lessening the evidence for God. For example, Auguste Comte writing his *Cours de Philosophie Positive*, published in 1839, held that the discovery of causal law by the sciences was one of the principal influences which were leading to "the irretrievable decline" of theology. He believed that the formulation of a causal law was an adequate explanation of the events described as effects. Belief in God had been useful to explain phenomena not yet accounted for by scientific law. But as soon as the sciences could extend the network of causality to cover all the phenomena of nature, belief in God would no longer serve any useful purpose.

But what is a causal law? What is usually called a causal law is plainly a formula. These formulas as we know them have been created by the minds of men. But clearly, all causal laws which are true were in operation before any men formulated them. Where and how did they have their being before men first discovered them? Did the elaborate formulas which together constitute

[5] Readers familiar with the history of philosophy will recognize here the solution known in the Middle Ages as one form of conceptualism, the view supported by Thomas Aquinas and many other thinkers. Its origin is not certain but the writer has not found clear evidence of it in writings earlier than Avicenna and is inclined to think that to this great Moslem thinker its historical origin must be credited. However, as was implied in the preceding footnote, it owes much to Augustine.

what we know as the law of gravity originally exist in stones? Do stones know all these intricate mathematical relations? Why does the water of the sea stir when the moon passes overhead many thousands of miles away?

Many thoughtless persons suppose that the law of gravity is a kind of power or substance which actually moves masses of matter about. But the law of gravity which we know is a system of meanings.[6] Now how should meanings be able to bring about actual events in the physical universe? This mystery can by no solution yet devised be fully comprehended. However, we do experience in our own minds the combining of ideas with the power of will. Often we plan orderly modes of procedure and then put these ideas into action through the exercise of will.

The relation between the great system of ideas which we know as causal law and the events of the physical universe becomes intelligible only when we conceive of the ideas as occurring, long before men discovered them, in a cosmic Mind in which idea and will are perpetually and intimately conjoined. Sir Isaac Newton declared that God must be a great mathematician. Until a better explanation of the universal order appears, the belief in a Supreme Intelligence is a reasonable faith.

D. Evidence from Apparent Purpose in Nature

For many centuries thoughtful observers have been struck by the remarkable adaptation of means to ends in the organic equipment of innumerable animals and plants. The protective coloring of many birds and other creatures, the oil sac and oiling instincts of water fowl, the remarkable relations of mutual helpfulness between bees and flowering plants, the intricate organization of the eye in all the higher animals, and many other examples suggest a creation by a mind deliberately devising means for the accomplishment of specific purposes.

Indeed this adjustment of means to end is so nearly universal in the biological world that when discovering some new organ within an animal body the student is almost sure to inquire, at least mentally, what is the purpose served by this structure relative to the organism as a whole. The substitution of the word "function" instead of "purpose" scarcely disguises the implication of telic direction.

The long movement of the entire evolutionary process from simple and passive structures to complex, active and freely self-directing creatures gives similar evidence of purposive guidance in the whole process. This directional movement of evolution is not adequately explained by the principle of the

---

[6] Cf. the recent trend of physical science as interpreted by Sir James Jeans in his book, *Physics and Philosophy.*

survival of the fittest. The superior powers of survival in the better equipped organisms are obvious enough. But the acute problem is not of survival but of origin. This problem is especially persistent when one faces the fact that in many organisms there are structures in which only the finely adjusted relationships of many parts give to the whole organ any usefulness at all in the struggle to survive. Henri Bergson has given an especially fine description of two diverse lines of development of the eye which illustrates this apparent purposiveness particularly well.[7] Pierre Lecomte du Noüy in his book, *Human Destiny*, has shown that the entire evolutionary process from the development of the most primitive organisms to the appearance of man is impossible to explain even in any single stage of transition without reference to purposive direction. His use of the principle of statistical probability, of which he is a famous master, is especially convincing, as he shows what incredible miracles on miracles must have occurred in the most bewildering succession—and all with no miracle worker—if no intelligent purpose guides the process.

The appearance is that there is a purpose operative in nature quite apart from the purposive efforts of human beings or any other creatures. How else shall this be explained excepting by reference to a purposive cosmic Person?

[7] See his *Creative Evolution*, pp. 60–88.

CHAPTER 6

Further Evidences

A. Evidence from Human Adaptation [1]

THE evidence is even more striking when we observe man himself in his relations with his natural environment. In five different dimensions of his life he is adapted to his environment in ways altogether impossible to explain apart from purpose in the process which has produced him and which sustains him now.

1. Biological Adaptation

The mere existence of the living human body is marvelous enough. The demands made upon the environment by such an organism are almost beyond comprehension. These requirements include the need for a range of temperature which in comparison with the heat and cold known to exist elsewhere is very minute; the dependence on never-failing supplies of oxygen, water and all those essential carbon compounds, minerals and vitamins known to the dietitian; the necessity of a certain kind of gravitational field, atmospheric pressure, freedom from noxious gases and many other complex circumstances. Man is equipped to live in this earthly environment with remarkable freedom and versatility. Any major portion of the human body will exemplify the intricate dependence of one organ upon others and the operation of all together as one organic whole. In the eye, for example, the sensitive retina would be useless without its relation to the optic nerve and without the transparency of cornea, aqueous humor, lens and vitreous humor behind which it lies. The fine adjustments of the pupil by the iris in response to varying light conditions would go for naught if there were no retina or if any one of the transparent structures behind or before the pupil were opaque like most of the body. These and all other relations within the body are simple as compared with those within the human nervous system, the crowning achievement of nature.

Yet, remarkable as this biological adaptation is which enables the human

---

[1] Indebtedness for the general conception in this section is acknowledged to F. R. Tennant's great work, *Philosophical Theology*.

race to survive here, there are other forms of adaptation which are much more subtle and marvelous, indeed are altogether beyond the range of mechanical or even biological description.

2. *The Cognitive Relation*

First among these must be mentioned that cognitive rapport which enables man not merely to live in the world but to understand it. The power of biological adaptation is a quite different matter from this intellectual adaptation. Many insects are well adapted to live in their environments and some are well fitted to live under conditions of very wide variety, but without evidence of understanding. Man, on the other hand, while living successfully in the world, is also able to view that world with such intimate understanding that he can predict its events with uncanny accuracy.

The demands of man's disciplined reason so parallel the realities of nature that again and again human thought has described things never observed, on the assumption that what man's reason required could be confidently assumed to exist. Thus Neptune was described before being observed, because without just such a planet the movements of Uranus could not be fitted into the mathematical formulas of human astronomers. It is especially significant that the most revolutionary recent advances in the scientific understanding of the material world have been made, not by the study of observed data, but by the purely theoretical study of mathematics. One might expect advances in physics and astronomy to be produced in laboratories and observatories. But the greatest recent advances in these subjects have been made in the brooding mind of Albert Einstein, a student of mathematical theory. Indeed, one of the greatest physicists, Sir James Jeans, writes,

What remains is in any case very different from the full-blooded matter and the forbidding materialism of the Victorian scientist. His objective and material universe is proved to consist of little more than constructs of our own minds. In this and in other ways, modern physics has moved in the direction of mentalism.[2]

The reader of such statements might be inclined, perhaps, to dismiss them as the fantastic abstractions of a theorist having little to do with the world of hard reality which we experience. But it is precisely through the discoveries by these abstract theorists that the way has been opened to the use of atomic energy. Much as we should like to shrug off atomic bombs as unrealistic theories they have become unmistakable and terrible realities.

Now why should men's abstract theories have such powers to comprehend the realities of nature? Why, indeed, unless there is a real kinship between our

[2] *Physics and Philosophy* (Cambridge: Cambridge Uni. Press, 1935), p. 216.

minds at their highest reaches of clear consistency and the order of nature? This kinship is altogether impossible to explain without belief in the governance of nature by a Mind in whose image our own minds are fashioned.

3. Aesthetic Rapport

Not unlike this harmony of the human intellect with the natural order is the answering of nature to our aesthetic need. The beauty we enjoy in a robin's spring song or the purpled mystery of the desert or the unapproachable majesty of a towering mountain peak is not to be explained in terms of biological utility. Indeed the aesthetic lures of desert, mountain summit, river rapids and ocean vastness have drawn many a man to his physical death. Here are no mere means by which men are biologically fitted to survive. Aesthetic experience is not so much a tool of existence as an end which makes existence worth while. Beauty belongs not to the means but to the meaning of life.

Consequently, to the thinker who does not believe in God, aesthetic experience must appear as a kind of inexplicable bonus dropped into our laps without any reason. Why the nature which has so remarkably produced and for thousands of years sustained human life and has strangely given us the power to penetrate knowingly many of its complex secrets should have added to all this beneficence the additional gift of aesthetic enjoyment is beyond all explanation excepting the account of the theist. It can hardly be denied that human beings have a natural love of beauty nor that nature, from the starry heavens above to the microscopic world of crystals and algae, fulfills and stimulates that love in innumerable ways. To the theist the beauty of nature is a sign of the likeness between man's aspiring soul and the Creator and an evidence of the power, beauty and love of God Himself.[3]

4. Moral Stimulus

This is not all. The natural order in which the human race is able to live, to learn understanding and to enjoy beauty serves remarkably, also, as "a vale of soul-making."[4] Despite all the pain and sorrow of our experience in this world, no, rather because these evils are present along with understanding, beauty and joy, this is a place where men can learn courage, self-discipline, loyalty and love. The proof that this is so is that such virtues are actually here. Our existence would seem tawdry and superficial if the whole moral dimension were to be removed. But whether we explain our moral experience as the expression of an inherent moral nature in man or the product of interaction

---

[3] See my article, "Natural Beauty and Theism," in The Personalist, Jan., 1939, pp. 63–73.

[4] This oft-quoted phrase of John Keats occurs in his letter to George and Georgiana Keats, April 28, 1818, where the context gives it heightened significance.

among men and between them and their natural environment or we resort to some combination of these theories, it will have to be admitted that the category of duty and moral good is an exceedingly important reality in human life.

What is the reason why this ethical dimension of meaning has been added to the biological, cognitive and aesthetic aspects of our lives? Has a blind process of chance brought forth all this? What coherence of meaning can be found between such vast meaningfulness of product, human experience, and the indescribable worthlessness of the cause, unknown and unknowing process? Coherence is gained in the account only when it is seen that such an intricate manifold of meaning and value is no accident of blind process but the creation of the God whose purpose governs the course of nature, both in the evolving of man and in the arousing of his moral sense to action.

5. Religious Nurture

One more level of significant interaction between man and the natural world remains to be examined. Human beings seem to be incurably religious. Throughout the world, in all ages they have sought help from unseen powers greater than themselves. Despite the exploitation of this religious concern by men who have sought to gain power or wealth by means of it the concern has persisted. Even when ruthless governments have sought by every conceivable device to stamp it out, religion has sprung up afresh in every generation.

However it may be explained, the appearance and persistence of religion among all peoples on earth is a fact. The thinker who does not believe in God must regard the religious interest as a product of men's relationships with their fellows and with their natural environment. Since on such a theory all men are themselves the products of the material world, we are confronted with a curiously incoherent belief. The nontheist must believe that an impersonal, blindly mechanistic world has somehow produced an organism which, in addition to its ability to survive, learn to understand the orderly laws of its environment, enjoy beauty and develop a moral nature, has also an apparently ineradicable aspiration for winning the favor of powers in a realm beyond the natural world. This aspiration has added a whole dimension of meaning to life. Moreover, where man's moral and intellectual life advances to high levels of attainment and his religious interest keeps in vital interaction with the rest of his culture, his religion shows a marked tendency to develop into an ethical monotheism. If there were no God this would have occurred by sheer chance in a world of blind process.

The believer in God has a more coherent explanation well expressed by St. Paul:

For what can be known about God is plain to them, because God has shown it to them. Ever since the creation of the world his invisible nature, namely, his eternal power and deity, has been clearly perceived in the things that have been made.[5]

The knowledge of God shown in men's other-worldly aspirations, however dimly perceived or darkened by priestly exploitation, they have "because God has shown it to them." Unhappy is the man who darkens what God has made plain.

B. The Objectivity of Moral Ideals

The fact that men have a sense of moral obligation and experience moral attainment in various degrees has been given notice. We have now to observe that in their strivings all persons are subject to a system of moral law which they did not create and which they are powerless to change.

It is often claimed that moral laws are identical with social mores or customary moral beliefs and sanctions and are therefore wholly relative to actual human societies. If this were true it would be obvious that moral laws were only products of human thought and experience. It is, of course, true that particular beliefs concerning moral law appear in particular minds or societies at particular times and places. These beliefs vary from nation to nation and even among individuals. Similarly there have been and are great numbers of contrary beliefs concerning causal law. Yet the true laws of nature are what they are, independent of human attempts to formulate them. There is good evidence that moral law too is real, independent of varying human opinions concerning it.

Actually the whole intellectual life of man, including natural science, rests upon a foundation of moral obligation. The superior claim of legitimate science to acceptance in preference to superstition and casual generalization rests upon the assumption that self-discipline is better than unrestrained emotion, that honesty is better than false or careless report and that patience is better than impulsive haste. All of modern science is thus seen to be a product of the acceptance by men of a system of ethical law.[6]

All evidence which could be secured on the question whether human beings were subject to a valid moral law could be evaluated, like evidence on any other question, only on the presupposition that belief ought to be committed under some conditions rather than others. If men will not acknowledge the obligation to choose the coherent rather than the incoherent they place themselves beyond

[5] Rom. 1:19-20.
[6] Cf. Kant's principle of "the primacy of the practical reason." Cf. also E. Brunner, *Christianity and Civilization*, Vol. 2, pp. 19-20, and Elton Trueblood, *The Predicament of Modern Man*, pp. 36-43.

man must accept that which is coherent in favor of that which is not if he is to derive any meaning from life.

FURTHER EVIDENCES   57

the reach of all argument on every subject. If they do acknowledge this obligation they acknowledge by implication a whole system of moral law.[7] If truth is ever independent of human opinion, then the system of moral law which must be acknowledged by implication in order to discover that truth must itself be a part of the truth which men cannot change. On the other hand, if truth is not independent of human opinion, then every belief including this one may be affirmed or denied with equal validity, which is to say with none. Such skepticism has been seen to be both self-contradictory and actually impossible to avoid rejecting in practice. When it is put aside by the barest affirmation of faith in any truth, the believer is implying, whether aware of it or not, that he and all men are subject to a system of moral law which they did not legislate and cannot revoke.

Of course everyone is subject to this moral law whether he believes in God or not. Max Carl Otto is quite right when he insists [8] that obligation is known to be real regardless of its metaphysical status beyond men. But *how* does it have its being? Whence comes this moral law which men are powerless to make or change? Could a system of obligation belong to a universe of blind necessity?

Moral law is not a law of necessity but a principle of evaluation. It is not a formula describing what is or will be but a judgment of what ought to be. Apart from mind and will there can be neither meaning nor being of such a judgment. Yet the moral law does have being and meaning which man does not create but to which he finds himself subject. Mores come and go but the true law stands forever beyond the power of man to change. But if it belongs necessarily to mind and will while having its home outside and above man so that man stands always under its jurisdiction, it is evident that it is the legislation of a Mind and Will more than human, under whose sovereignty we live. Human laws are imperfect, changing and often contradictory. But the law of God is perfect and eternal. It is of that law, the judgment of God Himself, that Jesus could truly declare,

For truly I say to you, till heaven and earth pass away, not an iota, not a dot, will pass from the law until all is accomplished.[9]

It is to that perfect law of God that we pay homage every time we ask which of two courses of conduct we ought to follow, which one of two social systems is truly better or even which of two theories, whether of ethics or physics, we are truly obliged to accept. Even those who claim that there is no moral law

[7] Edgar S. Brightman has drawn out some of this system in his extraordinarily significant book, *Moral Laws.*

[8] In his book, *Things and Ideals.*

[9] Mt. 5:18.

pay tribute to it willy-nilly by passing value judgments on ideas and upon one another.

Therefore you have no excuse, O man, whoever you are, when you judge another; for in passing judgment upon him you condemn yourself, because you, the judge, are doing the very same thing.[10]

By such judgments men "show that what the law requires is written on their hearts." [11] By our willing or unwilling tribute to the law we pay tribute also to the Lawgiver whose creatures we are and under whose judgments we stand.

C. Religious Experience

Probably the weakest of the valid proofs for the existence of God to be argued in words is the one which is strongest for him who experiences the evidence at first hand. Men and women of many types in many lands and in all ages have testified to their own experience of God. Some of them are among the most sober and self-critical persons to be found anywhere. Many have given evidence by their lives, that their report was trustworthy. Their calm courage, self-giving love and spiritual radiance have led many others who have not shared their experience of God to believe in their testimony.

The persons who have had such experiences are not all to be found among the famous saints or poets. Common men and women living quietly among their fellows in thousands of communities, by the testimony of their words and lives bring God nearer their friends than any ideational argument could ever do.

A student in a state university, after telling me how he and most of his companions had outgrown all religious belief now that they had learned "the scientific attitude" toward life, paused a moment and then added wistfully, "But a few of the students I know say that God is real to them and I'll have to admit there is a kind of clean glow about them that I wish I had." A verbal testimony supported by a "clean glow" is not to be shrugged off lightly.

But can we not give psychological descriptions and explanations of all such experiences and testimonies? Up to a point we undoubtedly can. Just so a father's vision of his newly born child can be described in terms of images and affections and the skeptic who has not seen what he sees could also "explain" it all as a hallucination due to an upsurge from his repressed desires for paternity. Yet the father standing there at the hospital nursery windows knows this is no hallucination.

I once attended a clinic in a great psychopathic hospital where a young woman was presented as a patient suffering from delusions of persecution. The doctors

[10] Rom. 2:1.
[11] Rom. 2:15.

who had been studying her case drew out her story by careful questioning. It was a fantastic tale of persecution and organized conspiracy against her. Now, she said, she had a case pending in court against a steamship company, a case which she was certainly going to win. The only question concerned the amount of damages she would be awarded. Since the amount would surely be very great her family had railroaded her into the hospital for the mentally ill, hoping to get their own hands on the money. Visibly distraught, she finally finished her story. Then the doctors, after gently ushering her from the room, returned to point out how perfectly the whole weird and fantastic tale fitted the diagnosis based on the symptoms of paranoid delusions. But the chief of staff ordered that a thorough investigation be made to discover just how many details of her strange account might be actually true to fact. I was present again in the same room when the report was made that nearly every part of the story had been checked and was, down to the most incredible details, literally true. I could not help pondering how the young woman must have felt when she was relating the things she had seen, heard and touched while the doctors solemnly took note of all these details as new symptoms of her "systematized delusions."

So a worshipper returns from prayer to report his experience of God, only to have every word translated by the skeptic, who has had no such experience, into terms describing various types of self-deception. If the skeptic can find no evidence beyond the word of the believer, perhaps he cannot be blamed. But he who bows in God's presence, experiencing the condemnation of sin by His purity, the perfect beauty of His holiness, the inrush of His power and the cleansing comfort of His love knows that this is no dream nor delusion. God lives and He is near.

PART TWO

THE BIBLE

CHAPTER 7

General and Special Revelation

WE HAVE now completed our examination of the general presuppositions of Christian theology. We are therefore ready to enter our study of theology proper, that is, the critical examination of the experience especially characteristic of Christians.

In determining where it is best to begin this major portion of our study it is instructive to observe where the new convert to Christianity must begin. The new convert who is to be instructed in the faith he has embraced must be introduced at once to the contents of the Bible. For the whole life of the Christian church has developed from the telling and interpretation of the Christian story with which it began and nearly all we know of that story is contained, together with accounts of its background and its earliest consequences, in the Bible. The church has therefore been and is today constantly dependent upon that book. The first problems to be faced by a person critically interpreting the experience of the church have, consequently, to do with the significance and authority of the Scriptures.

If the place of the Bible in the Christian community is to be rightly understood and evaluated, it must be placed in proper perspective, against the background of other channels of revelation by which God has declared Himself to men.

A. Our Dependence on Revelation for All Knowledge

Using the term "revelation," as before, to mean "any activity of God by which truth is disclosed to human persons,"[1] it is evident that we should have no knowledge at all without revelation.

All of our sensory experience is evidently due to the processes of the material world. But these processes are themselves willed and ordered by God. For the theistic evidences already examined point to a God who directs the whole order of nature so that causal laws are His orderly ways. Whether an idealistic metaphysics or a dualistic system be true, if the theistic evidences are valid then our experience of nature is due to God's activity. For even if His activity has been

[1] See p. 33.

63

exercised in relation to nature only by a creation *ex nihilo* in the beginning and by a sustaining or intervening will since then, so long as He is regarded as the one unconditioned Creator, cause or ground of all being, every experience we have of the material world results from His activity.[2]

Because much of our knowledge is a product of our sensory experience [3] and this experience is dependent upon the activity of God, much of our knowledge is dependent upon revelation. This must include all knowledge of the material world.

Since our communication with other human persons is mostly or entirely by means of material media, such as tongue, air and ear, the knowledge which we gain by such communication is evidently dependent upon God's activity and hence on revelation. It is by this means that we have learned languages and other symbols by which we not only communicate with one another but which we employ also to give precision and order to our own thoughts. Indeed, we cannot conceive how a human being could come to know anything at all, even if he could somehow exist, as he obviously could not, apart from any experience of the material world or any other influence from God.

There has been much talk in recent theology about the things which can be discovered by "man alone," as opposed to the things which he can learn only as God instructs him. Such talk is quite absurd among theists, since all theists agree that man could not even exist alone, let alone know anything. Every human being is dependent on God for his existence and for every increase of his knowledge, from the earliest comprehension of physical objects near him in infancy to the most elaborate scientific theory. If nothing ever happened in a test tube and men's minds were not made restless with longing for coherence, nothing would be learned by chemist or mathematician. That things *do* happen in test tubes and that men's minds *do* long for coherence is due to the activity of God. We learn only because He first sought to teach us.

B. The Distinction between General and Special Revelation

Traditionally, Christian thinkers have distinguished between general revelation and special revelation. General revelation has been thought of as including all disclosures of truth, especially truth about God and His will for men, through the regular order of nature. The evidences for theism from the observation of causal law and of apparent purpose in biological evolution are examples of such general revelation.

---

[2] We are not here raising metaphysical questions beyond the requirements of the present purpose. I maintain a personalistic philosophy and the position taken here is coherent with such a metaphysics. However, it will be noted that such a metaphysics is not presupposed in this volume.

[3] It is not implied that any knowledge is a product of sensory experience alone. Experience must be interpreted if there is to be knowledge.

Special revelation, on the other hand, has been regarded as a breaking of God's activity into the order of nature. Consequently, special revelation has usually been thought of as God's direct self-disclosure while general revelation has seemed indirect and remote.

It is doubtful whether this view of the relation between general and special revelation can stand the test of careful epistemological and metaphysical examination. If an idealistic metaphysics is correct, then all experience of the material world is induced directly by God Himself and special revelation could not be more direct than what has been called general revelation. But even if such a view is not assumed the distinction fades on strict analysis. For all theists are agreed that the order of nature expresses God's thought and that without His present sustaining will our experience of the world would cease. However, all agree (unless the pantheists are to be regarded as theists) that none of our experience is itself God or any part of Him. For idealistic and nonidealistic theists alike, then, our experience of nature is caused by God and expresses His thought. On the other hand, theists would agree that the most direct revelation possible in our own experience is caused by God and expresses His thought. The idea that special revelation to us is more direct than general revelation can hardly be maintained unless we either deny that the natural order is sustained by God's will and expresses His thought or else regard God as literally putting Himself or some part of Himself into the experience of a man, in special revelation, so that the "I" and "Thou" become blurred in a single consciousness. Even if we believe that God Himself literally walked the hills of Galilee and there spoke audibly to men, we were not ourselves there, so that whatever was spoken in those times must now come to us through the mediation of innumerable human minds and hands. In comparing the mediations of divine truth to us through the order of nature and through the Bible, however great authority we might ascribe to the latter, therefore, it could hardly be true to contrast, in John Calvin's words, God's use of "mute teachers" and the opening of "his own sacred mouth." [4]

Whatever distinction it may be useful to make between "general" and "special" revelation, the line cannot be drawn between nature and the Bible on the ground of the more direct, unmediated character of the latter.

C. Special Revelation

Nevertheless, there may be manifestations of God which are entitled, on grounds other than unmediated directness, to be distinguished by the title of special revelation.

[4] *Institutes* I.6.1.

For example, a particularly striking and enlightening event in the physical world might be so designated.

I may observe many actions of a human friend, read his letters and examine various things which he has made. Yet I may find him an enigma. I cannot understand the secret springs of his seemingly strange activities and expressions. Then, one day, a phrase in a letter, a symbol in his handiwork or a single act suddenly discloses to me his heart. Of such an occasion I later say, "It was a veritable revelation to me. In a moment I came to understand him." Of course the new datum which I have observed is no more of my friend's doing than are a thousand others. But *to me* it is more *instructive* in acquainting me with his purpose and character.

Similarly, a despairing boatman, worn by long travels over a dreary waste of water, may upon landing see a rainbow which is to him a sign of God's love and providential care. The rainbow is obviously as much a part of nature as the long familiar rain and sun. It is neither more nor less mediated than they. But its meaning to the long discouraged and fearful observer is much clearer, more intense and more helpful. It is understood as a veritable message from God to man.

If there should occur in the physical world an event which men could not fit into the formulas which we call causal laws, that event would be no more an act of God than would the ordinary processes of nature. As Jesus declares, it is God Himself who "makes his sun rise on the evil and on the good, and sends rain on the just and on the unjust." [5] It is God who feeds the birds of the air and clothes the grass of the field in flowering glory.[6] If God does these things which are plainly parts of the regular natural order, then no dividing of a sea nor halting of the sun in its visible march across the sky could be more completely a divine act. However, it may be freely granted that an unusual and spectacular physical event, especially if it occurred at an opportune moment in relation to felt human needs, might rivet attention and convey meaning as the familiar course of events could not do. The questions whether such miracles have actually happened and if so how they should be thought of in relation to the natural order are questions needing to be considered later. Just now we are concerned simply to point out that, in the light of our theistic evidences, if a miracle were to be properly called a special revelation it could not be so-called because of its being any more an act of God than are the ordinary processes of nature, but only because it was more revealingly meaningful to men.

Again, it would seem appropriate to designate as a special revelation any high moment of communion with God in which the worshiper is filled with the

[5] Mt. 5:45.
[6] Mt. 6:28–30.

sense of His presence, especially if through such an experience there is gained a new knowledge of God and His will for man. Moses at the burning bush, Isaiah in the temple, and the Psalmist under the star-dotted firmament all had such experiences. So also had Augustine in the garden, Wesley at Aldersgate and Kagawa in the slums of Shinkawa. Innumerable hosts of unknown people have likewise talked with God and had their lives changed by His forgiveness, His command and His power.

Finally, the name special revelation might be reserved for a particular historical movement in which various manifestations of God, manifestations of every kind, have been preserved in a single great stream of living tradition. Specifically, many Christians would give this title to the Bible and the events recorded therein. Some would include also in this body of special revelation the great utterances of the church. However, those Christians who would thus magnify the authority of the church would freely acknowledge that the church itself was historically rooted in the events and interpretations recorded in the Bible and that the authority of the church must be established by proving its continuity with the Biblical message.

For all Christians alike, Eastern Orthodox, Roman Catholic, Anglican and Protestant, the Bible holds a unique historical significance. Most of them would also grant to it a unique revelatory authority. It is therefore needful that our attention now be turned specifically to the examination of the Bible, its truth, inspiration and authority.

CHAPTER 8

The Fallibility of the Bible

IN THE experience of the Christian community the teachings and narratives recorded in the Bible have had a prominence and authority more universal and enduring, by far, than any other body of ideas. Despite the passage of many centuries, the accumulation of elaborate philosophical and theological traditions and the pride of our age in modern scientific learning, the Bible still retains for many millions of people a moral and religious authority not approached by any other literature.

It is noteworthy that many of the most devout students and defenders of the Bible's authority have nevertheless acknowledged that all within its pages was not invariably to be accepted as divine truth. Thus Martin Luther called the Epistle of James "an epistle of straw"[1] and John Wesley omitted some Psalms from *The Sunday Service* for American Methodists (1784) because they were "highly improper for the mouths of a Christian congregation." Others have been less candid but have nevertheless fastened their attention and loyalty on some passages while ignoring or explaining away the contradictions of others.

To the intelligent student who is more concerned with seeking out and declaring the truth than with maintaining a dogma it must be apparent that the Bible is by no means infallible. The signs of this fallibility are numerous. It will be sufficient to point out and illustrate six kinds of evidence.

A. INTERNAL CONTRADICTIONS

In regard to many facts of minor importance there are obvious contradictions within the Bible. For example, in Exodus 37:1–9 we read that Bezaleel made

[1] *Works* (Philadelphia edition of 1932), VI, p. 444. Luther was comparing the Epistle of James with "St. John's Gospel and his first Epistle, St. Paul's Epistles, especially Romans, Galatians and Ephesians, and St. Peter's first Epistle." In the original text Luther's words were: *"Darum ist Sanct Jakobs Epistel ein recht stroherne Epistel gegen sie; denn sie doch kein evangelisch Art an ihr hat."* The passage appeared only in the 1522 edition of his *Preface to the New Testament* after which it was omitted. It will also be observed that the evaluation is relative and not absolute. However, in view of the emphasis in Luther's theology, this explosive characterization seems undoubtedly to have expressed the spontaneous reaction of Luther's mind to the emphasis in the Epistle, so radically contrary to his own. It was natural that he should have preferred to omit later a statement so embarrassing to all who taught his general doctrine of Scriptural authority. The fact remains that if he had actually placed James alongside Romans and Galatians, as a book of comparable authority and had so used it, his theology would have been deeply altered.

the Ark of the Covenant, while in Deuteronomy 10:1-5 Moses reports that God commanded *him* to make the Ark and he says, "So I made an ark of acacia wood. . . ." When Joab was ordered to take a census, 2 Samuel 24:1 tells us that it was by God's command while 1 Chronicles 21:1 says it was by Satan's command. However, much of the reported conversation between Moses and Joab is verbally identical in the two passages, showing that the same census is being described. It is not strange that of two earnest, deeply religious men writing about a single course of action, one should interpret it as being the will of God and the other as exactly the opposite. But it does show that the writers and the works were not infallible.

Again and again the numbers of the people and of soldiers, the ages of kings at the time of coronation or death, and the sequence of events in 1 Kings and 2 Chronicles are flatly contradictory.

In the New Testament, inconsistencies between the accounts in the different Gospels have produced endless controversies and placed considerable difficulties in the paths of all who have tried to construct "harmonies" of the Gospels. But the difficulties are not solely to be found within the Gospels. The accounts of Paul's conversion are contradictory regarding the experience of his traveling companions. Acts 9:7 reports that they heard the voice but saw no man while Acts 22:9 says that they "saw the light, but did not hear the voice of the one who was speaking. . . ." Again the account of Acts 1:16-19 sharply contradicts the narrative in Matthew 27:3-10 regarding the manner of Judas' death and the way in which "The Field of Blood" came to be called by that name.

These uncertain details are of little moment unless one is interested in the truth or falsity of the doctrine that the Bible is infallible. But in relation to that doctrine they are decisive for any mind open to consideration of the evidence.

Even in narrating the events in sacred history which are of greatest religious significance the accounts are sometimes distressing in their differences regarding details. It is, for example, apparently impossible to work out a precise sequence of events surrounding and including the resurrection of Jesus which will not be contradicted by evidence from one or more of the accounts in the Gospels. In these important accounts the religious significance of the particular matters involved in discrepancy is minor. Yet the contradictions between the accounts show all too plainly that the narratives are not beyond all error.

B. Differences between Texts

A casual comparison between different English versions reveals the fact that there are questions about the proper translations of various passages from Hebrew, Aramaic or Greek to English or any other tongue. Some Christians in the mid-twentieth century resent the appearance of new translations because they suppose that the version ordered by King James and published in 1611 is the true Bible and that deviations from it are undue tamperings with the Word of God. But in the seventeenth century the people were under no such illusions. The translators, while devoutly seeking divine guidance, leaned heavily on the work by Tyndale and on previous revisions of his great translation, as well as on the manuscripts in the original languages and translations in various foreign tongues. They had set out to make "good" translations into "a better one," they announced in their preface, and this they believed they had accomplished.

Many of the differences in translations are traceable to differences among the best manuscripts in the original tongues. More than two centuries elapsed between the earliest writing in the New Testament and the oldest manuscripts now known, which, indeed, if we do not count the small fragments from the third century, date back only to the fourth century. In the copying during that lapse of time there crept in various errors and other changes so that among the most ancient copies we know there are many and sometimes important variations. An almost incredible amount of patient and skillful labor has gone into the collation of the various manuscripts. Critical studies of the differences discovered with due regard to the comparative age of the manuscripts, the evidences of skill and care of the copyists, the more probable directions of alteration in view of historical developments in doctrine and other factors, have doubtless brought to light ever closer approximations to the earliest forms of the sacred writings. Yet every textual scholar still finds it necessary to make many judgments on the basis of evidence which is far from decisive and the disagreements among authorities are many.

It is obvious, then, that the decision to accept one particular reading rather than another, in a given passage, must of necessity be based upon uncertain and quite fallible human judgment.

There is good evidence that some passages, whatever their original sources may have been, were inserted in the canonical books at comparatively late dates and not accepted for long periods in some traditions of textual transmission. For example, the passage which appears in some versions as Mark 16:9–19 is so poorly attested that the translators of the Revised Standard Version have put it in fine print, together with a very brief alternative passage supported by some ancient authorities. Similar is the treatment of John 7:53–8:11 which some of the ancient manuscripts either omit, place in Luke or vary considerably in wording. The latter passage bears an authenticity and authority not dependent upon the decision of textual critics as to whether it was in a canonical book at a given date or not. But if it is the infallibility of the Scriptures that is being defended, it is highly problematic, in this and many other instances, which writings are to be regarded as beyond criticism. However this question may be answered, the believer in infallibility will be taking his stand in support of some human textual critics or others.

Indeed, it must be pointed out that even the question what whole books are to be included in the Bible will depend on the believer's adherence to the traditions of an Eastern or Western branch of the church. It is hard to see how the infallibility of the Bible can be maintained without attaching a similar infallibility to the Councils by which the limits of the Scriptural canon were determined, a doctrine which few Protestants would care to defend.

C. Contradictions of Known Truth

Though the chief modern interest in the Bible is for its religious teachings, it deals also with many matters which are generally regarded today as well within the fields of the natural sciences. It can hardly escape the notice of the informed reader that concerning such matters the Biblical writers occasionally make statements which are based on long disproved mythology and false science.

When Laban had agreed that all the striped and spotted goats among his flocks were to be Jacob's as pay for his labor as herdsman, it is related in the "J" document (Genesis 30:35-43) that Jacob made all the stronger goats to have such progeny by keeping striped and spotted sticks in front of the breeding animals at their watering troughs. The ancient superstition that both human beings and animals are liable to be marked from birth by the images of things seen by their mothers is found, even in our day, among the ignorant, but has been thoroughly discredited among educated people. Every scientifically trained stock-breeding farmer knows that there is no such cause and effect relation as is assumed in the story. Plainly the narrator simply accepted the false science prevalent in his day.

Similarly, some or all Biblical writers assume the fixity of the earth, the actual movement of sun and moon from east to west, a space above the firmament reserved for God's dwelling and the demonological explanation of disease. Such views cannot be intelligently accepted as infallible teaching.

D. Evidences of Legend-making

Just as the Biblical writers were children of their own times in their scientific ideas, freely using current notions now known false concerning such matters as astronomy, heredity and disease, so also they used the legends of ancient times as vehicles of their religious teachings.

Thus the hero tales in the book of Judges have all the typical characteristics of the legends which have developed everywhere in the world among preliterate peoples. As the Greeks had their Hercules the Hebrews had their Samson. As the Greek legends were made to convey the doctrines of their polytheistic cults, so the legends of Jephthah and Samson were used to teach such ancient Hebrew doctrines as the conviction that solemn oaths to Yahweh must be kept at any cost.

In the Old Testament literature there appears often a strange admixture of deep probing into life's great mysteries and the childlike explanations of natural phenomena typical of oral tradition among prescientific people. Thus in the midst of the Genesis story of the Fall, which penetrates deeply into the mysteries of human sin and natural evil, there appears a mythological explanation of why the snake has no legs and must live in perpetual hostility to man.[2]

Again, in the setting down of oral tradition concerning human events which had occurred before written accounts were kept, the same kinds of exaggerations were transmitted as in similar conditions among other peoples. There have been many fruitless discussions of the great age attained by the ancient patriarchs according to the Genesis accounts. Actually these are paralleled by similar "histories" of kings and heroes among other peoples. For example, the Japanese histories describe the fabulously long lives of the earlier emperors, though the modern sovereigns live no longer than other men. It is notable that the transition to normal lengths of life in the Japanese imperial chronology occurs in the eighth century A.D., at precisely the time when the keeping of written records began.

The Hebrews were like other peoples in loving to tell of "the mighty men that were of old, the men of renown."[3] Like other ancient peoples they permitted their imaginations to embellish freely the oral traditions concerning the heroes of preliterate times.

E. Morally Unworthy Passages

Even if it be maintained that the Bible's infallibility is confined to matters of morals and religion the contrary evidence is decisive.

What Christian can defend as morally infallible a writer who boasts that he is morally perfect and goes on to gloat over the enemies whom he always kills before he turns back from pursuing them, whom he pounds to pieces and crushes "like mud in the street," who delights in the fawning, cringing homage of foreigners to himself and who attributes all this happy good fortune to God who has rewarded him with the murderous power he thinks he deserves?[4] While Jesus exhorts forgiveness to the repentant even "seventy times seven"

[2] Gen. 3:14-15.
[3] Gen. 6:4.
[4] See Ps. 18:20-24, 33-49.

times, the author of Psalm 109 not only prays that his enemy's prayer will be regarded as a sin but that no one will pity his children when he is dead. Similarly depressing are the portrayals of a narrowly nationalistic and bloodthirsty God in Judges, Nahum and elsewhere.

Of course, no earnest and intelligent Christian actually takes such passages of Scripture as morally authoritative for him. Doctrines of "dispensations" and distinctions between the present text and the unknown "autographa" are combined by desperate defenders of the theory of infallibility who know that some teachings in the Bible as we have it are not accurate representations of God's moral purpose for man. For practical religion the result still emerges that the Bible is not in all its parts an infallible moral guide.

F. The Testimony of Jesus

Jesus' exceedingly high regard for the Old Testament we shall have occasion to observe in the next chapter. But while we are treating the fallibility of the Scriptures we must note that Jesus unhesitatingly and repeatedly sets Old Testament teaching at naught.

Citing the Old Testament doctrines concerning the fulfilling of oaths, he did not stop with repudiating their authority with his emphatic "But I say unto you, Do not swear at all." He went on to give reasons for his command and they were reasons which had been as valid in the days of Deuteronomy, Leviticus and Numbers as they were while he spoke.[5] Similarly, when he denounced the doctrine of loving neighbors and hating enemies, substituting the law of love for enemies and prayers for persecutors, he again gave reasons the force of which is timeless. You are to love your enemies, he said, "so that you may be sons of your Father who is in heaven; for he makes his sun rise on the evil and on the good, and sends rain on the just and on the unjust." [6] It is obvious that God had been making the sun and rain to bless both evil and good men through all the centuries as well as in the time of Jesus' teaching.

G. A Collection of Human Writings

It is evident that the Bible is a collection of intensely human documents. These books were written by men who had their own characteristic education, interests, vocabularies and literary styles. Most of the events described are activities of obviously fallible human beings. Many passages contradict one another or well-established knowledge. Many of the moral and religious ideas, especially in the more ancient documents, are distinctly sub-Christian.

[5] See Mt. 5:33–37.
[6] Mt. 5:45.

The Bible is not such a book that a reader can safely assume the truth and authoritative moral validity of any given passage without critical examination in relation to other passages and to other evidence.

These considerations, however, do not constitute a denial of the inspiration and authority of the Bible in its more elevated portions or as a whole. We turn our attention next to the question whether there is any important sense in which the Bible may be called the inspired Word of God.

CHAPTER 9

The Inspiration of the Bible

THE human fallibility of the Bible does not preclude the possibility of its divine inspiration nor of its unmatched moral and religious authority. Although written by men with characteristic individual traits and typical human failings it may still have been written by men seized and impelled by the spirit of God. Although it tells of men who made serious mistakes and gravely sinned it may yet describe men to whom God revealed Himself in His forgiving mercy and wondrous power.

It contains many inconsistencies and inaccuracies, but it may nevertheless present truths of such profound worth as to make the inaccuracies seem inconsequential. Despite its composite and often uncertain human authorship there may be a high degree of continuity in the moral and religious message which evolves in this body of literature as a whole. Even though there are passages which represent low moral standards, those standards may have been relatively high in their own times. Moreover, they may be repudiated or corrected in the whole progression of thought and experience which the Bible represents.

The whole may thus represent a long process of revelation through which God showed increasing measures of His truth to humanity as men were prepared through progressive stages of understanding, obedience and humble spiritual sensitiveness to receive and declare that truth in word and life.

The evidence within the Bible itself and in its impact upon human history sustains the belief that all of these possibilities are in truth actualities. A full presentation of the evidence would require many books, as well as vast Biblical and historical learning. All that is possible here is a clarification of the claim that is being made with illustration of some kinds of relevant evidence.

A. MEANING OF INSPIRATION AS DEFENDED

Since the word "inspiration" as applied to the Scriptures has been made to convey many meanings it is necessary to define what is meant by it here. We may well begin by denial of some meanings *not* intended.

It should be clear to all readers of Chapter 8 that the present work is not defending either "mechanical" or "verbal" inspiration. The Bible was clearly not produced by a process in which the human writers were passive instruments or unimaginative amanuenses setting down the words given by a divine author. Neither was it produced by any method through which God insured the unfailing truth and usefulness of every word. Both the language and the substance bear the ineffaceable imprint of active human individuality in expression and thought.

Some theologians,[1] though conceding the untenability of verbal inspiration, defend still a doctrine of plenary inspiration. This view has about it a certain ambiguous flexibility which saves it from being so vulnerable to specific factual evidence as the theory of verbal inspiration. However, if it is meant (as it seems to be) to affirm still that every teaching in the Scriptures, when understood in context and in the sense intended by the writer, is strictly true, then it is as decisively even though not so simply refuted by the clear evidences of self-contradiction, error and low moral teaching.

Having cleared the way by repudiating doctrines of inspiration which overreach themselves with extravagant claims, we are now ready to state the view to be commended here. This doctrine is that the writing of the Bible as a whole was accomplished by an extraordinary stimulation and elevation of the powers of men who devoutly yielded themselves to God's will and sought, often with success unparalleled elsewhere, to convey truth useful to the salvation of men and of nations. This was possible mainly because they had truth of such extraordinary importance to convey. It is upon that truth that we must lay our principal stress.

Before each part of the Bible was written there were such events in the experience of the writers as to induce the writing. Inspiration is to be attributed primarily to these experiences and only secondarily to the passages in which they found expression. For example, Jesus' earthly ministry closed many years before Mark, the earliest of the Gospels, was written. The effective work of God in human history was primarily in and through Jesus and only secondarily in the account of that work written down several decades later. The life of the church is not rooted primarily in that and other accounts, but in Christ. This is shown by the fact that the church lived in great spiritual power before any of the Gospels were written. But the enlightenment and power of God, first expressed in His mighty acts in the lives of men, has been mediated to us both through the continuing life of the church and through the Biblical records by which the traditional memory of its origins is continually renewed and corrected.

[1] E.g., H. Orton Wiley, in his *Christian Theology*.

B. Evidences of Inspiration

Of Biblical inspiration in the sense just defined there are many persuasive evidences. Since our whole study will be based on the experience of the Christian community and that community itself is both product and depository of the message transmitted principally through the Scriptures, all the succeeding chapters will have a bearing on the inspiration of the Bible. If the experience of Christians has been rich in the producing of ideas which commend themselves as true and valuable, this fact constitutes especially important evidence for such a doctrine of inspiration as we are now considering.

However, we must call attention at present to some principal types of evidence which converge in support of such a doctrine. In doing so it will be assumed that the reader has sufficient knowledge of the Bible and of history to provide further illustration of the types and to evaluate the generalizations for himself.

1. Elevated Form and Spirit

Neither the form nor spirit of the Scriptures maintains an invariably high level of excellence. But with remarkable frequency the Biblical writings attain such heights of rhetorical beauty, dignity and power as have been equaled, if at all, only in other writings deeply influenced by these. Such nobility of mood and expression is often sustained through long passages.

Where else can be found such soul-searching prayers of penitence, such profound expressions of trust in time of adversity, such lofty hymns of joy and praise or such stirring calls to worship as are written in the great Psalms? Where is such blazing denunciation of hypocritical religion and social unrighteousness as the prophecy of Amos unless, indeed, it be in the words of Jesus? Is there a match for the sixth chapter of Isaiah in giving voice to the awe experienced before the presence of the righteous and holy God? What parable equals Jesus' story of the good Samaritan for teaching unlimited compassion? Who has answered the one serious objection to belief in immortality with such exalted thought and language as St. Paul exhibits in the fifteenth chapter of 1 Corinthians?

There are passages in every book of the Bible worthy of thoughtful exposition and memorable for richness of expression.[2]

It is small cause for wonder that writers in many tongues whose works have

[2] While in the pastorate I once preached, with some interruptions, a series of sixty-six sermons of which one was devoted to each book of the Scriptures. Again and again it seemed that the book for the day was written precisely for the most urgent need of the moment, as when the book of Amos fell due in the midst of a desperate struggle of the local shoeworkers against an extraordinarily brutal industrial management and there was no escape from centering the sermon on Amos 8:6. Never was there difficulty in finding in the book for the day an eloquently expressed teaching highly relevant to the people's needs.

endured for generations have found in the Bible models of literary excellence and inspiration for their own most powerful utterances. Such names as Dante, Shakespeare, Hugo, Tolstoy leap to mind. Neither is it strange that artists and musicians have found in Scripture the perfect symbols of countless human moods and aspirations.

2. *Great Thoughts*

The substance of thought in the Bible rises again and again far beyond the possibility of fully adequate expression even in the most exalted literary forms known to man.

In the fourth century B.C. when even the noblest ethical philosophers of the Greeks' golden age were taking infanticide for granted and showing hardly a sign of appreciation for the tenderness and beauty of loyal family ties, the Hebrews had already been reading for centuries Hosea's account of God's patient redemptive love for His wayward people under the figure of the prophet's tender love for his repeatedly disloyal wife and a father's patient concern for his little child, just learning to walk. While Rome's emperors hired soothsayers to search the entrails of butchered beasts for signs of favor or disfavor from their warring gods, Jesus was speaking confidently of the one heavenly Father whose will he both knew and did. Even today while millions of human beings wander homeless and starving and great scientists plan new means of vengeance upon any who dare to attack their native lands, the Scriptures speak across the ages of another road to peace under just law softened and strengthened by mercy and love. The prophets and the Gospels are still before us and not behind us. The faith and moral reason which they express still stretch our hearts and minds.

3. *Records of Uniquely Important Events*

The Bible contains the records of the most important events in the history of man. Here is the story of the aspirations, falls, struggles and the long climb of Israel, drawn by God's call, to the mountaintop of vision. It is out of this wonderful history of spiritual victory through tragedy that three of the greatest religions have come. For Judaism, Islam and Christianity all have their roots in the prophetic movement of Israel.

But here, too, is the story of Jesus. How unique and meaningful that is we shall be indicating in a later chapter. If the Christian faith is basically valid, then this story is by far the most important ever told, indeed is the one story which human beings really need to know. In the Gospels are answers to the deepest and most urgent questions of humanity. What is the purpose of our existence? Are men alone in their ideal strivings or have we cosmic support?

Can sin and death be overcome? What must we do to be saved? Here are answers to such questions, answers which have satisfied many of earth's wisest sages and brought triumphant joy on earth and hope of life to come to millions of the humblest toiling, suffering and sorrowing masses.

In the Bible, also, is the account of the founding of the Christian church which has brought to unnumbered multitudes all life's richest meanings.

Not only the form and thought of the Scripture, but likewise many of the lives and events described bear the marks of God's guiding hand. Indeed it is to those acts of God in human lives that we must refer for explanation of the extraordinary qualities which we find in the Bible itself.

4. Unparalleled Influences

The supreme evidence that the message of the Bible is inspired of God is its power to inspire men to seek and find God.

Other books have induced men to fight and plunder and destroy. It is a sad fact that many who have been deeply devoted to the Scriptures have done so. But no other book has conveyed a message with such demonstrated power to cleanse the soul and to create new levels of life as has the Bible. This life-giving message, conveyed to many through the Scripture, is properly called the Word of God.

The Word brought by the Bible has given rise to or helped greatly to advance such high values in human life as respect for womanhood and childhood, loyal monogamous marriage, hospitals and medical service for the poor, missions of mercy to strangers in distant lands, the ideal and the partial attainment of universal and free education and the only viable democratic governments which have given even lip service to equal rights for *all* men and women.

Surely these ideas and movements are of God.

Some of the theories concerning the inspiration of the Bible have been inept and ill-advised. But they have been framed in response to a great reality of history, the unique place of the Bible as guide of millions to experiences of such personal spiritual victory and social achievement as have been unparalleled where its message has not reached.

If our beliefs and practices do not acknowledge this unique, divinely inspired power within the Bible we shall be impoverishing ourselves and our children, destroying the church and undermining all that men of good will now hold dear. Besides, there is good reason to believe that in our failure we shall be missing the truth.

CHAPTER 10

The Authority of the Bible

T HE question of inspiration and the question of authority, though related, are not the same.

By authority is here meant rightful claim to be believed. Thus a specialist in mathematics has more authority regarding a question of analytical geometry than has a man with less knowledge of the subject. It occasionally happens that a man with less knowledge of a subject gives a correct answer to a question when the most learned man gives a false answer. However, this does not make the man with less knowledge a greater authority in the field in question. The probabilities of his being right concerning any new question in that field are lower than those of the expert. In general, unless we possess important contrary evidence of our own which he might not have, we do well in regard to a question of chemistry to take the word of the specialist in chemistry.

It is evident that authority occurs in various fields and in different degrees of reliability. We have, therefore, not only to inquire whether the Bible possesses authority, but also to ask how much authority and in regard to what kinds of problems.

A. AUTHORITY ACTUALLY ASCRIBED TO THE BIBLE

From the earliest beginnings of the Christian movement, Christians attributed very high authority to the canonical Scriptures. The extent of the canon, however, varied considerably. At first, of course, there was no New Testament so that the many references to the Scriptures in the Pauline Epistles and the Synoptic Gospels refer only to the Old Testament. Students of church history know how various books of our New Testament came, one by one, to be cited similarly as authoritative Scriptures, along with various other works such as I Clement and the Sybilline Oracles, how gradually some were added and others demoted until the fixing of the New Testament canon.[1]

[1] Indeed, the canon never was fixed by a general council, unless one is willing so to designate the Roman Council of Trent. The extent of the canon still differs considerably in the various branches of Christendom. It was historically established for most Protestants by the Westminster Assembly of 1643 and the Swiss Declaration of Faith in 1675.

Jesus, according to the Synoptic Gospels, attributed to various passages of the Old Testament the authority of God's own commands. With especially strong emphasis he affirmed and used the authority of Isaiah and of the Ten Commandments.[2] He came, he said, not to abolish the law and the prophets but to fulfill them.[3]

On the other hand, it must be recalled that in order to "fulfill" the law, he did in some instances plainly set it aside.[4] Apparently he distinguished between the true law of God which is the essential significance of the law and the prophets, on the one hand, and the specific written formulas on the other.

Among the Church Fathers the Scriptures were generally quoted as having decisive authority. However, as has been indicated, the bounds of the literature conceded such authority were often far from being identical with limits of the canon now received by any branch of Christendom. Moreover, the teaching accepted as the authoritative word of the Scriptures was often a doctrine obtained from other sources and drawn from a Biblical passage by devious allegorical construction.

From ancient times the authority of the Bible has been in practice modified considerably by being shared with other authorities, acknowledged or unacknowledged. For example, so Biblically minded a Father as Irenaeus declared that the authoritative exposition of the Scriptures was to be found in the church alone.[5] In effect, this was bound to transfer some of the authority from the written word to the interpreters in the church. Tertullian went further, saying that the Bible belonged to true believers only and others had no right to quote from it in behalf of their opinions. What, then, was to be the standard by which one might know who were the true believers? Tertullian was explicit and clear. Those only are true believers and have a right to quote the Scriptures who accept the Rule of Faith.[6] Although the Rule of Faith—in any of the several forms it assumed in the early church—was supposedly drawn from the teachings of the Bible, its language was not exclusively Biblical. At the very least Tertullian's principle would have the effect of setting up the particular Biblical ideas which were included in the Rule of Faith as possessing absolute finality and reducing every other teaching of the Scriptures to a relative authority dependent upon its relation to the Rule of Faith.

It is evident that whether acknowledged or not, considerations of similar

[2] Particularly interesting is his quotation from Isaiah in support of his condemnation of the Pharisees and Scribes for so interpreting some of the Ten Commandments, "the commandment of God," as virtually to substitute for them their traditions ("the tradition of men"). See Mk. 7:5–13 and Mt. 15:1–9.

[3] Mt. 5:17.

[4] Mt. 5:33–48.

[5] *Against Heresies*, IV.p.26.

[6] *Prescription against Heresies*, XVIII.

character have influenced the accepted authority of the Bible in every branch of Christendom down to the present time. Some churches, like the Greek Orthodox, acknowledge the decisive authority of the great catholic councils and where some passage of Scripture seems clearly to contradict the decision of such a council they give the council conclusive authority so that the Biblical passage must in some way be interpreted in conformity to it. The Roman Catholic Church, of course, finally gives to the *ex cathedra* utterances of the pope this power of decision regarding the teaching of Scripture and even the power to promulgate dogmas admittedly not taught in the Bible.

The Protestant churches, while not conceding any such absolute formal authority to any human person or body to interpret the Scripture and hence, in effect, to exercise an authority superior to it, all do in practice modify the authority of the Bible by the different cultural contexts in which they read and expound it. Lutherans tend to stress what Luther stressed and to give slight emphasis to teachings he considered of lesser value. Similarly, Calvinists read the Bible through Calvinist eyes, Baptists through Baptist eyes and Methodists through Methodist eyes, while Friends read as Friends. The very fact that there *are* various and often contrary traditions, even among the most conservative believers in Biblical authority, shows the great influence of the different cultural contexts in which the Bible is read. The staunchest defenders of the doctrine of the infallible Bible as the sole authority for faith do not escape these influences, but find themselves divided into Calvinistic, Lutheran, Arminian and other schools of theological belief, all thinking their own views to be the only truly Biblical systems of doctrine.

In modern times increasing numbers of Christians have come to ascribe only a limited though yet high authority to the Bible, believing that it is clearly fallible and that its teaching needs conscious, explicit correction and supplementation by evidence from other quarters.

B. Biblical Authority to Be Properly Acknowledged

Any candid examination must show that different parts of the Bible are radically unequal in inspiration and authority. Even Christian thinkers who have professed belief in Biblical infallibility have in practice leaned heavily on some portions and dismissed, ignored or adjusted the apparent meanings of others as best they could to avoid contradiction. While in some instances the choice seems to Christians who read in a different personal and cultural context indefensibly arbitrary, the general procedure of critical selection has much more to commend it in principle than has the doctrine of equal, because absolute, authority in every part of the Bible. No intelligent Christian would think of attributing high authority to the imprecatory Psalms nor to the legends of bloodthirsty heroes in the Judges if such passages had to stand alone and be judged on their own merits. The plausibility of the doctrine of absolute authority clearly rests on the exalted portions of the Scripture which have little in common with these. They do have one thing in common and that is their belonging historically together in the development of a great religious tradition. But it would seem reasonable to discriminate between the authority of the high points in that tradition and the inferior portions which are contrary in ideas and spirit.

The message of the Bible as a whole concerning its great central themes possesses high authority. A reasonable man concedes authority to the best books he can find on a given subject. If there is any book which should possess authority on any subject for a reasonable man, then religious authority should be conceded to the culminating deliverances of the Bible on the great themes to which it is most largely devoted. For there are no other books which have been tested so long by so many people as this one and no others can show such a record of salutary influence, of ideas sustained by the most critical examination and of personal experience confirming its most meaningful teachings.

Its authority is greatest at the center of its climactic development, that is, in the most characteristic spirit and teaching of Jesus Christ. For it is faith in Jesus which has been most heavily tested by critical thought and by personal and historical experience. It is precisely the teaching of Jesus and faith in the validity of his revelation of God that have inspired men and women to noblest achievement, sublimest courage and fullest coherent unity of life. Other teachings of the Bible must be judged to possess authority commensurate with their proximity in meaning to that climactic gospel theme, excepting as they can be independently supported by internal and external evidence.

Even as regards the most authoritative portions of Scripture it must be said that there is one higher authority. That is the totality of human experience, including the Bible, but including also the thinking of the most careful and critically disciplined minds, the records of secular and church history, the recorded religious experiences of mankind and the immediate experience of God in the heart of the reader himself. God has revealed Himself marvelously in the great events, utterances and insights recorded in the Bible, but not solely there. He seeks to reveal Himself also to all at all times. Especially significant are His revelations of Himself and His will in the experiences of those who most humbly and faithfully subject themselves to Him by faith in the highest single revelation we know—the Christ who is the culminating message of the Bible. To deny this would be to deny the doctrine of the Holy Spirit.

As has been pointed out, it is impossible, in any case, to read the Bible outside of any cultural context. If we would know all the truth offered to us by the self-revealing God, we need to read the Bible in the context most inclusive of all the evidence God has supplied through all the channels He has opened to men. Such a course is required both by the method of empirical reason defended at the beginning of our study and by a humble faith in the ever-living, ever-active God. Not to make a special effort at understanding in the most inclusive cultural context is to consent to reading the Bible from a narrowly provincial point of view from which much divine light has been excluded. But suppose it be denied that God has shed any light upon man outside the Scriptures? That could be determined, if at all, only by looking to see. Moreover, to believe so would be to deny some of the plain teachings of the Bible itself.[7] It would also be to contradict the obvious experience of the Christian community which has again and again been aided in the understanding and acceptance of the Biblical commands by secular movements and teachings.[8]

C. How This Authority Should Be Acknowledged

1. Reading

People who talk about the high authority of the Bible but do not devote much attention to reading and understanding it can hardly expect to have their professions taken very seriously. The acknowledgment of any considerable authority in a book which purports to give the answers to man's most profound and important questions obviously requires first of all diligent and thoughtful reading. The need for critical reading, in broad context, is no excuse for not reading.

Through the centuries the inspiration and guidance of the Christian community at its best have come primarily from the Bible. In churches where that reading has been neglected, the fires of devotion have slowly but surely died down. Even a superficial sociological description of the churches shows that one of the principal institutional symbols which hold a church together and give it distinctive place in the community is the reading of the Bible with instruction in its significance. Neglect of the Bible leads soon to neglect of the church.

2. Evaluation

If the real meaning and value of the Scriptures are to be appreciated, it is necessary that the reader examine critically what he reads, testing one part in

---

[7] E.g., Jn. 14:26; Rom. 1:20; 2:1–3; Acts 17:26–28.

[8] The recent interaction of Christian and non-Christian—even anti-Christian—influences in the rediscovery of the Biblical protests against the exploitation of labor and against war will serve to illustrate. In the ancient world the principle is well exemplified by the preparation of Augustine's mind by Platonic studies so that he was enabled to understand and receive the gospel which had previously failed to appeal to him.

relation to another, to his experience and to important relevant knowledge and opinion from other quarters. The influence of the Bible in history and the high themes with which it deals should draw from the reasonable reader a humble, sympathetic and prayerful search for truth in its pages. It should not lull his critical powers into thoughtless acquiescence. We have seen that the teachings of the Bible are not all of equal authority. Discrimination is therefore necessary. However, the earnest critical examination of what one reads from the Bible will go much further to show its actual relevance to the issues of personal and social human life than can possibly be learned by uncritical acceptance. It is a poor faith which is unwilling to test the teachings of Scripture quite open-mindedly in relation to the whole body of relevant evidence.

After finding, as most Christians have found, the exceedingly high average of dependability in the ethical and religious teachings of its finer portions and in its massive central trends of doctrine, the reasonable reader will learn to accept these as true unless and until disproved. In weighing the various evidences concerning a particular issue of religious doctrine the mere quotation of a Biblical verse will not be in itself decisive. However, a considerable body of Biblical teaching on the subject, particularly if that teaching appears in close conjunction with some of the most thoroughly tested and highly valued utterances, will be taken as very important evidence concerning the matter in hand.

3. Interpretation for Practice

The earnest seeker after truth concerning God and the way of salvation will wish to find the practical significance of the Bible for his own attitudes and actions and in relation to the problems of the world in which he lives. This will often require much hard thought to discover the principles exemplified in Scriptural teaching and to deduce from them the specific applications. The necessity of doing this will be inescapable if the Bible is to be given authority in practice, however emphatically the reader may reject all notions of "legalism."

One of the most able and forceful protests against legalistic interpretations of Christian ethics in recent years is Paul Ramsey's *Basic Christian Ethics*. Yet it is noteworthy that he carefully establishes by generalization from much Biblical material the principle that the Christian should always act in concern for his neighbor's need, whoever the neighbor may be. Then he devotes much careful thought to the question what such concern requires in various circumstances, as for example when the Christian confronts one neighbor abusing another.

There would seem to be only two alternatives to such procedures of generalization and deduction. One would be a literal conformity to Scripturally described examples and commands which would often miss and even contradict the original spirit and meaning of them. Thus the reader might feel obliged to give to a beggar whatever he asked in literal accordance with Matthew 5:42, even though this was clearly to result in the starving of his own family and though the beggar was predictably intending to use the donation as a means to the ends of debauchery and crime. Similarly, he might suppose that every man ought to wear sandals and a seamless robe and go as a homeless celibate from place to place because Jesus did so.

Another alternative would be, of course, to keep the stories, commands and doctrines of the Bible in a kind of sanctuary within the mind, well insulated from the practical business of living. Unfortunately, this is not so rare a procedure as it deserves to be.

4. Obedience

Having found what attitudes and action are implied by the Scriptural imperatives which have stood the test of thoughtful evaluation, the earnest man will place himself among those who are "doers of the word and not hearers only." [9]

5. Instruction

Finally, a proper acknowledgment of the authority of Scripture will require that it be taught to others also in order that its treasures may be shared in the love which it commands. The neglect of Biblical instruction cannot be excused by the need for critical interpretation and realistic application. Such need makes the task more difficult than would be that of an unimaginative literalism, but it does not reduce one whit the urgent necessity of it. Fortunately, there are hopeful signs of a new awakening to the duty and privilege of teaching the Bible.

[9] Jas. 1:22.

PART THREE

GOD AND THE WORLD

CHAPTER 11

The Unity of God

A. DEVELOPMENT OF THIS CONCEPTION

IN THE historic development of religion there is a tendency for thought to move in the direction of monotheism. Disregarding the more vague and impersonal conceptions of the supernatural [1] we may distinguish four main stages in this development. First is the primitive form of religion in which the dominant beliefs and practices are animistic, that is, concerning localized spirits supposed to inhabit individual objects such as a tree, mountain, river or man. At a second, more sophisticated level of culture, the tendency is to universalize various types of phenomena and identify with each a particular deity such as a god of storms, another of harvest and another of procreation. The pantheon of the ancient Greeks is the most famous example of such polytheism. Sometimes there develops out of polytheism some form of henotheism, in which the people of a tribe or nation regard only one god as worthy of their own faith and worship although it is assumed that the different gods of other peoples are also real. Henotheism leads naturally to monotheism in which existence is denied of any gods other than the one worshiped.

It must be emphasized that the stages of religious thought just described are not usually—perhaps ever—mutually exclusive, with the sole exception of monotheism which by its very nature implies the denial of all the others. Even among people who are conspicuously given to animistic beliefs and rites there is often an undercurrent of tradition regarding a single "Great Spirit" or "High God" who created and now rules over all the world.[2]

There are many evidences in the Old Testament of the long, hard struggle of the Hebrews to advance from polytheism to a steadfast belief in the one true

---

[1] E.g., the *mana* of the Polynesians.

[2] In showing that this was true Andrew Lang, in his book *The Making of Religion* (1898), corrected the oversimplified, unilateral view of religious development in E. B. Tyler's famous work, *Primitive Culture* (1871). The prevalence and sophisticated level of monotheism among primitive peoples are probably exaggerated, on the other hand, by Wilhelm Schmidt in *The Origin and Growth of Religion* (1931). See also Emile Durkheim, *Elementary Forms of the Religious Life*, J. G. Frazer, *The Golden Bough*, Paul Radin, *Monotheism among Primitive Peoples* and Horace L. Friess and Herbert W. Schneider, *Religion in Various Cultures*.

God, Yahweh.[3] Not only are there recorded countless protests by the prophets against the worship of various "strange gods," but it is evident that the accepted practice of the Hebrews before the time of Moses had been polytheistic.[4] Even when Joshua demanded that the worship of foreign gods cease he did not deny their existence. He demanded that a practical religious choice be made.

> And if you be unwilling to serve the LORD, choose this day whom you will serve, whether the gods your fathers served in the region beyond the River, or the gods of the Amorites in whose land you dwell; but as for me and my house, we will serve the LORD.[5]

There is here no suggestion that the other gods do not exist, but only that they should not be served by the Israelites. This monolatrous henotheism persists through much of the Old Testament literature. Most of the writers were little interested in theories concerning existence. Their concern was with practical religion. The existence of gods other than Yahweh might be granted so long as they were regarded as foreign and inferior. Hence we read, "Who is like thee, O LORD, among the gods?"[6] while in the Psalms He is praised as "a great King above all gods"[7] and it is declared that "our LORD is above all gods."[8] On the other hand, even in the earlier writings there are utterances which give to the Hebrews' God such pre-eminence as would permit to other gods at best a status comparable to that of good or evil angels. Thus in the Elohist document Abraham asks, "Shall not the Judge of all the earth do right?"[9] while the second creation story comes from the ancient Jahwist document.[10] When God is regarded as Judge or Creator of all the earth rival gods are hardly conceivable. The prophets of the eighth century so despised idols that they could not have had much fear of the deities which the idols represented. Amos attributed to Yahweh a guiding interest in nations other than Israel and Judah and taught that He used them to punish his own people.[11] However, it was in the late seventh century that a complete monotheism came to expression in Jeremiah's denunciation of his people's defection to gods which are "no gods,"[12] and in Deuteronomy occurs the most thoroughgoing and decisive statement,

---

[3] Readers unfamiliar with the artificial device which produced the hybrid word "Jehovah" will find a succinct account by R. B. Y. Scott in V. Ferm, *An Encyclopedia of Religion*. It should be observed, however, that even the vowel sounds in "Yahweh" are not certainly correct.

[4] See Josh. 24:2-3, 14-15; Ezek. 20:24.

[5] Josh. 24:15.

[6] Ex. 15:11.

[7] 95:3.

[8] 135:5.

[9] Gen. 18:25.

[10] Gen. 2:4-25.

[11] 9:7; 3:10-11.

[12] 2:11.

"Know therefore this day, and lay it to your heart, that the LORD is God in heaven above and on the earth beneath; there is no other." [13] In the sixth century the monotheistic theme was elaborated by Deutero-Isaiah and the false gods of the powerful nation which held the Israelites captive were denounced with impassioned argument and withering scorn.[14] Yahweh had created the heavens and the earth and He alone was God.[15]

The very heart of Judaism is the *Shema*, with its stout affirmation, "The LORD our God is one LORD." [16] This uncompromising monotheism is taken for granted in the New Testament as something which any rational person should know.[17] According to Mark, indeed, when Jesus was asked for the first commandment he replied with the first two verses of the *Shema*, adding the command of love for neighbor.[18] Despite the difficulties introduced into the thought of the church by doctrines of the Trinity, most people who have called themselves Christians have insisted that there is but one God and His self-unity is complete. The Christian religion is a monotheistic faith.

B. EVIDENCE OF THE DIVINE UNITY

It is no accident that as religious people increase in knowledge, in powers of discipline, in systematic thought and in depth of cultural experience they tend to move toward monotheism. There is considerable evidence that God is, indeed, one.

1. *Universality of Causal Law*

In an earlier chapter it was observed that one evidence for the existence of God is the rational system of causal law by which the entire material universe is governed. Such evidence not only supports belief in cosmic mind but also belief in *one* cosmic Mind as source of the world unity. For however far human knowledge penetrates into the vast interstellar spaces and however deeply it enters the intricate order of miscroscopic and submicroscopic processes, all is found to belong together in a single system of causal sequence. We live in a universe, not a multiverse. Corresponding to one rationally formulable system of causal law it is reasonable to believe in one God.

[13] 4:39.
[14] 44:9–20.
[15] 45:12, 18, 21–22. For an excellent treatment of Old Testament doctrine of God, see Albert C. Knudson, *The Religious Teaching of the Old Testament*. Cf. the similar, but more theoretical and less vital development of monotheistic conceptions in such Greek philosophers as Xenophanes, Heraclitus and Anaxagoras.
[16] Deut. 6:4.
[17] Rom. 1:18–23.
[18] Mk. 12:30.

2. *More Inclusive Universality of Abstract Truths*

It was seen that another evidence of God was to be found in the realm of abstract truths which human beings discover but are powerless to change. Euclidean and non-Euclidean systems of geometry, Aristotelian and non-Aristotelian systems of logic, all meaningful orders of thought are alike bound in one all-inclusive network of implication. Whether thought concerns material or spiritual being, all ideas which are formulated in quest of truth concerning "what is and what is not" [19] are alike bound by a single system of logical necessity which sets limits to possibility of meaning and of being alike. If we were right in attributing the being of such abstract truth to the Mind that has made us, we are justified also in concluding that that Mind is one and not many.

3. *Universality of Moral Ideals*

Again, the moral ideals, such as honesty, self-discipline and loyalty, on obedience to which the sciences of every kind depend, and likewise the other ideals which form a coherent system with these, are universal in scope. The moral law is by its nature valid for all persons or for none.

Such ethical universalism as has just been stated is foreign to polytheistic and henotheistic beliefs. If there are many gods it is natural to suppose that different ones make different demands on their devotees and that the gods themselves are in frequent strife because of their conflicting purposes. A single system of moral law implies a single source of moral authority. Indeed, the evidence for the *existence* of God which was earlier pointed out in the objectivity of ideal moral norms was evidence for the *unity* of God as well.

4. *The Historical Trend to Monotheism*

It cannot be argued with validity that an idea is true merely because for a given historical period there is a tendency toward the acceptance of it. But when the discovery of increasing measures of truth in many areas of thought and the enriching of culture with more varied and meaningful values appear in various times and places in reciprocal relation to a particular trend of belief and practice, that fact does have some evidential value. Now the trend toward monotheism does seem to be in such a reciprocal relation to advancing culture in many different parts of the world and in various periods of history.[20]

This trend is understandable in view of the rational evidences for the unity of God which we have indicated. The tendency itself gives added confirmation

---

[19] *Bhagavad Gita.* Note, however, that the *Gita* describes the deity as *being* both "what is and what is not."

[20] Cf. George Foote Moore, *History of Religions,* Vol. I, p. viii.

of the inferences. The fact that in the religions of many lands there is a marked tendency for the more thoughtful people to move toward monotheism and that monotheistic peoples have tended to advance more rapidly in the sciences, in education and in government gives added evidence of a superior comprehensive coherence of data in support of belief in the unity of God.

5. Religious Experience

The saintly men and women who have most convincingly witnessed by word and life to their experience of deity have shown a remarkable convergence of testimony on the unity of God. Whether reared in the traditions of a monotheistic faith like Judaism or of a polytheism like popular Hinduism, the great mystics show a striking tendency to return from their experiences of deity with the report that God is one. Mystical experience does, to be sure, show some inclination toward pantheism, but it moves very rarely, indeed, toward a compromising of the unity of God.

As Schleiermacher indicated, there is a kind of logic within religious experience itself which when fully developed leads to belief in one God, fully unified in His own being. Whether we accept Schleiermacher's understanding of religion as a feeling of absolute dependence or consider some such feeling to be only one aspect of true religion, it is undeniable that completely matured religion always involves an absoluteness of personal commitment. It is the whole self which is committed to God, whether in dependence, love or active devotion. Now if the worshiper believes several divine beings to exist, then while he prays to one such being, even though he never prays to any other, there must always be a certain degree of reservation. His faith in the god whom he serves must leave room for acknowledgment that there are other deities, too, to whom allegiance might be given. But when devotion to one deity becomes complete, no such reservation can be made. Indeed, it was this inner logic of religious experience which seems to have been the primary influence leading the ancient Hebrews into the understanding that there was, in truth, only one God.

Similarly, this absolute whole-commitment of self which a fully developed faith always experiences implies the unity of God within Himself. Any belief in conflicting or deeply disparate aspects of God's own nature would require that while paying the tribute of faithful devotion to one aspect of God a certain reservation must be maintained for the proper recognition of all that in God which was thought to be disparate. Only if God is conceived as fully one in His own nature can He be worshiped and served with wholeness of devotion. We can love God with all the heart, mind, soul and strength only if God is one.

6. *The Biblical Testimony*

On this matter the teaching of the Bible is unmistakably clear. Slowly, but forcefully, the vague and intermittent monotheism of the earlier writers gains in clarity and assurance until it triumphs over every kind of compromise in the *Shema.*[21]

It is true that there is nothing in Christian theology which is a greater stumbling block to thoughtful Jews than the doctrine of the Trinity, and this they often find repelling because it seems to them to compromise the divine unity and move toward polytheism. But it is clearly evident that any compromising of that unity of God stressed for all Jews in the *Shema* would be contrary to Jesus' explicit use of that very affirmation in circumstances which gave to it the greatest possible emphasis.[22] Any doctrine of the Trinity which is to be true to the original Christian teaching must be framed within the limits of that solemn utterance, the thought of which is assumed throughout the New Testament.[23]

C. Denials Implied by This Doctrine

1. *Polytheism and Henotheism*

The doctrine of the unity of God plainly implies both that only the one God should be worshiped and that only the one God exists. All polytheistic and henotheistic ideas must be firmly rejected as false.

2. *Tritheistic Interpretations of the Trinity*

Some conservative religious leaders, in trying to defend the historic doctrine of the Trinity, have so stressed the divisions within the godhead as actually to fall into tritheism. It is ironical that men especially solicitous for the defense of orthodoxy against heresy should proclaim a doctrine which amounts to a denial of the most basic tenet of the historic Christian faith. But that has happened again and again in recent years, especially in circles where there is little acquaintance with the history of doctrine.

It would appear altogether possible that doctrines long regarded as heresies may be true. Neither church councils nor long-standing traditions give convincing evidence of infallibility. However, to revive polytheistic denials of the unity of God would appear to be equally unpromising as a defense of orthodoxy and as a step toward larger truth.

[21] Deut. 6:4–9; 11:13–21.
[22] Mk. 12:29–30.
[23] Cf. Irenaeus, *Against Heresies*, III.8.9.

3. *Certain Analytical Conceptions*

The affirmation of the unity within the being of God stands opposed also to any views which by analysis conceive of God's nature as including utterly disparate aspects. Of course, thought may properly analyze so as to distinguish the righteousness and power or the knowledge and love of God. So long as the various aspects or attributes of God are regarded as harmonious and inseparable in reality, there is no denial of His unity. However, a belief in conflicting elements or in aspects so utterly different in kind as to constitute a real division within God would be opposed to such considerations as have been urged in support of belief that God is one.[24]

4. *Some Doctrines Concerning Powers of Evil*

The evidences supporting belief in the unity of God stand opposed also to such teachings as the ancient Manichaean notion, positing an ultimate dualism of good and evil powers. No less would they deny any doctrine ascribing to Satan or other evil spirits an ultimate metaphysical independence of God. The Biblical teaching concerning Satan as a fallen angel dependent upon God's sufferance and finally answerable to the divine judgment is not such a view and must be considered on its own merits. Popular thought does, however, often slip into belief in an ultimate dualism of superhuman good and evil powers, a doctrine which will not bear critical scrutiny. Such views would deny that unity of God which is so decisively supported by rational, moral and religious experience.

[24] Such ideas arise chiefly in relation to the problem of evil and are more specifically examined in the discussion of that subject.

CHAPTER 12

The Absolute Being of God

THE word "absolute" is used in various senses and may, therefore, lead easily to misunderstanding unless carefully safeguarded by definition. In the present work it must not be taken to mean all-inclusive, as in Hegelian terminology and much other philosophical usage. Neither is it intended to imply separation from the world and all categories of existence nor freedom from every conceivable limitation.

By "absolute being" is here meant being free from dependence upon or limitation by any other being. Instead of "absolute being" we might use the phrase "independent existence."

A. The Dependence of Men and of Material Things

While people sometimes speak of a "self-made man," the phrase is actually the height of absurdity. Not only is a man not the creator of his own existence but even those skills, powers and possessions to which we ordinarily understand the phrase to refer are the products of many influences most of which were quite independent of him. Ancestry, language, tools—these and countless other factors—point to chains of dependence reaching back hundreds of centuries into the hidden past.

But wherever in that chain of human influence an inquirer might wish to lay his finger he would find an equally dependent human being. That man, too, had a weak and helpless beginning and had it not been for something which preceded him he would not have existed.

If man be thought of as the product of matter, the explanatory principle is still within the realm of conditioned, dependent existence. Every material thing is a product of previous process, or rather is a kind of momentary convergence of various lines of process.[1] Every process which we confront in our experience is going on because of other processes and the order which connects all processes.[2] The nature of every material process is determined in large measure by the limits prescribed by other processes, just as it is impossible to define the

[1] Cf. Alfred North Whitehead's conception of "actual occasions."
[2] Cf. the doctrine of Heraclitus that everything changes excepting the law of change.

boundaries of a particular area without defining some boundaries of adjoining areas. No human being and a fortiori no material thing is self-explanatory or fully self-existent. Of each it must be said, "This exists and is what it is because of certain other things."

B. God the Unconditioned

In contrast to the whole realm of conditioned, dependent, creaturely being, God is, as Augustine declared, the one of whom alone it can truly be said without condition or qualification, "He is." [3] To be quite truthful a man must say, "I am a part of what my circumstances permit me to be." Only God has a right to say with unqualified meaning, "I am what I am." [4] The ground and explanation of His being are within Himself. Of no other being is this true.

The very fact that everything in the world of the senses was conditioned in being was the ground of the first three among the five arguments which Thomas Aquinas used to prove the existence of God. It may be doubted that Thomas gave adequate attention to the question whether the unconditioned being established by these proofs was the perfect being of his fourth proof or the purposive being of the fifth proof, much less the holy God. This identification is hardly established convincingly by such phrases as he adds to his inference of a first mover—"and this everyone understands to be God"—or to his proof of a necessary being—"This all men speak of as God." [5] However, if it be accepted, as was argued in our earlier discussion of theistic evidences, that God is the source of all other being, then the first three of the Thomistic proofs may be taken as quite legitimate proofs of His unconditioned being. Things that are actually moved by other things imply ultimately a mover which did not require to be moved. Observed events caused by earlier ones, in turn caused by others imply some cause which did not need to be caused. Being conditioned upon other being implies some being absolutely unconditioned and independent, not necessitated by something else but holding within itself the very ground of all necessity.

God is also unconditioned in the sense that He is the ground of those absolute ideal norms which give purposeful direction and meaning to existence. He is final cause as well as first cause, omega as well as alpha.

C. The Omnipresence of God

What does the absoluteness of God, as here defended, imply regarding His relation to space and time?

[3] *On the Trinity*, I.1.2.

[4] Ex. 3:14, margin. It is to be noted that the Hebrew verb used here is no mere copula, but an emphatic word meaning to exist, become or come to pass.

[5] All five proofs are given in *Summa Theologica*, I, Ques. 2, Art. 3.

Relative to space God has been traditionally described as omnipresent, that is, present everywhere. Now strictly speaking, God is not a spatial being. He has no length nor breadth, no height nor depth. Spatiality would imply divisibility, one part of Him being alongside another, and hence would deny His complete unity. The God in whom we have found reason to believe is a knowing, willing Person. It was in direct denial of the idea that worshipers should seek to locate God spatially that Jesus is reported to have said, "God is spirit, and those who worship him must worship in spirit and truth." [6]

God is real. Indeed, He is the most real, in the sense that He is the source and sustaining ground and meaning of all reality. So bound are human imaginations to spatial terms that undisciplined minds often find it very difficult to think of the truly spiritual as real. The ignorant frequently fail completely to grasp the conception of a God who is at once real in the fullest possible sense and spiritual. If they are to think of Him as real they feel compelled to think of Him, not only figuratively, but quite literally in terms of spatial form and location. At least one religious movement, the Church of the Latter Day Saints, has derived one of its characteristic doctrines from this identification of the real with the physical. Anyone who has heard Mormon preaching of the "God with flesh and bones and blood" as superior to the "mere spiritual God" of the "Gentiles" can hardly fail to have observed the strong motivation in the sense of divine reality. It must be said, too, that it is better for little children and the unlearned to think of God corporeally rather than to think of Him as unreal. Yet it is remarkable with what steadfastness the main stream of Christian thought has kept within the bounds of spiritual conceptions. Platonists, Aristotelians, Cartesians, Leibnizians, pragmatists and post-Kantian idealists alike, within the Christian church, have denied the corporeality of God and maintained that He is a nonspatial, spiritual being.

Yet there is a truth and an important one expressed in the somewhat misleading doctrine of the divine omnipresence. God is not a being that fills all space nor by some kind of magic is literally in every place at once. The truth of the doctrine of omnipresence is that God is not limited by space. The Scriptures, the universality of the truth and of the causal and moral laws grounded in Him and the witness of religious experience, all alike testify in support of this doctrine. His knowledge embraces all events, wherever located in our spatial experience. His interest is not centered upon certain places, varying inversely with distance therefrom, as ours tends to be. His activity is operative everywhere.

The Psalmist expresses the conviction of critical thought and of the religious consciousness alike when he declares in awed wonder,

[6] Jn. 4:24.

> Whither shall I go from thy Spirit?
>   Or whither shall I flee from thy presence?
> If I ascend to heaven, thou art there!
>   If I make my bed in Sheol, thou art there!
> If I take the wings of the morning
>   and dwell in the uttermost parts of the sea,
> even there thy hand shall lead me,
>   and thy right hand shall hold me.[7]

In that is both warning to the wrongdoer and consolation to everyone who would put his trust in God. No sin can be hidden from His judgment. But neither in this world nor in any other can we pass beyond the bounds of His active concern.

D. THE TEMPORALITY OF GOD

It is often supposed that the spatiality and temporality of God must be regarded as on the same footing. If God is believed to be nonspatial in His own being, then by the same token, it is supposed, the category of time must be thought inapplicable to Him. Actually, however, there are sufficient differences between the two categories so that His nontemporality cannot be inferred from His nonspatial spirituality.

This is true, first of all, because the relation of our own consciousness to time is far different from its relation to space. Although we are conscious of both spatial and temporal dimensions, our consciousness is not itself spatial in the same sense in which it is temporal. In experience of the spatial world we do necessarily take the viewpoint which our bodies afford. But our thoughts are not spatially extended. They do not occur side by side nor one above the other, though they do occur in time, one after the other. Our own consciousness proves that it is possible to be prolonged in time and yet not be spread out in space.

But does not the treatment of space and time together as space-time in modern physical science prove that the two categories are inseparable? Not so. The convenience of regarding time as a fourth dimension analogous to the three dimensions of space, for the formulation of many laws and problems of the physical universe, cannot gainsay our experience of our own real duration. The solution of mechanical problems requires the translation of time into spatial terms. But as Henri Bergson insisted so convincingly, such interpretations of time always involve a fictitious abstraction and they are so false as to be ludicrously absurd when living persons are involved.[8]

[7] Ps. 139:7–10.
[8] See particularly *Time and Free Will* and *Laughter*.

Since God is personal His nature must be far more closely analogous to our own than to that of material objects. It is for this reason that in the Bible God is likened often to human persons but rarely and only in much more limited fashion to material things. Hence the distinction between time and space so necessary in the understanding of human memory and will must be carefully maintained in thought about God.

A second reason why the categories of time and space are not to be similarly treated in relation to God is that space implies divisibility, and hence lack of complete unity, whereas time does not. To be sure, in thought we divide past from present. But this is no division in any concrete existing reality, for any past being which is not also present is not reality. Likewise, the future is not real, even though it will be. Hence if the category of time is applicable to God there is no division in His real being between His past, present and future, for His real being is only present. What He is is whole, a seamless robe of unity, and there never was nor will be a time when He is otherwise.

A third reason is that if God were a spatial being there would be places where any given part of Him was not. This would deny the universality of His availability to His children, attested by the Bible, the moral order and religious experience, and of His rational control of the material order described by the natural sciences. The idea that God is temporal, not in the sense of being perishable, but in the sense of living, in His own being, through an everlasting *durée réelle,* would involve no such limitation. It would imply, of course, that God was not now available to judge or forgive David in the hour of Nathan's ancient reproof of him. But David does not *now* need Him *then.* So long as there has never been a time when God was not, nor will be a time when He no longer exists, a temporal God would be as everlastingly available to meet every need as would be a God who existed somehow at all times at once in an eternal now.

On the other hand, there are important considerations favorable to the belief that time is grounded in the very nature of God.

First, if God is a purposive being, having certain ends in view for the persons whom He has made, as the theistic evidences indicated, then He must be seeking to shape the present to a future which is not yet. The category of purpose is meaningless apart from time. If God were a timeless Platonic perfection or an Aristotelian Pure Form, men might conceivably have purposes related to such a divine ideal, but such a God could have no purpose for men, since for God there would be no future in which purpose might be realized.

To the theistic evidences we should now add the testimony of the Bible in support of God's own purposiveness. Speaking of the destruction which is to overtake the ruthless Assyrians, Isaiah says,

> The LORD of hosts has sworn:
> "As I have planned,
> so shall it be,
> and as I have purposed,
> so shall it stand . . ."
> This is the purpose that is purposed
> concerning the whole earth . . .
> For the LORD of hosts has purposed,
> and who will annul it? [9]

So again and again we are told in the New Testament of God's purposes, as when St. Paul writes,

And we know that in everything God works for good with those who love him, who are called according to his purpose.[10]

Second, God as He is presented in the Scriptures is far too intimately concerned with the sequence of events in the world to be thought of as timeless. Time enters into the whole warp and woof of the Biblical testimony concerning God. In the first chapter of Genesis God is described as creating in temporal sequence. In the last verse but one in the Revelation it is reported that Christ promises, "I am coming soon," and the writer adds, "Amen. Come, Lord Jesus!" The whole of the Scriptural record has to do with God's dealings with men from the temporal acts of creation to the consummation of His kingdom. Even after that consummation the faithful are not described as leaving time behind for sheer timelessness. Rather, it is said that "the Lord God will be their light: and they shall reign for ever and ever," or, as the ARV marginal reading literally translates the Greek, "unto the ages of the ages." There is certainly no suggestion here of an absence from time. Rather there is promise of time without end. The God of the Scriptures is no Pure Form untouched by men's sin or sorrow, simply being in perfection while men toil and strive. According to John, Jesus said, "My Father is working still, and I am working." [11] A deity outside of time is a ghostly product of man's abstraction, not the God who is "clearly perceived in the things that have been made" [12] by Him, who enters deeply into the affairs of history and who communes as Father with His children—the only God of whom there is empirical evidence, sensory or spiritual.[13]

Third, if God is aware at all of the changes which occur in the world, as the theistic evidences, the Scriptures and the experience of prayer attest, there must be changes in His own consciousness. Two replies might be attempted. It

---

[9] Is. 14:24–27.   [10] Rom. 8:28.

[11] Jn. 5:17.   [12] Rom. 1:20.

[13] Cf. E. S. Brightman, "A Temporalist View of God," *Jour. of Relig.*, 1932, 12:545–55, and the articles on "eternal," "eternity" and "time" by Charles Hartshorne in V. Ferm, *An Encyclopedia of Religion*.

might be argued that the changes in the world actually did not occur, but were purely illusory. But such a Parmenidean notion would be too flagrantly contradictory to experience to merit much consideration. That we experience change is evident enough. If it be said that the experience is illusory then the changing illusions must still be acknowledged and nothing more is needed to refute the theory. On the other hand, it may be more plausibly objected that even though change is real enough, God is aware of past, present and future all at once and hence His own consciousness does not change. But even if it be supposed that the past, present and future are equally well known to God, the content of His consciousness must be continually changing while events known as future change to events known as present and then as past.

E. The Supertemporal Eternity of God

While the category of time must be applicable to God's own life, there are some respects in which God may be regarded as above time.

First, of God and God alone can it be said that there never was nor will be a time without His existence. All other being is relative to time while God is co-eternal with time. He alone is "from everlasting to everlasting." [14] Usually when anything is spoken of as "temporal" some limitation in time is implied. But in this sense God's eternity is rightly contrasted with the temporality of all other being.

Second, His fundamental nature must be as unchanging as the timeless laws of implication which are grounded in Him. He may in this sense be spoken of as eternal in contrast to all things which change with the passing of time. If it be thought that His knowledge of the future is not complete, particularly so far as men's free acts are concerned, then His total knowledge must be considered to increase with the passage of time. Still His knowledge of all that is or has been real may be presumed to be always complete so that while His knowledge is increasing it is always perfect. Not to know as real or as sure what is not yet real or sure is no imperfection. Likewise the reason, character and ultimate purposes of God are as unchanging as the perfect truth to which we aspire. Rightly does the Psalmist say,

> Of old thou didst lay the foundation of the earth,
>   and the heavens are the work of thy hands.
> They will perish, but thou dost endure;
>   they will all wear out like a garment.
> Thou changest them like raiment, and they pass away;
>   but thou art the same, and thy years have no end.[15]

[14] Ps. 90:2.
[15] Ps. 102:25-27.

Finally, if there were no being there would be no time. The idea of an utterly empty time, a time in which nothing either changed or endured, is only an abstraction representative of no conceivable reality. Accordingly, since God is the source of all being, He is also the ground of all time. By being and creating, God makes time to be real. He may thus be thought of as the author of time, not that there was a time before He made time (a patent self-contradiction), but because in all its infinity time is constituted by the active being of God. Therefore, even though in some ways God may be thought of as subject to time, even more meaningfully must time be regarded as subject to God. Not only "our times" but all time is in His hand.[16]

[16] Cf. Ps. 31:15.

CHAPTER 13

The Power and Knowledge of God

ONE of the historic doctrines of the Christian community is the belief in the omnipotence of God. Indeed the description of God as all-powerful or almighty was taken over by the primitive Christian church from the more ancient teachings of the Hebrew Scriptures. One of the oldest names given to God by the Hebrews was *Shaddai* or *El Shaddai*, that is, "the Almighty" or "God Almighty." [1]

Strictly speaking, there is a certain ambiguity which has always attended these attributions of power to God. The Hebrew *Shaddai* is simply the plural of excellence of *Shad*, meaning strong or powerful. Hence the Hebrew word does not necessarily imply power of absolutely infinite degree but rather power beyond all other powers or power over all. The Greek word by which *Shaddai* was translated in the Septuagint and which appears also in the New Testament is *pantokrator*, which means literally all-ruling.[2] Both the Hebrew and Greek words are translated in the Vulgate by *omnipotens* which, like the English "omnipotent," means all-powerful. But just how much power does that imply? Does "all-powerful" mean powerful over all, having all the power there is, or having all the power abstractly conceivable?

The Bible is concerned with the sufficiency of God's power to meet all contingencies in the care of His children and frequently stresses the difference between men's power and God's.[3] The main interest of the writers being practical and not metaphysical, many of the problems raised in later speculation were not so much as mentioned in the Scriptures.

A. God's Power As Limited

It can hardly be affirmed without qualification that God can do everything abstractly conceivable. To state that He can do so is to invite such riddles as

---

[1] E.g., in Gen. 49:25 and the later passages found in Gen. 17:1 and 28:3; also Ex. 6:2; and throughout Job, as 5:17; 6:4; 8:3, 5.

[2] In the New Testament it appears principally in Rev., as, e.g., in 1:8, 4:8, 11:17, but also in 2 Cor. 6:18. The last, however, is an echo of Old Testament usage.

[3] See especially Rom. 8:28; Job 38; Mt. 19:26; Eph. 3:20.

have called forth many absurd discussions. If God can do everything which may be mentioned, then, of course, He can now make it so that the reader of these words has never committed a sin nor made a mistake in his life. Likewise He can make weights so big that He cannot lift them—though, of course, He can lift them. And by such omnipotence God could make Himself cease to exist and then, while not existing, make Himself to have twice the unlimited power He had before.

If the reader protests that such ideas are nonsense this will be quickly agreed. But it must be added that they are nonsense implied in the nonsensical notion of an unqualified limitlessness of power.

There are also more practical and religious implications of such an abstract notion. If God can do anything we can conceive, then He can accomplish all the good ends which He purposes to achieve, without permitting any of the evils which we experience, including all sin, pain and sorrow. But if God is able to accomplish His perfect ends without any of these evils then He must will the evils with no compensating advantage whatever. He is then preferring for their own sake, the pain, sorrow and sin we experience. But such a deity could not be called good in any intelligible sense and there is no value in using the word "good" in an unintelligible sense. Certainly men could not regard a God who for no purpose at all preferred that they sin and suffer, as being the deeply concerned Father revealed in the New Testament.

B. His Power Not Limited by Other Being

On the other hand, the power of God must not be limited by any being ultimately independent of His rational will. It was to the grounding of all existence in the rational, creative will of God that we traced the rational structure of reality itself, including all causality and even the necessity of rational implication itself. If, therefore, there were any being not dependent upon that rational will, its existence would not imply any effect upon the will itself and would constitute no limitation. Such limitations of God's power as there are must, then, be either limitations of that power in itself or limits imposed by the divine purpose or by other beings dependent upon God's creative will.

C. The Divine Self-limitation

There would seem to be three kinds of limitation to which God's power is subject, although all are of such character as might lead to the objection that they should not be called limitations at all. They are, nevertheless, specifications of the meaning to be intended by saying that God is all-powerful and they are of such a character as to put a check on the speculative fancy which when unbridled sometimes draws from the doctrine quite foolish inferences.

1. *Voluntary Limitation*

Every decision includes a limitation. To choose change is to limit changeless-ness. To choose love is to limit hate. To choose to create a world is to reject the alternative of not creating a world.

Specifically, if God has chosen to create human persons and maintain toward them those attitudes and relationships which Jesus described by calling Him "Our Father," He has thus imposed upon Himself the restriction of not being indifferent to men, like the mythical gods of Epicurus. Again, if He purposes, as will be later contended, to give men some freedom of responsible choice, He has made of this human power a limitation upon His own.

It has seemed to some Christians that any freedom of the human will would be such a serious external limitation of God's power that it must be denied if we are properly to glorify God. However, it would actually seem more of an evidence of His power than a detraction from it. That God can make instru-ments without free will is evident enough. The creation of beings possessing such power, even power to share in some measure with Him the responsibility for their own and their fellows' well being, would be an added glory.

Emil Brunner, although his various utterances on free will are difficult to harmonize, is quite clear on this subject. He says,

That God is Lord means either that He *wills* to be known and acknowledged by man or that He *is* known and acknowledged by man as the One to whom man un-conditionally belongs. Because God *wills* to be and can be Lord only in this way, He places Himself face to face with an independent creature. For only an independent creature can know and acknowledge. God wills to be acknowledged as Lord in freedom, since it is by virtue of such free acknowledgment that He is Lord in the highest sense.[4]

Such limitations as we have been discussing are not restrictions on the ulti-mate power of God. The fact that a man of firm purpose will avoid doing things which negate that purpose is not a sign of metaphysical weakness but of moral strength. He could do the things which He will not do. So the volun-tary self-limitation of God is not a metaphysical finitude of power but a moral exercise of power.[5]

[4] *The Divine-Human Encounter* (tr. by Amanda W. Loos, Philadelphia: The Westminster Press, 1943), p. 56. Cf. his statement that "when one believes . . . that to uphold the honor of God he must belittle man's independence and freedom or even defend Determinism, he does not serve the God who has revealed Himself in the Holy Scriptures. . . ." *Ibid.*, p. 54.

[5] Cf. Anselm's statement, "Even God cannot raise to happiness any being bound at all by the debt of sin, because He ought not to." *Cur Deus Homo*, 21. (Of course Anselm did not believe that God therefore passed by the poor sinner. Rather, He sought to release the sinner from this debt by the atoning cross.)

2. *Limitation by His Rational Nature*

If we are to avoid nonsensical notions of God's power, it is necessary also to deny that He can contradict His own nature. He cannot make Himself not to exist and while not being at all create a thousand deities, each one an uncreated being greater than He.

But why not? The very contemplation of such ideas is an abstract reference to possibilities beyond the range of all possibility.

To say that a thing is impossible is to imply a frame of reference by which it is contradicted. Thus, to say that it is impossible for a baseball player to reach second base from home plate in five seconds means that to do so would contradict a combination of data including the official rules of baseball and the maximum running speeds which are ever attained by men as we know them. In some other frame of reference, with the size of baseball diamonds changed or man's speed of running considerably increased, the feat might be quite possible. Again, it is impossible for sound to travel faster than light, in the frame of reference of the present causal order, for to do so would contradict some causal laws. Impossible in *every* frame of reference is a contradiction by real being of the very laws of contradiction. A realm in which real contradictories were actual would be a realm in which being was the same as nonbeing and concerning which no judgment was more true or more false than any other.

The supreme frame of reference in which meaning and being can be conceived is the structure of rational implication itself. This rational net of possibility we have attributed to the rational nature of God's own will. Could God violate it if He chose? The widest possible meaning of "could" concerns the question whether any given x is contradictory to rationality, that is, to the rational nature of God's will. Hence to ask whether He *could* violate that rational nature is to ask whether to violate it would be to violate it. Of course the answer is unmistakably yes, which is to say that such violation would be impossible in the widest sense of the word which would have any meaning.

This impossibility represents no subordination of God's will to some other being or even to some other aspect of God's own being, but only means that God's will is what it is and not something else. God is true to His own nature. The recognition of such a limitation is not a denial of God's omnipotence in the historic sense. No theologian in Christendom has been more clearly insistent on the infinite perfection of every divine attribute than was Anselm. Yet Anselm explicitly acknowledged that God could not act contrary to His own perfect being. Thus he wrote in the *Proslogium*:

But how art thou omnipotent, if thou art not capable of all things? Or if thou canst not be corrupted, and canst not lie, nor make what is true, false—as, for example, if thou shouldst make what has been done not to have been done, and the like—how art thou capable of all things? Or else to be capable of these things is not power, but impotence. For, he who is capable of these things is capable of what is not for his good, and of what he ought not to do. . . . He, then, who is thus capable is so not by power, but by impotence. . . . Therefore, O Lord, our God, the more truly art thou omnipotent, since thou art capable of nothing through impotence, and nothing has power against thee.[6]

3. *Limits of His Own Being*

God as He has been described can properly be spoken of as omnipotent. For He is the source of all being and all power. All things are under His sovereign control. No being limits His action excepting as God wills to permit it. In that sense His power may also be described as infinite. It is also infinite as inexhaustible in time. Of course, the worshiper naturally expresses the indescribable difference between his own absolute dependence and God's unconditioned, absolute being by the use of such honorific terms as "infinite." This is altogether appropriate.

Yet when we are seeking to give precise, disciplined expression to truth, as in theology, we are obligated to define our meanings with all exactness possible. The terms we use have theological value only so far as their intent is clear. It is not always clear precisely what is meant by describing a positive existent or even all existence as infinite. In one sense it would appear that any existing process or being, even God, must be regarded as finite. He is all that He is but not more. The resources of His creative imagination and will can never be exhausted. Nevertheless, He must have been unable to accomplish the highest ends He has conceived without cost of suffering to others and without sin having become actual, else He would have done so. No man knows the problems confronted by God as He devised the cosmic order He has created. His imagination, as well as the power to actualize what He imagines, surpasses our powers of understanding. Yet even such power must be all that it is and not more. Though not limited by any other being it is limited by its own bounds, however unsearchable, beyond which is no reality nor concrete possibility.

D. The Omniscience of God

Omniscience is implied by omnipotence. If God can do all that can be done He can know all that can be known. If He can control all things according to His purpose, so far as He wills to control them, He must know all things so far as He wills to know them. For knowing is one kind of doing and purposive control of a thing could not be more complete than knowledge of it.

[6] Ch. 7.

The knowledge of God, however, must be limited by His own nature and purpose, much as we have seen His power to be. His knowledge may thus be presumed to be limited by the rational nature of His own being. Likewise, it may be supposed that voluntary limitations of His power in accordance with His own purpose entail corresponding limitations of His knowledge. For example, if He has put a check on His power to give man freedom of will, then He must have limited somewhat His knowledge of the future. He doubtless knows all things. But what is not yet and indeed is still within the possibility of never coming to be must hardly be knowable to God as future actuality.

If God knows now every choice any man will ever make, then every choice is already determined and freedom is an illusion. It may be objected that God's knowledge of the future is not through inference from present reality but is an immediate transtemporal perception and hence does not imply a present determination of the future. However, this is actually to regard the future as already present. It is to treat time as a form of space, denying its reality as time, a procedure we have already shown to be insupportable.

Of course men, even with the little knowledge they have, are able to foresee as probabilities many of the voluntary acts of their fellows and we have every reason to suppose that God's powers of prediction are far greater. But if men have any margin of free will whatever, then God's foreknowledge of some of their choices must be a knowledge of probabilities, not of certainties.

CHAPTER 14

The Holiness, Righteousness and Love of God

A. HOLINESS

JEWS and Christians have so moralized the conception of God that the word "holy" is often taken to imply simply perfect goodness. However, this is not the original meaning of the word, nor is it the complete meaning today in precise usage. Properly speaking, holiness has always to do with special prerogatives, characteristics or influences of deity, as contrasted with man and the common, earthly objects of his experience.

The Hebrew word, *kodesh*, translated as "holy thing" or "holiness," was derived from *kawdash*, which had to do with a ceremonial cleansing or a setting apart as taboo.[1] From the earliest times it implied a sense of mysterious awe. Like other ancient words having to do with the most elemental religious experience, it referred to the absolute powers which men were utterly unable to comprehend or withstand but to which they felt themselves unconditionally and properly subject.

Mysteriousness alone does not constitute anything as holy in this sense. Some great and mysterious forces primitive peoples sought to manipulate and control for their own purposes. But such practices constituted magic rather than religion and the powers thus dealt with were occult rather than holy. The holy is not possessed and managed. A man seeks rather to be possessed and controlled by it. While an occult power might be coerced by secret formulas, a holy being may only be beseeched, placated or served. Thus magic is an attempt to subordinate occult powers to one's own purposes, while religion is a subjection of self to the holy.

The classic Biblical passage attributing holiness to God is in Isaiah 6:1–8.[2] In this passage, very ancient though it is, the idea of holiness has come to marvelously complete expression. The mysterious otherness of God is expressed in the descriptions of the strange seraphim attending Him. His power is so great that even the voice of one of His attendants shakes the foundations of the

[1] Cf. A. C. Knudson, *The Religious Teaching of the Old Testament*, ch. 6.
[2] Cf. Rev. 4:8–11.

temple and the prophet trembles before Him. So worthy of reverence is He, that even these great superhuman seraphim cover their faces in His presence. His purity is so transcendent that before Him the prophet is overwhelmed with the sense of iniquity in himself and his people. So absolute is His rightful authority that the prophet eagerly volunteers to serve Him without asking what he will be required to do.

The attributing of holiness to God is a response to an experience of His presence rather than an inference from thought concerning Him. Like the beauty of a symphony or the crushing sorrow of bereavement, yet more, holiness is a quality which must be felt to be understood and yet when felt is known to be beyond description or even adequate comprehension. The holy is the ultimate of all value qualities, known immediately as absolute and inexplicable in other terms.[3]

Yet after such experiences of God's holiness or after reports of such experiences from others it is proper to ask what truths about God and our relation to Him are represented by them. To raise this question is to ask whether any characteristics of God, in which we have reason to believe, would warrant such a unique, complex and overwhelming feeling toward Him as comes over us when we confront God as holy. No such account could approach completeness. To explain the holiness of God would be the fantastically presumptuous task of explaining God. But there are certain ideas concerning God which are favored by evidence from other quarters and which give intellectual warrant for regarding God as holy. Such ideas are in turn supported by the experience of His holiness. It is an integral part of the theologian's task to give some account of these ideas.

1. *Source of Our Being*

When we acknowledge the holiness of God we speak as befits creatures in the presence of their Creator. "It is he that hath made us and not we ourselves."[4] We turn to Him in recognition that without Him we could not even exist, much less find our way to the destiny for which He made us. Since He made us and sustains us our lives are rightfully His. We owe all to Him, not only as a man owes his life to his parents or to his teachers or to a friend who has rescued him from imminent death, but with an obligation inclusive of all these and much more. For God made also the parents, the teachers and the friend and likewise all the generations upon whom they depended. He is author also

---

[3] Cf. Rudolf Otto, *The Idea of the Holy*, and Robert F. Davidson, *Rudolf Otto's Interpretation of Religion*.

[4] Ps. 100:3, AV, marginal reading in ARV. Cf. RSV margin.

of the very idea of humanity itself and of all that framework of logical and causal law, sensory experience and social communication in which we have our being. He alone is Creator.

We turn to Him as we return home from wanderings in strange places. For from Him we have come. He knows the innermost secrets of our being. All the powers upon which we finally depend are in His hand. In Him alone is complete security, understanding and peace.

Since He knew how to make both ourselves and all else upon which we depend, He must know also how to preserve us and to direct us according to His purpose. Every other guide and stay must of necessity be partial and finally inadequate because dependent at last upon forces beyond understanding and beyond control. Only God knows and can control all things according to His will. Therefore, He alone can be worthy of our absolute submission and trust. In His presence we rightly declare, "Thou only art holy." [5]

2. Supreme Lawgiver

God is the one giver of law worthy of absolute obedience. Only the law of the holy God is holy.

People in all lands know that prudence requires the paying of some deference to human lawmakers. Legislators have the power to determine what one must do or refrain from doing to avoid the onus and penalties which fall upon the lawbreaker. But conscience may contradict prudence. Legislators are often corrupt or arbitrary and laws are frequently unjust. To do one's duty sometimes requires the violation of law.

It is quite otherwise when the law of God is concerned. As far as prudence is concerned, undoubtedly it is infinitely more important to obey God than to obey men. For while human lawgivers can control only some conditions of our earthly life, God controls, so far as He wills, all the conditions of all life here and hereafter.

Yet sheer power, even absolute power for the endless ages, does not in itself guarantee the rightfulness of law. We have observed that only a being with absolute knowledge and power *could* be worthy of absolute submission. But such a being might not be *actually* worthy of such submission. The moral validity of law is not necessarily co-ordinate with the power of the lawgiver to impose sanctions. Even infinite power would not in itself guarantee perfect right.

The law of God is worthy of complete obedience because it is the true norm by relation to which all other laws and all of life ought to be judged. It is not a foreign standard imposed arbitrarily or externally upon us. God's rule is not,

[5] Rev. 15:4.

to use Kant's term, heteronomous. It is the law of our being. This does not mean that when men pursue their own inclinations or even when they are true to the best principles they can rationally discern they will always be obeying God's perfect law. Far from it. Both human ignorance and the distortions due to human sin must be taken into account. But God's way is the final cause of our existence. We find fulfillment of our own deepest needs in obedience to Him. In that obedience alone is our lasting health and satisfaction. We may interpret our needs in many contrary ways and seek satisfaction in many a far country, just as men may pursue perverted tastes and thirsts to the ruin of their bodies. But our real needs are for the life for which God designed our very nature. We can finally be true to ourselves only by being true to Him. His law is not merely power: it is truth [6] both for men and for nations.[7]

Hence God is the one Lawgiver worthy of absolute obedience. Many legislators are relatively good. Many are endowed with relative power and relative moral authority. God alone possesses absolute power and absolute moral authority. God only is holy.

3. Source of All Good

God does vastly more than prescribe the principles to which all that is to be good must conform. He creates the good. Indeed, if there is one idea of deity so essential that no religious person of any place or time could think of any god at all without it, it would seem to be this, that from deity issues good. Whether divinity be regarded as lord of battle,[8] founder of the world government in which alone justice and peace can be secured [9] or author of our salvation here and hereafter,[10] always the notion of divinity implies a source of something regarded as good. This is true even in the thought of Epicurus whose gods enjoy all their blessings themselves without so much as a moment of concern for man's unhappiness and in the antitheistic philosophy of John Dewey. However poor may seem the good which some men have attributed to their gods and however inadequate may be such conceptions of deity as have been set forth by men like Dewey [11] actually to account for religious experience or any other value, this uniting of men's thoughts of deity and of good is significant. In this persistent tendency the Christian may well see the effect of God's own Spirit upon men. For every path of good which enters our lives leads back to Him.

When I delight in the majesty of the starry heavens, the grandeur of snow-clad summits or the grace of a swallow's flight, I should rejoice the more in

---

[6] Ps. 119:142.
[8] Cf. Ps. 24:8.
[10] Rom. 8:31-39.

[7] Cf. Is. 2:3-4.
[9] Is. 2:3-4.
[11] See A Common Faith.

the divine wisdom that has made these and all the beauty of earth. If I am gladdened by loyal love of friends my gratitude should go up to Him whose love put into mankind the very capacity for love. If some heroic act of a brave man or woman quickens my pulse and calls forth my admiration I should pause to praise also God who is the author of all courage. If in hours of thought I contemplate the ladder of truth in which Plato so delighted I should look in humble praise to Him whose very thought is truth and who put into my soul this vision.

But even though we should list all good things we have ever experienced and give to God the praise for each one and for the sum of them all our gratitude would be inadequate. For besides all these there are the greater goods which we have missed by our waywardness and the endless, exquisite delights which will flow from His bounty for all eternity to all who seek Him in love.

We may thus contrast every good which is created and finite with Him who is holy, from everlasting to everlasting the fountain of all good.

B. Righteousness

While the righteousness of God is very closely related to His holiness as conceived in Jewish and Christian thought, it is sufficiently distinct to merit a brief separate discussion.

There are three senses in which God may be properly spoken of as righteous.

1. Righteous Lawgiver

The very ground and meaning of all righteousness is in God's perfect law. As giver of the supreme righteous law He is righteous with a holy righteousness completely transcending all that is possible for men.

2. Faithful Keeper of His Own Law

God is righteous also in the fidelity of all His acts to His own perfect law. He does not require that men be ruled by His law and then act toward them in the whimsical fashion of an irresponsible tyrant. To infer from the conception of God's absolute sovereignty that He acts in such arbitrary and irrational fashion is a case of indefensibly anthropomorphic thinking in which the holy sovereignty of God is confused with the petty pretentiousness of a man who can rule others but cannot possess his own spirit.

It is evident that righteous fidelity to His own law would not mean for God the following of those relatively specific patterns of conduct which are rightly required of men. It is true, even of men with different responsibilities and different skills, that the same principles of conduct will imply different acts. For a garage mechanic to put a knife into the body of his neighbor is a crime before both man and God. But for a surgeon to do so may be both an everyday occurrence and a solemn duty.

God is Lord of all life on earth and in the world to come. He has the right to remove His children from one sphere of His care to another. For men, to whom the veil of death is drawn between this world and the next, the voluntary removal of a human soul from this earthly scene has a radically different meaning. But the principles of God's action are the same principles which He has given to men.

Indeed, it is by His honesty that He has taught us the obligation of honesty. If God's active governance of His world were not honest and faithful to His own principles we should not find any such dependence of scientific discovery upon moral law as we have pointed out. By His faithfulness He summons men to faithful obedience. Again, "we love because He first loved us." [12] Any righteousness ever experienced by men is derived from the perfect righteousness of God.

3. Perfect Judge of All Men

Finally, God is righteous in the sense that He is the just Judge of all men. He who is the giver of the perfect law is also Judge of all by the law. However, since the very idea of divine judgment raises so many complex and important issues for which the discussion to this point has not made adequate preparation, the whole subject will be considered in a later chapter.

C. LOVE

The supreme righteousness known to the Christian community is love. Preparation for the understanding of God as loving Father had been given by Hosea, Isaiah, Jeremiah and some of the Psalmists. But through Jesus Christ this divine love came to have new meaning.

The meaning of love in the Christian sense, the relation of God's love to His justice and the work of grace to which His love gives rise must be discussed at length after we have confronted the figure of Christ. To avoid repetition the elaboration of these themes must be omitted at present. It is to be observed, however, that in the Christian interpretation of God's righteousness and in our whole understanding of His being, love is central.

God is not an abstract deity nor one who lives out His life in aloof preoccupation with Himself. He is one who gives Himself in creation of other persons to share His bounty and in reconciliation to win their faith for this sharing. All that we know of God we know through His love. It is through His going forth in creation and other revelations of Himself that He is shown to us.

[12] I Jn. 4:19.

The whole of our study is concerned in one way or another with the love of God. As we hinted at the very beginning and are to elaborate later, the Christian community is a community created by and devoted to that love. The first four parts of this book anticipate, in this and many other respects, the doctrine of divine love, while the last two parts are entirely devoted to this theme and its consequences. The Christian gospel is good news of God's love, in the double sense that His love produced the gospel and is also the subject about which the gospel tells.

CHAPTER 15

The Transcendence and Immanence of God

HIGHLY important in Christian thought of God is His relation to the world. What we know of Him must necessarily be learned through this relationship since we are in the world and any path our thought may follow must begin here, just as any revelation which is to reach us must come into the world. Likewise, this relationship is of the greatest practical significance to us since it is God's relation to the world which actually affects us.

In the history of thought, both Christian and non-Christian, concerning this subject, men's ideas and likewise their religious attitudes have tended often to stress the great gulf between God and the world even to the point of a deistic[1] denial that God ever acts upon the world since its creation. On the other hand, some men have emphasized His constant activity in the world, sometimes even to the point of a pantheistic denial of any difference between God and the world. The vitality of both tendencies suggests that there may be truth in both. This suggestion is underlined by the further observation that at the two furthest extremes of deism and pantheism religious life appears to lack some essential ingredient so that it becomes sterile and finally vanishes altogether in theoretical speculation. The doctrine of transcendence seems to need the tension or balance provided by the doctrine of immanence. Likewise, although pantheism is capable of more emotional warmth than is deism, the doctrine of immanence requires the tension or balance of belief in transcendence to maintain a vital historical religious movement.

These empirical observations do seem, in fact, to be associated with the truth that the doctrines of the divine transcendence and immanence are both half truths, alike partial glimpses of a more inclusive real relationship.

[1] In what is here written concerning deism and deistic tendencies, the fact is not overlooked that most men who were called deists in the eighteenth century believed that God did continue to act upon the world since creation. However, the term "deism" has come to connote the denial of such action and with this connotation it is accurately descriptive of such a system as the monadology of Leibniz.

A. The Transcendence of God

There are several ways in which, according to the evidence of Scripture, religious experience and philosophical considerations alike, it seems that God does transcend the world.

1. *He Is More Than His Creation*

God is more than all that He has created. For He continues to act creatively, both in nature and in history.[2] His resources are not spent. We and all the things we observe are being continually displaced by other persons and things. At no point in time has God shown forth all His creative power. He alone creates new existents. The eternal Creator transcends all His temporal creation. The Biblical writers concerning the creation of the world seem to have been largely motivated by a concern for stressing the contrast between the God who creates and all other being.[3] The testimony of religious experience is similar. Men of all ages, in communion with God, have sought and often found in Him a source of strength far transcending the uncertainties of earth.[4]

2. *He Is Other Than Ourselves*

Although Christians sometimes speak, either figuratively or carelessly, as if God were enclosed within themselves or they enclosed within God, such sayings are seldom meant seriously and literally. God is one who has created us and redeemed us, who confronts and addresses us and to whom we give thanks and pray. In all these relations He is shown as the divine Other. Indeed, so far as identity is concerned He is the Wholly Other, though this must not be taken to imply an absolute unlikeness. No man created himself nor redeemed himself. In the divine-human encounter [5] a human being does not confront and address himself. It is not to ourselves that we give thanks and pray. To say that any of these transactions occurred simply in a man's relation to himself would be to deny the gospel in its entirety and reduce the Christian religion to a delusion. It would also obviously contradict the theism in which we have already found good reason to believe.

It will be observed that even those Christian mystics who seem most completely to affirm an identification of themselves with God address Him as "Thou," contrast their own finite weakness with His infinite power and call upon God's boundless mercy to forgive their sins. At most the Christian mystic considers himself to have been received by God's love into His own life so that

---

[2] Cf. Augustine, *The City of God*, 12.25.

[3] Cf. Gen. 1 and 2; Neh. 9:6; Job 9, 10, 26, 28, 37–39; Ps. 19:1–6, 24:1–3; Acts 4:24; Eph. 3:9; Heb. 3:4; Rev. 4:11.

[4] Cf. Ps. 46.

[5] Cf. E. Brunner's fine book by that title.

the man shares in the life of God. Yet despite the most extravagant assertions of identity there is a continuing assumption, apparent in many other utterances, of a profoundly real difference between the mystic and God.[6]

The churches have often treated the mystics with unbecoming harshness. In other areas of life words spoken in expression of feeling unusual in intensity or descriptive of emotionally overwhelming experiences are interpreted with considerable latitude. It should be expected that when people whose whole lives have been poured into the quest for God find Him, their descriptions of the experience might bear more resemblance to the extravagant poetry of lovers than the precise formulas of psychologists or the conceptual language of systematic theologians. By their rapturous testimonies the mystics have often stirred the churches to new purity and ardor in both their prayer and their social practice. Considering this inestimably great service they have been met with inexcusable suspicion, condemnation and even outright persecution.

Nevertheless, in one particular the opponents of mysticism have been right. Wherever the line of distinction between man and God has been blurred, truth and sound religion have been brought into peril. Taken literally, a mere man who declares, "I am become God," makes himself both foolish and blasphemous.

3. He Is Other Than the Material Universe

The doctrine of the divine transcendence affirms, too, that God is not to be identified with the physical universe which we experience in sense perception and interpret in the natural sciences. It is not necessary that the Christian theologian take his stand for a specific metaphysical theory, although he is, like other men, at liberty to do so if he wishes. But if he is to be true to the implications of Christian experience he must necessarily exclude some kinds of metaphysical theory. Although the consideration of God's relations to the material universe might readily lead into a full-blown metaphysical treatise, the issues particularly relevant to the distinctive experience of the Christian community and hence of concern to the Christian theologian as such can be examined without any attempt to decide many of the metaphysical problems involved.

The material world of human experience is a spatial order of things many of which Christians as well as all other people find it necessary or useful to subordinate to their own needs and wills. Thus we eat carrots, burn coal, chop logs, walk upon the ground, domesticate cows, battle against forest fires and kill microbes. Isaiah pointed out the absurdity of worshiping as God a thing subject

[6] Cf. below, pp. 358–359.

to hewing and burning at the hand of the worshiper.[7] It was of man's dominion over material objects and the lower forms of life that the Psalmist spoke when he gratefully prayed, "Thou hast given him dominion over the works of thy hands; thou hast put all things under his feet." [8] Now it is clearly not God who is put under the feet of man. There are open to the Christian many possible philosophical accounts of the relation between God and the material world and the choice between them will have to be made, if at all, on metaphysical grounds. But an outright identification of the things in our sense experience with God or the regarding of them as any part of God would result in absurd and blasphemous contradiction. It will hardly be said that we ought to worship the same object which the very continuance of our lives requires us to eat, walk upon, domesticate or kill nor that we should worship other objects of similar stuff— even though they are beyond our reach like the moon or voluntarily let alone like most song birds.

We must exclude, then, any such pantheism or apotheosis of nature as would induce a man simply to look at the physical world and call what he sees "God." If an idealist were to say that the very objects we experience constituted part or all of the being of God he would be opposing the implications of Scripture and Christian experience. Actually, however, it is doubtful whether any idealist has meant to do that. An idealist may, like George Berkeley, say that nature is "the divine language" or like Tennyson that it is "the vision of Him," though a vision distorted, like "a straight staff bent in a pool." [9] But always it is represented as an emanation or effect going forth *from* God into human experience, never as God Himself as He is.

The Bible and Christian tradition have generally maintained further that the material world known to men was not a pure expression of God's perfect purpose. It is a world distorted, scarred and full of strife and pain resulting from or in some way associated with men's sin. We are, therefore, bidden to look back to a primeval paradise or forward to the Heavenly City to see an environmental order fully expressive of God's pure purpose. The present world is "cursed" so that it brings forth thorns and thistles.[10] "We know that the whole creation has been groaning in travail together until now." [11]

This imperfection of the world as known to us has caused great perplexity to Jewish and Christian thinkers from Job to our contemporaries. But the acknowledgment of it has been well-nigh universal. No one could be a sensitive and discerning theist, let alone a Christian, and believe that a world made tragic and unjust by earthquakes and disease—not to speak of men's own

---

[7] Is. 44:16–20.
[8] Ps. 8:6.
[9] "The Highest Pantheism."
[10] Gen. 3:17–18.
[11] Rom. 8:22.

devastations—was the final, perfect word of God. Only partially and intermittently do the reason and loving purpose of God appear to us in the natural order.

God far transcends the world.

B. The Immanence of God

In balancing tension with the doctrine of divine transcendence must be placed the truth that God is also immanent in us and our world. This may properly be affirmed in several senses.

1. He Now Sustains Us

An exclusive dwelling upon the transcendence of God moves the believer further and further toward the deistic doctrines of a divinity no longer active in the world which He once made—or even toward the Epicurean notion of deity completely unconcerned, from eternity, with the affairs of earth. But the God of Christian theism is not such an aloof being. He sustains us and continuously we are dependent upon Him.

Through the prophet Isaiah He says,

> Fear not, for I am with you,
>   be not dismayed, for I am your God;
> I will strengthen you, I will help you,
> I will uphold you with my victorious right hand.[12]

Not only did He create the world at the beginning, but He also acts in sustaining His creatures now. He now makes the lilies to grow and feeds the birds of the air. With yet greater concern He cares for His human children from day to day.[13] It is to Him that we pray, "Give us this day our daily bread," for all food is produced by His sustaining providence. Without the support of His will none of us could exist even for an hour.

2. The Norms of Our Right Thoughts Are Ordained by Him

Since God is the ground of logical, moral and causal law, whenever our thoughts are true and right they conform to God's own thought. To be sure, our ignorance, error and sin are vast and even at our best moments we are unworthy to stand in His presence. Nevertheless, at those moments, however fleeting, when we choose rightly or think truly we may quite properly join with Johann Kepler in crying out, "O God, I am thinking Thy thoughts after Thee." At such moments some judgments grasped by our own thought are judgments first affirmed by God Himself.

---

[12] Is. 41:10.   [13] Mt. 6:26–30.

A Platonist might hold that at such times the being of man and God actually overlapped. But it would seem that we ought to distinguish between judgments affirmed and the psychological processes by which they are affirmed. When a man thinks a thought of God after Him, no identity of process or being is implied, but only an identity of meanings apprehended.

A sharing of truth is, however, no mean kind of sharing. In the apprehension of God's thoughts we experience significant divine immanence.

3. He Knows Our Very Thoughts

God may be thought of as dwelling within us in the sense that He observes what passes in our conciousness. It is written, "I know their works and their thoughts." [14] This immediate divine knowledge of our thoughts is implied in the belief that we can properly pray to God in silence, and likewise in the confidence that He knows our every purpose. While men must judge by appearances and outward acts, God, we are assured, knows fully our secret intentions so that the sincerity or hypocrisy of our repentance and faith are an open book to Him.

4. His Activity Continually Affects Our Experience

If the world be conceived of in the terms of an objective idealism it is obvious that every sense perception is an effect of the divine activity. But even if a dualistic metaphysics is espoused or if, eschewing metaphysics as far as possible, no specific ontological interpretation of the material world is attempted, this is still true. For it has already been shown that all being is continuously dependent on God's sustaining will. Whether we suppose that God acts upon our consciousness immediately, to produce our sense perceptions, as many idealists would maintain, or indirectly, through a long or short chain of mediate causes, His purpose is finally affecting us in all our experiences of the physical order, however seriously that order may be marred by the sin of His creatures.

5. He Appears Immediately to the Religious Consciousness

We have affirmed that our innermost thoughts are open to the direct observation of God. No man can lay claim to any such vision of God. The ancients believed that no man could see God and live.[15] Certainly anyone who could see God in the fullness of His being would no longer live as man. A little child could not observe even a fair sample of the mathematical thought of Einstein and still be a little child. He could be shown certain symbols on paper or in spoken language but these would not transmit the meanings they were intended to convey, much less give the child an immediate view of Einstein's

[14] Is. 66:18.   [15] Cf. Ex. 33:20.

consciousness. Yet the difference between the child and Einstein is infinitesimal as compared with the difference between a man and God.

However, God does frequently confront a human being, immediately, within his personal consciousness. When we are so confronted we do not understand the one whom we meet. We are likely to carry away from such an encounter so little increment of discursive knowledge about God that we may be taunted with our continuing ignorance of Him. Yet we have been given something more precious than discursive knowledge. We have been made aware of His presence. But the mystic's experience is not of a mere "that" with no qualitative distinction from other experienced being. The effulgent love, the all-consuming power, the infinite beauty, the sublime goodness, the absolute holiness, some or all of these, known to identify the One called God, are overwhelmingly felt in the One encountered. His full glory must always pass man by, but even the glimpse of Him occasionally given as He passes can change a life and history.[16]

[16] Cf. Ex. 33:21–23.

CHAPTER 16

Some Issues Concerning
The Divine Government of the World

A. Providence and Miracles

1. *Historic Faith in Special Providence*

THE Christian community has, through the centuries, clung steadfastly to the belief in a special providence attendant upon our deepest needs. It is altogether obvious that there is no provision whereby we are kept from pain, sorrow, temptation and death, nor would that be maintained by any intelligent Christian. The live question is whether God does exercise a guiding control over human affairs with the deepest interests of individuals, as well as of all peoples, being given specific consideration. Christian faith has always affirmed such a concerned and guiding providence. The God who holds all the heavenly spheres in their courses is the same one by whom "even the hairs of your head are all numbered." [1] Prayers of petition imply such belief as do also all prayers of thanksgiving for specific blessings. It is likewise involved in the conception of special revelation and of divine acts in history.

Henry Bett somewhat overstates the case when he makes all living religion completely dependent upon belief in special providence and miracles.[2] It is certainly true, however, that without belief in special providence the Christian religion would be without its historic personal warmth and would have lost much of its power. It would, in fact, be scarcely recognizable.

2. *Difficulty Introduced by the Sciences*

In our day the historic belief in special providence is called into question chiefly because of the modern scientific notion of an all-embracing system of causal law. If everything from the weather to the incidence of disease is determined according to a rigorous system of causal laws, then, no matter whether

---

[1] See Mt. 10:29–30. Cf. Rom. 8:28.
[2] See his able and helpful book on the subject entitled *The Reality of the Religious Life.*

God legislated the laws or not, there appears to be no room for Him to act upon a specific concern for particular individuals at particular times and places.

3. The Difficulty Not Decisive

Despite the system of causal law it is not unreasonable to believe in special providence. Our common experience makes it plain that whatever causation is, it does not prevent a *man* from affecting the experiences of his companions by acting upon specific concerns for them from moment to moment. If one believes at all in such a God as we have been speaking of, it is preposterous to suppose that He is powerless to express love for individuals in the world of His own making where men express their particular concerns every hour of every day.

Causal law is not the rigid framework which by a kind of imaginative apotheosis we often suppose it to be. A causal law in the scientific sense is not a thing, a power or a process. It is an abstraction, a formula or a set of relationships represented by a formula, in accordance with which certain kinds of sequences invariably occur. The discoveries of recent physics have shown that no causal laws represent in precise rigidity the actual processes to which they refer. They represent rather statistical probabilities and the limits within which real events occur. Since single variations from the averages stated in the laws are so small as to be detected only by very precise methods of observation and measurement, it might be argued that they could not affect the practical concerns which we are considering. But actually there are many points at which practical variables in the physical world are set on very fine pivotal points. Hence, just as the movement by an inch or two of a rail in a switch may change the course of a train by a thousand miles, so minute movements of electrons at crucial points, which would, if observed, be seen to fall well within the prescribed physical limits, might, in cumulative effect, alter profoundly the course of a human life or of history.

All causal laws are the orderly ways of God's action in the spheres in which they are discovered. No law, taken by itself, defines the course of actual events. Every event in the real world represents the convergence of many forces and could be accurately and fully described only by such complex formulas as would represent all of the orderly ways of God relevant to that event. God is faithful to His own ordered plan. But the ways of Him "with whom there is no variation or shadow due to change" [3] include constancy of concern for each of His children. Scientific knowledge of causal law sustains no reason for doubting the faith supported by so much of our knowledge about God and the

[3] Jas. 1:17.

experience of millions, that this divine concern has room for effective expression within the order He has ordained.

4. *Miracles*

The belief in miracles originated long before the belief in a divine creation or the doctrine of one God reigning over all the world. In those primitive times both the gods and men were regarded as dwelling in a world not of their making, the existence and ultimate nature of which were taken for granted. In this world, however, despite its being in a sense foreign to the wills of gods and men alike, the gods, with their superior power, were able to intervene, on occasion, and do mighty wonders on behalf of their favorites. Most of the time the world took its natural course, but just as men acted in the world, so now and then the gods acted also. Then the natural world proceeded again on its own way.

With the rise of monotheism and creationism the idea of miracles thus formulated became an anachronism. If the world is itself a mighty act of God, the idea that He acts occasionally within it and then leaves it to go its own way is obviously absurd. The notion of a divine breaking into the world from outside for an occasional work does not make sense if from the beginning and without ceasing He has been at work in the world. If, as we have maintained, He is omnipresently active, then nowhere would He need to intervene from without.

Yet if we take "causal law" to mean the usually dependable formulations describing certain of His ways without reference to His purpose, there is still a very significant sense in which the word "miracle" may be used.

We should hardly suppose that God accounts the physical system as prior in importance to the purpose for which He has ordained it. The means will scarcely be elevated to superiority over the end. If His purpose is a loving concern to create persons and to establish over them His reign so that they will choose joyfully to serve Him and share in His glory, He will surely not let the orderly procedures He has adopted as means prevent Him from doing what He sees is needed for the accomplishment of that purpose.

If, then, it happened—whether once or frequently—that God acted in such a way that no mechanistic, impersonal formulation of causal law such as the natural sciences discover, could possibly have predicted what would occur, and, moreover, so that, on the basis of such probabilities as those formulas could establish, it would have been confidently predicted that this event would *not* occur, it might properly be called a miracle.

It is not to be thought that such events would be common. If they were, the formulas of the natural sciences would not be plausible at all. Moreover, a reasonably dependable, even apparently mechanical causal order is highly beneficent in our development as moral beings. Only in a world where the sun shines and the rain falls on just and unjust alike can the life of a responsible rational being be developed. God, it may be presumed, has ordained the orderly sequences discovered by the sciences for these and other purposes and will not lightly contradict the formulas by which He intended for men to predict and partially control events.

Even if God has, on occasion, contradicted such causal laws, it must not be supposed that He has contradicted His system of governance over the world. The only complete statement of causal law would have to include the entire system of His ways of dealing with His creatures, in which system impersonally mechanical formulas of invariable sequences would constitute only a part and His total purpose would be all-inclusive. Of this larger order there is no disruption, no "shadow of turning." [4]

In reports of miracles there are, of course, innumerable instances of fraud and of self-delusion. Many events called miracles are actually wonderful events altogether in accordance with known impersonally formulated causal laws. Others do contradict causal laws as best formulated by the science of the time, but are quite in accord with later formulations.

Whether at any given time an event which would seem incredible to a scientific mind has or has not actually occurred is to be determined, if at all, only by examining all the scientific and historical evidence available. Even then it could hardly be known conclusively whether that event was in fact a miracle in the full sense we have defined. For though it may flatly contradict natural laws in which we have the utmost confidence at the time, later scientific developments may completely eliminate the contradiction or even enable the prediction and control of such events in the future.[5] Nevertheless, there is no evident good reason for discounting the possibility that some such events may be forever, in principle, beyond the reach of such developments, even though we cannot be sure of any particular instance.

B. ARE THERE SUPERHUMAN CREATURES?

1. The Traditional Belief in Angels

In the Christian community until recent times it was taken for granted that there were in existence many personal beings greater in power and knowledge than men but like men owing their being to God's creative act. Sometimes, in the ancient church, polytheistic deities were explained as real, but as inferior

---

[4] Jas. 1:17, AV.

[5] Such possibilities are convincingly argued and illustrated by Henry Bett, op. cit.

to the true God and as being, in fact, rebellious angels. When God's transcendence was extremely emphasized, angels were regarded as intermediaries between heaven and earth. Moreover, the belief in angels has obviously added much of variety, color and beauty to Christian art and tradition.

2. Implications of Modern Theology

The stress on the immanence of God, so characteristic of modern Protestant theology, has tended to reduce both the interest in angelic beings and the credibility of their existence. If God is everywhere active, if He is concerned with the innermost life of every one of His children and if He immediately confronts the human person in divine-human encounter, there is little occasion for interest in messengers between heaven and earth. If "he is not far from each one of us," if "in him we live and move and have our being," [6] we have no need to communicate with Him from afar through intermediaries, nor is there need to believe in such intermediaries to account for experiences of divine illumination.[7]

Other modern practical and theoretical religious developments likewise tend to minimize the place of belief in angels. Most Christians are now so far removed from any living polytheistic faith that they feel no inclination to grant any credence to the existence, in any form, of pagan deities other than the one true God. The pressure felt by Christians from the surrounding world is toward the elimination, not the multiplication of superhuman beings. The aesthetic attractiveness of belief in angels is still felt by many, but it is often accepted as purely imaginative, to be used in symbolic stained-glass windows and stories of the nativity for children at Christmas, but not to be taken seriously.

3. Reasons Still Favoring Belief

Despite all the trends noted above, it must be observed that there are still no decisive disproofs and there are some positive evidences favoring belief in superhuman personal beings.

1. Some human beings have attained within their earthly lives a striking pre-eminence over their fellows, both in sanctity and in wisdom. If we believe in the life of such persons after death under conditions favorable to continued growth, a belief which will be later defended, these great saints and sages must,

---

[6] Acts 17:27-28.

[7] It may be objected that belief in the divine immanence, while characteristic of liberal theology, is discounted in such recent theologies as that of Karl Barth. That is true. Nevertheless, by his doctrine of the incarnation and especially of the *"revealed Word"* and other teachings, Barth actually recovers enough of the practical religious significance of immanentism so that he has no such practical need for angelic mediaries as appears in the ancient apocalyptic literature and in modern popular Roman Catholicism.

within a comparatively short time after death, develop well beyond the highest level of human attainment on earth. Some of these noble spirits must, in fact, be now "personal beings greater in power and knowledge than men but like men owing their being to God's creative act." They would thus conform precisely to our definition of angelic beings.[8]

2. It is reasonable to believe that human souls are not the only persons God has created. The great variety of other known creatures and the vast scale of the spatial universe suggest strongly that the God whose vast resourcefulness thus appears creates other persons more powerful than men and with means of gaining greater knowledge than we possess.

3. It is evident that human beings often abuse their powers and irresponsibly cause grave injury to other people—sometimes to vast numbers of them. We can hardly dismiss the possibility that persons of superhuman power have, like men, responsibilities affecting deeply other persons in their own society and also creatures of lower orders. Such a hypothesis might be a part of a total explanation of the problem of natural evil in human affairs.

4. Some of the most exalted passages of Scripture refer to angels in ways which make it difficult to eliminate them without seriously marring the lofty form and thought.[9]

It seems probable that some created superhuman persons formerly human beings of earth, and perhaps others too, do exist. Some such beings may have responsibilities which affect us for weal or woe as the Scriptures teach. But in any event, our final trust is in God. History shows unmistakably grave dangers which accompany a preoccupation with other superhuman beings, good or evil, real or imaginary. God alone is the source of our being and fashioner of our salvation. He is ever near at hand in unfailing concern for us. It is unseemly that we should address our reverent petitions, thanksgivings or praises to any other.

[8] Cf. Mt. 22:30; Mk. 12:25; Lk. 20:36.
[9] E.g., Lk. 2:8–15; 15:10; 22:43.

CHAPTER 17

God and Natural Evil: Analysis

A. THE PROBLEM

THE greatest theoretical difficulty confronting the Christian faith is the problem of evil. If God is good how can it happen that evil is everywhere in the world which He has made and which He now sustains? If He loves His human children why does He inflict or permit to be inflicted upon them pain, sorrow and death?

At present we are to be concerned only with what has been traditionally known as natural evil, as contrasted with moral evil. We are asking now, not the question, Why do God's creatures sin? but the question, Why do they suffer?

B. TYPES OF SOLUTIONS OFFERED

For more than twenty-five hundred years monotheists have labored with this problem. From the ancient interpreters of Israel's national tragedies and the writer of the Book of Job to the present day, suffering believers have sought to know why the most faithful lives were often accompanied by trouble and sorrow. Many answers have been proposed.

Some proffered solutions are so superficial or obviously contrary to fact as to warrant little consideration. One of these is the denial that sin, sickness and death occur at all, such apparent evils being regarded as mere illusions or errors of mortal mind.[1] Such a theory leaves to be accounted for the presence of error, no mean problem in a system of doctrine which maintains that all is God and God is truth.[2]

No more helpful is the view frequently held by uncritical minds that all suffering is a beneficent warning of greater evil. Thus it is often pointed out that if burning did not produce pain we should be in much graver danger of serious injury or death by fire. Of course, the serious injury and death are left to be explained.

[1] Mary Baker Eddy, *Science and Health with Key to the Scriptures* (1934 edition), pp. 229, 482.
[2] *Ibid.*, pp. 113, 115.

Occasionally it is glibly asserted, usually by some well-protected youth, that all suffering must be the fault of the sufferer since God is just and rewards all according to their desert. Sometimes it is added, as by Zophar addressing Job, "God exacts of you less than your guilt deserves."[3] But experience does not support such a view. The candid observer must confess with the Psalmist that it is often the wicked man who is "overbearing, and towering like a cedar of Lebanon," while the upright are cast down, poor and needy.[4] Jesus spoke for honest men of all time when, being told of the Galileans whom Pilate had just slain, he said,

Do you think that these Galileans were worse sinners than all the other Galileans, because they suffered thus? I tell you, No; but unless you repent you will all likewise perish.

Then, as if anticipating the inference that tragedies due to "natural" causes were, on the contrary, selective and just punishment of sinful individuals, he added,

Or those eighteen upon whom the tower in Siloam fell and killed them, do you think that they were worse offenders than all the others who dwelt in Jerusalem? I tell you, No; but unless you repent you will all likewise perish.[5]

A modern revision of the view which Jesus thus repudiated blames not so much the sins of men but rather their imprudence, ignorance or lack of psychological skill in self-management. According to this view, preached from many pulpits, all suffering results from violation of "God's laws," meaning causal laws affecting health and safety. We need only learn how to predict more accurately every peril, from earthquakes to emotional disorders, and learn to escape or prevent them. God has arranged everything perfectly for our health and pleasure. We need only to use the proper techniques and all will be well. For this purpose the essential instruments are, of course, the sciences, and above all psychology.[6] But even if one could believe in such superficial panaceas, overlooking even the inconvenient fact that everyone, even the psychiatrist's most faithful client, sooner or later dies, it still remains to be explained why the world was so ordered that countless millions of people have gone down to death without ever having opportunity so much as to hear of the sciences.

When it comes to the more serious solutions of the problem why pain and death exist in God's creation, thought takes generally one of two directions.

---

[3] Job 11:6.   [4] Ps. 37:35, 14.
[5] Lk. 13:1-5.
[6] All honor to the sciences for their magnificent achievements! They would be worthy of valiant defense if they needed it. But when ministers set them up as solutions of such ultimate problems as we are discussing, they do them no credit, while making themselves ridiculous.

Some views would stress the limitation of God's power, others its transcendent absoluteness. On the one hand, it is held that some or all natural evil is contrary to God's will and its existence is due to some uncreated force, being or aspect of being which opposes, limits or partially obstructs that will. On the other hand, it is stressed that God's power and knowledge far transcend our understanding and that even the worst of the pains we suffer have some good reason in relation to the ultimate purpose of God. Because the one type of view stresses the limitation of God's power it may be designated as finitistic, while the other, emphasizing the difference between our perspective and God's, may be designated as absolutistic.[7]

Each of the two types appears in many forms, varying greatly in critical thoroughness and cogency. However, each type has certain characteristic advantages which can be set forth with only occasional references to its specific representatives.

C. Advantages of Finitistic Theism

1. Simplicity

One clear source of appeal in the finitistic type of solution is the simplicity of its answer to the central question. If it is asked why God did not make the world without its anguish it is replied that He was unable to do so. No answer of the absolutist can equal this for simple directness and intelligibility. We have all had many experiences of wanting to accomplish good or destroy evil beyond our powers. Hence even the unlearned person can understand this explanation without difficulty.

2. Placing God Unconditionally with the Sufferer and against the Pain

When a person is suffering from sorrow, fear or pain, he wants allies in his struggle. The finitist assures him that God did not choose that he should suffer, that God, in fact, battles against the same forces which have produced his affliction. Hence there is given clear assurance of divine sympathy, comfort and aid far surpassing that of any man.

3. Clear Defense of God's Goodness

Since evil is experienced it seems apparent that either God could not or would not make the world without it. If He could but would not, it looks as if

---

[7] The word "finitistic" as used here does not imply a belief in a "small" God. A finitist in the special sense of the word here employed may conceive of God in positive, concrete terms of richness and magnitude far beyond the conceptions of some who would here be called "absolutists." Neither does it imply necessarily belief in some uncreated being other than God. On the other hand, the designation "absolutistic," be it noted, does not here have anything to do with belief in an all-inclusive philosophical "absolute," nor even necessarily in a God altogether without limitations.

He preferred to do evil along with good. Hence doubt is cast upon His perfect goodness. But if He lacked power to accomplish His purpose in all its perfection, then He is free from blame, so long as it is believed He has done as well as He could.

4. *Explanation of Other Irrationality in Experience*

The finitistic views, while offering an account of the afflictions which beset humanity, serve to explain at the same time some other features of the world, particularly the appearance of profligate and irrational waste in the unimaginably great proportion of seeds and eggs which never develop to maturity, the many species which have become extinct or which mark "dead ends" in the evolutionary process and the vast cruelty and destruction by the preying of different creatures upon one another. Some finitistic theories, particularly those of Plato and Edgar S. Brightman, give account also of the sheer stuff or material of our experienced world as contrasted with its meaningful forms.[8] The theory of Paul Tillich ought probably to be put in the same class. His method and language seem often to be absolutistic in the extreme and yet in relating the nonrational and evil aspects of experience to God as "abyss," he employs an idea strikingly similar to, though much less clear than Brightman's doctrine of "the Given."[9]

D. Advantages of Absolutistic Theism

1. *Clear Avoidance of Ultimate Dualism*

If natural evil is attributed to some being or aspect of being not subject to full control by the rational will of God it seems impossible to avoid the objections inherent in any ultimate metaphysical dualism.[10] This is especially apparent in a theory like Plato's, in which the retarding factor is regarded as altogether independent of God and of the eternal Ideas which are the ultimate forms of rationality. The difficulties of relating ultimate rational forms to metaphysically independent nonrational being were effectively stated by Aristotle and, indeed, were anticipated, though left unresolved, by Plato himself if he actually wrote the *Parmenides*.

It is hard to see how such objections can be met even in the thought of men

---

[8] For Plato's doctrine of the Receptacle see his *Timaeus* and *Philebus* and Raphael Demos' fine book, *The Philosophy of Plato*. For Brightman's theory of the "Given," see his *A Philosophy of Religion* and *The Problem of God*.

[9] See Tillich, *Systematic Theology*. See also the article by Georgia Harkness, "The Abyss and the Given," *Christendom*, Vol. 3, pp. 508–20.

[10] While some of these objections beset the philosophy of Thomas Aquinas, his view is not here relevant. It is not an *ultimate* metaphysical dualism, since according to Thomas matter was created by God. The Thomistic account of natural evil is of the absolutistic type.

like Brightman and Tillich. In Tillich's view the relation between God as *abyss* and God as *logos* is left so completely in mystery that it is unclear why the two should both be called God. Indeed, there appears to be no connecting link between them other than the mystery of the rational or "regular" and the nonrational or "irregular" in our experience, and this mystery is problem rather than solution.[11]

Brightman's theory attributes natural evil to the "nonrational Given" as content of God's consciousness, in contrast to His "rational Given" and His will. This view has the effect of putting Plato's Ideas inside God's own being as "rational Given," the Receptacle becomes the "nonrational Given" and Plato's God or "demi-urge" becomes for Brightman the divine will. This appears to mark a great metaphysical gain over Plato's view by reducing the ultimate threefold metaphysical division into a merely relative division within one single being, God. Moreover, instead of the unrelieved mystery which Tillich leaves between the *abyss* and the *logos* Brightman explains the relationship of the three aspects of God as analogous to our experience of unformed sensory qualia to reason and will in our consciousness. The great advantage in intelligibility is obvious.

However, this view would seem finally to deal with the problem of this relationship in our experience by attributing the same relationship to God. This has the effect of moving the problematic situation from man's consciousness to God's where it is in principle insoluble since there is no further being to whom we may look for explanation.

In short, if all meaningful relationships in the world are attributed finally to a rational will, rational Given or *logos* in God and one speaks of some *abyss*, nonrational Given or other nonrational source of the "irregular," then any meaningful relation of this source to rationality, will or anything else has been made *ex hypothesi* impossible. Not only is belief in such an extrarational kind of ultimate being a barren hypothesis from which nothing can be inferred, but it postulates gratuitously a new self-contradictory relationship at the very source of being.

The absolutistic views, on the other hand, finally attribute all being, directly or indirectly, to the perfection of God's good purpose, even though in ways which we can but partially understand. This method does involve the acknowledgment of a margin of mystery, but it leaves no relationship in complete mystery, much less in self-contradiction. For it can be readily understood from our experience that much of pain and trouble which in the narrow perspective of the time seems devoid of any good proves later, when a larger perspective is

[11] See, e.g., Tillich, *op. cit.*, Vol. I, p. 119.

possible, to have added greatly to the depth and richness of life. Since the widest perspective ever open to a human being is infinitesimal as compared with God's range of view and depth of wisdom, it is in principle intelligible that even the miseries which seem most completely dark have a place in the totality of His all-encompassing purpose which fully warrants their occurrence. There are many acts of parents, physicians and other adults which to a small child seem only distressing and altogether unreasonable but which are seen in the later perspective of maturity to have been wise and good. It would be a mystery, indeed, if from our limited human perspective we could unfailingly appreciate the value of all the hard experiences which God knew to be for our good.

In principle this general mode of explanation is coherent and the margin of mystery it leaves, while wide, is no more than we should expect in matching our limited knowledge against a problem involving infinite time and divine wisdom. This path is open, moreover, for unlimited further exploration without any sign of an end blocked by self-contradiction or problems inherently insoluble.

2. Doctrine of Absolute Dependence

Finitistic theism would represent God as a sympathetic fellow sufferer, who, like ourselves, must put up with various evils which He is unable to prevent or eliminate. There is no doubt that such a view would justify that kind of familiar camaraderie with God which some people fancy they should expect. However, it is doubtful that it would encourage the kind of absolute dependence or unconditioned trust in the holy God which we have found—along with Augustine, Schleiermacher, Kierkegaard, Rudolf Otto and other penetrating observers—to be characteristic of religious experience at its more profound and creative levels. Not only great Christians of famous names, but also millions of humble believers with great faith have reached their depths of assurance and sense of the divine presence precisely when they have accepted suffering or loss as God's holy will. The grim and hard-set jaw which would follow logically from belief that God shares our partially ineffective struggle with evil He cannot prevent may be admirably courageous. But it is more closely akin to the heroic spirit of Henley's "Invictus" than to Jesus' acceptance of the cross as the Father's will or St. Paul's interpretation of that cross and of his own "thorn in the flesh." [12] This implication is softened in Tillich's thought

---

[12] See Mk. 14:35–6; Rom. 5:6–12; 2 Cor. 12:7–10. Of course, the personal piety of finitistic Christians, nurtured in a Christian community predominantly absolutistic, is not here under discussion. Our practices are often different from the logic of our ideas, especially our newer ideas.

by the great stress on the awesome mystery of God's being and in Brightman's by the emphasis on "the control of the Given." Nevertheless, an admission of the mystery of God or the belief that God can partially control evil is not the same as the acceptance of pain or death as His holy will.

3. Interpreting Suffering as Redemptive

Much of the Scripture rests upon the faith that all pain, death and sorrow, whether personal or national, was willed by God for His own purpose. This is assumed in the historical books and the early prophets, as the writers seek to interpret the meaning of Israel's constantly changing vicissitudes. Without the assumption that even such tragedies as defeat and captivity at the hands of evil human foes expressed a divine purpose, the sublime prophecies of the exile never would have been written. It was not open to the second Isaiah or to Jeremiah to believe that God could not have prevented Israel's sore trials. It was precisely because they were confident that God could have prevented these afflictions that they had to search for a deeper meaning of suffering and found it in the profound message which was to have so great a part in preparing both Jesus and his contemporaries for his work of redemption. The writers of Job and many of the Psalms would have been saved their anguished searching for God's purpose in human pain if only they had believed God could not prevent it, but the world would have been deprived of incomparable poetry, wisdom and creative faith.

If Jesus had supposed that the Father could not save him from the cross he would not have had to view it as the Father's will. If Paul had doubted that whatever pain and sorrow occurred were willed or permitted by God he would not have found the cross at first a stumbling block and then the means of salvation. How much of the Bible would have been written if evil had been explained by the ancient Hebrews in the finitistic manner?

It is true that the Christian defenders of finitistic views believe that God partially controls and uses as best He can the evils He cannot prevent. They can, therefore, quite logically look in every situation for whatever good may be retrieved or even gained from conditions which God, as well as they, must deplore. But would anyone with a background of generations of belief in such a view actually have plumbed such depths of spiritual wisdom as the sacred writers knew? The problem that gave rise to the books of Job, Hosea, Jeremiah and the Epistle to the Romans was not the problem how the most good could be derived from a bad situation. It was how the anguish could be interpreted within the single, all-encompassing, holy purpose of God.

Such creative soul searching in prayer as the writers of Scripture presented to God as an open channel of divine revelation did not cease when their work was done. The same kind of questionings in darkest hours still serve for many devout persons as windows through which appear the most creative and redemptive visions of the Most High. The faith upon which is based man's preparation for such redeeming revelations is preserved in the absolutistic type of thought.

CHAPTER 18

God and Natural Evil: Toward Solution

T HE time has come for proposing a solution of the problem of natural evil, or rather the direction which the development of a solution ought to take. The suggestions which follow are offered in the hope that the truths in both absolutistic and finitistic solutions may be conserved and clarified in a single coherent view awaiting fuller development.

A. RELATIVE SUBORDINATION OF PAIN AND PLEASURE

It is no accident that the revival of interest in finitistic solutions of the problem of evil has come at a time when a sensate hedonism is dominant in our civilization. At a time when the value-dimension of pleasure and pain is taken generally as the primary dimension of significance, even the devout Christian is likely to give to the experiencing of pain or sorrow a depth of intrinsic importance well beyond what is merited. It then becomes intolerable to suppose that such experience can be within the purpose of God.

In any adequate theistic account of natural evil, and particularly in a Christian solution, it is necessary first of all to get a proper sense of proportion regarding the dimension of pain and pleasure as related to the dimension of sin and sanctification. In our time the importance of pain and pleasure looms so large that even in preaching, the practice of sin, prayer and faith are often presented as important chiefly for their effects on health and other material values. In the Christian perspective precisely the contrary is true. Christians have believed through the ages that it was the reign of God which was to be sought first. Other things have their chief importance as instrumentally affirmative or negative in relation to that.

In the individual's experience sin is the chief intrinsic evil, in comparison with which the intrinsic disvalue of pain is of minor importance, just as sanctification is of supreme worth and pleasure a trifle. In the long run of eternity it matters little to me whether my earthly days are long or short, since even a century is but a passing moment. But it matters everything what stewardship I give of the days at my disposal. Whether I am today suffering pain or enjoying pleasurable health will make little difference a thousand years from now. But how my pain or pleasure, weakness or health are related to faith and love will make all the difference.

In short, while the pleasure-pain dimension has undeniably some significance in itself, its supreme importance, beside which the greatest agony and most pleasant rapture fade like the oldest memories of them, is their instrumental relation to "the pearl of great value," the reign of God in our hearts, minds and wills.

B. Causation of Much Natural Evil by Sin

The relations of natural evils to sin are exceedingly varied and complex. But among all these relations one which has far-reaching ramifications is this, that much pain and trouble is quite specifically and plainly caused by sin.

God does not will that men hate and murder one another. But in their sin they do both inflict these and other injuries and provoke others to such action. Must not the ravages of war, with all its consequent fear, starvation and disease, be charged to the many human sins which cause this madness? Similarly venereal diseases produced by sexual immorality, and again the floods and droughts which follow the recklessly greedy exploitation of forest lands, these and many other ills human beings in rebellion against God bring upon themselves and their fellows.

In another way, too, much of our pain is caused by our sin and faithlessness. Just as Kant showed the deep dependence of our perceptual experience upon the organizing forms which our own minds supply, so recent psychology and medicine have brought forth one evidence after another that much of the character of our experience which we attribute to the objective world is actually due to the operation of our own attitudes. Not only in the diseases treated in our psychopathic hospitals, but also in many sufferings which afflict "normal" people, fear and distrust have profound effects, aggravating until almost unbearable some pains which faith, hope and love could reduce to insignificance. If a doctor can train the attitudes of an expectant mother so that she can bear her children without drugs and literally in triumphant pleasure—and this has been demonstrated in a great number of cases [1]—how much of earth's pain might be removed if individuals and the whole society in which they live were rid of the fear, hate, guilt feelings and self-pity which sin has engendered? We do not know, but it would undoubtedly be a vast quantity.

C. The Cost of a Causal Order

Much of the inequitable distribution of suffering in our present world is obviously due to a causal order in which sunshine and storm, health and plague

[1] For an account of some, see Grantly Dick Read, *Childbirth without Fear.*

are distributed in a regular and apparently impersonal way, falling upon just and unjust alike. It is plainly impossible that there should be any such dependable regularity of cause and effect in our environment without the wicked often seeming—so far as earthly pain and pleasure are concerned—to receive the smiles of chance, while it is the righteous who fall under "the slings and arrows of outrageous fortune." [2]

Why, then, did God ordain such a causal order? Why should there be any trouble in the world? Or, if pain and sorrow be needed as instruments of some good purpose, why were they not so distributed as to be experienced in precise accord with justice or with the needs of each individual? Why this mechanically regular and hence inequitable distribution which bears down with crushing weight upon some while others dwell in carefree, irresponsible ease?

If the goal of existence were pleasure, as Omar Khayyám supposed, it would be readily seen that any intelligent creator could order our "sorry scheme of things" in a way much "nearer to the heart's desire." [3] But if the training of immortal souls for heroic faith and love be the purpose, that is a different matter. How would a created person learn courage if there were no peril of real injury? How come to know the deep joy of self-giving love if, with no pain or death, there were no hard sacrifice to make? How learn responsible community if each must bear alone the penalties of his own sin without power to increase or heal real sufferings in others? How would we be incited to self-disciplined, responsible maturity, were it impossible to predict with fair accuracy many consequences, at least, of our acts?

It is plain that such a mechanical causal order as that in which we live is not fitted to be the last word of a good God. But no one who has condemned it has suggested an alternative which would serve so effectively as a school to prepare created persons for the higher revelations of His purpose to be enacted both within and after their historical experience within it.

D. Transmutability of Suffering into Good

All natural evil, when confronted with faith, prayer and courage, can become a means to good. Thus out of the anguish of the whole ancient nation, Israel, came the sublime revelations of the exilic prophets. Even the most radically unjust suffering ever inflicted upon human flesh, the torture of Jesus upon a cross at the hands of sinful men, became the supreme channel of divine revelation and redemption. It must be observed that neither in the prophets nor in Christ was good thought to be achieved merely in spite of suffering, but rather

---

[2] *Hamlet*, Act III, sc. 1.
[3] *The Rubáiyát of Omar Khayyám*, tr. by Edward Fitzgerald.

precisely by means of suffering. Countless men and women, both great and humble, have experienced in their own persons a similar transmutation.

It is noteworthy that Brightman, with all his dramatic emphasis upon "surd evil" as evidence of the nonrational Given, has corrected an earlier apparent denial and agreed that every natural evil can be made instrumental to good.[4] Finitistic and absolutistic theist alike agree that in God's sight not a single distressing experience of any human being is final. Because God lives evil never has the last word.

E. Correction of Earthly Injustice in the Life to Come

It often *seems* that suffering has the last word and to our sight death always has. The necessities of this earthly stage in God's preparation of men for His kingdom bring many individuals to the grave, bearing, in proportion to their fellows, far more than their share of life's most grievous burdens. But the Christian's appraisal of any life reaches beyond death to the life hereafter where, in the long reaches of eternity, all the inequities of this present world are righted as the judgments of God have the lasting and final word.

F. Limitations of God's Power

Would not God, in His perfect righteousness, choose, if He could, to achieve *all* the good which He purposes without any of the suffering, perplexity and sadness which now beset us? Granting that no man can prescribe how such an end could be achieved, if God could bring to pass the perfect fulfillment of all His highest purpose without the evil, would He not do so? If in any sense that has positive meaning for us we are to say that God is good our answer must be yes. Indeed, we have already observed, in discussing the power of God, that His omnipotence, although it is power over all, is limited by His voluntary delegation of power to some of His creatures, by His rational nature and by the bounds of His own being, however unimaginably great.

The acknowledgment of such limitation marks the view here defended as in a sense finitistic. It is a denial that God is in all conceivable respects infinite. On the other hand, it is to be observed that two of these kinds of limitation were acknowledged by so thoroughgoing a defender of God's infinite perfection as Anselm.[5] The third, the limitation of His being by His own vast bounds, beyond which is no reality nor possibility, seems to be acknowledged, though not stressed nor elaborated by Albert C. Knudson [6] whom, so far as the present

---

[4] Cf. the first and subsequent editions of his *A Philosophy of Religion*, p. 246, and "Shall We Be Reasonable" in *Zions Herald*, Vol. 127 (1949), p. 923.

[5] See *Proslogium*, 7, and *Cur Deus Homo*, 21.

[6] See *The Doctrine of God*, p. 269.

issue is concerned, Brightman has regarded as representative of the absolutism which he opposes. According to our initial characterization of the two types of solutions, such divine limitation as has been defended in this work does not constitute this a finitistic view, for it is not here held that evil is due to any "uncreated force, being or aspect of being which opposes, limits or partially obstructs" God's will. It is one thing to say that the divine will or God as *logos* confronts a Receptacle (Plato), nonrational Given (Brightman) or symbolically indicated potentiality (Tillich).[7] It is another thing to say that God's will confronts nothing which He has not created (as man's free will) or fully approved (as God's own rational nature), but that the will is limited simply by being all that it is and not more.[8]

In terms of practical religion there is a great difference. On the finitist's terms, if followed through in practice, we should have to suppose that God Himself was unable to prevent some specific natural evil and that it must therefore be treated as something in spite of which we ought to do the best we could with God's help. On the other hand, on the view being defended here, every natural evil must be regarded as having a positive place in the purpose of God. It is, therefore, not to be treated as something *in spite of which* we do the best we can. On the contrary, we are to treat it, as the prophets dealt with the exile and as Jesus and Paul interpreted the cross, that is, as something *by means of which* God's will is being done and hence great new good coming to pass, *good worth much more than all the cost.*[9]

But above all, God is limited by our own sin which He did not will but which He foresaw as our abuse of freedom and for which He made provision. Here Schleiermacher saw part of a truth. He taught that the doctrine of the original perfection of the world has to do not with history but with the truth that had there been no sin there would have been no need of suffering, although natural evil has probably been in the world from the beginning because God foreknew that men would sin.[10] What he seems to have missed is that the peril and reality of suffering must be instrumental to advance from innocence to mature and righteous faith as well as from sin to redemption.

This present world is not the best of all possible worlds. It is not in accord with the *final* purpose of God. It is only in accord with His *provisional* purpose. It is not the best He can give to His children. It is only the best He can give to His children while they are moving from innocence through sin into

---

[7] See his *Systematic Theology*, Vol. I, pp. 246–47.

[8] Here is limitation, not by "nonbeing" (the *me on* of classical Greek philosophy) but by sheer not-being, that is, nothing at all, either real or possible (the *ouk on* of the Greeks.) Cf. Tillich, *Systematic Theology*, Vol. I, pp. 187–89.

[9] Cf. Rom. 8:17–18.

[10] *The Christian Faith*, p. 243.

the early stages of redemption and while most of them remain thoroughly preoccupied with their own sinful purposes. This is not "the glory which shall be revealed" [11] when we enter the kingdom that is to be.[12]

G. Mystery

There must always be a vast margin of mystery when we confront the ways of God. It could not be otherwise, else we should be God. When confronting in experience the actual pains and sorrows which beset us we can at best see "through a glass darkly." We can only "know in part" [13] what God means to do for us.

Indeed, if we could understand the whole meaning of suffering, perhaps it would fail fully to serve its purpose for us. We must not think there is any complete solution for the problem of evil while any neighbor anywhere remains in distress which we could ameliorate. It is probably God's own purpose that we must be perplexed and plagued, intellectually as well as practically, by the very existence of pain and trouble as long as we need them. For their purpose is served only so long as we cannot be at peace with them in our own persons or in any others. Struggle with them we must, at every level, until we enter the heavenly city where sin has no place and all tears are wiped away.

Yet when we do not know why or how this pain or that crushing loss is meant to aid us we can trust Him who in the hour of anguish assures us, as He did St. Paul, that "in everything God works for good with those who love him." [14] And in that trust we find a foretaste of His peace.

---

[11] Rom. 8:18.
[12] Cf. the teaching of Nels Ferré in *Evil and the Christian Faith.*
[13] I Cor. 13:12, AV.
[14] Rom. 8:28.

PART FOUR

MAN

PART FOUR

MAN

CHAPTER 19

The Origin and Nature of Man

A. ORIGIN

IN Genesis is expressed the great truth that "in the beginning God created the heavens and the earth."[1] That man owes his being to divine authorship is attested not only by the Scriptures but also by an abundance of other evidence. There is much additional profound truth expressed in the first chapters of Genesis concerning the divine image in man, for example, and concerning sin and its tragedy.

On the other hand, it cannot be reasonably maintained that Genesis is authoritative concerning the chronological sequence of events nor the means employed in the creation of man or his world. Not only are these matters outside the field in which we find the Bible to speak with authority, but there are also quite specific evidences of human error within these particular passages.

In the first place, there are two narratives concerning the creation of man, written centuries apart and flatly contradicting each other.[2] According to the first chapter of Genesis, living creatures appeared in the following order: (1) vegetation, (2) fish, (3) birds, (4) land animals and (5) men and women. The much earlier second chapter, on the contrary, reports that man was created first, then the useful plants, then animals and birds, then woman and finally the annoying weeds.

Concerning such matters we do well to consult the great body of information amassed by the natural sciences. For the great antiquity of human life on earth and the distant animal ancestry of the human organism there is a convergence of testimony, including evidences from the examination of fossil remains, comparative anatomy, embryology and experimental animal breeding. These evidences are decisive for any mind not closed by contrary dogmatic assumptions. This discovery was enough to cause at first a kind of panic among many Christian leaders. It was feared that the apes were replacing the divine Creator

---

[1] Gen. 1:1.

[2] This is true even though the priestly editor may have had a studied religious purpose in mind when he placed the narratives together.

acknowledged in Genesis. Then it was observed that, far from displacing God, the apes, or rather some common ancestors of apes and men, represented only a stage in the forming of the "dust" into man.

It is true, of course, that in the sciences, as elsewhere, faith and reason must be joined. If a man does not believe in the basic trustworthiness of the senses, of disciplined human reason and of careful communication, there is nothing to prevent him from denying the plainest implications of scientifically ascertained fact. But if he denies them he should recognize that he is at the same time cutting the lines of communication by which he might hope to transmit his own beliefs to others.

From the scientific studies related to biological evolution we know that there have been creatures upon earth which were, anatomically speaking, at least, recognizably human, for at least twenty-five thousand years and probably for a half million years or longer.[3] Of this vast period we can recover history, in any proper sense, of only about seven thousand years and for that length of time only when we are concerned with the oldest advanced cultures, such as the Egyptian. Yet the whole period of human life, great as it has been, is very brief as compared with the ages in which lower forms of life have existed on the land and in the waters of the earth. Even after human beings arrived on the scene many millenniums passed before they developed those tools, utensils, weapons, wearing apparels and variously designed artificial dwellings which to the senses most conspicuously distinguish human societies from the flocks and herds of animals.

B. The Nature of Man

1. Behavioristic Psychology

It is commonly supposed that scientific psychology is capable of deciding what is truly the nature of man. Such a claim is made especially in behalf of a purely external or behavioristic type of study. This kind of psychology arose from the determination to attain a body of knowledge concerning human individuals which would be as public and as exact in measurement as the knowledge which we have in physics and chemistry concerning their proper objects. After experimenting with animals for a time, John B. Watson turned his method to the examination of human beings. Until that time he had carefully refrained from any suggestion that there was a subjective aspect to animal behavior. Similarly, in describing the responses of human beings, he eschewed all references to thinking, sensing, purposing or affective feeling, on the ground that

---

[3] Cf. Sir Arthur Keith, *The Antiquity of Man*, and Alfred Louis Kroeber, *Anthropology*, pp. 93–94.

there was no public, scientifically verifiable evidence that any such subjective factors existed. Hence, the human individual was described exclusively in terms of the material body in its various patterns of behavior, made up by the conditioning of reflexes.

Now it is evident that any such doctrine of man is quite contrary to the concerns and experiences of which the Christian community has borne witness through the centuries. Faith, prayer, love, joy—with these the Scriptures are continually concerned and of these Christians have spoken in all times and places where Christians have been found. All are unseen. None is subject to public scrutiny. None can be verified by the laboratory methods of the natural sciences. In short, a thoroughgoing behavioristic conception of the human individual and acceptance of the most persistent testimonies of the Christian community are mutually exclusive.

However, the behavioristic denial of man's spiritual being is contradicted also by the experience of all men. All that we know about the body and its activities we know through sensation, thought and the projection of our purpose into action. Yet sensation, thought and purpose are all subjective experiences. A strange phenomenon is the behaviorist, who, in loyalty to a nonspatial, mentally apprehended ideal of scientific method, thinks about the meanings of his observations and solemnly pronounces the judgment of his thought that mind, ideals and thoughts are unknown to him. John B. Watson, the founder of behavioristic psychology, once had misgivings about his position to which he and his followers have since paid too little heed. He openly faced the question whether mental images relatively remote from stimulation and beyond the reach of behavioristic description might actually be decisive in determining some actions. Watson suggested that behaviorists might well admit the existence of such images while choosing to specialize in research on stimulus and response, so leaving the images for others to study. But he added,

. . . and yet we dislike to admit anything which may be construed as an admission of even partial defeat. Feeling so, it seems wisest, even at the cost of exposing the weakness of our position, to attack rather than to remain upon the defensive.[4]

Weakness, indeed! What greater weakness could a scientist admit than that he decided which side he would take on a crucial issue, not by concern to side with truth but by fear of being construed as admitting "even partial defeat"?

In view of the grave contradiction of experience in the behavioristic position itself it need not be regarded as a serious threat, in the long run, to the faith of the Christian community.

---

[4] *Behavior* (New York: Henry Holt and Co., 1914), p. 17.

2. *Other Mechanistic Views of Man*

More plausible is the modified behaviorism which would freely admit the occurrence in experience of sensations, ideas and purposes, but would deny that such subjective events had any causal efficacy. An airplane's passing is accompanied by the movement of its shadow on the ground far below, without being retarded, advanced or directed by it. So, it is argued, the motions and changes of the human organism produce an accompanying consciousness, with its succession of images and affections, without being in the least influenced by these subjective events. The causal connection between body and mind is thus regarded as a strictly one-way affair, the mind affecting nothing.

This view has the advantage over Watson's behaviorism of admitting the manifest evidence that mind occurs. However, it still leaves unmodified the doctrine which Watson himself admitted having maintained for polemic purposes despite doubt as to its justification by the evidence. If consciousness is only an effect and not a cause, then the thoughts and feelings which are stirred in the mind of a reader engrossed in Shakespeare's *Macbeth* are not results of any expression of Shakespeare's imagination. We are left to infer that we can never communicate our ideas to other persons. The writing of words on a page is not to the slightest degree directed by or expressive of the thoughts in the mind of the writer. Rather, it can merely be said that some of the thoughts in writer as well as reader are caused by the physical events involved in the writing. The writing itself is a series of physical events caused solely by other physical events without influence by thought or feeling in any mind. The idea that the classics of literature, science or philosophy have been produced without benefit of any influence from the thoughts of the authors hardly commends itself to reason. It looks like a tour de force to save a mechanistic presupposition. Moreover, if such a view be true it is evident that there is no mind capable of judging it to be true. For any mind which thinks it is weighing the evidence for and against it is actually experiencing only a series of mental sparks struck off by the mechanisms of the body. Even when thought seems to be guided by considerations of logic and the ideal of truth it is actually guided only by the mechanical forces of matter in motion. There appears no good reason why anyone should pay serious attention to a person's announcement of such a theory. For on its own terms the announcement is not the expression of a thoughtful judgment but only the effect of certain mechanical motions.[5]

3. *Psychological Monisms*

Any theory of man, whether materialistic or idealistic, which would eliminate any real difference of identity between his soul and body would be in conflict

[5] Cf. below, pp. 172–173.

with the implications of Christian experience. It is true that in the Scriptures the possibility of a living human body without a soul is never entertained and it seems often to be assumed, even in the New Testament, that for a man's soul to live his body must live also. But this assumption may well be attributed to old habits of thought and speech, to the difficulties of representing reality without the imagery of sense and to the indubitable necessity that the consciousness of a man have its context of communication provided through some medium. On the other hand, many passages indicate a breaking away from the ancient Hebrew tendency simply to identify the individual with the living body. The accounts in Matthew and John of Jesus giving up the ghost or spirit, accentuated in Luke by the cry, "Father, into thy hands I commit my spirit," clearly imply a separation of one part or aspect of his being from another.[6] St. Paul, in one of his great discourses on immortality says, "I tell you this, brethren, that flesh and blood cannot inherit the kingdom of God."[7] It is true that he describes the future "spiritual" body as a miraculous transformation of the present body. Yet it is hardly clear that anything of the old body is to remain. He seems rather to expect the soul to be clothed in a "spiritual body" which is to displace the "flesh and blood" we now inhabit. In that other great discussion of the life after death, in 2 Corinthians 4 and 5, Paul makes it crystal clear that he anticipates a separation of the immortal soul from "our mortal flesh."[8] One day, he promises, we are "to be absent from the body, and to be at home in the Lord," though even then the Lord will remember "the things done in the body."[9]

It is not only in connection with the life after death that the New Testament distinguishes soul and body, however. According to Luke, Jesus warned his hearers, "Do not fear those who kill the body, and after that have no more that they can do."[10] If nothing were to live after death of the body there would obviously be nothing more to fear.

Corliss Lamont contends[11] that such psychological dualism has become quite untenable in the world of modern thought. Pointing out the strong trends of modern philosophy toward a metaphysical monism of one kind or another, and showing the theoretical advantages of such monism, he concludes that it is not reasonable, in the light of present knowledge, to regard soul and body as distinct and separable, however intimate the interaction conceded. Unfortunately for his argument he fails to observe consistently the distinction between

---

[6] See Mt. 27:50; Jn. 19:30; Lk. 23:46.
[7] 1 Cor. 15:50.
[8] 2 Cor. 4:11.
[9] 2 Cor. 5:8, 10.
[10] Lk. 12:4.
[11] See his book, *The Illusion of Immortality.*

quantitative and qualitative monism and between the latter and psychological monism.[12] It is one thing to say, as most recent philosophers other than Thomists do say, that all being is basically of one *kind*—whether material, personal or neutral. It is quite another to say that all being is one individual entity and this is something most recent philosophers have not said. It can be quite reasonably maintained that all being is ultimately of one metaphysical *kind* while it is still insisted that there are many entities of this kind representing various degrees of complexity and value, variously interrelated and capable of entering into interaction and being withdrawn from it. Among these the body and soul of man may well be examples.

4. Philosophical Psychologies Coherent with Christian Experience

Following our adopted policy, we do not here enter upon the examination of the metaphysical problems which confront us at this point, excepting in so far as they are of quite direct concern in the interpretation and evaluation of the experience of the Christian community. It is clear that materialistic or other mechanistic doctrines of the human individual would imply that the whole concern of Christians as Christians was false. But we have seen that such views should also be rejected on other empirical and rational grounds. On the other hand, it is not of direct concern to the theologian whether the body be regarded as a form of material substance created by God and subject to His governance, as the metaphysical dualist would maintain, or whether it be considered as an appearance in human experience of certain activities of God, as the objective idealist would contend. The soul may be conceived of as the subject of consciousness,[13] as the whole of personal consciousness which recognizes its own self-identity,[14] as a spiritual substance which is the subject of consciousness[15] or as some other kind of reality of which all that is observed in consciousness is the activity.[16] The relation between the activities of consciousness and the behavior of the body may be regarded as one of interaction,[17] or as two appearances of a single process which is in and for itself as it appears in consciousness but which appears phenomenally in spatial patterns of behavior.[18]

The Bible, the centuries of experience in the Christian community and likewise the common moral and intellectual experience of mankind attest the validity and responsibility of the thinking, willing self as an existent deeply

[12] E.g., see *ibid.*, pp. 102–3.
[13] Cf. the doctrine of Lotze.
[14] Cf. the views of Brand Blanshard, Edgar S. Brightman and Gordon Allport.
[15] Cf. the Neo-Thomists.
[16] Cf. the "Personal Realism" of James Bissett Pratt.
[17] Cf. Borden P. Bowne, Ralph Tyler Flewelling and Peter A. Bertocci.
[18] This view is elaborated and defended in my metaphysical (not theological) article entitled, "A Personalistic Re-examination of the Mind-Body Problem," *The Personalist, Winter,* 1953.

related to the realm of physical causation yet in some respects and to some degree, at least, transcending that realm. It is with this responsible subject of our thinking and willing to which we refer in theology when we speak of the human soul. It is not some peculiarly religious aspect of man's experience nor something at present unknown within him. It is the thinking, feeling, willing self, the subject of all our experience, however much more it may be thought of as being and in whatever terms it may be metaphysically described.

C. Role of the Body in the Life of the Soul

1. *In Creation of the Individual*

It appears that the creative act of God which produces each human soul is at least closely related to the divine activity which projects the new infant organism into the world. It may be that the creative activity of God which gives being to the new soul is the very same as appears spatially in the development of the fertilized ovum into the lively new-born body. In any event there is apparent the closest kind of correlation between the development of the body and that of the soul, both as to temporal sequence and as to quality. Only when the body, particularly the nervous system, has attained a certain level of maturity, and only when the nervous system is within certain broad limits of proportion and of physical and chemical condition is there evidence that a new young subject of thought, feeling and will exists.

Closely related is the whole problem which has been debated between creationists and traducianists. For laws of heredity such as make possible certain predictions regarding the bodies of children born with specified types of ancestry, also enable us to make some predictions, within wide limits, regarding the intelligence and other qualities of their souls. These facts have often led to the traducianist supposition that God created the souls of the first human parents only and that all other human souls have been generated from them. But this would be to attribute to God's creatures a kind of creative power quite incoherent with the view of His relations to the world which we found most tenable, and it would seem poorly supported by experience. It is all too well known to millions of parents that they cannot by taking thought of the matter determine even the sexes of their children, to say nothing of the more subtle but even more important capacities of intelligence and feeling. It seems clear that there is a creative power coming into action on certain occasions of marital intercourse and resultant conception, a creative power which is not the parents themselves and which is far from lending itself wholly to their control. God has ordained that in the processes of creating a new life, as in all the other processes of the world, certain orderly sequences and relations should be observable. But it is not to be supposed that the events or the kinds of children which may be predicted to follow upon certain other events or kinds of parents have been therefore created by those events or parents. Every soul should rather be regarded as having been made by the one Creator, in accordance with the order of relationships which He has ordained.

2. *In Communication*

The body is obviously an instrument by which the soul expresses its thoughts, affections and volitions in such form as to be discernible by other souls through the perceptual apparatus of their bodies. Our bodies are thus seen to be instruments of reciprocal communication between souls. Through such communication is made possible the education of the individual and the forming of human society. By means of this communication and by the experiences of the non-human world of nature through these same bodily organs, the soul is enabled also to learn of God and to be led into communion with Him.[19]

3. *In Moral and Religious Development*

The body provides for the soul a system of predictable order which makes possible the development of rational thought, intelligent foresight and meaningful moral purpose. In the body also, with all its variability of condition and perceptual stimulation, is the source of infinite changes and surprises which serve to awaken the soul from lethargy and spur it on to new adventure and growth. It is likewise the body which provides a large portion of the pains and pleasures which first excite the soul to action, which continue to provide the pedagogical foundation for all value experience and which furnish many of the encouragements and obstacles for the incitement and disciplining of faith.

4. *Valuable Instrument*

The body, then, is not to be despised. It is not evil. When St. Paul contrasted spirit and flesh and condemned the latter he was not contrasting soul and body. What he called "the flesh" was rather the whole aggregation of lower, sinful impulses which beset the soul and which rule it excepting as men accept the grace of God and are reborn. When Paul lists "works of the flesh," many of them turn out to be sins scarcely connected with bodily desires. Although he includes lasciviousness and drunkenness, he includes also idolatry, dissension and party spirit.[20] The very fact that he uses the term "the flesh" as he does indicates a certain association of the body with sin in his mind, an association which seems foreign to the teachings of Jesus. However, this is more a matter

[19] Cf. Rom. 1:8 and 1:20.
[20] Gal. 5:16-21.

of association in experience and of mere terminology than of serious conviction. Nowhere in literature is there a more emphatic and exalted assertion of the rightful sanctity of human bodies than the passage in which Paul depicts them as "members of Christ." [21] He seems even to imply that the body is rightfully so sacred that a sin against it is worse than a sin of the soul in which the body is not involved. At the climax of his denunciation of fornication he says, "Every other sin which a man commits is outside the body; but the [sexually] immoral man sins against his own body." [22] And in conclusion he cries, "Do you not know that your body is a temple of the Holy Spirit within you, which you have from God? You are not your own; you were bought with a price. So glorify God in your body." [23]

On the other hand, the body is not to be loved as an end in itself. It is a temple, an earthly tabernacle, an instrument, not the Holy Spirit to whom the temple belongs nor the rightful ruler of the soul. "I pommel my body and subdue it," says Paul.[24] The Master himself teaches that it is better for the health and wholeness of the body to be sacrificed than that it bring the soul into bondage and so drag the whole life down to hell.[25] The body has a very high purpose in the divine plan. But this purpose is fulfilled only when by the grace of God the soul firmly rules the body and uses it for the high vocation to which every child of God has been summoned. When the body is exalted to be served by the soul both are brought low. Only by being subjected can the body be glorified as God intended.

[21] 1 Cor. 6:13–20.   [22] 1 Cor. 6:18.
[23] 1 Cor. 6:19–20.   [24] 1 Cor. 9:27.
[25] Mt. 5:27–30.

CHAPTER 20

Man's Limitation

A. His Existence Dependent

THE human individual has not always been. He has a known personal history, beginning in complete ignorance and helplessness. Theories about the pre-existence of human souls are only vain speculations unsupported by memory, developed skill or any other convincing evidence.[1] The temporal dimension of man's life is limited at one end—the past.

He is a creature of God. In contrast to the Creator's unconditioned, absolute being, man exists only by virtue of the divine will. He is born in inescapable and total obligation to God who has made him and by whom his very existence is sustained.

Every man owes his being also to his parents and to the larger human society. In the origin of his life, in nurture and protection through infancy and childhood and in the provision of the instruments for both his physical and his mental life, he is dependent upon other human beings as well as upon God. The language, the concepts and the attitudes which so largely constitute the content of the personal consciousness itself, all represent the influence of society. The individual's indebtedness to mankind is tempered by the wrongs inflicted by others. Yet, if he values his life at all, this indebtedness is greater than he can ever discharge.

B. Subjection to Causal Determination

It is evident that we live within a causal order in which the range of possible events is narrowly limited. The accuracy of much scientific prediction and the impressive achievements of technology attest the validity and the wide scope of the category of causation. Not only planets and molecules, but sensations and emotions are predictable to a degree, in spite of the rudimentary and uncertain stage of our psychological knowledge.

---

[1] The attempt by J. E. M. McTaggart to revive the ancient Platonic doctrine of pre-existence has seemed strange and anachronistic to most readers and apparently convinced no one. See his books, *Some Dogmas of Religion* and *Hegelian Cosmology*.

Indeed, if we could not predict with fairly high accuracy the effects of events within the consciousness of other persons we should not be able to act toward them in any responsible fashion. With the best of intentions we should not know how to behave in relations with others if we did not have some notion whether our acts of certain kinds would cause them laughter or tears, angry rage or friendly confidence. But whenever we predict such effects we assume that the inner lives of all human beings are largely subject to causal determination. Especially is this true in the dealings of parents or teachers with the children whom they seek to train.

This assumption is well supported by the observations of very high positive correlations between certain hereditary and environmental conditions on the one hand and characteristics of temperament, mental ability, tastes and achievements on the other. Sigmund Freud has shown us that even when we are making choices which we regard as the freest conceivable the causes of those choices may be apparent to a trained and discerning observer.[2] Indeed, the development of psychology, even to its present relatively unsatisfactory stage, would have been quite impossible if there were not discoverable causal sequences in human thought and behavior. There are demonstrably predictable and manipulable relations between the intensity of stimuli and the quantitatively measurable unlearned or conditioned reflexes, between the quantities of specific hormones in the blood stream and the qualities of sensation, emotion and thought. But it is not only in such instances, where the causal formulas include material factors, that causal determination is at work. Likewise the studies of "free association," forgetting, dreams and errors in thought, all show that we are bound by forces within ourselves which are often quite out of harmony with our conscious purposes, explicit reasons and emphatic volitions.[3]

St. Paul declared,

I do not understand my own actions. For I do not do what I want, but I do the very thing I hate. . . . I can will what is right, but I cannot do it. For I do not do the good I want, but the evil I do not want is what I do.[4]

It will have to be admitted that we still do not understand these distressing experiences very well. But many of them have been catalogued and classed in regular causal sequences by the depth psychologists of the twentieth century. More distressing than all the obstructions and coercions which press upon our spirits from the outside are these bonds which enslave us from within ourselves.

[2] See S. Freud, *Psychopathology of Everyday Life*, pp. 275–338.
[3] Cf. H. Lotze, *Microcosmus*, Vol. I, pp. 137–50.
[4] Rom. 7:15, 18–19.

C. LIMITATION OF KNOWLEDGE

Each human individual must begin his life with no actual content of knowledge, whatever may be his potential capacities and the intensity of the curiosity he may early develop. Beginning at zero he builds a certain store of information and understanding within the years which are his lot upon earth.

Even in the longest spans of earthly life, though endowed with the richest opportunities and abilities ever vouchsafed to men, the data of knowledge are narrowly limited. The time itself is so short that only a minute sampling is possible of the vast currents of reality within which we live. We have learned to multiply our possibilities by recording our findings and transmitting them from generation to generation. Yet the whole period in which men have been inclined and able to do this has been very brief in comparison with the geological ages of earth or the far longer stretches of astronomical time, to say nothing of the infinite life of God who is "from everlasting to everlasting." Moreover, any one individual can in his own brief years learn from the beginning only a few of these bewilderingly complex and numerous, yet quite inadequate facts, together with the skills required for their understanding and interpretation. His resources are clearly bound to be unequal to the adequate comprehending of the whole or of any parts in proper relation to the whole of this vast reality.

The human sensory equipment conveys to us but limited impressions of the real world. By means of various instruments and techniques, our photographic telescopes, electronic microscopes, spectroscopes and electroencephalographs, for example, we extend our sensitive powers for the reception of impressions from many forces which would otherwise be inaccessible. But most of these means of observation have only been in use for a century or less and the exploration of the world by means of them has barely begun. Moreover, they are all of kinds extending the powers of our senses into closely analogous fields. What undreamed of ranges of reality may lie at hand without having aroused any suspicion of their presence we do not know.

No sane man believes that his own consciousness is the only center of personal awareness that exists, however often philosophers accuse one another of embarking on journeys that must lead to solipsism. Yet no man has immediate experience of the contents of other minds.[5] We assume familiar knowledge of many persons and yet no one of us can collect data concerning another's own consciousness by firsthand observation.

---

[5] This is true even though a few ideas may be transmitted by some kind of extrasensory perception. Like ordinary communication such transmission, if it occurs, is an induction by one individual of ideas analogous to his own in the mind of another, rather than an actually unmediated internal observation of one mind by another.

As far as knowledge of God is concerned, many persons do have intuitions of His presence. But even if we did not take account of His incomprehensibly vast inclusiveness of being, we should have to admit that all the experiences we have had of Him were but a glimpse as He passed by.[6]

Moreover, the sheer complexity of the data from all the specialized sciences, the reports of many kinds of individual experience, added to all the intimations of our own private spheres of consciousness, constitute an overwhelmingly vast maze of evidence beyond our utmost capacities properly to synthesize. Some sense of intellectual mastery can be gained only by a mind which deliberately leaves most of life out of account for the sake of a narrow specialization.

The greater our knowledge and the more refined our rational precision the more this insufficiency is borne in upon us. It is for that reason that the greatest ages of *knowing*, in ancient Greek thought and in modern science, have given rise to the deepest and most persistent *doubting*, in ancient Academic skepticism and modern logical positivism.

D. Limitations of Power

Knowing is one kind of doing and the ability to know is one kind of power. The limitations of knowledge which we have noted are themselves, therefore, limitations of power.

These limits of knowledge set limits also to our other activities. We cannot launch and guide actions for purposes we do not know. Even when we have chosen ends for which to strive, we cannot then choose to use means of which we have not knowledge. It is this knowledge of means that we usually have in mind when we say that knowledge is power and it is this which has increased so greatly in our technological age. Yet today scientists and technicians in ten thousand laboratories are trying to find the answers to questions *how* certain specified, proximate ends can be achieved. In fact, every new scientific discovery or invention widens the perimeter of this seeking and raises a new brood of unanswered questions, every one a sign of our still limited power.

The physiological equipment with which we work inevitably limits our powers. We grow tired in the midst of labor. We require food, drink and rest. We are compelled to take time out from other tasks while we provide clothing, warmth and relaxation for our bodies. By modern technology we have sought to reduce to a minimum the need for work to produce our physical necessities and luxuries. Yet it is doubtful whether there ever has been a time when more people than now have found themselves driven by the economic demands of their bodily wants to spend their working hours in tasks which they inwardly despised. A man who works all week for the hour when he can punch a clock

[6] Cf. Ex. 33:20–23.

and draw his check so that he may then do what he wants to do is experiencing toil more as a limitation of his personal powers than as an expression of them.

Limited and limiting as our bodies are, even in their healthiest and most serviceable state, most of us go through large parts of our lives with more serious physical fetters. Through hereditary defect, accident and disease we find ourselves unable to use our eyes, hands, legs and backs in the way we should consider "normal," for physiological normalcy is a rarity. And if we escape all other forms of physical breakdown, there is old age always before us, promising that soon even our little strength must succumb to weakness and our uncertain life end in death.

To the bounds which nature sets to our powers, we have all added others by our own past mistakes and sins. Many of us can point to particular defects of our bodies which resulted from indulgence, carelessness, folly or neglect in our own past performance. Doubtless, other weaknesses have been caused or augmented by our acts without our having become, even yet, aware of the fact.

What restricting habits of body and mind we have also fastened upon ourselves! Habits of indolence, careless speech, disorderly management, wandering attention, needless dependence on artificial internal or external stimulation, self-pity, jealousy, easygoing dishonesty of thought, anger, pointless daydreaming and even inefficient method—all these and more take their daily toll. When we think of our follies and sins our attention is further diverted from tasks in hand and that self-confidence is impaired without which we can never hope for maximum achievement. But if we avoid thinking of our error and wrongdoing we sink steadily deeper into inefficiency, complacency and willing mediocrity.

Even when we think that we are in fullest mastery of our personal powers we are often self-deceived. Sometimes what seems to me a necessary rational inference or a freely postulated hypothesis is actually a deposit of dark forces within me but beneath the level of conscious observation and control. Here the evidences of Freud and a host of workers in the fields of psychology and psychotherapy are quite unanswerable. My own past and the past of the community in which I live have left their marks in the dark subterranean passages deep within my soul.

Can such a being as man, limited from without and within, deceived and self-deceiving, be regarded as having any freedom at all?

CHAPTER 21

Man's Freedom Questioned

A. THE CONFLICTING TRADITIONS

AS John Calvin began the exposition and defense of his doctrine of predestination he confessed,

To many this seems a perplexing subject, because they deem it most incongruous that of the great body of mankind some should be predestinated to salvation, and others to destruction. How causelessly they entangle themselves will appear as we proceed. We may add, that in the very obscurity which deters them, we may see not only the utility of this doctrine, but also its most pleasant fruits.[1]

Such has been the division of thought among Christian men ever since the time of Augustine. A doctrine which affirms the absolute predetermination of every person's choices by the sovereign will of the Creator, with some predestined to salvation and others to damnation, has seemed to some to be not only true and useful but productive of "most pleasant fruits." On the other hand, the same teaching has appeared to others "most incongruous." In fact that is an understatement. Arminius, like many of his disciples, thought that Calvin's doctrine, besides being incongruous, was

repugnant to the NATURE OF GOD, but particularly to those ATTRIBUTES of his nature by which he performs and manages all things, his wisdom, justice, and goodness.[2]

Of the contradiction between predestination and the divine goodness, Arminius declared,

. . . For this doctrine states, that God willed to damn; and, that he might be able to do this, he willed to create; although creation is the first egress of God's goodness towards his creatures. How vastly different are such statements as these from that expansive goodness of God by which he confers benefits not only on the unworthy, but also on the evil, the unjust and on those who are deserving of punishment, which trait of Divine Beneficence in OUR FATHER WHO IS IN HEAVEN, we are commanded to imitate. (Mt. 5:45.) [3]

[1] *Institutes,* III.21.1.
[2] *Declaration of Sentiments* (tr. by James Nichols), I.3.vii. Emphasis from Arminius.
[3] *Idem.*

The controversies within Christendom which have centered upon the issue of human freedom versus absolute divine sovereignty have been among the most complex in the history of religious thought. D. M. Baillie, with good reason, speaks of it as "this endlessly difficult subject."[4] Every possible combination of ideas on the subject must have been defended by someone. In the literature are innumerable subtleties to trap the unwary. Thus such radical opponents of Augustinian determinism as the Pelagians defended the belief in "foreordination" founded on God's foreknowledge of the decisions which men would freely make. On the other hand, we find Augustine, even in the context of his most radical denial of our freedom, defending the proposition that sin can be attributed only to a being which has freely chosen evil rather than good. But this, he insists, all human beings did in Adam who originally possessed genuine free will. Hence, when we are born we are already sinners, although in our own individual lives we have never been and never will be free to choose between sin and righteousness.[5]

Especially subtle and confusing have been the controversies on this subject within the Roman Catholic Church. It is true that Thomas Aquinas stated precisely and clearly the doctrine that the providential government of God "does not deprive the will of liberty."[6]

Notwithstanding this clear statement and many others, Thomas did not directly challenge the contrary teaching of Augustine and that remained to provide authority for the heresy of Baius and Jansen in the seventeenth century.[7] To refute the Jansenists without questioning the authority of Augustine required all the devious subtleties of which the Jesuits were capable, and the dispute over many related problems still goes on among Jesuits and Dominicans.

The difficulty of resolving the centuries-old controversy concerning free will, within Christendom, has been due in no small measure to the fact that the Bible can be persuasively quoted on both sides of this intrinsically obstinate problem.[8] It is to the Biblical evidences that we must next turn, noting first some important passages which appear to imply the denial of human freedom.

B. APPARENT BIBLICAL DENIALS

1. Principal Passages

Frequently it is affirmed or implied in the Scriptures that all men are in fact sinners. The most emphatic statements of this doctrine occur in the third

---

[4] Scottish Journal of Theology, June, 1951, p. 113. [5] See On Rebuke and Grace, 11.
[6] Summa Contra Gentiles, III.73.
[7] See Nigel Abercrombie, The Origins of Jansenism.
[8] Some evidence of its inherent difficulty is to be found in the voluminous philosophical and psychological literature on the subject. The names of Leibniz, Kant, Lotze, Renouvier, James, John B. Watson and Freud should be sufficient to call it to mind.

chapter of Romans, quoting from Psalm 14 the assertion that "no one does good, not even one," and later adding, "For there is no distinction; since all have sinned and fall short of the glory of God." [9] If all men sin does that not appear to be an unavoidable necessity? Wherein, then, lies their freedom?

In Romans 9:10–24 the doctrine of a divine election which leaves men unfree to choose their own manner of life seems to become much more explicit. Here we read,

So then he has mercy upon whomever he wills, and he hardens the heart of whomever he wills.

You will say to me then, "Why does he still find fault? For who can resist his will?" But, who are you, a man, to answer back to God? Will what is molded say to its molder, "Why have you made me thus?" Has the potter no right over the clay, to make out of the same lump one vessel for beauty and another for menial use?

Again, in Romans 11:7–8, Paul writes,

Israel failed to obtain what it sought. The elect obtained it, but the rest were hardened, as it is written,

> "God gave them a spirit of stupor,
> eyes that should not see and ears that should not hear
> down to this very day."

Seeking to comfort his persecuted and suffering brethren in the church at Rome, he declares,

We know that in everything God works for good with those who love him, who are called according to his purpose. For those whom he foreknew he also predestined to be conformed to the image of his Son, in order that he might be the first-born among many brethren. And those whom he predestined he also called; and those whom he called he also justified; and those whom he justified he also glorified.[10]

So, too, in his letter to the Ephesians, we read Paul's praises to God for all spiritual blessings,

even as he chose us in him before the foundation of the world, that we should be holy and blameless before him. He destined us in love to be his sons through Jesus Christ, according to the purpose of his will, to the praise of his glorious grace which he freely bestowed on us in the Beloved.[11]

Finally, we must recall Paul's famous confession of his moral impotence experienced before his conversion, from which quotation was made earlier.[12]

---

[9] Rom. 3:9–12, 23–24.
[10] Rom. 8:28–30.
[11] Eph. 1:4–6.
[12] Rom. 7:14–25. See above, p. 157.

2. Limiting Considerations

There are several considerations which together greatly limit the force of
these passages, despite the apparent vigor and clarity of their denial of freedom.
First of all, it will soon be observed that they run counter to other passages of
the New Testament, some of them by Paul himself and at least one (Rom.
11:13–24) in the same context as the most vigorous statements already introduced. It must also be observed that most of the passages which have been cited
and those most often quoted by the Augustinians and Calvinists occur in the
first eleven chapters of Paul's letter to the Romans, where his main problem
concerns not the freedom or bondage, sin or righteousness, salvation or damnation of the individual, but rather the meaning of the contemporary roles of
Jews and Gentiles relative to the hearing, obeying and transmitting of the
gospel. It is one thing to write of God's plan for the place which different nations are to take in the historical process, as vessels serving the divine purpose,
"one vessel for beauty and another for menial use"; it is another to speak of the
choices and eternal destinies of individuals. It can hardly be gainsaid that in
dealing with philosophy of history here Paul has made a number of statements
which directly concern personal salvation, too, and in so doing has given strong
verbal support to the predestinationists who would deny freedom of the human
will. But in view of Paul's tendency to reckless rhetoric and to intense concentration of attention upon one subject at a time, these utterances are not so
decisive in establishing his own considered position on the issue before us as is
sometimes supposed.

3. Paul's Experience

On the other hand, the manner of Paul's own conversion surely influenced
greatly his whole view of the relations between God and individual men. That
experience was the one sure landmark of his faith and to Paul what happened
on the Damascus Road was not only an act of God and not of his own, but also
an act contrary to his desert and expectation. This seems natural enough and
such humility on his part is even admirable. Yet it can with good reason be
questioned whether, practically and emotionally involved as he was, Paul was
ever in a position to give a just account of his part in the proceeding. There is
good evidence, for example, that he had been deeply sincere in his persecution
of the Christians. He had sought to serve God at whatever cost to himself or
others. Recent experiences must have shaken him profoundly, particularly the
way in which Stephen had met his martyrdom. Such experiences had left a
deep perplexity and a heavy sense of guilt upon his earnest and sensitive conscience. Had Paul himself, then, nothing to do with the meeting of Christ in

the vision near Damascus? Would a careless man with no concern for God or righteousness have been so confronted and would he have responded as did Paul? We can only answer that it was not in fact such a man who *did* have the experience nor has such a man ever within our knowledge had such an encounter.

C. Biblical Affirmations

1. *Important Passages*

Much of the New Testament seems to presuppose the ability of hearer or reader to choose his way even as did Joshua in his cry, "If you be unwilling to serve the Lord, choose this day whom you will serve," [13] and Elijah, when he demanded, "How long will you go limping with two different opinions? If the Lord is God, follow him: but if Baal, then follow him." [14] Jesus' many admonitions, instructions, warnings and persuasive appeals seem made to free wills rather than to human puppets predetermined in their courses.

James not only makes many such appeals for righteous action, but defines sin as a responsible act of a person who knows better. For immediately after insisting on recognition of our dependence upon God for our lives and many of the conditions they confront, he says, "Whoever knows what is right to do and fails to do it, for him it is sin." [15]

Paul himself, the very Paul who is quoted so much against freedom, writes to deny that anyone is compelled to sin, as he warns of the need for constant vigilance. "Therefore," he says,

let anyone who thinks that he stands take heed lest he fall. No temptation has overtaken you that is not common to man. God is faithful, and he will not let you be tempted beyond your strength, but with the temptation will also provide the way of escape, that you may be able to endure it.[16]

God will always "provide the way of escape," but God does not guarantee that it will be used else there would be no need to "take heed." [17]

Indeed, even in the midst of that great discussion of philosophy of history so often cited in favor of a strict predestinarianism, Paul makes an emphatic affirmation of the need for a responsible use of freedom. Addressing his words "to you Gentiles," [18] he warns that the Jews who have rejected Christ may yet turn to accept him.

---

[13] Josh. 24:15.
[14] I Kings 18:21.
[15] Jas. 4:17.
[16] I Cor. 10:12–13.
[17] It is true that he is here addressing "those sanctified in Christ Jesus" (I Cor. 1:2). But compare the passage to be next discussed.
[18] Rom. 11:13.

For if their rejection means the reconciliation of the world, what will their acceptance mean but life from the dead? . . . They were broken off *because of their unbelief*, but you stand fast only through faith. So do not become proud, but stand in awe. For if God did not spare the natural branches, neither will he spare you. Note then the kindness and the severity of God; severity toward those who have fallen, but God's kindness to you, *provided you continue in his kindness*; otherwise you too will be cut off. And even the others, *if they do not persist in their unbelief*, will be grafted in, for God has the power to graft them in again.[19]

It is not being contended that a man saves himself by his own free will nor is any evidence from the Scripture being adduced in favor of such a view. Certainly, according to the New Testament, God initiates our redemption and He completes it. Yet, if we are to base our judgment on the last passages cited, we must acknowledge that to be saved it is necessary for us to accept freely the grace that is offered to us.

So Arminius wrote, quoting St. Bernard,

No one, except God, is able to bestow salvation; and nothing, except free will, is capable of receiving it.[20]

2. *Intensifying Considerations*

Three characteristics of the passages to which reference has been made as favoring belief in free will make these passages particularly emphatic evidence.

First, the exhortations and appeals to choose righteously which appear in the teachings of our Lord are very numerous and especially so in the Synoptic Gospels which are the records believed most closely to reflect his own actual utterances. For the Christian the teachings of the Master himself carry a special weight of authority. The Epistle of James is so similar in tone that the reader who passes straight through the New Testament is likely to feel as he begins reading that Epistle that he is back in the Synoptic Gospels once again, reading the stern admonitions of the Master.

Second, one of the most emphatic passages favorable to free will appears in the very midst of one of those very few discourses which seem to throw human freedom of will seriously in doubt; that is, Paul's long discourse on the philosophy of history in the Epistle to the Romans.

Third, since the pleas for righteousness, calls to repentance, numerous promises and warnings, conditional on human choice [21] are in the central stream of the entire Biblical message and are constantly recurrent from beginning to end, they must be given precedent consideration.

[19] Rom. 11:15, 20–23. Italics mine.
[20] Disputation "On the Free Will of Man and Its Powers."
[21] Such as, e.g., Rom. 11:22–23; Jn. 3:16; Mt. 5:3–11; 11:28; Rev. 3:8–11.

But what has other evidence, outside the Bible, to show us concerning human freedom? These other evidences not only affect the cultural context in which the Scripture is read and understood but they are also important as throwing further light on the problem itself.

D. Naturalistic Determinism

1. *Allied with Calvinism*

Jonathan Edwards formed a mighty synthesis between the Calvinistic doctrine of predestination and a philosophical determinism resting upon the common assumptions of the natural sciences. Thus, in his *Inquiry into the Freedom of the Will*, he argued that "nothing ever comes to pass without a cause." [22] Indeed, to believe otherwise, he insisted, is to deny the possibility of knowledge.

> We immediately perceive nothing else but the ideas which are this moment extant in our minds. We perceive or know other things only *by means* of these, as necessarily connected with others, and dependent on them. But if things may be without Causes, all this necessary connection and dependence is dissolved, and so all means of our knowledge is gone. [23]

Even one event without a cause would, he argued, overthrow the assurance of our reasoning from causality and hence all our knowledge.

> And if once we allow that such a sort of effect as a Volition may come to pass without a Cause, how do we know but that many other sorts of effects may do so too? [24]

We are therefore justified, thought Edwards, in explaining all creaturely events as effects of prior causes and finally as due to determination by the purpose of God Himself.

Most of those who deny human freedom of will today on the ground of universal causation do so without any reference to Calvinism or, indeed, to God. For the great present stronghold of determinism is in naturalistic philosophy rather than in such metaphysical idealism and awe of the divine sovereignty as were present in the mind of Edwards. [25]

---

[22] Pt. 2, sec. 3.
[23] *Idem.*
[24] *Idem.*
[25] D. M. Baillie observes that among philosophers the more skeptical and naturalistic thinkers, generally hostile to Christian belief, have usually been the ones to deny freedom of the will, while those who have defended belief in God and immortality have defended freedom also. "Philosophers and Theologians on the Freedom of the Will," *Scottish Journal of Theology*, June, 1951.

2. Chief Grounds

The most convincing evidences of naturalistic determinism are to be found in the natural sciences. The scientist's great principle of explanation is causality. There is a practical motivation in search for this kind of explanation. It is by determining causal relations that man is enabled to predict and control physical events. Not to know the cause of A is not to be able to produce A on occasions when A may be wanted, as in the case of electric lighting and atomic explosions, or to predict it when it may be useful to prepare for its coming, as a hurricane or an earthquake.

The scientist as scientist presupposes that every event has a cause. This is true not only of material things but also of events in thought and volition. If a psychologist be asked why Mr. S beats his wife he is expected to reply in terms of previous habits, prior acts of repression or earlier imitations, tracing the causal chain back through environmental influences to an inherited infant organism. Where in all this can be found a place for an act of free will? If it be said that Mr. S beat his wife today because he freely chose to do so, was it not *he*, the kind of man he was who chose and would not a different kind of man have chosen differently? And was he not this kind of man because of prior acts under prior influences and so on back to his conception in his mother's womb? Where can the freedom be?

The actual success of scientific discovery and invention based on this presupposition of universal causality gives great weight to its claims upon our credence. Every new formulation of a causal law validated by prediction, observation and manipulation constitutes one more evidence favorable to the doctrine that all events are under the complete reign of such law and that the lacunae in our causal explanations are due wholly to our remaining ignorance.

3. Limiting Considerations

Albert Einstein writes,

Today, faith in unbroken causality is threatened precisely by those whose path it had illumined as their chief and unrestricted leader at the front, namely by the representatives of physics.[26]

According to the modern theories of physics, says Einstein, "the natural-law foundations are themselves not causal, to begin with, but statistical." Hence,

These theories maintain: were I to know with all imaginable precision the circumstances of an atom, it would nevertheless, in principle, be impossible for me, on

---

[26] "Beyond Newton: the New Physics" in Charles G. Abbot *et al.*, *The Drift of Civilization* (London: Allen and Unwin, 1930), p. 136.

the basis of natural laws, to calculate when the atom will really go over into condition "B." This means waiving causality "in principle." All natural laws are therefore claimed to be, "in principle" of the statistical variety, and our imperfect observation practices alone have cheated us into a belief in strict causality.[27]

As Einstein and Leopold Infeld put it in the summary at the conclusion of their survey of *The Evolution of Physics,*

> Quantum physics formulates laws governing crowds and not individuals. Not properties but probabilities are described, not laws disclosing the future of systems are formulated, but laws governing the changes in time of the probabilities and relating to great congregations of individuals.[28]

Such scientists as Sir Arthur Eddington and even the more reserved Sir James Jeans have been quick to see in this modern development of physics an answer to the grim determinism represented earlier by such men as La Place. Thus Eddington writes on "The Decline of Determinism," [29] and Jeans says,

> The old physics showed us a universe which looked more like a prison than a dwelling-place. The new physics shows us a universe which looks as though it might conceivably form a suitable dwelling-place for free men, and not a mere shelter for brutes. . . .[30]

Earlier, Jeans wrote of the "loose-jointedness" which physicists now see throughout the universe, a "loose-jointedness" which *destroys the case for absolutely strict causation.*" [31]

On the other hand, Max Planck, who is second only to Einstein, if to him, in the influence he has exerted in bringing about this recent scientific revolution, vigorously opposes such inferences. He regards the "loose-jointedness" as due to the inadequacy of men to understand fully the implications of the new methods now being used and the data now obtainable. "Our picture is not in perfect accord with our observational results," he says, and adds,

> I am convinced that the bringing about of that accord must take place, not in the rejection of causality, but in a greater enlargement of the formula and a refinement of it, so as to meet modern discoveries.[32]

Yet it is a chastened physics which is represented even by Planck, a science moved by faith rather than by rigorous proof, in its loyalty to the principle of causality. Moreover, it is not insignificant that Planck maintains stoutly that

[27] *Ibid.*, p. 142.
[28] *The Evolution of Physics* (Cambridge: Cambridge Uni. Press, 1938), p. 313.
[29] Chap. IV in his *New Pathways in Science* (Cambridge: Cambridge Uni. Press, 1935).
[30] *Physics and Philosophy* (Cambridge: Cambridge Uni. Press, 1943), p. 216.
[31] *The Mysterious Universe* (New York: The Macmillan Co., 1930), p. 24.
[32] Max Planck, *Where Is Science Going?* (New York: W. W. Norton, 1932), 221.

the individual person is justified in regarding himself as the one exception to the universal reign of causal determinism. He says,

The fact is that there is a point, one single point in the immeasurable world of mind and matter, where science and therefore every causal method of research is inapplicable, not only on practical grounds but also on logical grounds, and will always remain inapplicable. This point is the individual ego.[33]

This idea of Planck's seems close to Henri Bergson's conception though Bergson extends it much further. Bergson points out that a causal law is a formula of invariably repeated succession. A situation which by its very nature is not capable of even approximate repetition is not subject to any possible causal law, although certain repetitive aspects of it may be. But this is precisely the case of the human self in its moments of conscious choice. If one single self were to experience two such moments as near as possible to being absolutely alike, the two situations would still be radically dissimilar in a most important aspect. For one situation would be the first such situation to be experienced by that person and the other would be the second and a person who has had such an experience before is very differently equipped for it than a person to whom it is new. The fact that through conscious and unconscious memory a human self continually takes up its past into its present guarantees that the complex of significant factors in any given situation of choice will be impossible to repeat.[34]

[33] *Ibid.*, p. 161.
[34] See Bergson, *Metaphysics* and *Time and Free Will.*

CHAPTER 22

Man's Freedom Affirmed

A. Evidences for Freedom

IN setting forth the problem as it has arisen in the Christian community, we have already spoken of Biblical evidences in support of belief in free will, evidences which are not canceled by the passages which appear to deny freedom. We turn now to other affirmative evidences and then to the effort to formulate more precisely a defensible view.

1. *Immediate Intuition*

Max Planck, after stating his doctrine that the individual ego is immune to the generally inclusive causal determinism of the world, adds,

I might put the matter in another way and say that the freedom of the ego here and now, and its independence of the causal chain, is a truth that comes from the immediate dictate of the human consciousness.[1]

Now it is possible that in such a matter we may be self-deluded. But the burden of proof is on those who say we are. We have seen that even physics, the most highly developed of the empirical sciences, lacks proof of universal determinism and indeed has been moving away from confidence in the possibility of such proof. If determinism is ever to be established by empirical science it will have to be done by appeal to evidences of perception. Just here Eddington has a relevant word:

Just as a theory of matter has to correspond to our perceptions of matter so a theory of the human spirit has to correspond to our inner perception of our spiritual nature. . . . If I can be deluded over such a matter of immediate knowledge—the very nature of the being that I myself am—it is hard to see where any trustworthy beginning of knowledge is to be found.[2]

That some freedom of self-determination is attested by immediate intuition seems hardly open to question. After a choice has been made, the chooser can

---

[1] *Op. cit.*, p. 165.
[2] *New Pathways in Science* (New York: The Macmillan Co., 1935), p. 90.

look back and interpret the choice as having been made of necessity just as it was made. But such interpretations are speculations well removed from the most relevant empirical evidence. At the moment when a man is making a deliberate conscious choice between alternative courses of action he feels free and his anxious thought about the choice he has to make presupposes his freedom so that the choice itself, *as he makes it*, is an *assertion* of his freedom. Such empirical evidence is not to be taken lightly.

2. *Postulate of Moral Life*

Whenever I say that I ought to perform act A or when a neighbor condemns me for not performing act A, it is presupposed that I am or was free to choose act A. Despite all of the efforts to prove that a man is blameworthy and guilty for the following of courses of action which he was as powerless to avoid as a bomb is powerless to avoid falling when it is dropped from a plane, the very meanings of "blameworthy," "guilty" and the like deny any such possibility. St. Paul pointed to the fact that men who have known neither Christ nor Moses do actually blame other men for their sinful actions, as proof that they themselves were responsible to God for their own sins.[3] So we may do well to observe that intelligent men knowingly attribute to others responsibility only within the bounds of their powers.[4]

The nature of right is to be always within reach, otherwise there is no obligation. . . . The sinful situation is not a failure to reach what was by some organic law beyond reach; it is a defection from what was within my power.[5]

If God is just, we can believe that we are responsible to Him only so far as Paul's words are true that

God is faithful, and he will not let you be tempted beyond your strength, but with the temptation will also provide the way of escape, that you may be able to endure it.[6]

3. *Postulate of Intellectual Life*

It is not the moral life only, important as that is, which presupposes some freedom of the human will. So also does the whole intellectual life.

Suppose, for the moment, that all of my reasonings and their conclusions are completely bound to the wheel of causal necessity. Anything I may say or write or even think is then not to be taken seriously as a genuine weighing of reasons

---

[3] Rom. 2:1-3.

[4] Cf. the principle of sound administration that responsibility and power must be commensurate. This is due to the fact that people rightly resent being held responsible for events which they are powerless to control.

[5] W. E. Hocking, *Human Nature and Its Remaking*, p. 127.

[6] 1 Cor. 10:13.

in loyalty to the purpose of discovering truth. For I am but a machine driven from behind by an inexorable determinism. Everyone who presumes to observe and interpret my utterance is in exactly the same predicament.

A partially free seeker after truth may, to be sure, use a calculating machine as the instrument of his purpose. But calculating machines left to their own devices would never discern between the true and false solutions of a single problem. Only a being sufficiently free of bondage to impulses from the past to govern some of his present action by reference to a future goal of truth can give to a machine "problems" and interpret the results of its movements as "answers."

If all reasoning is mechanically determined by the past, then any proof advanced to show that it is so determined is likewise so determined and no mind is free to weigh evidence for or against this belief. A society of calculating machines, however intricate, would have no way of knowing that it was a society of machines, though the maker of the machines, if he were free to pursue truth, might know it. In short, the doctrine that all reasoning is but the rationalization of rigorously predetermined, causally driven mechanisms is a hypothesis which implies the impossibility of any mind ever discovering that any proposition was either true or false or even more probably true or false. That would include, of course, the proposition affirming universal mechanism.[7]

4. Reinforced by Christian Experience

The experience of the Christian community has added greatly to the weight of evidence favoring belief in human freedom of will. When life seems hollow and senseless, a "sound and fury signifying nothing," it is easy to believe that all present experience is but the unwinding of a scroll upon which the last detail was entered before the worlds began. In such a deterministic view there is much in common with the cyclical views of history so common in the Orient and among our ancient forebears. Both imply a world-weary despair of any fresh emergence of worth in human life. Out of the same mood comes the monotonous assertion,

> What has been is what will be,
> and what has been done is what
> will be done;
> and there is nothing new under
> the sun.[8]

and the despairing cry,

---

[7] Cf. Borden Parker Bowne, *Metaphysics* (1882), pp. 397–98.
[8] Eccles. 1:9.

I have seen everything that is done under the sun; and behold, all is vanity and a striving after wind.[9]

Christians have not so experienced life.

Christians have found life profoundly meaningful. The acts they have performed, the words they have uttered and even the thoughts they have entertained have seemed, in the presence of Christ, to take on ever-renewed significance. As Jesus said, "My Father is working still and I am working," so his disciples are aware of a divine calling to fulfill the responsibilities of their special tasks and stations as in God's sight and every day lived in that spirit is full of novelty and fresh adventure. To the Christian, life is not "a tale that is told" and so remains only to be droned through in every one of its already established crises, denouements, nuances and inflections. Each day he seeks again from God his daily bread and prays anew for the doing of the divine will on earth as it is in heaven. As he prays and works he hopes and expects always the establishment of "a new heaven and a new earth" but he knows also that his choice may bring untold tragedy. He lives continually at the *krisis* which is both parting of the ways and judgment [10] and at that *krisis* he decides issues which make *all* the difference for present and future.

In the Christian community God has been known as good and just. He cannot be good and His justice is indistinguishable from injustice if He predetermines that this man must sin, must refuse redemption—which is offered by the very Creator who also predetermines him to reject it—and must bear all the burden of guilt and suffering, as if this scheme for his life had originated with him. Verily, such a predetermination would mean a reversal of the Christian gospel. Instead of God's suffering for human sin it would present man as suffering and bearing the guilt of a being who by some blasphemous perversion was called a deity.

Even those Christians who have done most to teach doctrines of predestination have been able to see at times the folly and evil implicit in the denial of human freedom. Thus Augustine took pains to attribute the evils of man's sinful career to the free will of one man, Adam. Accordingly, when speaking of the essential and persistent goods of man's nature, he was able to say,

But the flaw which darkens and weakens all these natural goods, so that it has need of illumination and healing, it has not contracted from its blameless Creator—but from that original sin, which it committed by free will.[11]

---

[9] Eccles. 1:14.
[10] Jn. 3:19–21.
[11] *On Nature and Grace*, 3.

Augustine thought he could maintain a doctrine of predestination without libeling God, by holding that Adam, at least, was free and in him we all, therefore, freely chose to sin. But only a Platonic fallacy of the universal enabled him to suppose that anyone but Adam could have sinned in Adam's choice.

Calvin had not even that poor escape, since according to his teaching even Adam, too, was subject to the immutable decrees of the Creator. Without intending to do so, Calvin pronounced the best judgment of the Christian conscience upon his own doctrine, as Georgia Harkness shows in her excellent book, *John Calvin: The Man and His Ethics*.[12] As she points out, Calvin complained of the pantheistic Spiritual Libertines,

After having forged a single spirit, destroying the nature of the angels in heaven and the devils in hell, and likewise human souls, they say it is this one spirit which does everything. Not meaning what the Scripture does, when it speaks of God, that all creatures live and move in Him, are subject to His providence and serve His will: but that everything which happens in the world is to be directly regarded as His work. In so doing they attribute to man no free will, any more than if he were a stone; and they remove all distinction between good and evil so that nothing can be done wrongly, in their opinion, since God is the author of it.[13]

The logical implications of such a view, thinks Calvin, are terrible.

Example: Some one has committed adultery? One cannot chide him for it; for that would be to blaspheme God. A man covets his neighbor's wife? Let him enjoy her if he can; for he would only be doing the will of God, and even that would be a divine act.

Indeed, from the Libertine doctrine that man has no free will, Calvin says,

Three dreadful consequences follow. The first is that there would be no difference between God and the devil—indeed, the god they forge for us is an idol worse than a devil in hell. The second is, that men would no longer have any conscience to avoid evil, but like brutes would follow their sensual appetites without discretion. The third is, that everything would have to be adjudged good—whether adultery, murder or theft—and all the worst crimes imaginable would be regarded as praiseworthy acts.

Calvin seems to have believed he could escape his own strictures by denying the pantheistic identification of the human and divine wills and hence denying that men's acts should "be *directly* regarded as His work." [14] But it is hard to see what *moral* difference it makes whether the acts are regarded as directly or

---

[12] New York: Henry Holt and Co., 1931.

[13] Translated and quoted by Georgia Harkness, *ibid.*, p. 75, from John Calvin, *Contre la Secte des Libertins*, III.183. The following quotations are from the same passage.

[14] See first excerpt from Calvin above. Italics mine.

indirectly God's work so long as it is believed that God's irresistible will decreed that they be done. Hence it is fittingly that Georgia Harkness comments:

Seldom have the logical consequences of the destruction of man's moral freedom received keener analysis! Calvin could see clearly what it meant, when he was talking about the Schoolmen or the Libertines, to rest everything in the absolute power of God. But to few of us is it given to see ourselves as we see others. This gift was not granted to Calvin.[15]

B. Freedom As Gift of God

1. *The Divine Order As Condition of Freedom*

The freedom here defended is no mere contingency, but the power of choice between meaningful alternatives. In a world of sheer contingency there would be no such freedom. Responsible freedom cannot consist of choice between alternatives of indistinguishable outcome. If freedom is to be meaningful it must be exercised within a meaningful setting of predictable order. If there were no assurance, even to the degree of some probability, that thrusting a dagger into a man's chest would have an effect different from addressing to him a Christmas greeting, there would be no responsible freedom in choosing between the two acts.

The predictable order of nature, all that vast network of intelligible causal law, in the context of which we live, makes possible both the system of our knowledge and the meaningfulness of our voluntary choices. That order we have seen to be the work of God. Through it God limits our freedom of choice at any given time to narrow margins of possibility. But through that same order God gives to us the conditions necessary to any meaningful freedom which could be possessed by finite, dependent creatures like ourselves.

2. *Freedom Itself As Divine Endowment*

God has made us and hence all the powers we have are His gifts to us. "It is He that made us and not we ourselves." [16] Among these gifts must be included our freedom of self-determination. But in this freedom is to be seen a special mark of the divine creativity, something which may well be taken as one aspect of the divine image in the human creature.

By affirming freedom of the will it is not for a moment suggested that some events happen without a cause. It is conceded, indeed it must be emphatically insisted, that a man's free act of will does have a cause; namely, himself. But it is insisted that he is a cause of such a kind that within narrow limits he

[15] *Op. cit.*, p. 77.
[16] Ps. 100:3, margin.

determines which of alternatively possible effects he will bring forth. At his moments of free choice there is a degree of emergent novelty. His free act is no mere act of repetition but a continuance of creation in a present moment of growth. That this act is propelled from behind—from all the past of the individual and the race and even the progenitors of the race—there is no doubt. But the original propulsion and present governance of the entire process is of God. Instead of keeping all the powers of determination in His own hands, He has committed some of the power of causation to the persons whom He has made. To be sure, we have not that power of original causation which belongs to the Creator alone and the exercise of which alone is called, in the strict sense, creating. But we do possess, as stewards, a derived and dependent power to direct, in some measure, the onflowing development of our own lives and of the continuing creative process of which we are a part. Like the irrigating farmer, we cannot produce the life-giving streams which flow from the gleaming summit of His creative love; but while sustained by those very streams we can channel them into Dead Seas of stagnation or into fields where new flowers may bloom and new groves bring sustenance and joy to others of His children. We thus stand at the yet unfinished edge of His creation where we are given a significant part in determining what is to be.

C. FREEDOM AS PRESENT ACHIEVEMENT

1. *A Self-determined Variable*

Freedom is not a fixed quantity. The significant self-direction of an infant is yet unfounded or at least small, indeed, as compared with that of the intelligent, self-disciplined man or woman. The child senses the difference and supposes it to be due to external circumstances. If only the restraints of parents and teachers were removed, he thinks, then he would be as free as the adults he admires. But if he runs away and even if no one pursues him, he is likely to find soon that, lacking economic skills, the understanding of the world around him and disciplined powers of self-control, he has much less freedom, not more, than he enjoyed under the direction of his elders.

So likewise the self-indulgent slave to his own passions knows but little of freedom as compared with the saintly servant of God. A Schweitzer at Lambaréné may freely choose to bring more new, meaningful experience into human lives in a day than some poor wretch enslaved to narcotic drugs has it in his power to choose in a year.

The student choosing faithful work with books and pen or an easygoing kind of "campus life" is choosing also the extent of freedom which will be his to use in years to come. The day will appear when with more knowledge and more disciplined habits he could do many things which now lie beyond his powers. So, within the context of our common daily lives, we are all continually broadening or narrowing the limits of our own freedom by the ways in which we employ the freedom already possessed.[17]

2. Determined by Other Forces

It must not be supposed that since God's initial gift the scope of our freedom is altogether self-determined. Much depends upon environmental circumstances beyond our physical powers to change or beyond the scope of our knowledge to improve by responsible choice. The infant burned to death in an incendiary air raid on his village never had much free choice nor choice of freedom in this life. Neither has the small child whose nervous system is so shocked by the overwhelming catastrophes of modern warfare that he is never able to rise above the level of a disordered mind. On the other hand, many a person long confined within narrow limitations of his own making has been given opportunity for release by the wise and patient ministrations of some good physician, pastor or friend. Indeed, not infrequently some convergence of events unplanned by any human mind brings new stimulation and opportunity to a person long bound within narrow confines. Some will say the release came by a happy coincidence, others will bless the fateful stars, while yet others will give the praise to a merciful God. Yet all must agree that it was by no merit of his own choosing that new life was offered to the captive, however important was his own response when the offer came.

3. Renewal of Freedom through God's Grace

It is apparent that all men labor under limitations which are the consequences of sin committed by themselves or others. How large a proportion of our potential skills and opportunities have been squandered in jealousy, or crushed beneath unjust and hateful gossip, or turned into useless channels by senseless social customs, or destroyed in internal conflicts arising from selfish greed or hate, we may never know. But even in the best and most fortunately situated lives, such loss of freedom must be appalling.

Now just as all our freedom, as we have seen, is at first committed to our stewardship by God's creative love, so our impaired freedom is renewed by His forgiveness and can be daily increased by communion with Him who alone is the source of creative power and hence of true freedom.

But before we shall be in a position to understand even that little which we may hope to understand of these renewing, redemptive processes of God, we must examine the nature, origin and consequences of that great destroyer of freedom which we call sin.

[17] Cf. William Ernest Hocking, *The Self: Its Body and Freedom*, pp. 167–73.

CHAPTER 23

The Nature and Prevalence of Sin

A. THE MEANING OF SIN

I T must be evident to any discerning reader that the word "sin" is used both in the Scriptures and in subsequent theological literature to convey many divergent meanings. Not a little verbal strife and confusion have resulted from this fact.

The difficulty of definition is not purely verbal, however. There are different levels of responsibility for one's choices and their consequences, and as the depth and breadth of insight into the nature of moral responsibility and of moral failure increase, the meaning of the term "sin" seems bound to broaden also. For with the refusal to apply to any act of mine the term "sin" is likely to go a refusal to acknowledge my need to repent of it. As Reinhold Niebuhr writes, "In fact the sense of guilt rises with moral sensitivity." [1] With this rise of sensitivity and hence of the sense of guilt goes a broadening of the concept of sin. On the other hand, it does not follow that it is a mark of virtue or truth in the theological writer to have the broadest possible definition of sin. A place can be reached where a further extension of the term will have the effect of reducing or eliminating its moral signification and making it synonymous with evil in general, including natural evil, or even with finite existence.

There evidently is no simple way out of the resultant difficulty. Probably the most useful procedure, at least in such a brief treatment as is possible in a work of this kind, is to begin by observing the most limited and indubitably moral use of the word and then, as we observe the moral experience of the Christian community, to extend the concept as much as the facts may warrant.

1. Acting Contrary to Acknowledged Ideals

"Whoever knows what is right to do and fails to do it, for him it is sin," reads the Letter of James. [2] If the proviso be added that the failure is freely chosen and not, for example, due to an irresistible psychopathic compulsion, we probably have here the definition of a kind of choice which is most widely

[1] *The Nature and Destiny of Man*, I, p. 257.
[2] 4:17.

acknowledged to be rightly subject to moral condemnation. I can hardly defend as right a choice of mine which I at the same time acknowledge to be a wrong kind of choice. To act contrary to my own judgment of what I ought to do is to me sin.

Yet it is hard to restrict the definition of sin to this formal meaning. The very fact that I hold a judgment of what I ought to do implies the belief that there is a truth about what I ought to do, a truth which my judgment is intended to represent. If I do not believe that there is a truth about what I ought to do then I can have no judgment or opinion on the subject, but only a preference. Preference, as such, does not establish moral obligation and to do what I generally prefer not to do would probably not be considered by anybody to be sin. The fact that I generally prefer cauliflower to spinach does not make it a sin for me to choose spinach over cauliflower on some occasions. Implicit in the holding of a judgment concerning "what is right to do," then, is not only the obligation "to do it," but also the obligation to represent the truth by my judgment. Hence, sin is seen as violation of my own judgment concerning a *tertium quid*, a norm or standard of right independent of my judgment. When I violate my moral judgment, so committing what is for me sin, it is sin for me because I believe that it is contrary to some norm which is not of my making but to which my moral judgment and action are rightly subject. This discovery leads beyond the first conception of sin to a second.

2. Disobedience to God

For the members of the Christian community the supreme norm of obligation is the will of God. To be sure, Christ is often spoken of as the norm, but that is true only because and so far as the will of God is found in him. Jesus himself said emphatically, "Not everyone who says to me, 'Lord, Lord,' shall enter the kingdom of heaven, but he who does the will of my Father who is in heaven." [3] Similarly, the fourth Gospel reads:

So Jesus answered them, "My teaching is not mine, but his who sent me; if any man's will is to do his will, he shall know whether the teaching is from God or whether I am speaking on my own authority." [4]

Indeed, the Christian views a man's violation of his own moral judgment as sin in this second sense—a case of disobedience to God's law—for God wills that men should be true to their own moral convictions. Thus Paul writes:

Therefore you have no excuse, O man, whoever you are, when you judge another; for in passing judgment upon him you condemn yourself, because you, the judge,

[3] Mt. 7:21.
[4] Jn. 7:16–17.

are doing the very same things. We know that the judgment of God rightly falls upon those who do such things. Do you suppose, O man, that when you judge those who do such things and yet do them yourself, you will escape the judgment of God? [5]

The conception of sin as disobedience to God runs through the entire Bible. The act of Adam is described in Genesis 3:17 as condemned of God for this reason:

Because you have listened to the voice of your wife, and have eaten of the tree of which I commanded you, saying, "You shall not eat of it. . . ."

So Paul says,

For as by one man's disobedience many were made sinners, so by one man's obedience many will be made righteous.[6]

Hence, we read in 1 John the clear definition: "Every one who commits sin is guilty of lawlessness; sin is lawlessness." [7]

But there is a serious problem here. There is many a man of whom it may be said, in the words of the fourth Gospel, that his "will is to do his will," that is, to do God's will, but who, with the best of intentions, is led astray by ignorance of what God's will really is. Is a person blameworthy for doing the best that he knows? It may be objected that he could have known better if he had taken advantage of some earlier opportunity. This may be so or not. But in any event to raise that question is to change the subject from the evaluation of one choice to the evaluation of another which may have preceded it. The question must not be evaded nor another question substituted for this one: Is it a sin to choose what one believes to be the will of God, if through ignorance one has been led to misconstrue God's will?

Let no one answer by citing the principle of criminal jurisprudence that "ignorance of the law is no excuse"—a principle by no means absolute, even in criminal law. We are not here discussing what judgments men pronounce or have found practicable to pronounce in courts of law. We are asking what judgments are *right* as *moral* judgments. In other words, we are asking no less than the question how we are to believe a righteous God judges. Are we to suppose that God condemns as implying moral guilt the acts of a man who is earnestly doing what he mistakenly believes to be God's will?

To such a question the enlightened Christian conscience seems bound to reply with an emphatic denial. What good human father will not put to his son's credit as a faithful son an earnest attempt to carry out his father's will, even though he has misunderstood and so been led in all sincerity to do some-

---

[5] Rom. 2:1–3.
[6] Rom. 5:19.
[7] 1 Jn. 3:4.

thing with quite dreadful consequences? Has God less understanding and regard for the secret intent of the heart? Surely not.

But such a denial involves further difficulty. We are here speaking not merely of a father's personal judgment within the larger context of an established law. We have now to do with the judgments of the Creator, whose will is the very legislation of the law. If a child is taught to steal or to hunt human beings of other tribes as fair game to provide food for cannibalistic meals, and does so with sincere loyalty to the best life he knows, does God then consider stealing and cannibalism in this case morally good? To believe so would be to imply that moral sincerity was the only norm of the divine moral judgment. Neither in the Scriptures nor in moral philosophy can such a notion be supported. Even such a formalist as Kant found in his categorical imperative many implications absolutely binding upon all men, yet certainly not explicitly recognized by all, indeed sincerely disbelieved by many. As for the morals of common sense, do we not hear that "Hell is paved with good intentions"?

There seems no escape from holding to two different, altogether proper uses of the word "sin." It may mean the willful act of choosing contrary to self-acknowledged obligations. This we propose to call *formal sin*. On the other hand, it may mean choosing contrary to the actual will of God, whether that will is known or not. This we will call *material sin*. Which kind of sin is the graver offense depends on the kind of gravity or offense one has in mind. A material sin committed by a man having the most sincere moral intentions might have the most tragic consequences. Many acts of Saul of Tarsus in persecution of the Christians may have been of this kind. His participation in the stoning of Stephen was a ghastly wrong which must have brought deepest grief to God as well as to many Christians. Yet the wrongdoer may have been as earnest as any man alive in doing what he believed best under the circumstances. On the other hand, if we were right in believing with St. Paul that formal sin is always condemned by God (Rom. 2:1-2), then we cannot give an example of a formal sin which is not also a material sin. However, we may imagine that some friend of Saul the persecutor shared fully his convictions, yet, out of sheer indolence or because he had found an especially pleasant amusement that day, was not present at the stoning of Stephen and did not give his approval to it. There may even have been another occasion on which his similar failure to act on his convictions had the effect of saving some Christian's life. Surely in that event God must have rejoiced at his absence and its happy consequences, and yet He must have condemned thoroughly the failure of the idler to be true to his own convictions. In quality of soul at the time, as well as in the light of subsequent events, was not Saul, the actual persecutor, closer to God?

Augustine had a true insight when he bore down so mercilessly on his out-wardly trivial act of stealing pears,[8] while paying less attention to other deeds which must have had far worse effects upon other persons, but which had not been at the time of commission so clearly understood as inexcusable wrongs or which had been incited by such temptations of passion as concealed the per-versity of will. One could wish, however, that, with less one-sided preoccupation with the state of his own soul, he had given more thought to the cruel injury he had done to the mother of Adeodatus.[9] He might, then, have come to a finer appreciation of womanhood and of marriage, with inestimably salutary effects on the subsequent history of theology and of the family in Christendom.

It will not do to dwell on the gravity of formal sin to the neglect of adequate concern about material sin. Indeed, such a course always threatens to lead to a subjectivistic, egocentric morality quite in contrast to the outward and God-ward reference predominant in Biblical and historic Christian teaching.

3. The Attempt to Reduce Sin to Pride

There is a third and quite different way of approaching the meaning of sin. If virtue be the state of soul in which "any man's will is to do his will" who is his rightful Sovereign, then the essence of unrighteousness is the contrary spirit. This contrary spirit is sometimes described as a willful pride, a deter-mination to assert one's own ideas, desires and will as a law to themselves.

According to the Genesis story of the Fall, a proud desire to be "like God, knowing good and evil," [10] was prominent in the motivation of the first sin, though desire for food and aesthetic pleasure also played their parts. [11] In the recorded utterances of Jesus there is never any such violent denunciation of sensuality as of proud pretension. Even greed and cruelty are most sharply condemned when joined with presumptuous egotism, as when men dare to use even the Temple of God for dishonest business or pretend to be paragons of righteousness while evicting widows from their homes.

St. Paul greatly varies his emphasis from time to time, stressing sensuality, factionalism, idolatry or pride, according to the demands of the occasion. In the Johannine writings lack of faith and lack of love are selected for most charac-teristic condemnation, although pride appears, in various guises, in many cata-logues of sins throughout all the Scriptures.

Augustine, Luther and Calvin agree in making pride the prime root and basic nature of sin. Although there is frequent denunciation of pride in the

---

[8] *Confessions*, II.

[9] Even when he wrote, in the *Confessions*, of sending her away, he dwelt on the tragic effects upon himself rather than upon her. See *Conf.*, VI.

[10] Gen. 3:5.

[11] Gen. 3:6.

New Testament and we shall see that it has a particularly important role in the causation of sin, it would seem that the three theologians mentioned and many recent writers, as well, have given to it a prominence quite out of proportion to the realities of moral experience and to the teachings of the Bible.

Augustine says,

For there would have been no evil work, but there was an evil will before it: and what could begin this evil will but pride, that is the beginning of all sin? [12]

Similarly, Calvin, commenting on the first chapter of Romans, writes,

But lest any should exculpate them, he [Paul] adds that they were deservedly blinded, because, not content with the bounds of sobriety, but arrogating themselves more than was right they willfully darkened and even infatuated themselves with pride, vanity and perverseness. [13]

Like positions are taken by many contemporary theologians, including Karl Barth, Emil Brunner and Reinhold Niebuhr. Niebuhr says,

We have previously considered the Biblical definition of basic sin as pride and have suggested that the Pauline exposition of man's self-glorification ("they changed the glory of the incorruptible God into an image made like unto corruptible man") is really an admirable summary of the whole Biblical doctrine of sin. [14]

He grants that Christian thought, so far as it has been influenced by "the classical view of man" has failed to maintain consistently the theory under discussion. But he adds, "The definition of sin as pride is consistently maintained in the strain of theology generally known as Augustinian." [15]

However, such an interpretation seems seriously to oversimplify the Biblical view. Even in his quotation from Romans which he says "is really an admirable summary of the whole Biblical doctrine of sin," Niebuhr has made his position more plausible by interrupting the quotation after the word "man," whereas the Apostle goes on to say, "and to birds, and fourfooted beasts, and creeping things." [16] Paul is not, then, condemning men for having given to themselves or their own likenesses, alone, the glory due to God. He is tracing their sensual sins not so much to pride as to idolatry—any and every worship of false gods. It is not at all clear that the worship of animal or bird forms is a proud practice. It is a false practice. Any turning away from God, whether to self or to other creatures or to vainly imagined, nonexistent beings, is deleterious in effect, as well as sin in itself. This view is commonly found also throughout the Old Testament. It is clear that Paul ridicules and condemns the pride of these fool-

[12] *Conf.* XIV.13.   [13] *Institutes,* I.4.1.
[14] *The Nature and Destiny of Man,* Vol. 1, p. 186.
[15] *Idem.,* n. 1.   [16] Rom. 1:23, AV.

ish sinners, but his condemnation seems to fall at least as heavily on their foolishness as upon their pride. Their fault is that they are proud of a wisdom which their foolish turning from God shows that they do not possess. This is quite in keeping with the Hebrew prophetic tradition.[17]

Even in the Genesis account of the Fall the sin may as well be interpreted as a listening to serpent and woman in preference to God. Is there more pride involved in Adam's listening to Eve than in listening to God? Moreover, it is explicitly stated that there were three different kinds of appeal which the forbidden fruit made to Eve—"good for food . . . a delight to the eyes . . . and . . . to make one wise." [18]

The fact is that there is no single, universal definition of the basic motive of sin in the Scripture, from which all other sinful motives are thought to be derived. The Greek Apologists' ideas of sin as irrationality, idolatry or sensual passion and the modern liberal ideas of it as greed or folly or denial of love are not simply imported into the Christian stream of thought [19]; they were all there from the beginning.

Sin is a suppression of truth (Rom. 1:18), a foolish refusal to honor the God who is known and the failure to manifest in life the wisdom professed (Rom. 1:21–22), or men's acting contrary to their own moral judgments (Rom. 2:1–3; Jas. 4:17). It is obedient service to idols or to the devil (Gal. 4:3, 8–9; Col. 2:20; Eph. 2:1–2; 1 Jn. 3:8). Again, sin is slavery to sensual passion (Rom. 7:5, 23; Jas. 4:1–3). In the teachings of Jesus the sins most emphatically condemned are generally hypocritical pretense (Mt. 6:2, 5, 23:13–33; Mk. 7:6; Lk. 11:42–46) and selfishness.[20] The latter may take the form of preoccupation with material possessions (Lk. 12:13–31). This teaching may be compared with the emphatic denunciation of the desire for wealth in 1 Timothy 6:6–10, climaxed by the unequivocal generalization, "For the love of money is the root of all evils," and with Jesus' repeated warnings to the rich (Mk. 10:23–25; Lk. 6:24). On the other hand, it may be seen as neglect of persons in need, as in the parable of the last judgment (Mt. 25:31–46). Indeed, in this parable Jesus divides all men into only two classes, the "righteous" who minister to the needy and the "cursed" who do not. In the Letter of James greed and cruelty are combined to receive by far the harshest condemnation uttered in that work, pronounced against the rich who have exploited the poor for profit (Jas. 5:1–6).

The attempt to reduce all of these kinds of sin to the single sinful motive of pride is not supported by the Scriptures. Jesus and the Biblical authors did not fall into such abstract oversimplification.

[17] See especially Is. 44:9–20.   [18] Gen. 3:6.
[19] Contrast Reinhold Niebuhr, *op. cit.*, Vol. 1, p. 186, n. 1.
[20] But cf. Mt. 15:19.

The deviation of man from obedience to God may, to be sure, take the form of a proud self-assertion. It may, on the other hand, take the form of abject slavery to some contrary person or idea. It is true that when a child of Christian parents plunges into a life of sin, whether sensual or "respectable," proud self-assertion is likely to be prominent in the process. But on the other hand, a youth who leaves a home degraded by sensuality or by smug sophistication and gives himself to Christ is likely to be more self-assertive in the process than his brother who easily drifts along in the family's pattern of life. Moreover, many lives most completely in bondage to sin are powerless, not through lack of humility, but through lack even of such self-respect as is necessary for any act of commitment. Deliberate efforts by others to develop in them some minimum of self-esteem may be prerequisite to any further steps in their redemption. These facts are well-known in every evangelistic city mission and every effective reformatory. Some men may have to be bowed low before they can hear the voice of God, but others may need first to be set upon their feet. The fact that the people who write or read theological books are far more likely to need a humbling than a lifting of self-esteem does not alter the essential truth of this matter. There may even be some things which God wishes to reveal to theologians, as to Ezekiel, which they cannot receive while preoccupied with the need for groveling in the dust before Him.[21] Moreover, since pride is not the only motive of sin, preoccupation with its peril may both blind us to other incursions of sin and deafen us to the voice of God.

4. Sin As a State of Soul

Often sin is spoken of in the Bible as a condition giving rise to evil acts, rather than as the acts themselves. It would be generally agreed, among philosophical moralists as well as among theologians, that morality has to do with the will and its intents rather than with the motions of a human body as such. Jesus is especially emphatic in his stress on the inwardness of good and evil.[22] But some passages seem to go well beyond the identification of sin with the evil choices of the will, to imply rather that sin is a condition which causes those choices. Thus, Paul says that "all men . . . are under the power of sin"[23] and exhorts, "Let not sin therefore reign in your mortal bodies, to make you obey their passions."[24] He speaks of men without Christ as "slaves of sin"[25] and complains that sin makes such a man do what is hateful to him. "So then," he says, "it is no longer I that do it, but sin which dwells within me."[26]

For some purposes of rhetorical exhortation it is, of course, quite legitimate

---

[21] See Ezek. 2:1–2; 3:24.
[23] Rom. 3:9.
[25] Rom. 6:17, 20, 22.

[22] E.g., see Mt. 5:27–28; 23:25–26; Mk. 7:14–23.
[24] Rom. 6:12.
[26] Rom. 7:17.

thus to dramatize the conflict between good and evil within the soul. Sinful choices are certainly joined together by ties of habit and association, often forming a powerful system which may well be thought of as a single obstruction or foe of my righteous resolves. But any part of that resisting system or condition which is not volitional is not subject to moral judgment. Thus my finiteness and my embodiment in an organism with various impulses and habit-forming proclivities, however clearly they may provide conditions and occasions of sin, are not my sin, for they are of God's making and not mine. Strictly speaking, then, the resistant system may be properly called sin only so far as it is an aggregate of *sins*, i.e., specific evil choices. Among such evil choices, certainly the willing acceptance of a proud, selfish or sensual spirit is an especially grave and consequential sin, giving rise to many others. Even such a prevailing emotional set or habit is not properly regarded as in itself a sin, but the various choices which have given rise to it, acquiesced in it and strengthened it were sins.

Accordingly, however justifiable rhetorically and homiletically other usages may sometimes be, the only meanings of sin which are acceptable in strict theological discourse are the first two discussed, which we have designated as formal sin and material sin.

B. The Prevalence of Sin

1. *Biblical Testimony*

The universality of sin is an often reiterated New Testament doctrine. Indeed, Jesus is citing an already familiar idea which can be taken for granted when he says, "No one is good but God alone." [27] Indeed, this doctrine is one aspect of the teaching, at the heart of the New Testament and of the church's message, that all men are in need of salvation. Thus Nicodemus is told that "unless one is born anew, he cannot see the kingdom of God." [28] It is "since all have sinned and fall short of the glory of God," that "they are justified by his grace as a gift, through the redemption which is in Christ Jesus." [29]

It must not be supposed, however, that all human action is painted by the Scriptures in an even black. From the doctrine that all men are sinners in need of redemption it does not follow that every human deed is a sin nor even that sin prevails in every life. In fact, a contrary teaching is altogether explicit and plain. No book of the New Testament more systematically and consistently maintains the doctrine that all men are sinners than does Paul's Letter to the Romans. Yet in that very letter, Paul writes:

[27] Mk. 10:18b.
[28] Jn. 3:3.
[29] Rom. 3:23–24.

When Gentiles who have not the law do by nature what the law requires, they are a law to themselves, even though they do not have the law. They show that what the law requires is written on their hearts. . . .[30]

In Jesus' parable of the Last Judgment he not only seems to assume that there are "righteous" people to be praised and rewarded, but he describes "the righteous" in concrete terms of such caring for the needy as all of us have seen fulfilled by actual men and women on specific occasions.[31]

Yet whatever good deeds any person has done, who can claim to have fulfilled the command to "be perfect, as your heavenly Father is perfect"?[32] While acknowledging that men do good as well as evil, the Scripture clearly teaches that "all have sinned and fall short of the glory of God."[33]

2. Empirical Evidence

It does not require very long or close observation to discover evidence that all human beings who live to maturity are probably involved in material sin. The life in which we are all involved in the world, with its war, competitive greed, discrimination of race and class, divisive pride of religion, sensuality, drunkenness, political hypocrisy, corruption and compromise, marital disloyalty and petty personal jealousy—this is surely not the life which God intended we should have together. There are some persons who have, to be sure, renounced all these evils. Yet who can say that he is both free from all of them and is doing all he possibly could do to prevent and relieve the suffering and guilt which are everywhere in evidence as their awful products? Even if someone is convinced that he is now in this condition of freedom from active participation or acquiescent involvement in sin, our capacities for self-deception are so great that it is at least highly probable that he is not in fact so, and much more that he has not always been so.

Again, can any man claim to know the will of God for him at every moment? Imperfect in knowledge as we are, we may make a choice with the best of intention to do God's will and yet miss the mark, perhaps with most destructive consequences, affecting even those persons whom we love most dearly. As we grow in spiritual understanding it is our common experience that again and again we awaken to the wrong of something which we have hitherto done without insight into its real character as contrary to the will of God. It is highly improbable, to say the least, that in any of us this process has come to perfect completion so that our insights into the character of our acts now accord absolutely with God's judgments.

---

[30] Rom. 2:14–15.
[32] Mt. 5:48.

[31] Mt. 25:31–46.
[33] Rom. 3:23.

Moreover, only in doing the perfect will of God can we find complete harmony within our own wills. When our moral understanding is immature, our judgments and our wills are brought into internal contradiction. So in carrying out what we conceive to be our duties we find ourselves running counter to other known duties. Thus, in being generous to our children we neglect sufficiently generous charity to starving and homeless children far away—or, more rarely, in caring for others we fail to see the hungry bodies and love-starved souls in our own households.[34] Again, in prophetic battle against entrenched social evil we lose a generous and charitable spirit toward those who oppose us —or, in persistently pursuing the way of humble love, we become speechless and cowardly in the face of wrong. Lacking complete, assured understanding, we betray ourselves through the unwitting violation of God's will into contradiction even of our admitted obligations. Thus material sins of ignorance pass into formal sins of willful self-contradiction.

When we are fully aware of the whole breadth and subtlety of sin we find it hard to escape the conviction that the Scriptures speak truly to the condition of us all in portraying us as sinners, every one.

[34] Cf. Pearl Buck's portrayal of her missionary father in *The Fighting Angel*.

CHAPTER 24

The Origin of Sin

APART from belief in God no coherent metaphysical account has been offered of moral good-and-evil as a valid category.[1] But for the person who does believe in God one of the hardest things to understand is how there happens to be sin in the world, especially such universally experienced sin as we have found to be actually present. How did sin get into a world created by a good God? Let us put the question contemporaneously and in more personal form. When I sin what makes me do it?

To be sure, we have contended that we are free, within narrow margins, to choose our acts. But why do we ever choose evil instead of good? Why, indeed, does it seem extremely difficult to avoid sin? As William James pointed out, the man of duty often

speaks of conquering and overcoming his impulses and temptations. But the sluggard, the drunkard, the coward, never talk of their conduct in that way, or say they resist their energy, overcome their sobriety, conquer their courage, and so forth. . . . And if a brief definition of ideal or moral action were required, none could be given which would better fit the appearances than this: *It is action in the line of the greatest resistance*.[2]

Why should this be so?

A. Interpretations of the Cause of Sin

1. *The Law*

Paul, at times, attributes sin to that very law of God which as a Jew he had always regarded as offering the way of salvation. Guarding carefully against the error of condemning God's law, he says,

What then shall we say? That the law is sin? By no means! Yet, if it had not been for the law, I should not have known sin. I should not have known what it is to covet if the law had not said, "You shall not covet." But sin, finding opportunity in the commandment, wrought in me all kinds of covetousness.[3]

---

[1] Cf. above, pp. 54–58. See also E. S. Brightman, *A Philosophy of Religion*, pp. 250–72.
[2] *Psychology*, ch. 26, "The Will."   [3] Rom. 7:7–8.

It is not only the Mosaic Law of which Paul is speaking. It is the moral law ordained of God, no matter in what form made known to men. For Paul has already pointed out that Gentiles who have not the Mosaic Law nevertheless accuse each other of wrong and sometimes "do by nature what the law requires" and thus "show that what the law requires is written on their hearts." [4]

To find a creature completely without the law we should need to observe an animal with no inkling of a moral sense. The behavior of such a creature, how- ever cruel or greedy it might appear to a morally awakened person, would not be sin. This is true not only because it would be unjust to charge with sin an agent incapable of discerning between good and evil, but also because the behavior of such an agent is not willfully rebellious in motivation and intent.

Paul uses another illustration, having to do with one particular prohibition. Before a man knows that it is immoral to covet, he may lustily seek to gain his neighbor's property for the sake of the property only. But after he has learned that God forbids covetousness his coveting partakes also of an angry, willful animus. Instead of a formally innocent, though materially evil, desire for a good thing—the property—it is now a formally sinful desire for an evil thing—success in getting what he knows he has no right to take from his neighbor and self- assertive defiance of God's law. Knowledge of the law has thus made possible willful sin and become the means by which the former material sin brought the unhappy man into open rebellion against God.

That the knowledge of moral law may have just such effects upon a person is shown clearly by experience. Yet we must agree with Paul that "the law is holy, and the commandment is holy and just and good." [5] If it were not good it would not be truly the moral law and if we did not know the law we should be merely innocent, amoral animals, not moral agents called to become the children of God.

2. *The Devil*

"He who commits sin is of the devil; for the devil has sinned from the begin- ning. The reason the Son of God appeared was to destroy the works of the devil." [6] In this and many other passages of the New Testament, the devil (*diabolos*, false accuser, slanderer) is spoken of as father of evildoers,[7] or tempter [8] or otherwise as source or head of the forces of evil.[9]

However, no clear or consistent doctrine concerning the devil appears. The headship of the forces of evil is sometimes attributed to Beelzebub, sometimes to Satan, and elsewhere, as in the passages cited above, to "the devil." Accord-

---

[4] Rom. 2:1, 14, 15.
[6] 1 Jn. 3:8.
[8] See Mt. 4:1-11.

[5] Rom. 7:12.
[7] E.g., in Jn. 8:44.
[9] E.g., in Mt. 13:39 and 25:41.

ing to the solemn judgment of Paul, Satan seems once actually to have done good by sending him his "thorn in the flesh." [10]

Probably Paul thought of this spiritually helpful affliction as having been sent upon him by Satan with evil purpose but permitted by God for good purpose. Nevertheless, this passage shows something of the blurred outline of the whole conception of the devil in the New Testament. Apparently regarded as a veritably real superhuman personal being, the figure of Satan serves more as a dramatic symbol of sin, pain, temptation and their causation than as a distinct explanatory principle.

Indeed, if we attempt to make of a personal Satan a serious explanation of sin, we are driven either to an inacceptable ultimate dualism or to the question why God created such a being and permits him to continue his nefarious work among men. This question simply repeats the original problem of the cause of sin in God's world, but in a form just so much more perplexing than the problem of man's sin as Satan is presumed to transcend man in sinfulness, power and inaccessibility for our study.[11]

3. Bodily Passions

It has been pointed out that prominent among the sins condemned in the Scriptures are the sins of sensuality. It is obvious that the natural appetites of the body provide much of the motivation of these sins.

As we have seen, passions and appetites of the body are not to be regarded as evil in themselves, but rather as intended by the Creator for good ends. Yet, like every limited value, when it usurps the throne and rules in the place of God, the body is an incitement to great sin. Its rightful place is in subjection to the God-ruled will and it must be kept in its proper place of subordination. It then becomes the carrier of high spiritual meaning.

4. Prior Acts of the Sinner

Any person who determines to free his life of sin finds that one of the worst obstacles he has to overcome is the bond of habit. Wrongdoing in which he has engaged before tends to be repeated, especially if it was formerly accompanied or followed by pleasure. Sin thus perpetuates and multiplies itself.

Albert C. Knudson and some other theologians have found in habit one of the chief explanations of the origin of sin in the individual life.[12] The small child, it is pointed out, engages in activities which, if indulged by a normal

---

[10] 2 Cor. 12:7.

[11] For a thoughtful recent treatment of the problem of evil, using the doctrine of Satan as symbol and clue, see Edwin Lewis, The Creator and the Adversary. "The Adversary," as finally interpreted, however, bears little resemblance to the personal devil of the Scriptures.

[12] See Knudson, Principles of Christian Ethics, p. 84.

adult, would be generally and properly condemned as morally wrong. When a baby has temper tantrums or asserts its own demands with no regard for the convenience or health of others it is intending no evil. But the habits thus formed tend to persist after the child has become clearly aware that he ought not to indulge in them. Upon first arrival at an age of moral self-awareness, a child thus finds his freedom of choice already weighted by certain habits which compel him to struggle against the current for the virtuous life to which he may aspire.

Some of these behavior patterns can hardly be regarded in the tiny child as even material wrongdoing, let alone formal or willful sin. His egoistic preoccupation and lusty self-expression seem so clearly to belong to a stage through which every human being needs to pass to attain meaningful personal freedom, that they are evidently parts of God's own plan for the child's maturation. Yet they do develop habits which, at a later age of discretion, resist efforts to discipline the self in obedience to God's will.

5. Social Influence

The individual discovers himself as a responsible self, a person capable of good and evil choices, only in social context, that is, as one person in interaction with others. In many ways the sins of his neighbors and forebears put their mark upon the child. His struggles against unfair domination develop angry resentments and attitudes of rebellious self-assertion. His imitation of his elders leads directly to sinful practices. Social sanctions which place a premium on conformity to custom press him to acquiesce in grossly unjust racial and class discrimination, and to accept materialistic standards of sensuous self-indulgence. If he resists such pressure he becomes a self-assertive rebel against many accepted standards of his society. While the former alternative leads plainly to sin and must be resisted, the latter course brings with it its own temptations to a contentious, egotistical self-righteousness which may be no less wrong.

Many sinful practices have become crystallized into institutions which are evil and at the same time in some respects inescapable for the individual. For example, the taxpayer under a highly militarized and corrupt government may, so long as he lives within its domain, be unable to avoid providing means for the perpetuation of its bureaucratic tyrannies, military brutalities and dishonest practices. Even if he finds ways to obstruct the collecting agencies so as to make his taxpaying a liability and not an asset to the government, he may only make his neighbors' burden heavier. Finding that he cannot avoid contributing to causes which he regards as evil, he is tempted to give up all resistance to them and accept them as an inescapable and normal part of life. He thus becomes an accessory to wrongdoing, an accomplice in sin.

Similar is his involvement in the economic order. There is no economic system in present existence nor in lively prospect which can be regarded as even approximating Christian standards of social relationships. Yet it is impossible for a person to live in the modern world without active participation in an existing system. By participation in it he becomes, however unwillingly, a partner in its injustice and its idealization of greed. If an American gains a fair degree of prosperity he is also sharing in the plundering of peoples exploited by colonial policy, racial discrimination, misleading advertising and sharp practice. Even if he is a financial failure, so long as he *tries* to succeed in the order of which he is a part he is hardly relieved from the moral responsibility of a partnership to which he aspires, though vainly. On the other hand, not to try for a fair degree of economic success would mean for most men to choose that their families be kept in want.

Some of our institutions seek deliberately to stir the lowest passions of the people in order to exploit them for profit. Examples of such organized agencies of temptation are the advertisements of beverage alcohol, of betting tracks and salacious entertainment. Magazines, books and theaters catering to sensual passion serve similarly as deliberate promoters of sin for profit.

The youth growing up in such a world as this knows all too well how insistent and diabolically effective are the incitements to evil thought and action and how hard it is to run the gantlet to a chaste, honest, generous, and socially responsible life.[13]

6. *Misunderstood Freedom*

When it is said that the freedom of man's will is the explanation of his sin, all that is usually meant is that since he is free to choose between alternative courses of action he may sometimes choose evil rather than good. This is, of course, true. But what needs explaining is not merely the possibility of sin but its excessively prevalent actuality.

It is sometimes added that in view of the vast number of choices made by a human being in the course of a full lifetime it is not strange that sometimes his choice should be evil. But although there is some truth in this observation it is in danger of treating moral choices as if they were only the drops of a flipped coin. To treat the freedom of the will as if it were only a gamble, subject to the laws of chance, so that after several instances of "heads" or right choices it is probable that soon "tails" will come up or a wrong choice be made, is to deny the very meaning of freedom and of moral choice. Sheer chance and moral responsibility are mutually exclusive.

However, there is a way in which freedom in a finite, dependent creature

[13] Cf. Walter Rauschenbusch, *A Theology for the Social Gospel*, p. 67.

loads its own balance against the good. This is an observation which has been made by such radically different students of the moral life as Immanuel Kant and Sören Kierkegaard, though it has been variously interpreted.[14]

It seems to come about in some such fashion as this. A child begins life under the dominance of physical impulses or instincts. In this age of innocence he is acting neither sinfully nor virtuously, for he is not making moral choices at all. Before he can make such choices he must awaken to the possibility of making them; that is, he must discover his freedom. But how is a child to know that he has the freedom of a responsible individual? Does he not learn it by experiencing the power to rebel against the pattern of behavior set for him by his elders? Yet simultaneously with this discovery and implicit in it is temptation. He cannot mature as a responsible person without coming to know his freedom. But he knows his freedom by asserting it. To assert his freedom as an individual is to affirm himself by denying the not-self, and especially, in the time of discovery, the other person—any and every other person.

Now to assert oneself is not necessarily to sin. But in the wonder of discovering his freedom the individual is not likely to keep his use of it within bounds. Seeing the void of indeterminism before him, he does not see the conditional and responsible nature of it. In the excitement of discovery he is attracted to the thorough exploration of its possibilities by asserting himself to the limit and indeed he beats lustily upon every barrier which his freedom encounters. He not only asserts himself but he denies every other self. Thus, in the very act of discovering his freedom—so good and necessary to his being a child of God—occurs also the act of self-assertive and rebellious use of it.

This discovery does not occur all at once in full maturity. It occurs repeatedly at different levels, each with its characteristic type of rebellion. It appears as the monotonously repetitious "No" of the toddler and the more discriminating and skillful, subtle and self-conscious resistance to family regulations by the eleven-year-old.[15] Most significantly it bursts forth in the comprehensive, meaningful, often absolute and life-determining crises of adolescence. At each of the earlier stages the adventure into the unknown of free self-determination is closely limited by the dependence of the child upon others for his very sus-

[14] See the first part of Kant's *Die Religion innerhalb der Grenzen der blossen Vernunft,* translated in Thomas K. Abbott, *Kant's Critique of Practical Reason and Other Works on the Theory of Ethics* under two titles, the more descriptive one being "On the Radical Evil in Human Nature," and Kierkegaard's more persistent and searching work, *The Concept of Dread.* Edward T. Ramsdell writes that Kierkegaard's work was written "almost certainly under the stimulus of the Kantian analysis." *The Christian Perspective* (New York and Nashville: Abingdon-Cokesbury Press, 1950), pp. 140–41. I am indebted to Ramsdell for pointing out the logical relation between the teachings of the two so radically different thinkers.
[15] Both of these earlier stages of self-assertion are especially well described in the studies published by the Gesell Institute of Child Study at Yale University.

tenance and by his relatively quick discovery of his inability to match his strength of mind and body against his elders. Yet he is likely to suppose that he is only lacking mature strength to do absolutely as he pleases. So the illusion of absolute freedom is repressed to bide its time rather than corrected by the discovery of the inherently conditional and dependent character of all human freedom.

Sometimes with the more mature discoveries of freedom come experiences of a fearful insecurity attendant upon the blazing of new paths in the unknown wilderness of the future where rewards beckon but where the infinite darkness of death also threatens. As Kierkegaard taught, this dread, so far from keeping the pilgrim from wandering, actually lures him with a strange, wild fascination all its own. Reinhold Niebuhr and others have shown many of the ways in which this dreadful sense of insecurity leads to the seeking of false self-assurance in wealth, social power, military force and other earthly idols. But such search is unending. Only an infinite defense will serve since the perils of the future to a finite creature are limitless. Hence, however great the wealth or power achieved, the insatiable demand continues unabated. So arise the monstrous competitions and conflicts for self-advantage which are continually blighting every community and periodically laying waste ever-greater portions of the world.

It is difficult, indeed impossible for a man to say at what moment in this dire evolution of self-discovery as a free person into unrestrained egoistic struggle for advantage sin has begun. We cannot tell precisely where material sin began because we do not know precisely how much of the child's self-assertion was part of God's own plan for him and at what point it overreached the needs of healthy growth and, running contrary to God's will, began the process of self-destruction. No more can we say when formal sin first occurred because when we are mature enough to ask the question we cannot remember the answer. But we can say with assurance that sin has come and, in its evolution in the individual and in societies large and small, the mistaking of freedom for un-conditioned, absolute autonomy such as no finite creature could have has had an important part. Significantly involved in this development of sin is the fail-ure of nerve which occurs because men think they walk alone into a vast, un-known future uncharted by purpose and unattended by love which knows the way.

B. The Doctrine of Original Sin

1. *Traditional Doctrines*

The Biblical basis for the traditional Christian doctrines of original sin is laid chiefly in the Pauline writings. Especially important are his words,

Therefore as sin came into the world through one man and death through sin and so death spread to all men because all men sinned—sin indeed was in the world before the law was given. . . . Then as one man's trespass led to condemnation for all men, so one man's act of righteousness leads to acquittal and life for all men. For as by one man's disobedience many were made sinners, so by one man's obedience, many will be made righteous.[16]

Upon this teaching of St. Paul have been erected a number of elaborate doctrines purporting to show how one sin of one man could actually make all human beings guilty of sin in the eyes of the just God. Some theologians, like Augustine, have leaned heavily on discussion of "human nature" or "man," as if Adam and the child of my neighbor next door were only different appearances of a single entity which was itself a true bearer of moral responsibility.[17] The flagrant fallacy of abstraction in this attributing to an abstract universal of moral responsibility in which all concrete individual men participate was made plausible by the Platonic modes of thought to which these Christian thinkers were habituated. At the same time Augustine set the dominant pattern for Christian thought in many subsequent centuries by describing sin as a corruption of nature transmitted by heredity through the evil of sexual reproduction and continually renewed and supplemented by the actual sins occurring in every individual life. Many have been the attempts to prove that God justly condemns every newly born infant for the sin which Adam committed. It is then contended that if he dies without the removal of this guilt by baptism he is punished by eternal torment or by banishment from God's presence (the Roman Catholic teaching). On the other hand, if he lives the condemnation will be compounded by the actual sins which will express the inordinate lusts of pride and sensuality by which God punishes him.

Despite the antiquity of such contentions and the great names associated with them, they must be firmly rejected by anyone who wishes to combine some degree of rational consistency with belief in the goodness of God. It is appropriate in this connection to quote an eminent defender of the traditional doctrine. Pascal wrote,

For it is beyond doubt that there is nothing which more shocks our reason than to say that the sin of the first man has rendered guilty those who, being so removed from its source, seem incapable of participating in it.[18]

Yet he adds, in the spirit of much theology now current,

Certainly nothing offends us more rudely than this doctrine, and yet without this mystery the most incomprehensible of all, we are incomprehensible to ourselves.[19]

---

[16] Rom. 5:12–13, 18–19. Cf. 1 Cor. 15:21–22.
[17] E.g., see Augustine, *On Nature and Grace*, 3.
[18] *Pensées*, 434.
[19] *Idem*.

But how can it be supposed that we have explained ourselves to ourselves by pronouncing a hypothesis which "shocks our reason" more than anything else could do and which is itself "incomprehensible"? When it is further considered how little meaning can be left to the affirmation that God is "good," "just" or a "loving Father" if He is thought to hold little children guilty of a sin committed by a man long dead and completely unknown to them, we must say that *such* a doctrine of original sin is both irrational and blasphemous.

There is no such teaching to be found in the Bible, no, not even in the writings of St. Paul. The apostle does, however, teach that "sin came into the world through one man." It is clearly true that sin does beget sin both within the sinning individual and in those whom he influences. All this deep, powerful current of sin which moves down through history like a treacherous muddy flood obviously began with the first sin committed. The nature of the first sinful deeds are unknown to us and the names of the first sinners likewise unknown except that the first sinful man was, indeed, Adam (Heb.: "Man") and the first sinful woman must have been truly Eve (Heb.: "Life") to all the race. It can hardly be denied that from the first sinners both sin and its dire consequences have, in fact, as Paul said, "spread to all men because all men sinned." His other expressions on the subject are likewise rather descriptive of such evident experiences of himself and of the race than they are attributions of guilt by "imputation" or by heredity.

2. Truths Symbolized

The traditional teaching that

> In Adam's fall
> We sinned all

does represent the effort of many earnest Christians to formulate real and important truths. Many critics who see clearly how ill-conceived and self-contradictory it is neglect the deeper, spiritually valuable insights which have been conveyed to countless lives by this clumsy but capacious vehicle. Some of these insights have already been presented without reference to the traditional doctrine. They will be mentioned briefly along with others in the following summary statement:

1. Every human being is born in indebtedness to God for whatever of value life may offer him. Since God has given to him his very self this indebtedness of gratitude is absolute. It is impossible to repay. For whatever he may do to further God's purpose in the world will make his own life the richer. Even in most fully losing his life for God he finds it. This, too, is of God and so his debt of gratitude increases. In such a relationship all thought of living on terms

of personally achieved solvency, to say nothing of doing more than he ought, of performing "works of supererogation," contributing to a treasury of merit applicable against the debts of others, must be forever put aside. By the very nature of his existence he lives solely by the grace of God.

2. All human beings suffer temptations to sin and disabilities in resistance to it which result from the sins of past generations. Some of the very people who are most contemptuous of the notion that Adam's sin could possibly affect the present moral situation declare that the youth of the present (any) generation are not so much to blame for their evil conduct as are their parents. They apparently overlook the fact that their parents were little less and little more able to pass the responsibility back to *their* parents and so on straight back to the parents in whom the possibility and actuality of sin first occurred.

3. In our experience, from the dawn of moral consciousness, we do not find it equally as easy to be true to our duty and to be false to it. To relax moral effort and "let nature take its course" is to drift into indolence, sensuous indulgence, cowardice and selfishness. We do not drift into industry, purity, courage and loyal generosity. Movement toward moral perfection is upstream.

4. Our own inner experience, our observation of others and the accounts of many discerning minds make it reasonable to believe that all human beings who have long lived at a responsible level of development are actual sinners.

5. We need to repent not only of our formal sins, the choices we have made in contradiction of our own ideals, the deeds we thought at the time to be contrary to God's will. Repentance must go further, to include the violations of God's purpose which we did not at the time of commission understand to be such. Even if I have performed an act which I have believed to be my solemn duty to God but which I now understand to have been contrary to God's will, I must repent of it. This psychological, moral and religious necessity is often overlooked by rationalistic moralists preoccupied with formal sin and righteousness.

Such repentance is psychologically necessary because otherwise there is left an unrepudiated emotional self-identification with a choice which is now rationally negated. A contradiction will remain within the personality until there has occurred that purgation and emotional reorganization of memory which only repentance can bring about. It is morally necessary because if I do not now repent of the materially sinful choice which I once made in ignorant sincerity, I am now easily winking at a choice which I believe to be contrary to God's will. What was at the time of commission a material sin thus becomes, at the time of my later easygoing recognition of its true character, the occasion of a formal sin. Repentance of such material sin is religiously necessary because my act has been finally recognized as an act against God. If I am truly concerned about God's purpose I am bound to feel now a deep sorrow and contrition for having betrayed it—however ignorantly.

To illustrate all of these necessities we may well take the case of St. Paul. Suppose that in all his persecutions of the Christians prior to his conversion he was utterly sincere in the belief that he was doing the will of God. Imagine then that after his conversion he might have said simply, "I now see that I was mistaken about all this business. If I had known that God favored these Christians, of course I would not have persecuted them. It is too bad that they suffered all these things and especially that Stephen was stoned to death with my consent. But after all I meant well at the time, so I have no reason to feel guilty about it."

Can anyone imagine that psychologically such a response to his new insight would have constituted the radical reorientation of his whole soul required to reintegrate him as a whole man? Would he have been morally justified in such an easygoing attitude toward his own past violation of God's purpose which he now believed supremely good and important? Would he have been brought by such means into that sense of deep communion with God and identification with Christ which he actually experienced thenceforth?

6. For similar reasons we need to repent of the sins of others with which we find ourselves identified—much as with our own past deeds—by sharing in their economic or other advantages, by our loyal self-identification with groups that have sinned and by our involuntary but deep emotional involvements, often beneath the level of conscious awareness. Isaiah shrinks before the vision of God's holiness not only because his own lips are "unclean" but also because he dwells "in the midst of a people of unclean lips." [20] Toyohiko Kagawa, despite his personal resistance to the Japanese aggression against China, goes to the mainland and as a Christian Japanese citizen begs the Chinese people for forgiveness. The appropriateness of such expressions is immediately evident to anyone whose empirical sensitiveness to spiritual realities is not dulled by formalistic theory.

7. Our acts do not spring from a vacuum. They express systems of habits, ideas and motives highly organized within our personalities. If we are really heartily ashamed of our sinful acts we shall be deeply contrite also about the corrupt sources within us from which they come. Indeed, since these habits, complexes, attitudes and other "sets" within us are so persistently identified with ourselves and may also give rise to repeated evil choices, many of the more sensitive and thoughtful souls have dwelt more sorrowfully upon their sinful *condition* than upon any particular deeds. This is as it should be, so long as the connection with sinful choice is kept clear and strong.

[20] Is. 6:5.

CHAPTER 25

In His Image

SINFUL as man is, he is not content to regard his condition as normal. To be sure, many people apparently make little effort to escape the clutches of sin and rise to a higher level of life. But even while remaining at a low level and resisting every suggestion that they ought to do differently, they are beset by feelings of guilt. Their very protestations of innocence show by their combined ardor and deviousness the lengths of self-deception to which they have been driven by secret self-reproach. "The lady doth protest too much"[1] is a line which might be truly spoken of every lady and of every man as well. But that is proof not only of universal sin, but also of the universal conflict between that sin and a higher norm deep set in every human conscience. However far an individual may drift from true righteousness, he can never shake himself quite free for wholehearted enjoyment of sin. The storms of temptation may drive him far from port but he never ceases to drag anchor.

In one mood of piety many Jews and Christians have vied with one another in condemning their common humanity. Prostrating themselves before the holy God, they have sought to exalt Him by contrasting His righteousness with the wretched depravity of men. Now we are all, in truth, sinful enough. Yet the mood of religious self-abnegation must not be mistaken for accurate and balanced description.

If human depravity were really total, men would simply call evil good and be content. In actuality they cannot quite do this, though they often try. At worst they remain restless and discontented, wandering fearfully through the dark passages of their own souls, haunted by the vague but chilling specters of their guilt. On the other hand, countless millions of men, representing every region of earth and every period of history, have openly tried to learn whom they should worship and what they should do and then, despite interminable disappointments and failures, have sought to obey the call of duty.

The observer of the human scene may look only upon the sins and failures of men. If, as he observes, he uses the standard of Christlikeness for measure, he will see a frightfully dismal picture of hypocrisy, cruelty, licentiousness,

[1] *Hamlet*, Act 3, sc. 2.

moral blindness and self-deception. But the same scene may also be viewed in another perspective, and without loss of the measure of Christ. No less impressive than men's sins are their groping efforts to make amends for them. The sons of Adam are not only hypocrites but also the exposers and despisers of hypocrisy. They are not only cruel but also kind. They are not only licentious but also self-controlled. In moral blindness they yet grope for light. In self-deception they betray their dissatisfaction with what they are.

The theologians may refuse to credit man with these finer attributes of his own historic life, assigning all good rather to the gracious work of God and condemning "fallen human nature" as wholly lost in sin. But the arbitrary abstraction of such procedure should be apparent to anyone. To refuse to call the good of a Gautama or Jeremiah, Gandhi or Schweitzer a human good, on the ground that whatever virtue was theirs was the gift of God, is no more true than to say that no such thing as human life exists because that is the gift of God. Of course, it is God who gives us life and it is He who empowers us for every good work. But for all that we do live and we both aspire and in some measure attain to righteousness. We show more gratitude to God by giving Him thanks for these endowments of our common humanity than by gloomy denials.

The Scriptures, with all their stress upon the sinful ways of men, emphasize also the higher aspect of man's nature. According to Genesis, "God created man in his own image, in the image of God he created him; male and female he created them."[2] After this we are told that "God saw everything that he had made, and behold it was very good."[3]

With even greater fervor the Psalmist declares, "You are gods, sons of the Most High, all of you."[4] According to the fourth Gospel Jesus once quoted this passage in defense of his right to call himself Son of God.[5]

Paul sometimes uses the phrase "image of God" to refer specifically to the perfect image he sees in Christ.[6] Yet on occasion he not only speaks of the image as present in other men but regards it as rightful ground for man's rejecting some expressions of humility. Thus, speaking of coverings for the head in prayer and prophecy he says, "For a man ought not to cover his head, since he is the image and glory of God."[7]

Recognition of this inherent dignity of divinely created men lies scarcely

---

[2] Gen. 1:27.   [3] Gen. 1:31.
[4] Ps. 82:6.   [5] Jn. 10:34-36.
[6] As in 2 Cor. 4:4 and Col. 1:15.
[7] 1 Cor. 11:7. The exclusion of woman from this honor implied by Paul's added word, "but woman is the glory of man," can be defended only by ignoring the explicit inclusion of the "female" in the genus "man" in the passage of Genesis upon which his argument is based. See Gen. 1:27, quoted above in the preceding paragraph but one.

beneath the surface of the great prophetic pleas for justice and mercy. But it becomes most explicit as reason for respectful treatment of other human beings in the New Testament. In the famous passage of the Letter of James, denouncing misuse of the tongue, we read, "With it we bless the Lord and Father, and with it we curse men, who are made in the likeness of God." [8] This logic carries far. If it is an obvious inconsistency and hence an evil to bless God and curse men "who are made in the likeness of God," it would seem similarly inconsistent and evil, while praising God, to indulge in such unrelieved disparagement of humanity as may be found in some censorious theologies.

What may we rightly think of as "the image of God" or "likeness of God" in man? There has been so much discussion of this issue that a historical survey doing justice to all the theories would go far beyond the limits possible in such a work as this. However, before setting forth a doctrine which seems defensible it may be useful to explain why some views are being rejected.

A. INACCEPTABLE VIEWS OF THE DIVINE IMAGE IN MAN

1. As Physical Form

If we were primarily concerned to know what was in the mind of the ancient priestly writer who spoke of the "image of God" in Genesis, it might be argued that he could have envisioned a likeness of physical form, though there is good reason to think he did not.

However, our concern here is to ask in what sense man may be *truly* regarded as being, possessing or reflecting the likeness of God. To answer that question in terms of physical form would be to leave behind millenniums of spiritual religion and critical thought and subject oneself to the rightful scorn of Hebrew prophet and Greek sage alike. "God is spirit." [9] Any likeness of God to be observed in man must certainly be found in some aspect other than the form of the human body.

2. An Original Perfection Now Gone

It is sometimes taught that although man was created in the image of God this likeness was lost in the Fall. As he came from the hand of the Creator man was perfect in righteousness, either by a supernatural image added to the natural or by an intrinsic perfection of his own nature as originally formed. But with the first sin, it is believed, this pristine perfection was lost. Although man was originally like God and hence in open, untrammeled communion with Him, this likeness no longer exists. Some, such as Irenaeus and the Roman Catholic theologians, would maintain that the lower, or natural image was

[8] Jas. 3:9.   [9] Jn. 4:24.

still present but the supernatural gift of righteous perfection was lost through the Fall. Others would insist that since God is essentially and perfectly holy, it is presumptuous folly to suppose that any sinful being such as man could in any proper sense be likened to Him. For such thinkers the "image of God" in man has true reference only to his original perfection now long lost, to the perfection of Jesus Christ and to the perfection restored or to be restored to sinful men through the atonement of Christ. The phrase is thus used only with historical and eschatological reference, not as applicable to the present state of fallen natural man.

It was mentioned earlier that Paul sometimes spoke of the image of God as referring specifically to Christ. Thus he writes of "the gospel of the glory of Christ, who is the likeness of God." [10] Similarly, he speaks of him as "the image of the invisible God." [11]

On occasion Paul speaks of the divine image also in eschatological expectation. Thus he writes,

But we all, with unveiled face beholding as in a mirror, the glory of the Lord, are transformed into the same image from glory to glory, even as from the Lord the Spirit.[12]

Now any Christian would surely believe that Christ was more like God than were other men and we all aspire hopefully to bearing also a greater likeness in our own persons. However, it seems quite false to suppose that a perfect, god-like righteousness was originally borne by man and was lost in the first sin. Before "knowing good and evil" [13] neither the first man nor any other could properly be called righteous or godlike. The innocence of infancy is not to be confused with the positive virtue of maturity, much less with the strong righteousness of God. That neither the first man nor any of us once possessed a perfect love of right and abhorrence of evil is proved by the fact of sin. Surely the mere lack of experience in sin before the dawn of moral insight is not to be compared even with the imperfect but strong loyalty to good in many a present man or woman, let alone likening it to the eternal goodness of God.

3. Mere Reflection of a Perfect Nature Alien to Man

It is sometimes taught that the image of God is not a quality of man's being, not a similarity between sinful man and the God who is the Wholly Other, but only a reflection in man of the perfect divine nature from which he is alienated. The image is then a *relationship* of divine mercy and grace to man, not a *condition* of man himself, just as a mirror does not resemble a human face but

[10] 2 Cor. 4:4.
[12] 2 Cor. 3:18, ASV.

[11] Col. 1:15-17.
[13] See Gen. 3:5. Cf. verses 10-11.

may yet receive and reflect the image of a face while that image is given to it by a man who stands before it.[14]

But if it be asked how it is that a man may receive and reflect God's grace as a stone or a tree may not, it is apparent that it is due to man's nature as a conscious rational being, a being therefore subject to categories of moral distinction and in this respect, at least, like God. As Paul Tillich says,

> Certainly man can have communion with God only because he is made in his image, but this does not mean that the image can be defined by communion with God. Man is the image of God in that in which he differs from all other creatures, namely, his rational structure. . . . Man is the image of God because his *logos* is analogous to the divine *logos*, so that the divine *logos* can appear as man without destroying the humanity of man.[15]

B. The True Divine Image in Man

If we follow the clue just suggested we find that there are a number of observable human characteristics which mark man, in his concrete reality, as like God. Before elaborating them it must be emphasized again that to attribute these traits to human beings is not to deny that God Himself is the source of them. Since man's very existence is due to God's creative and sustaining love it would be quite pointless to speculate on the question what attributes would belong to such a fictitious entity as "man alone" or "man apart from God." We are here concerned with man as he is, sustained by God's power and love. That he is sinful we know all too well, but sinner though he is, he bears upon his person the stamp of his Maker. This is seen in four persistent qualities of human life.

1. *Spiritual Being*

First of all, we observe that a human person has a spiritual nature which distinguishes him from the lower creatures and likens him to God. Unlike sticks and stars, men are able to think, to feel, to will. Whether and to what degree any of these characteristics are shared with other creatures of earth or other orders of being we may speculate but without much clear evidence. This limitation, however, does not affect our self-knowledge. As Augustine and Descartes demonstrated, we cannot doubt the fact of our own thinking without exemplifying and affirming it. Moreover, if we are to trust any experience whatsoever, we can hardly deny that we experience desires and exercise our

---

[14] For a recent able defense of this view, see Paul Ramsey, *Basic Christian Ethics*, pp. 249–84.

[15] *Systematic Theology*, I, p. 259. Unfortunately, Tillich's conception of God is so ambiguous as regards His personal nature that his total theological system provides a hardly adequate context for this doctrine.

wills. God, too, is a spiritual being, though vastly transcending ourselves in wisdom, power and righteousness. We know not how many other attributes He may have, unknown to us and perhaps beyond all possibility of our comprehension. But unless He is less and not more than we ourselves, He knows and desires and wills. The attributes of thought, affection and will have generally been unhesitatingly applied to the Divine Being by Christian thinkers and for this there is reasonable warrant.[16]

2. Sense of Moral Obligation

Acknowledgment must be made that a great gulf divides the original righteousness of God basic to the whole creation from the uncertain, changing and imperfect moral sense of man. But this should not blind us to the godlikeness implied in man's power of moral discrimination and his persistent concern with the moral dimension of life, evident even in his repressed feelings of guilt. We may describe deserts and songbirds in the valuational categories of beauty and utility. But human beings are like God in being subject also to rightful description in the ethical category of righteousness, however low on that scale man may sometimes fall. This is no small matter. Without this dimension of his being man would not be a real or potential child of God, called to be like Him.

It is often falsely supposed that the variety of content in man's moral judgments must prove his sense of moral obligation to be an essentially illusory synthesis of nonmoral affections. It is certainly true that the moral judgments of men differ greatly from individual to individual and from culture to culture. This fact shows indubitably that our moral sense is not infallibly trustworthy in its contents. But it no more shows that the sense of duty or longing for righteousness is itself illusory than the contradictory variety of men's tastes in food proves that hunger is illusory or that no discrimination between healthful and unhealthful foods is needed. Social experience has a large part in developing and conditioning man's moral sense. That sense is, however, an inextricable part of his human nature. It cannot be left undeveloped or eradicated without leaving an immature or dismembered humanity.

3. Longing for Union with God

The human race seems incurably religious. Restless and discontented with themselves and the visible order, the peoples of all the world have found or devised objects of reverence and devotion.

Much idolatrous religion, like some Christianity as actually practiced, is

---

[16] Cf. the analogy between human and divine self-consciousness in 1 Cor. 2:11. Cf. also the series of analogies in Augustine, *On the Trinity*.

doubtless an incongruous blend of self-subjection and self-assertive pride. Yet it is easy for the outsider to exaggerate the element of pride in idolatry. In its deeper significance for our present subject, it is not so important as a symptom of sinful pride as in witness to the unsatisfied and unenlightened but irrepressible longing for the one proper object of absolute reverence. So persistent is this inward yearning for God that when it does not find its proper object it attaches itself to human heroes, living or dead, to animals elevated by imagination to superhuman status, to the forces of nature or to monstrous products of mythological art.

So intimate is the proper relation of man's nature to God that without Him no human being can gain the completion of himself. When this completion is not found, all the races of the world persistently keep up the quest.

4. Aspiration to Goodness

In the study of sin it was observed that effort is required to be loyal to the right whereas anyone can drift easily into sin. But it is remarkable that the effort is so persistently made. The aspiration to good and the condemnation of evil are present in the most primitive societies known. They are so persistent that the most monstrous evil movements of the world have to gain their following and their power by masquerading as good. The most cruel and unprovoked aggression must be launched in the name of justice and peace, while the shackles of the most abject slavery are fastened on the wrists of willing subjects by tyrants who call them to "freedom" and "brotherhood."

The life to which God calls us requires the ready laying down of the old life. Yet the best to which we are called is known as having life "more abundantly," the perfecting or maturation of our humanity itself, not the destruction but the fulfillment of the law known before.[17]

The call of God to the higher life comes to men from the great Other, it is true. Yet it is not a summons to a strange land where humanity finds itself alien and insecure. It is an invitation home to our only peace.

[17] Cf. Jn. 10:10; Mt. 5:48 (noting the Greek, τέλειοι); Mt. 5:17.

CHAPTER 26

Man, Mortal and Immortal

A. Introduction

1. *Historic Emphasis*

CHRISTIAN preaching and teaching, from the earliest times, have emphasized both the mortality and the immortality of man. On the one hand, man has been urged to acknowledge that he is destined to die. The uncertainty of life and the fact of death have been held before him, in order to induce in him a humility and awe proper to a dependent creature standing before God. The resulting sobriety and earnestness have helped to support in many persons a disciplined life of faith and virtue. Stress on human mortality has likewise shown the urgent need for immediate decision and ceaseless work. On the other hand, it has been steadfastly insisted that death is not the end of our being.

The central importance of the doctrine of Christ's resurrection in the whole of the Christian gospel and the integral relation of that doctrine to the belief in the general resurrection is well illustrated by Paul's words to the Corinthians:

Now if Christ is preached as raised from the dead, how can some of you say there is no resurrection of the dead? But if there is no resurrection of the dead, then Christ has not been raised; if Christ has not been raised, then our preaching is in vain and your faith is in vain. We are even found to be misrepresenting God, because we testified of God that he raised Christ, whom he did not raise if it is true that the dead are not raised. For if the dead are not raised, then Christ has not been raised. If Christ has not been raised, your faith is futile and you are still in your sins. Then those also who have fallen asleep in Christ have perished.[1]

By the Christian assurance that "those . . . who have died in Christ" have *not* perished, martyrs of the faith have gone singing to their deaths, not only in the first centuries but also in the present times, and by this faith comfort has been brought to millions who have therefore not grieved "as others do who have no

[1] I Cor. 15:12–18.

hope." [2] Indeed, the emphasis upon the life after death has been so great that the church has often had to bear the reproach of being "other-worldly."

2. Recent Neglect of These Teachings

In many churches the historic stress upon the imminence of death and the reality of the future life has been greatly softened, of late, or has even disappeared. In many pulpits these subjects are seldom mentioned and many laymen confess that the Christian teachings concerning a future life have little meaning for them.

There are many discernible causes for this lack of interest. It is in part a wholesome reaction against unreasonable and immoral teachings of some churches preoccupied with the life after death. Such teachings include the mercenary exploitation of grief in selling supposed assistance to souls in purgatory. Not much better is the selling of tracts containing some ingenious but poorly supported interpretations of prophecy which the salesmen say we must read and accept or be forever lost. Experiences with such practices, however sincere may be their defenders, have quite understandably caused revulsions of feeling against all religious concern about death and the life beyond.

Quite rightly many persons are insisting that the Christian life is a present giving of self in obedience to God and in love for His children on earth and that such a life is intrinsically good now, whatever the future may hold. When such emphasis becomes extreme, in reaction against an irrational and enervating other-worldliness, it sometimes leads to the complete exclusion of the Christian hope of immortality.

Undoubtedly the prevailing naturalistic mode of thought likewise discourages belief in a life beyond the range of our present sense experience. Closely associated with this naturalistic trend are the methods stressed in much recent religious education, with the supposed necessity of "learning by doing," and keeping all instruction tied immediately to present experience. It requires more imagination and skill to teach about the future life through such means than to handle other subjects; indeed, it is impossible if these prescribed methods are taken altogether literally—unless teacher and pupil were to find themselves together in the actual presence of death, and even then it is doubtful whether the "doing" could be adequately managed. Only the dying actually make the crossing and experience life's continuation and we cannot depend on them to provide the instructed membership of our churches on earth!

Recently some writers on eschatology have furthered the decline of interest in immortality by disparaging remarks about it intended to focus attention on other forms of the Christian hope.

[2] 1 Thess. 4:13.

3. Continuing Inquiry and Need

Despite the widespread lack of interest and teaching in the churches, the need for Christian instruction concerning the future life continues undiminished. The percentage of people who must face death at the end of their own lives is undiminished by the remarkable and beneficent advances of medical science. It continues to be the absolutely universal experience. The loss of others bound closely by ties of love, blood and friendship is likewise as soul-shaking as ever. Many a disillusionment with all religion begins when the churchgoer finds himself suddenly standing unprepared beside an open grave.

But it is not only for sorrow and for death that the person without the Christian hope is poorly prepared. It is also for life. Is the whole of the human venture a play on which the curtain will one day fall, leaving everything as it was before any child was born? Is the fatal cancer or heart failure the last word of God to faithful men and women? If the answers are affirmative then at its very core life is untrustworthy.

An ultimate seriousness in our concern with sin and righteousness depends on an undergirding conviction that being is good. A genuine sense of sin comes only to the man or woman who feels the obligations of gratitude to God. No one has a sense of contrition for having disobeyed God without having first felt that God was worthy of being obeyed. But if death is God's last word to man, how can He be so regarded? Joseph Haroutunian says discerningly,

> There is an elemental bitterness in being threatened with nonbeing, and this bitterness persuades the creature that the Creator has no claim upon his loyalty. Under the circumstances, neither the goodness nor the justice of God is impressive. On the contrary, when the creature faces extinction, he feels that the source of his being is neither good nor just; whence it follows that there is no sin against God.[3]

There is a vitally important connection between recent neglect of the Christian hope and the prevalent lack of concern to repent and seek victory over sin. Haroutunian rightly observes that the "elaborate disquisitions on sin" by many recent theological writers have "made us more 'realistic' and readier to admit our involvement in social evil" but have still "failed to induce a conviction of sin before God." [4] True repentance can arise only where there is a grateful conviction that God is worthy of absolute trust. That cannot come to most people without belief that God has overcome death for us. Until it has come, the realistic analysis and portrayal of sinful pride in our hearts is more likely to bring enervating discouragement than life-restoring repentance.

[3] "From Joseph Haroutunian," *Religion in Life*, Spring, 1952, p. 195.
[4] *Ibid.*

People have a right to expect from the church an answer to their ultimate needs and fears. Such an answer must certainly speak clearly concerning the overwhelming human fact of death. When this answer does not come from the churches of the open Word, many turn pathetically to séances in dark places, to the elaborate Roman apparatus for purchasing postmortal insurance or to the innumerable foolish sects which thrive on promises of occult glimpses into the future with little relevance to present earthly tasks.

What have we as Christians to say about death and the future life?

B. Man's Mortality

1. Stressed in Scripture

The contrast between the fitful brevity of human life and the sure eternity of God is a frequently recurring theme of the Old Testament. "What man can live and never see death? Who can deliver his soul from the power of Sheol?" [5] asks a Psalmist. More eloquent are the familiar words,

> As for man, his days are like grass;
>   he flourishes like a flower of the field;
> for the wind passes over it, and it is gone,
>   and its place knows it no more.
> But the steadfast love of the Lord is from everlasting to everlasting
>   upon those who fear him. . . . [6]

In the Letter to the Hebrews it is written that "it is appointed for men to die once," even though this is said in order to add, "and after that comes judgment." [7]

2. Inescapable Fact

The victory and joy of the gospel is never understood until the grim face of death is openly confronted. Many are the efforts to avoid, evade or gloss over the shock of death to life. Even ministers sometimes say assuringly, "God does not want you to be ill," and in lieu of sermons give psychosomatic lectures on the health that comes with faith and love. Doubtless it is true that many are ill when they should be well and God does heal through faith, today as well as in ancient Palestine. But to be honest the minister and his people must face the larger fact that all, even the most faithful, loving and, in the best sense, healthy-souled individuals, are still going to be sick or suffer violence, and die. We are created mortal and plainly death is a part of God's plan for us.

[5] Ps. 89:48.
[6] Ps. 103:15–17.
[7] Heb. 9:27.

3. Our Need for Recognition of This Fact

It is curious that just when the psychologists are bringing up evidence on every hand that it is unhealthful both to mind and body for us to repress or in any way evade fearful thoughts which we must sooner or later, in some form, face, at this very time has come a strange reluctance to admit that we are going to die. We pride ourselves on being realistic. We talk about evils of many kinds and boast of our plain speech. Yet in the matter of facing death the Christians of no other generation have shown themselves so reticent or evasive. Perhaps our fathers talked too much about the uncertainty of life and the inevitability of death. We want, we say, to speak of life instead and live it to the full. Good! But we ought not to submerge into a nameless, repressed dread the knowledge of the fact that this life is of a few uncertain years, that death may come at any time and it will come in the end. If we are to live life to the full we must know it for what it is. It is not so known when death is left out of the account.

The fact of death is of incalculable moral significance. It means that in this whole earthly situation, at least, we have not forever to decide and to act. Indolence and procrastination will not do. Life is a limited quantity and must be used before it is gone. Death gives a peculiar urgency to life.

Death also makes of relative commitments and half-faiths a delusion. However hard we try to reserve judgment, delay decision and avoid "going out on a limb," our lives go and they go with finality. We do, willy-nilly, give ourselves absolutely to something or many things great or small and to delay is still to decide.

It is within this setting of a life bounded by both birth and death that we learn those tenderest meanings of human existence—the love of parents for fragile and ever-imperiled little ones and heart-searching sympathy and concern for the aged whose days with us are seen to be nearly numbered and especially priceless for our expressions of love.

Our mortality shows to us also the absoluteness of our dependence upon God. However we may boast of being "self-made men," however proudly we may lay up our treasures for future security, however mighty we may think ourselves by virtue of office or worldly power, there is always facing us that certain and absolute insecurity. Death lies ahead and how will it be then? Then all depends upon God. Facing that fact we know that all the while everything really depended upon God. Always there is the voice of plain truth, saying, "This night your soul is required of you," and always the man or woman is simply a "fool" who "lays up treasure for himself, and is not rich toward God." [8]

---

[8] Lk. 12:20–21.

4. *Mortality of the Race As a Whole*

It is often said that nature is careless of the individual but solicitous for the species. Yet many species, too, have passed into extinction. It is an amazing fact that for so long the exacting conditions required for human life have continued to be present upon earth. The whole race is delicately balanced between the possibilities of a new and all-encompassing ice age and a return of such heat as once gripped the earth in fiery lifelessness. A brief glance at the cataclysms of geology or the novae and "dead stars" of astronomy shows that the very possibility of human life on earth hangs on contingencies over which we have no control—even if we do not destroy the race by our own clever folly.

We may not, then, console our injured self-sufficiency by saying that although we must die we shall leave a legacy to our children and our children's children. The time set for the total life of the human race is not for our knowledge fixed within such definite outward limits as the life of each individual. But the race, too, is mortal and, in every century of the continuing human species, is absolutely dependent upon God. All that we can observe of stars and atoms indicates that one day all human life will be only history. But wait! not even history, for there will be no historian. Rather, as the candid naturalistic philosopher, Max Carl Otto puts it,

It is predicted that as the earth now sleeps every year for a winter, as we sleep every day for a night, so by and by the earth shall refuse to awake, as we rest at last in the sleep that nothing disturbs.[9]

That is, all will be so, unless—unless there is in very fact a life after death. But the Christian church has made, through the centuries, precisely this daring affirmation.

C. *Definition of Immortality*

Our concern here is not with some supposed inherent immortality of "man without God." We have seen how absolutely dependent is man for his existence at every moment. He neither creates nor sustains his own life. How could he leap over death and live again, this time by his own powers? No Biblical writer nor the church in any age has ever dreamed of affirming the immortality of man apart from God. Indeed few modern philosophers of the Occident have been impressed by arguments for the intrinsic immortality of the human soul as such. Many have pointed out the fallacies and dubious presuppositions of Plato's "proofs" and only one prominent philosopher of the West in the last

[9] *Things and Ideals* (New York: Henry Holt and Co., c.1924), p. 293.

hundred years has defended belief in human immortality apart from a doctrine of God.[10]

Neither are we concerned with any of those spurious substitutes which have been ceremoniously ushered forth under the falsely assumed name of immortality. The "genetic immortality" of the germ plasm or the mere "immortality of influence" will utterly fail for all who beget no children and who exert influences distorted by later generations. They will fail for all men in the common mortality of the human race. Little better is the "eternity of the truth" within us. The timeless truth of true ideas grasped by a human mind is meaningless apart from mind. Even in the mind of God it will continue to be, after a man has lived, just as true and no more true than before. The time will thus come when his discovery of it will have made no difference.

At later times we shall be considering the doctrine of the Judgment, the condemnation of sin and the qualitative meaning of "eternal life" for the faithful. We are not discussing these matters at present. In this and the succeeding chapter we are deliberately abstracting from all other considerations the one specific question whether there is to be a future for the individual human person after death and through the everlasting ages. It may be objected that for the Christian these considerations cannot be separated and none can be understood apart from Jesus Christ whose person and work we have not yet considered. It is true that in a coherent system of thought, including systematic theology, nothing is fully understood apart from everything else and especially apart from the person and events which have given the clue to that whole interpretation of life which is being presented. It is true that for the Christian nothing is fully understood apart from Jesus Christ. However, it is also true that Jesus Christ is not fully understood apart from all else—especially apart from God and from man with his sinfulness, his mortality and his intimations of immortality.

The first disciples did not come to Jesus from a background of this-worldly naturalism. They had behind them centuries of spiritual training. They had heard Job ask, "If a man die, shall he live again?" And they had heard both negative answers, as from Ben Sirach and the thirtieth Psalm, and affirmative ones from Ecclesiastes 12:7 and the twenty-third Psalm. In the dispute concerning this issue between the Pharisees and Sadducees Jesus unequivocally took the side of the Pharisees and in terms of their common Mosaic heritage argued that the dead rise and live again.[11] It is noteworthy, too, that from the

[10] I refer to J. E. M. McTaggart. See his book *Some Dogmas of Religion*. For analysis of other arguments concerning immortality, see my unpublished Ph.D. dissertation, *Presuppositions of Arguments Concerning Immortality in Thirty Ingersoll Lectures (1896–1935)*. Boston University Graduate School, 1935.

[11] Mk. 12:18–27.

Scriptures, which Pharisee and Sadducee alike accepted, Jesus argued the question of the future life on its own merits. He did not ask first whether, in the test case of the Sadducees' story, the woman and her seven successive husbands had been righteous or faithful, nor did he at that moment raise the question whether they were raised to condemnation or to glory. It was plain to see that there was not much use in talking to men about God's judgments or glorious gifts to those who are risen from the dead, so long as his hearers saw death as absolute and final annihilation.

In the twentieth century there are great multitudes of Sadducees. For many the doctrine that death ends all seems so firmly grounded in the whole modern, scientifically oriented interpretation of the world that there can be no question of a future destiny and the story of Jesus is dismissed in advance because there is a resurrection in the heart of it. To them the resurrection may continue to be a stumbling block until faith in Christ has changed all of life, but we can at least follow the example of Jesus in seeking to lower the barrier and prepare for faith. Though Jesus be the keystone of the arch of faith in life hereafter, there are other solid stones of evidence, too, and these may well be laid in place in preparation for his coming into his own.

CHAPTER 27

Evidences Concerning Immortality

A. Objections to Belief

BEFORE presenting positive evidence which makes immortality credible it is necessary first to speak of the objections which in many modern minds loom so high as obstacles to belief. Aside from frivolous and wholly fallacious arguments [1] there are only two objections. Both have been urged from ancient times, but from the standpoint of the prevailing modern mood both are weighty.

1. Sensory Evidence Lacking

We have not seen the dead returned triumphant to life. In an age which demands scientifically verifiable evidence and which usually conceives of that evidence in terms of data presented by the senses, this is a difficult stumbling block to belief. To reply that other men did see Jesus after his resurrection will not answer this objection. The scientific appeal to sensory evidence requires present verification by such evidence, not an appeal to reports by men of a prescientific age.

The spiritualists will make reply that present sensory proof is available and will offer to stage their séances with departed persons as demonstrations. Despite the great amount of fraud and obvious delusion which have had their part in so-called psychic phenomena, the literature of psychical research does indicate that conventional psychology has not adequately explained all communication among the living nor accounted for all successful cognition. But the inference that the poorly explained phenomena are due to the present agency of departed loved ones is highly questionable. [2]

The lack of direct sensory evidence would be a decisive refutation of belief in immortality if sense perception were the one valid test of truth. But near the beginning of our study we found that such a test could not be defended either by appeal to itself or by broader considerations of reason. If it were to be

[1] See my article, "Immortality: Arguments for and against," in V. Ferm, ed., *Encyclopedia of Religion*, and also the analysis in my unpublished Ph.D. dissertation referred to above.

[2] For some of the most persuasive statements favorable to the belief in psychic communication with the dead, see Sherwood Eddy, *You Will Survive after Death*, and the sources there cited.

accepted, then we should have to doubt the present existence of any thought in the mind of our most healthy and visible friend. For who ever saw a thought or a mind? Indeed, the extreme behaviorists and the logical positivists would doubt that there are such things. But so long as they continue to commend their views to the thought of other minds by books and lectures, most men will take the faith expressed by their actions as representing their more serious convictions and suppress a smile at the contrary content of their teachings.

Is it, then, being contended that there are no reasons for believing in the reality of mind or that we should believe some things without reason? Not at all. If there were no reason for belief in a life after death, then of course such belief could not be commended to minds concerned with discriminating between truth and falsehood. But we may rightly appeal to the broader evidence of comprehensive coherence which we found earlier to be the most adequate test of truth. Some evidence will be presented after discussion of the other objection to belief.

2. Intimate Relation of Soul and Mortal Body

The human body is observed to die and to disintegrate in decay, some of its materials to be taken up again in the great cycle of other earthly life. Now it is argued that this body was so intimately bound up with the conscious, thinking, feeling, willing soul that the obvious disintegration of the one must entail likewise the doom of the other. Since ancient times it has been noticed that the condition of the soul varied in some respects with the strength and health of the body. Both begin in weakness and dependence. As the body grows to mature strength, so does the thinking self. Often, with physical decline into senile weakness comes also a childlike dependence of thought and purpose. What could be more obvious, some say, than that the soul and body which share a common time of beginning and common periods of rise and decline must fall likewise into a common final death?

Modern studies in psychology, neurology and endocrinology have added greatly to the precision and detail of predictions that certain changes in neural structure or in blood chemistry will be accompanied by definite changes in personality. So intimate is the correlation between the neural and mental series of events that increasing numbers of psychologists prefer to describe mind and body together as a single "psychophysiological" individual.

It cannot be denied that the series of events which anyone can observe introspectively in his own consciousness correlates closely with the series of events which may be observed in the movements and changes of the physical organism. But even if they are, respectively, more and less intimate appearances of the same series they do not prove that the end of the body dooms the soul.

Probably anyone will grant that the motion of my face to form a smile, as that motion is observed in a mirror, is the same motion which I feel myself making. If I am sitting, like the guard in some large banks, with my back against a heavy steel wall and with my eyes on a great curved mirror before me, what I see, either of my own face or of the activities in the bank, and hence the intelligence of what I do, depends upon the condition of the mirror. Likewise, the view which people in the lobby have of my face will depend on this same mirror. Yet if a gangster, intent on robbing the bank, looks up, sees me reaching for my telephone, and shoots at the clear image of me, completely shattering the mirror, he does not end nor even injure any part of my body but only the mirrored images which we see of each other.

As William James pointed out in his famous Ingersoll Lecture,[3] the functions of the body in relation to the human soul may be, as far as our evidence shows, transmissive rather than constitutive. In other words, the scientific facts can all be accounted for on the supposition that the body serves as a means of communication, a mirror, imaging the soul to the outside world and the outside world to the soul. Determining the quality of the soul's communications, it affects profoundly the soul's own inner experience and the relevance of its responses to its environment *so long as the soul remains within it.*

But if *this* system of communications can be dispensed with, *some* such system is required for the continued life of the soul. Neither the Biblical teachings nor considerations of critical thought lend any support to the notion of a disembodied soul living on in solitary abstraction from the rest of reality. Paul expresses the critically defensible Christian hope when he says,

For we know that if the earthly tent we live in is destroyed, we have a building from God, a house not made with hands, eternal in the heavens. Here indeed we groan, and long to put on our heavenly dwelling, so that by putting it on we may not be found naked. For while we are still in this tent, we sigh with anxiety; not that we would be unclothed, but that we would be further clothed, so that what is mortal may be swallowed up by life.[4]

What reason have we to suppose that any such "building" will be forthcoming to replace this "earthly tent"? As if anticipating this very question Paul answers in the next verse, "He who has prepared us for this very thing is God, who has given us the Spirit as a guarantee."[5]

Similarly, when Paul confronts the skeptical question, "How are the dead raised? With what kind of body do they come?"[6] his answer avoids both the suggestion that it is *this* body and the notion of a disembodied soul. The body which is buried is like the seed grain which is sown.

[3] *Human Immortality.*
[5] 2 Cor. 5:5.
[4] 2 Cor. 5:1-4.
[6] 1 Cor. 15:35.

And what you sow is not the body which is to be. . . . But God gives it a body as he has chosen. . . .[7]

The vast resourcefulness of God, evident in the variety of His visible creation, shows us that He can provide a body suited to each kind of existence which He purposes to sustain.[8] Paul does not tell us much about the "spiritual body" which is to be. And with good reason. We can no more anticipate the kind of body with which we shall be "further clothed" after death than we could have described in advance this present body, even if we had somehow possessed all our present mental ability before entering our present life. But the God who did anticipate and create this present "earthly tent" can be trusted to provide also that "house not made with hands" which is to serve our future needs. We do not know the future. But we know Him and so we are content.

B. Positive Reasons for Belief

Our ground of affirmative belief is in God alone. In Him is centered all our ultimate hope for this life and the next. Man alone neither exists here nor could have any hope of existence hereafter. But given our confident trust in God the Father, our reasonable faith which has been brought to us through Jesus Christ, the ground of our hope is sure.

1. *Experience of True Value*

All our experience of the deeper values denies that they are ephemeral, fleeting things. Yet if death were the end, then all would one day be as if no man had ever loved or stood firm for truth, a day when Jesus and Judas would have come to a common annihilation. Faith in God at its very minimum is, as Höffding pointed out,[9] belief in the conservation of true values. Every courageous stand for truth or righteousness is an assertion that the achievement of knowledge or justice has a true worth set deep in the heart of things. Such assertion implies an affirmation at once of God and immortality. Particularly when human beings choose death in preference to cowardice or disloyalty they affirm in the most convincing way their faith that the value of courage and loyalty transcends this mortal life. Who is prepared to deny the rightness of such heroic choice or to assert that this rightness is opposed to truth?

2. *God's Goodness Assures Some Compensations*

The good God whom we know through theistic thought, through the Scriptures and through the common experience of the Christian community assures us that some inequities of the present earthly life will be corrected. We see the

[7] I Cor. 15:37–38.   [8] I Cor. 15:39–40, 42–44.
[9] In *The Philosophy of Religion*, pp. 215–19.

wicked "overbearing, and towering like a cedar of Lebanon," and we see Job
suffering in his righteousness. Often death interrupts both the prosperity of the
evil man and the suffering of the faithful. Is such inequity the last word of a
righteous God? "Shall not the Judge of all the earth do right?" [10] Especially
certain is our confidence that God has not at death spoken the final word to
the child born in poverty, infected with disease and going early to the grave
before he has had a chance to learn life.

3. God Assures Infinite Time for Obedience to Infinite Commands

God has set in our hearts such aspirations for truth, for beauty, for goodness
and for reverent fellowship with Him as constitute the common vocations of
all men. Not all understand clearly what it is to which they aspire. But all
think they ought to discover a little more truth or to experience some more
beautiful music, some lovelier scene or artistic creation, or they aspire to overcome some bad habit or to spend another hour in more reverent communion
with God. All of these aspirations are actually impossible to bring to final and
complete fulfillment at any point in time. Every new satisfaction of any one of
them carries with it the yearning for more. These calls to higher vision and
attainment are plainly both invitations and commands from God Himself.

Will He who invites and calls us to limitless privileges and endless tasks cut
us off with but limited time? Will He who has set our feet on a trail to infinite
heights and who bids us go all the way, give us less than infinite time for the
ascent?

4. Life Can Trust Him for Preservation of Life

In all ages men and women who have come to know God have been led to
trust Him as their supreme protector. In the Psalms this trust is expressed over
and over again:

> God is our refuge and strength,
>   a very present help in trouble.
> Therefore we will not fear though the earth should change,
>   though the mountains shake in the heart of the sea . . .
>
> Those who trust in the LORD are like Mount Zion,
>   which cannot be moved, but abides for ever. [11]

Especially has Jesus taught millions to put their trust in God as their heavenly
Father, who cares for each of His children with a holy love. Will this Father
who always gives good things to those who ask Him [12] send them into the final

---

[10] Gen. 18:25.

[11] 46:1-2; 125:1. Cf. 4:8; 23; 121:7-8.   [12] See Mt. 7:9-11.

dark night of nothingness in which they could receive no good things of any kind because they would have no being at all?

5. *Continued Life Not Enough*

If one is to experience any good whatever one must at least have being. But merely to be, though we should be forever, is not enough. Even to continue conscious, personal life forever might be a dubious good. Men need redemption not only from the nothingness of eternal death but also from the worthlessness of sin, futility, loneliness and despair.

Length of life will be worthy of our aspiration only if the *quality* of life is secured. Indeed, it is the qualitative rebirth of life experienced by Christians which makes immortality a living reality to them. But before we can examine this Christian meaning of eternal life, which is qualitatively as well as quantitatively different from the mortal life of the flesh, we must first see Jesus. For he first lived victoriously and then triumphed over death. It is he, "our Savior Christ Jesus," who has "brought life and immortality to light through the gospel." [13] Notice the order. He brought to light first life and then immortality. To him we now turn our thought.

[13] 2 Tim. 1:10.

PART FIVE

CHRIST AND RECONCILIATION

CHAPTER 28

The Humanity of Jesus

FROM earliest times, the church has found need to insist emphatically upon the humanity of our Lord. The desire to glorify Christ has led some Christians to deny that Jesus was a man. Possibly another motive of such denials has been to provide a ground for refusing in practice to use the standard of his life as a judgment upon men's own mediocrity. In any event the denials of his humanity have occurred frequently from the first century to the present and repeatedly the councils and other authorities of the church have denounced them as heretical.[1]

In our time the tendency to minimize or even deny the manhood of Jesus comes mainly from two sources. One of them is the practical instruction of Roman Catholics.

The official Roman Catholic teaching affirms the humanity of Jesus plainly enough, and the great stress upon the figure of the dying Jesus might be expected to impress this doctrine clearly enough upon the consciousness of the lowliest layman. However, it is taught that the humanity of Jesus was an "impersonal humanity," his *persona* being the Second Person of the Trinity, so that he was God assuming an impersonal human nature. Moreover, the emphasis upon the "holy mysteries" in the life of Christ, on his awful judgments to come and the need for mediation by the saints and priesthood of the church tend to set him further and further away from humanity.

The other source of theological movement away from the historic insistence on Christ's humanity is in conservative reaction against the exclusively humanitarian trend of some modern Protestant teaching. In their zeal for what they imagine to be orthodox Christianity, many Americans emphasize the full deity of Christ in such a way as to deny by omission and implication that he was really a man at all. Some of these persons, in ignorance of Christian history, think that they are defending the traditional doctrine when they teach that Jesus was simply God in a human body. Doubtless the etymology of the word "Incarnation" has sometimes encouraged such a view.

[1] Donald M. Baillie truly says that "in the story of the controversies which issued in the decisions of the first four General Councils it is impressive to see the Church contending as resolutely for His full humanity as for His full deity." (*God Was in Christ*, p. 11.)

The truth about the humanity of Christ is a matter concerning which all of our important sources of information are in the New Testament. Hence it is to that record we must now look.

A. TAUGHT IN THE GOSPELS

1. *Bodily Humanity*

According to the record of the Gospels Jesus' body was fashioned in the womb of a human mother and he was born into helpless infancy.[2] In the Scriptures there is no suggestion of that infant prodigy who was believed by some ancient Christians to have possessed all the wisdom and power of God, instructing the wise and performing miracles from his crib. Instead he is described as the "babe lying in a manger," being carried here and there by his parents and gradually growing toward manhood.[3]

In his mature ministry his bodily humanity was evident. He is reported to have grown tired[4] and slept.[5] He became hungry, not only after a long fast[6] but on other occasions as well.[7] He grew thirsty[8] and once used his thirst as a common human bridge of communication.[9]

What is more human than to die? All four Gospels report his death in circumstantial detail. There is no thought anywhere in the Gospels of a theophany such as the Hindus love to describe, in which the suffering and death would be only apparent, the drama of divinity showing men how to suffer and die but without real suffering and death.[10] Mrs. Eddy interprets the pain and death of Christ described in the Gospels and many times over in the other books of the New Testament to mean only an "illusion,"[11] but there could be no flatter contradiction of the Biblical record.[12] If there is any fact concerning Jesus which can be established beyond reasonable doubt it is known that his body was a human, mortal body and that he was tortured to death on a cross.

2. *Humanity of Soul*

But the Jesus of the New Testament record was human not only in body but also in soul. Not only his flesh but also his thoughts, emotions and will were human.

---

[2] Lk. 2:5–7, 12, 16, 27–28; Mt. 1:18, 25; 2:13–14, 19–21.
[3] Above references and Lk. 2:40, 52.
[4] Jn. 4:6. [5] Mt. 8:24; Lk. 8:23.
[6] Mt. 4:2. [7] Mt. 21:18.
[8] Jn. 19:28. [9] Jn. 4:6–7.
[10] Cf. Swami Akhilananda, *A Hindu View of Christ.*
[11] Mary Baker Eddy, *Science and Health with Key to the Scriptures*, "Death," in the "Glossary" of Biblical terms.
[12] See Lk. 22:44; Mt. 27:27–50; Mk. 15:15–37; Lk. 23:26–46; John 19:16–30; 2 Cor. 1:5; Heb. 5:8; 1 Pet. 3:18; 1 Cor. 15:3; Heb. 12:2.

His soul, as well as his body, grew from infant weakness to manly strength. At the age of twelve, it is true, according to Luke, he seized an opportunity to talk with the leading teachers of his people in the temple, "listening to them and asking them questions." But though "all who heard him were amazed at his understanding and his answers," [13] there is no suggestion of a precocity more than human. Moreover, after this event he returned to Nazareth with his parents and, so far from assuming the role of superhuman teacher, he "was obedient to them." [14]

a. Grew Spiritually

Especially significant is the picture of Jesus' youthful growth presented at the end of Luke's account of his boyhood. Here he writes, "And Jesus increased in wisdom and in stature, and in favor with God and man." [15] Of the four categories in which his growth is here affirmed, one is physical or merely chronological,[16] while three have to do with the development of the soul. Only a person of limited wisdom grows in wisdom and only a person not already in maximum favor with God and man could increase in such favor. The account seems to imply that God's confidence and delight in the youthful character of Jesus grew as the lad met the ever harder tests of his successive years, with steadfastness and increasing maturity.

b. Attracted Limited Attention in Youth

Apparently there was nothing about the youthful activities of Jesus which set him apart from his fellows in any absolute sense. For when in his mature ministry "he came to Nazareth, where he had been brought up," [17] and, after reading the Scriptures, he spoke in a remarkably gracious but also authoritative way,

many who heard him were astonished, saying, "Where did this man get all this? . . . Is not this the carpenter, the son of Mary and brother of James and Joses and Judas and Simon, and are not his sisters here with us?" And they took offense at him.[18]

Such an incident does not contradict the belief that he had been an unusually intelligent, good and devout boy. But plainly all of his actions in Nazareth had been of a kind to fall within the bounds of unmistakably human life.

c. Experienced Typical Human Emotions

In his fully developed manhood, during his active ministry, the Gospel writers describe his emotional responses to the various situations in exalted and yet altogether human terms. When his legalistic foes watched to see whether he

---

[13] Lk. 2:46–47.   [14] Lk. 2:51.

[15] Lk. 2:52.   [16] Note the marginal reading, "years," in place of "stature" in RSV.

[17] Lk. 4:16.   [18] Mk. 6:2–3.

would violate the law by healing on the Sabbath and met with stony silence his challenge to say whether it was "lawful on the sabbath to do good or do harm, to save life or to kill," it is reported that "he looked around at them with anger, grieved at their hardness of heart." [19] Moreover, he is reported to have uttered such condemnations of the Scribes and Pharisees as we cannot imagine being spoken without anger.[20]

According to Matthew's Gospel, after John was beheaded by order of Herod, "when Jesus heard this, he withdrew from there in a boat to a lonely place apart." [21] In so few words is told in eloquent simplicity the story of Jesus' lonely grief at the martyrdom of the great prophet who was also his own kinsman, forerunner and friend.

Especially familiar is the account of Jesus' grief after the death of Lazarus.[22] The Christ of the Gospels is no stranger to human emotion, even anger and sorrow, sometimes considered to be particularly typical of human frailty.

What of fear? Was that, too, a part of his experience? Certainly he did not succumb to it, but the steadfast courage with which he went to the cross would be far less impressive without the deep emotional distress which had come upon him with such crushing force in the Garden of Gethsemane.[23] Despite what would appear to be the obvious occasion of the distress, there has been reluctance in some quarters to believe that Jesus could have been in such dread of his own impending death. Many brave men confront death with much less sign of emotional agony than appears in this account. Hence it is thought "the cup" which Jesus dreaded and which he implored God to remove must have been something else, such as the burden of the world's sin. If this theory refers to a unique bearing of guilt by Jesus as a necessity of his vicarious atonement, it will hardly stand even the examination of the Biblical accounts. For Jesus is reported to have asked the sons of Zebedee explicitly, "Are you able to drink the cup that I am to drink?" and to have told them, "You will drink my cup." [24]

However, the meaning which impending death has for a man depends on the meaning which life has for him. Life becomes so burdensome and dreary for some that they seek death as a welcome relief. A courageous husband and father, with the responsibility of a beloved family upon his heart, thinks of approaching death, not so much as it affects himself as an individual, but rather with deep sorrow and concern for his wife and children. For Jesus life meant healing and teaching, especially the training of a few men to carry the good news of the Father's kingdom on and out to an ever greater company. That work seemed just begun. Jesus probably had long expected that his course

[19] Mk. 3:5.
[20] See especially Mt. 23:13-33.
[21] Mt. 14:13.
[22] Jn. 11:32-36.
[23] See Mk. 14:32-36; Mt. 26:36-42; Lk. 22:39-44.
[24] Mt. 20:22, 23.

would lead to ever-intensifying crisis and finally a violent death. But now? So near the beginning of his work? Was *this* faith, too, required of him—that he should now be sent to the death of a convicted criminal when he was seeing only a few uncertain signs that some disciples might be catching a glimmering of the word to be entrusted to them? Was he to die now, betrayed by one of that little select group he had chosen and begun teaching so that they might be entrusted with being the leaven of the kingdom?

Only one who had taken upon himself such a responsibility as Jesus bore, and whose life therefore had such vast dimensions of meaning, could know what it meant to him to die in the beginning of his ministry. But for all its unfathomable depths, the agony of this prayer in the Garden, with its struggle of faith and repeated renewal of submission to the Father's will, was an intensely human experience.

d. Possessed Limited Knowledge

That Jesus was limited in his knowledge during his youth has already been pointed out. But in his maturity his knowledge was still limited. According to the earliest Gospel he said on one occasion that he did not know what the Father knew.[25]

The limitations of his knowledge are also evident in his accepting the limited forms of language and thought belonging to his time and place. He customarily handled the Old Testament in ways familiar to his age and he accepted without criticism the demonological interpretation of nervous disorders.

e. Was Tempted

Three of the four Gospels give accounts of Jesus' being tempted in the wilderness at the beginning of his public ministry, two of them dwelling on the story at length.[26] At the close of the account in Luke it is reported, "And when the devil had ended every temptation, he departed from him until an opportune time," which suggests, at least, that there may have been other temptations later. Perhaps they were renewed even in the shadow of the cross, and drove Jesus to his knees in the agonized but victorious prayer of Gethsemane. The wilderness temptations, directed as they were to desires for food, for a spectacular short cut to success and for worldly power, were all appeals to a thoroughly human being, although a human being aware of a most extraordinary divine calling.

f. Subordinated Himself to God

According to the Gospels Jesus prayed most earnestly to God. On one occasion, at least, he was so concerned to separate himself from every distracting

[25] Mk. 13:32.   [26] See Mt. 4:1–11 and Lk. 4:1–13. Cf. Mk. 1:12–13.

influence that he sent the disciples off in a boat, dismissed the crowd that had followed him and then, "after he had taken leave of them, he went into the hills to pray." [27] At another time he slipped away "to a lonely place, and there he prayed" while many people looked for him in vain.[28] After healing the epileptic boy, he told his disciples that this kind of healing could not be done "by anything but prayer." [29] The disciples apparently recognized the importance of prayer in the Master's ministry as in that of John the Baptist and so they begged him to teach them to pray.[30]

In the fourth Gospel, where, most of all, the unique prerogatives of Jesus are emphasized, Jesus is nevertheless quoted as insisting that he had no power nor authority of his own and as distinguishing explicitly between his will and the will of the Father. "Truly, truly, I say to you, the Son can do nothing of his own accord, but only what he sees the Father doing," [31] he says, and again:

I can do nothing on my own authority; as I hear, I judge; and my judgment is just, because I seek not my own will but the will of him who sent me.[32]

In the Garden of Gethsemane his victory was won, not in the affirmation of self-will, but in the subjection of himself to God, as he prayed, "Yet not what I will, but what thou wilt." [33] A clearer, more explicit affirmation of the distinction between the consciousness of the man who prayed and the being of the God to whom he prayed would be hard to imagine, even while the will of the man Jesus was subjecting itself by faith to the purpose of God.

3. *The Doctrine of the Virgin Birth*

To all that has been pointed out in the Gospels making clear the humanity of Jesus some may reply by raising the question whether the teaching that he was born of a virgin by miraculous conception does not prove that he was only part man and by birth part God.

It must be replied that this teaching is nowhere in the Gospels presented as a denial of Jesus' humanity, nor has it any essential relation to the doctrine of his divinity. Indeed, though all of the Gospels teach that he was the Son of God, all likewise teach plainly that he was wholly and not partly a man subject to God's rule. Only two Gospels, Matthew and Luke, mention a virgin birth. In Matthew the significance of this miraculous birth is presented as a fulfillment of Isaiah 7:14.[34] Only in Luke is there a suggestion that this birth constitutes the

---

[27] Mk. 6:45–46. Cf. Mt. 14:22–23.
[28] Mk. 1:35–37.
[29] Mk. 9:29.
[30] Lk. 11:1.
[31] Jn. 5:19.
[32] Jn. 5:30.
[33] Mk. 14:36.
[34] Mt. 1:23. The Hebrew of Is. 7:14 does not certainly imply virginity but may refer to a young matron.

meaning of his title, "Son of God," and even there the wording may mean simply that by reason of this miraculous birth his divine sonship will be attested or made known.[35]

It is plain that the development of Jesus' body from a fertilized or unfertilized or miraculously fertilized ovum is not the subject being discussed in the great councils which dealt with his divinity nor is it intrinsically important to his moral authority, his spiritual power or the meaning of his death and resurrection. Those who have thought sexual procreation to be the one means by which original sin was passed from generation to generation have seen in the virgin birth the means of insulating Jesus from the hereditary Fall. But there is in the Scriptures little warrant for such an Augustinian view of sex and the Bible contains no such interpretation of the virgin birth. Moreover, the Roman Catholic Church, which has especially emphasized it, has been so ill satisfied with it as to have conjured up the additional doctrine of a miraculously "immaculate conception" of Mary in *her* mother's womb to place an additional barrier between Jesus and the Fall as well as further to exalt Mary herself.

On the other hand, those who profess to find either some disproof or some substantiating evidence of the virgin birth of Christ in the natural sciences might better be saved their pains. Scientists know about this essentially what everyone knows, namely, that there is no well-authenticated parallel case of an unfertilized ovum developing into a human body. All who believe in the virgin birth should not only agree with that assertion but should insist upon it, since if there were parallel cases Jesus' birth would lose its uniqueness. In other important respects the life of Jesus was unique and no natural scientist, using the powers which God gave him, can, by observing the world which his Creator made, set the limits of God's power to stir hope of such a unique life by a miraculous birth, if that were His will. When the question is raised whether or not Jesus was actually born of a virgin, the issue for a theist turns not on the limit of God's power but on the historical evidence.

The evidence in the text of the New Testament is not very convincing. The fact that only two books so much as mention such an event is important but not decisive evidence against it. The silence does indicate that it was no part of the Christian tradition as known to Paul and the authors of Mark, John, Hebrews and the other New Testament writings, or else it indicates that they were too skeptical or indifferent to record it among all the tributes they paid to the Master. But more important are other, more positive evidences. Both the genealogies, in Matthew and Luke, bear evidence of tampering. For if, as Matthew reports, the genealogy given traces only the lineage of "Joseph the husband of Mary, of whom Jesus was born," [36] then it is not, as promised, "the

[35] See Lk. 1:35.   [36] Mt. 1:16.

genealogy of Jesus Christ, the son of David, the son of Abraham." [37] Even more suspicious is the parenthetical phrase introduced by Luke. For if Jesus was only "the son (*as was supposed*) of Joseph," [38] then it is hard to see why a writer who knew that Joseph was *not* Jesus' father would have traced a genealogy through him. The parenthesis looks like an insertion into a genealogy already in circulation, to harmonize it, rather lamely, with the birth story which had come into the tradition at a later time. Probably the birth story itself had arisen as a further tribute to his divinity and to his fulfillment of the ambiguous prophecy in Isaiah 7:14.[39]

The same two Gospels which give the birth stories report that the neighbors in Nazareth thought Jesus to be Joseph's son and give this common assumption as one cause of their astonishment that he should speak as he did in maturity.[40] The neighbors plainly knew nothing of a virgin birth. Luke reports that Mary herself, speaking to Jesus, called Joseph his "father." [41] The same writer calls Joseph and Mary Jesus' "parents" and says that in his youth Jesus "was obedient to them." [42]

The pattern of life in the carpenter's family seems not to have been affected by remembrance of a miraculous birth. Whose life, then, are we to suppose was different because of it? The obvious answer, at first thought, would seem to be the life of Jesus. But in what respect is it to be supposed that God made him different as the son of one human parent than He may as well have made him as son of two human parents? His body was evidently fully mortal and human in every respect. Would a soul joined with such a human body be any different for that body's procreation by one than by two parents? Could God provide a man fit to be the Savior of men only by giving to that man a body from a virgin mother? [43]

But after raising the last question we must hasten to add that the New Testament, for all the teaching of his divinity, is unequivocal in affirming the completely human nature of Jesus, both soul and body. We have cited some testimony to that effect in the Gospels. It remains to point out other affirmations of his full humanity elsewhere in the New Testament.

B. Other Assertions of Jesus' Humanity in the New Testament

That there are abundant materials in the New Testament inviting the later development of a metaphysical doctrine setting Christ far above all other men

[37] Mt. 1:1.   [38] Lk. 3:23. Italics mine.

[39] Of course, the statement that the marriage of Jesus' parents had not been consummated (Mt. 1:25) at the time of his birth is an integral part of the birth tradition itself. The frequent claim, therefore, that to deny his birth of a virgin is to affirm his illegitimacy is even more pointless than it would otherwise be.

[40] Mt. 13:55–56; Lk. 4:22.   [41] Lk. 2:48.

[42] Lk. 2:43, 51.   [43] Cf. Heb. 7:15–16.

and even identifying him with God can hardly be gainsaid. Yet it is also true that alongside the passages which affirm or suggest a "high Christology" there are others which explicitly affirm his humanity.

Thus Paul writes,

For as by a man came death, by a man has come also the resurrection of the dead. For as in Adam all die, so also in Christ shall all be made alive.[44]

This teaching implies much, not only concerning Christ, but also concerning our own rightful destinies. We are called, says the same apostle, to take our places alongside the Savior as "heirs of God and fellow heirs with Christ, provided we suffer with him in order that we may also be glorified with him." [45]

In the Letter to the Hebrews both the fact and the religious significance of his full humanity are emphasized.

For surely it is not with angels that he is concerned but with the descendants of Abraham. Therefore he had to be made like his brethren in every respect, so that he might become a merciful and faithful high priest in the service of God, to make expiation for the sins of the people. For because he himself has suffered and been tempted, he is able to help those who are tempted.[46]

Like other men, Jesus found his salvation, not in himself, but in God and like other men he had to learn obedience to Him.[47]

The New Testament pictures Jesus as the mediator who reveals God to men and reconciles men with their Creator. But this mediator is no third kind of being suspended midway between heaven and earth. As Paul writes, "For there is one God, and there is one mediator between God and men, *the man* Christ Jesus." [48]

[44] I Cor. 15:21–22.
[45] Rom. 8:14–17.
[46] Heb. 2:16–18. Cf. 4:15–16.
[47] Heb. 5:7–10.
[48] I Tim. 2:5. Italics mine.

CHAPTER 29

The Son of God: Historic Testimony

NOTHING that is to be written here will contradict or detract from the teaching that Jesus was fully human. That he was wholly a man is the truth. But it is not the whole truth. There is more which must be said.

The Christian faith includes a high regard for the worth of man and a lofty conception of what God intends that he should become. Jesus the man is symbol and evidence of this valuation and this hope. Christians are also reminded by the human life of Jesus how far they have fallen short of what a human life can be. Were it not for the humanity of Jesus he would not be the clear revelation *to men* that he is. That Jesus was a man must be affirmed and insisted. But it is not all that must be affirmed.

Although the Christian faith does include a doctrine of man, it is not primarily a faith in man. It is primarily a faith in God. Jesus is important to his followers not only as the revelation of what man may become but even more as the revelation of what God is and of what God has done, is doing and will do for men.

From the first century until now Christians have spoken of Jesus both as man and as Son of God. We have now to consider what truth is implied in the historic affirmations that Jesus Christ is the Son of God. We begin by observing the character of those affirmations.

A. TEACHINGS OF THE SYNOPTIC GOSPELS

The earliest record of our Lord's life and ministry is the Gospel According to Mark. The first words of this Gospel are: "The beginning of the gospel of Jesus Christ, the Son of God." Even though a number of the most ancient and reliable manuscripts we possess omit the phrase "son of God," [1] it is clearly apparent that the whole Gospel was written in the belief that this designation was true. Within the first chapter it is narrated that, at the baptism of Jesus, "a voice came from heaven, saying, 'Thou art my beloved Son; with thee I am well pleased.'" [2] Mark's Gospel attributes to Jesus the assertion of his authority

---

[1] In the standard edition of the Greek text edited by Eberhard Nestle and revised by Erwin Nestle the phrase υἱοῦ θεοῦ and the variant υἱοῦ τοῦ θεοῦ are relegated to a footnote.
[2] 1:11.

to forgive sins,[3] and a parable sharply distinguishing between other messengers from God and His own beloved Son.[4] Many other teachings and acts are described which set him above the rest of mankind. At the climax of all is the story of his resurrection.

Matthew and Luke likewise make the loftiest claims for his unique filial relationship to God. Especially important are the following words attributed to Jesus himself:

All things have been delivered to me by my Father; and no one knows the Son except the Father, and no one knows the Father except the Son and any one to whom the Son chooses to reveal him.[5]

In the reports of one important utterance, there is a crescendo of affirmation of divinity as the reader passes from the version given in Mark, through the Lucan account to that in Matthew. Mark reports that when Jesus asked, "But who do you say that I am?" Peter replied, simply, "You are the Christ."[6] Luke's version of the reply is, "The Christ of God."[7] But Matthew gives the response usually quoted: "You are the Christ, the Son of the living God."[8] Matthew has also added a further response by Jesus in which he praises Peter's confession as divinely revealed and speaks of the church to be built upon "this rock."

The events of the miraculous birth, not mentioned outside of Matthew and Luke, are also narrated in these two Gospels with clear intent to provide further evidence of Jesus' unique relationship to God. Indeed, they appear in these Gospels as seals of God Himself placed upon Jesus at the beginning of his life, just as the voice in the baptismal scene and at the Transfiguration serves at the commencement and in the midst of his ministry, and as the darkness of the crucifixion hours and the glory of the resurrection serve at the end.

All through the first three Gospels the assumption of a unique status held by Jesus is perfectly apparent.

B. Other Affirmations in the New Testament

According to the Acts, as soon as Paul, after his conversion, began to preach, "immediately he proclaimed Jesus, saying, 'He is the Son of God.'"[9] This doctrine was obviously at the center of the message upon which the churches were built from the beginning. It is implied throughout the letters of Paul and is explicitly declared over and over again.

Paul entitles the gospel he is called to preach, "the gospel of God. . . . , the

---

[3] 2:7–12.   [4] 12:1–9.
[5] Mt. 11:27. Luke presents a variant account, but the essential idea is the same.
[6] Mk. 8:29.   [7] Lk. 9:20.
[8] Mt. 16:16.   [9] Acts 9:20.

gospel concerning his Son, who was descended from David according to the flesh and designated Son of God in power. . . ." [10]

Likewise the Letter to the Hebrews testifies to "a great high priest who has passed through the heavens, Jesus, the Son of God." [11] This is the faith of the whole New Testament.

But most of all, the Gospel and First Letter of John make this faith explicit and most emphatic. Indeed, by its own testimony the fourth Gospel was written "that you may believe that Jesus is the Christ, the Son of God, and that believing you may have life in his name." [12]

John has been the favorite Gospel to millions of Christians and the epitome of the Christian message has been most often stated in the words of that Gospel,

For God so loved the world that he gave his only Son, that whoever believes in him should not perish but have eternal life.[13]

The popularity of the gospel in this form is no accident. For in the midst of our mortal life, with all its temptations and insecurities, its frustrations and perils, its vast evils and its ever-impending death, everyone feels in his heart the inadequacy of any salvation which human wisdom or power can offer. Men and women of every class and nation, in their strife and sorrow, long for assurance that the power on which the very world is founded is on their side. Only good news of *God* is the absolute good news sufficient for our absolute need. The Gospel of John, more than any other book of the Scriptures, emphatically, constantly and persuasively teaches that we have precisely *that* gospel, the good news of God in Jesus Christ his Son. It is also to the Gospel of John that we are indebted for the interpretation of Jesus as the divine Word, to which we shall devote careful attention later.

C. Limiting Considerations

Confronted with such testimony it would be easy to leap to the conclusion that Jesus was a kind of heavenly being altogether incompatible with our earlier affirmations of his humanity. We have not yet reached the place in our undertaking for the attempt to state in our own terms the meaning of Jesus' divine sonship. However, before we leave the Biblical testimony for a time, some restraining considerations must be noted.

1. We must recall that the testimonies that he is the Son of God occur in the New Testament alongside the most explicit and numerous affirmations of his humanity. One more example may be cited. Only five verses after Paul writes

---

[10] Rom. 1:1–4. Cf. Rom. 5:10; 8:3, 32; Gal. 2:20; 4:4.   [12] Jn. 20:31.
[11] Heb. 4:14. Cf. 6:6; 7:3; 10:29.   [13] Jn. 3:16.

that "we were reconciled to God by the death of his Son," he says that "the free gift in the grace of that one man Jesus Christ abounded for many," and in the next four verses he refers to Jesus three times as "man." [14] The doctrine of Jesus' humanity is not to be denied nor minimized by the teaching that he is the Son of God.

2. Even within some Biblical affirmations of Jesus' unique divinity, a distinction is made between Jesus and God, with Jesus clearly subordinated. For example, in the reported prayer of Jesus for his disciples, in John 17, a prayer repeatedly affirming an especially high Christology, Jesus represents his "power over all flesh" as "given" by the Father, and speaks of "eternal life" as knowing "thee the only true God, and Jesus Christ whom thou hast sent." It is noteworthy, in view of later developments of doctrine, that here Jesus is represented as placing deity wholly in the one whom he addresses in prayer and speaks of himself as "sent" by that "only true God." [15]

3. It is doubtful that anywhere in the New Testament Jesus is directly said to be God. It is true that repeatedly in John he is quoted as saying that he and the Father are "one," and these passages are often cited as proving that the New Testament affirms the "full deity" of Jesus. But in the same context with some of these affirmations, Jesus is described as praying repeatedly that the disciples may have the same kind of unity which he has with his heavenly Father. Thus:

Holy Father, keep them in thy name which thou hast given me, that they may be one, even as we are one.[16]

Surely the author of the fourth Gospel does not mean to represent Jesus as praying these three times that the disciples should lose all their individuality as distinct and different human beings. It is not metaphysical unity that he is asking. It is a unity of the most intimate sharing in understanding, purpose and love. In the fourth petition for the unity of the disciples this is made clearer:

. . . I in them and thou in me, that they may become perfectly one, so that the world may know that thou hast sent me and hast loved them even as thou hast loved me. . . . O righteous Father, the world has not known thee, but I have known thee; and these know that thou hast sent me. I have made known to them thy name, and I will make it known, that the love with which thou hast loved me may be in them, and I in them.[17]

---

[14] Rom. 5:10, 15-19.   [15] Cf. Jn. 5:30-31; 6:38-40.

[16] Jn. 17:11. Cf. 20-22.

[17] Jn. 17:23, 25-26. If it should be objected that Jesus is not here addressing God, but rather the first person of the Trinity, and that his own identity as God is therefore not at stake, it must be pointed out that it is in this very prayer that Jesus distinguishes between himself and "thee the only true God" (17:3).

Christ may possibly be called God in Romans 9:5. But the Greek text is ambiguous and the majority opinion embodied in the text of the Revised Standard Version is probably correct. The verse, according to this reading, comes to a full stop, then closes with a doxology, "God who is over all be blessed forever. Amen."

Anyone who supposes that the committee preparing the Revised Standard Version was averse to translating a passage in a way to affirm directly that Jesus is God will be disabused of that idea by comparing the earlier renditions with the Revised Standard Version of Titus 2:13, where the latter version presents the phrase, "the appearing of the glory of our great God and Savior Jesus Christ." Again the Greek is ambiguous but here the renditions of the Authorized Version and the American Standard Version seem more natural. The latter reads, "the appearing of the glory of the great God and our Savior Jesus Christ."

In Colossians we read, "For in him the whole fullness of deity dwells bodily." But it is one thing to say that God was *in* him and another thing to say that he was God. This is especially true when it is observed how flexibly and mystically the phrase "in him" (ἐν αὐτῷ) is used. Indeed, in the very sentence from which the first part has just been quoted, precisely the same phrase appears in the next clause where it is quite impossible to take it in a metaphysical sense: "and you have come to fullness of life in him." [18]

Probably the nearest the New Testament ever comes to asserting explicitly that Jesus is God is in the words of Thomas to the risen Christ, as narrated by John, where we read, "Thomas answered him, 'My Lord and my God.'" It must be observed that the words are addressed to the risen Christ who, according to the same Gospel, was so different from Jesus as known before the crucifixion that even his best friends had great difficulty in identifying him as the same person.[19] It might also be argued whether the phrase "my God" was literally addressed to Jesus himself or to God as Thomas sensed His presence with or *in* Christ. But the author of the Gospel was, at least, not concerned with making any such distinction clear.

There are passages which when placed together provide premises from which may be drawn the conclusion, Jesus is God. But it is highly significant that in all the New Testament literature, continually seeking to exalt Jesus in every possible way, the inference is exceedingly rarely, if ever, drawn and stated. It remained for later generations of Christians to make such a conclusion an article of faith.

4. The phrase "son of God" is not strictly reserved for Jesus. Adam is called

[18] Col. 2:9-10.
[19] Cf. Jn. 20:14-15.

son of God in the Lucan genealogy.[20] Jesus once called the blessed dead "sons of God," [21] and he used the term in an exalted sense implying a place "equal to the angels." More important still, when Jesus' right to call himself "the Son of God" was challenged, according to a report in John, he defended his right on the ground that Psalm 82:6 had called the chosen people "gods." [22]

5. Some of the attributions of a unique divine sonship to Jesus in our New Testament accounts may be due to later exaggerations of things said by Jesus and others during his lifetime. The possibility can be well illustrated by comparison of the words spoken by the centurion at Calvary, as reported by Luke 23:47 and by Mark 15:39 and the differing translations of the latter passage. In the King James Version of Mark, the centurion's words are, "Truly this man was the Son of God." In the Revised Standard Version, as in the margin of the American Standard Version, the words are, "Truly this man was a son of God." Now in the Greek neither a capital letter nor definite article is present to justify the translation, "the Son." The natural reading of the Greek, then, is "a son." But in many other passages where the Greek text is exactly the same, the Revised Standard Version reads "the Son of God." Why not here? The problem is obviously to know what the original narrative meant. Here Luke may be appealed to for support of the reading "a son." For in Luke's account the centurion says, "Certainly this man was innocent!" or (AV) "Certainly this was a righteous man." In view of this fact, the reading "a son" is much the more plausible. In how many other instances may an emphatic expression concerning Jesus' righteous, filial loyalty to God have been colored by later oral tradition, writing or translation, so as to assert finally a doctrine of superhuman divinity?

D. Historic Doctrines in the Church

1. Views Generally Rejected

a. Compromising the Divine Nature of Christ

In the second century, several theories concerning Jesus were rejected by the authority of the church because they were believed to deny that it was truly God Himself who was known in him. Among these it was especially clear that the church could not accept semipagan, syncretistic views, like that of Carpocrates, which assigned to Jesus a supernatural, divine nature but made similar

---

[20] Lk. 3:38. In the Greek the word υἱός (son) is understood from v. 23. The definite article is not used in the original text. On the other hand, the English reader must not suppose that the use of the capital letter in the passages calling Jesus "Son of God" has evidential significance, for the capital does not appear in the corresponding Greek passages.

[21] Lk. 20:36.   [22] Jn. 10:34–36.

affirmations concerning such men as Plato and Aristotle. The church had no intention of making Christ a member of a new pantheon. A more serious influence was exercised by the Ebionites. To them Jesus was the long-awaited Messiah, endowed uniquely with the Spirit of God, either from birth or from the time of his baptism. The Ebionites denied the doctrine of pre-existence and assigned to Jesus a human nature only.

Under Ebionite influence there developed late in the second century the view of Theodotus known as adoptionism, which was brought to full development by the third-century bishop of Antioch, Paul of Samosata. He accepted the doctrine of the virgin birth and believed that from birth Jesus was superior in endowment and goodness. Through the impersonal Word, taught the bishop, God elevated Jesus to such an ethical union of will with Himself that at his baptism he was given a divine status which was finally perfected by his resurrection. This view came near, at least, to constituting a story of the making of a second deity, an idea not calculated to be well received generally in the Christian church. As Albert C. Knudson says, "Though initiated in the interest of the divine unity it turned out itself to be a kind of di-theism and to verge on mythology." [23]

A more famous heresy, one which shook the whole church, and gave rise to much intense doctrinal—and political—activity in the fourth century, was Arianism. Arius was an Alexandrian presbyter who taught that Jesus was the incarnation of a pre-existent being generated before anything else in all creation, but nevertheless subordinate to God and not, like Him, existent from eternity. Despite the superior character and skill of Arius and his willingness to pay to Jesus the homage due a deity, this teaching was decisively rejected at the Councils of Nicaea (325) and Constantinople (381). Monotheism was too thoroughly established at the heart of the Christian faith to permit any doctrine about a divinity other than the one true God. Moreover, it was precisely God, and not a god, whose presence was believed to have been known in Christ and about whom the Christian gospel was good news.

b. Docetism

On the other hand, the church could no more accept an attempt to solve the problem concerning Christ by the device of affirming that he was simply God appearing *incognito* as a man, masquerading as what He was not in very truth. Accepting the idea that God had veritably appeared on earth in the form of Jesus Christ, but quite logically finding it impossible to believe that one and the same being could be truly God and man at once, such men as Marcion (second century) sacrificed the notion of real humanity. The God of love,

[23] *The Doctrine of Redemption*, p. 289.

Marcion held, descended to earth, appeared in an illusory body and only seemed to suffer on the cross.

Another thoroughly inacceptable view was the fourth century Apollinarian theory that the body of Jesus was a genuine human body animated by a human life (ψυχή), but that in him the divine Logos took the place of a human rational soul (νοῦς or πνεῦμα). The doctrine of Eutyches, a century later, was similar in its compromising of Christ's humanity, for Eutyches denied that Jesus' body was of the same nature with our own and was ambiguous about the human nature of his spirit. However, the dismissal of Eutyches from office (448) and the promulgation of the Chalcedonian Creed failed to stamp out his doctrine and Monophysitism[24] in various forms continued to be an influential theory for more than two centuries, occasioning some of the most immoderate and unchristian tempers in the history of theology.

Indeed, although the early Councils repeatedly declared, against the docetic and quasi-docetic doctrines, that Jesus was fully human, still great numbers of Christians, both learned theologians and untutored laymen, have been reluctant to draw the inevitable inferences of limited knowledge, moral struggle and spiritual growth in the life of the Master. As D. M. Baillie says,

> The cruder forms of docetism were fairly soon left behind, but in its more subtle forms the danger continued in varying degrees to dog the steps of theology right through the ages until modern times.[25]

2. *The Traditional Doctrine*

From the controversies of the first four centuries after Christ there emerged as the official, orthodox position of the church the doctrine that in Christ a completely human nature and the nature of God Himself were united. But these two natures were not regarded as so separated in him as to prevent his perfect unity, as the teachings of Nestorius (c.451) were thought to imply. Rather they must be thought of as completely united, yet without reduction of either the humanity or the divinity. The classic formulation of this paradoxical doctrine is in the phraseology adopted at the Council of Chalcedon in 451, which reads:

> Following, then, the holy Fathers, we all unanimously teach that our Lord Jesus Christ is to us One and the same Son, the Self-same Perfect in Godhead, the Self-same perfect in Manhood; truly God and truly Man; the Self-same of a rational soul and body; consubstantial with the Father according to the Godhead, the Self-same

---

[24] The doctrine that there was but a single nature in Christ, regarded as a fusion of the divine and human, but in reality compromising his humanity.

[25] *God Was in Christ*, p. 11. This book is an excellent Christological study and I am much indebted to it.

consubstantial with us according to the Manhood; like us in all things, sin apart; . . . acknowledged in Two Natures unconfusedly, unchangeably, indivisibly, inseparably; the differences of the Natures being in no way removed because of the Union, but rather the property of each Nature being preserved, and (both) concurring into One Prosopon (Person) and One Hypostasis; not as though He were parted or divided into Two Prosopa, but one and the Self-same Son and Only-begotten God, Word, Lord, Jesus Christ.[26]

In this document, it will be observed, there are three main doctrines affirmed, without effort to resolve the flagrant internal contradictions which seem to result. The first is that Jesus Christ was "truly God," the second that he was "truly Man" and the third that his Godhead and his humanity were kept completely distinct and unchanged while being perfectly united "without separation" in one person.

This formula can hardly be regarded as explaining anything. Indeed that was not its purpose. It was a compromise of ecclesiastical politics, much concerned with the harmony of the church, with its several lines of cherished traditions and with several doctrines which were of great practical religious value. It was little concerned with logic or real intelligibility. It satisfied few even in its own time. From that day to this the theologians who have accepted it have taken it, not as a satisfactory Christology, but as a statement of the basic problems and the elements to be included in a satisfactory Christology which remained to be thought out and made intelligible.

Moreover, the creeds and other formulations of doctrine constructed in ancient and medieval times do not generally gain very effective leverage on modern minds. They sound archaic in language and give the impression of trying to solve problems which are now of only antiquarian interest. This is true because of the fact that the frame of reference of those statements is in a philosophical world foreign to our thought. They are to us utterances in a foreign tongue, not so much because they were written in Greek or Latin, which can be readily translated, but because the concepts for which such words as (in translation) "nature," "consubstantial," "person" and "hypostasis" then stood are concepts saturated with metaphysical assumptions belonging to Platonic, Aristotelian and Stoic philosophy which few of us are today ready to accept even when we understand them.

[26] T. Herbert Bindley, *The Oecumenical Documents of the Faith* (4th ed., revised by F. W. Green. London: Methuen & Co. Ltd., 1950, pp. 234-35).

CHAPTER 30

The Son of God: Christological Reconstruction

IF a doctrine of the Person of Christ is to be of maximum intelligibility and service to us, we must confront anew the historical and living reality of Jesus and face for ourselves his question, "But who do you say that I am?" For the Christian no question is more personal and none more impossible for another to answer in his stead. But on the other hand, it is also impossible for one to answer the question aright without sharing in the experience and thought of others, for Christianity is a social religion and the discovery of truth is a social enterprise. Hence, without presuming to suppose that author and readers will think alike, we must seek to face together some of the pitfalls into which some studies of our problem have fallen, then consider some constructive suggestions pointing toward a solution.

A. Pitfalls in Christological Thought

1. Outright Identification of Jesus As God

If Jesus be regarded simply as God, then we encounter his own emphatic contrary teaching, as recorded in the Gospels, even, or rather especially, in the fourth Gospel. For as we have noted, according to that Gospel he prayed earnestly to God, addressing Him on at least one occasion as "the only true God" and as the one who "didst send me," steadfastly declared his own complete dependence upon the Father's power and the subjection of his own will to His will.

Some modern theories of Christology seem to fall into this pitfall, as did the ancient Apollinarian doctrine. For example, Emil Brunner distinguishes between every man's empirical, historical personality, observable by introspection, on the one hand, and his hidden, ultimate ego, the *subject* and never the object of his observation, on the other. He then goes on to say that in Jesus the empirical self was human but the ultimate subject was God the Son. But in addition to the dubiousness of thus elevating into metaphysical entities the subject-self and object-self of epistemic analysis, Brunner's view encounters the irreconcilable Gospel accounts of Jesus' frequent praying to God. For obviously it was precisely Jesus as subject who prayed.[1]

Another theory attempting to avoid docetism while yet identifying Jesus with God fares little better on examination. I refer to the Kenotic Theory, which attempts to develop Paul's words in Philippians 2:5-7 into a literal and complete Christology. According to this view, when the eternal God became incarnate on earth he "emptied himself" (ἑαυτὸν ἐκένωσεν) of all the attributes which essentially distinguish God from men. Hence God lived on earth without His infinite power, knowledge and space-transcendence (omnipresence). But Baillie's criticism is quite decisive as he points out that on this view there was, during Jesus' lifetime, a complete and crude separation of the Persons of the Trinity, with God the Son actually (or else in dramatic, deceptive pretense) stepping out of the Godhead and ceasing to be divine but later turning into God again. Such a view is neither orthodox nor more plausible than the mythological theophanies of paganism.[2]

2. Explanation As a Religious Genius and Saint

At the opposite extreme from the docetic views is the common notion that Jesus is to be explained simply and exclusively as a man of unusual religious insights into the nature of God and man, who with high purpose devoted his great powers to the teaching and healing of men until his unswerving loyalty to his ideals led him to martyrdom. If this doctrine were true, then the Gospel would not be gospel ("good tidings of God"). The story of Jesus would show what a heroically good life a man could lead, and that would be highly significant. But it would not be good news of God, the news we need most of all to hear, nor the word on which the church has been built.

Moreover, we could not accept Jesus, the religious genius and saint, as our example and guide without going further. For it is he himself who continually turns attention from his power to God's power, his limited knowledge to God's perfect knowledge, from his subordinate will to God's supreme will. If we are to imitate the man Jesus and take his teaching seriously, then we must first of all see in him not so much the good man, though he is that, as the working of God's power and purpose.

3. Substituting Other Problems for This One

Occasionally, and with increasing frequency of late, theologians have sought to substitute for doctrine about Jesus an account of the faith of the early church

[1] See Emil Brunner, *The Mediator*, and also D. M. Baillie's conclusive criticism in *God Was in Christ*, pp. 88-90.

[2] Cf. Swami Akhilananda, *A Hindu View of Christ*, where Jesus is held to be God in a theophany similar to others believed in by the Hindus of the Ramakrishna Society.

or a teaching about "the Christ of faith." Now surely no one should object to any truth being discovered and taught which any scholar can find out about the faith of the early church. Indeed, such discoveries have added greatly to our evidence concerning the very question now in hand, the question about Jesus. But this question is not answered by changing the subject.

An example is found in the thought of Rudolf Bultmann. This New Testament scholar and theologian tells us that our sources of information are so fragmentary, uncertain, and saturated with polemic doctrinal concerns that we can know scarcely anything about the historical life of Jesus. But he thinks this does not much matter, for the historical figure of Jesus is of no great interest. It can hardly be denied that Jesus provided the occasion for the faith of the church, or at least a part of that occasion.

> But neither in the earliest Church nor anywhere in the New Testament is Jesus looked back upon as a deed of God by which—as by Abraham, Moses or David—He showed "mercy" upon the People. Of course not! For Jesus' importance as Messiah—Son-of-Man lies not at all in what he did in the past, but entirely in what is expected of him for the future.[3]

Such a view can, of course, be maintained only by a very radical and highly selective criticism of the New Testament writings. Bultmann's *Formgeschichte* provides such criticism and in it his own theology seems often to be decisive in his dating and interpretation of the text. But even when he discusses the faith that the Jesus who had been crucified had risen again from the dead, he does not attempt to explain why this faith arose *concerning this one man Jesus*, rather than any other. How desperate are the lengths to which Bultmann's hypothesis drives him is shown by his writing concerning the faith of Paul:

> Paul is interested only in the fact that Jesus became man and lived on earth. *How* he was born or lived interests him only to the extent of knowing that Jesus was a definite, concrete man, a Jew, "being born in the likeness of man and being found in human form" (Phil. 2:7), "born of woman, born under the law" (Gal. 4:4). But beyond that Jesus' manner of life, his ministry, his personality, his character play no role at all; neither does Jesus' message.[4]

To most readers of the New Testament it seems undeniable that in the faith of the early church, Paul included, it was precisely the teachings, character and works of Jesus which first focused attention on his crucifixion. Could any carpenter, chosen at random, have drawn to himself such disciples and become the central figure in their faith? It is ironical that such men as Bultmann and Barth should especially identify their own faith with the faith of the

[3] *Theology of the New Testament* (tr. by Kendrick Grobel), p. 36.
[4] *Ibid.*, pp. 293–94.

ancient church and yet believe the central historical figure of that historical faith hardly worthy of serious historical study.[5]

On the other hand, if it be desired to distinguish between the historical Jesus and God as the creative Word revealed in him and to call the latter "the Christ of faith," no serious objection should be made. However, whatever may then be said about "the Christ of faith," there will still remain the question of Jesus, "But who do you say that I am?"

B. Elements to Be Included in Any Adequate Christological Reconstruction

If the doctrine of the person of Jesus Christ is to be even approximately intelligible as an explanation of the data at hand, it must take account both of his thoroughgoing humanity and of several factors not associated with any other human being.

1. *The Moral Authority of Jesus*

First is his unique moral authority. Millions of men and women, including many of the wisest and best, have confessed that in him they found the norm, inspiration and guide of their own lives. Christians of all the centuries would confess that they could compare their lives with their neighbors and remain complacent or even be reassured, but when, in imagination, they have placed themselves in his presence they have been driven to repentance and renewed moral aspiration. Other men of history may shame us in this or that particular aspect of life, but only Jesus has stood the test of being made the norm of life itself, from its very center.

2. *His Own Filial God-Consciousness*

Only by a method of Biblical criticism which judges the evidence by preconceived theory can we eliminate from the Gospels the records of a singularly clear, all-pervading sense of God's present love and power in the consciousness of Jesus. This filial consciousness gave to him such a sure confidence in his vocation and the divine authority of his teachings and acts as to be without historical parallel and yet without arrogance, narrowness nor claim of immunity from the greatest hardships of life.

3. *His Wisdom and Power*

The teachings of Jesus have long provided and do still afford such suggestive insights into the relationships of human beings with one another and with God as to be unmatched. But he did not stop with teaching. He also performed many acts of healing which showed a strange and wonderful power over the

[5] See Karl Barth, *The Doctrine of the Word of God* (tr. by G. T. Thompson), p. 188.

sin-ridden, despairing souls and sick bodies of men. Granting that the oral traditions transmitted by his enthusiastic followers must have added considerably to the stories of his "mighty works," his reputation is still extremely impressive. Moreover, the maladies reported as healed by him are preponderantly of the psychosomatic type in which the impact of a powerful personality, combining deepest understanding and sympathy with utmost confidence and authority, might be expected to have most dramatic influence. The record is the more impressive because it is apparent that the narrators had not the remotest idea of any explanation other than the attributing of this mysterious power to God, and yet, in contrast to the usual legends of past wonder-working heroes, stressed precisely the kinds of miracles which best conform both to the portrait of his character and to what we have learned about faith healings.

4. Other Men's Finding of God in Him

In the New Testament we have the writings of a number of men of high ability and sensitive discrimination who were alike in believing that Jesus was the supreme revelation of God. It does not suffice to say that these records were the deposit of faith rather than the statement of historical truth. They purport to be both. But if we take them as simply the testimony of faith we have still to face the question why there should have been such faith in the minds of those persons, centered in that one carpenter and obviously a powerful creative force within a generation of his own lifetime. If this faith were so prejudiced in his favor he must have made it so.

Moreover, this particular faith, the faith in Jesus Christ as the Son of God, had from the beginning a cleansing, creative power unparalleled in all the world. Drawing men and women of many tribes and classes, it fused them together into a close-knit community of mutual sharing, unconquerable courage and self-disciplined purity never seen before. Nearly two thousand years later the lifting and cleansing power of this faith has survived every kind of savage and subtle attack from without the church and the most perfidious betrayal from within and yet rises again and again with undiminished strength.

Any Christology to be true must be in accordance with these elements of truth from the life and historical influence of Jesus.

C. Toward Solution of the Christological Problem

It is easier to point out the inadequacies of other views on a difficult, complex problem than to set forth a constructive proposal for solution. In this instance one might plead that unless and until we can better explain our own personalities and our relations with one another, to say nothing of knowing more about God, we should not be expected to explain the relation between the Jesus of long ago and the God whose being is still so shrouded in mystery. That plea is true, if we are asked for a complete and finally satisfying explanation.

Yet no one who has once confronted seriously the question, "But who do you say that I am?" can leave it so easily unless he turns his back on Christ himself. And surely the theologian, dedicated to the discovery, organization and defense of truth implied in the experience of the Christian community, has no right to beg leave from the drawing of some inferences concerning the church's emphatic faith in Christ as the Son of God.

1. Preparation and Calling by God

The first part of the story of Jesus concerns God. The Gospel of Christ, like the story of creation, starts with "In the beginning. . . ." At the beginning, the Gospel, too, finds God's Word, "Let there be light!" going forth in creative initiative.[6]

At the start of every human life is God. However dark and perplexing are the historical circumstances of a child's birth, however veiled in mystery is the divine purpose, there *is* such a purpose to the fulfillment of which that life is summoned. Not one lost coin of earth's human resources, not one wandering sheep, not one rebellious, wayward boy is outside the Father's plan. Otherwise He would not be the Father, the God in whom our reasonable faith is fixed.

With every vocational plan for which God prepares a human child and to which God calls him, the Father prepares in some time and manner the strength to fulfill that holy calling. But though providing the initial resources, He calls; He does not compel. Whether the vocation is fulfilled or not depends on the response of the child of God who is called.

While everyone is called to take a special, individual place in God's kingdom, Jesus was called to reveal to men the kingdom itself. He was not only to perform a particular task in one time and place and for certain people around him—though he did that as a carpenter of Nazareth and as friend and minister to certain individuals. He was also to perform the universal task for all peoples who were yet to be in any age or nation, the task of living the total purpose and meaning of the reign of God. Jesus was called to be not only, before God, subject to that reign, but also to be, before men, Lord of the kingdom. He was to show in word and life the purpose, spirit and power of God issuing forth in human life. He was thus not only to *teach*, but to *be* the highest of all teachings. He was not only to heal but to be the norm of true health. He was not only to lead in worship but to show in his own person, as no words nor ritual nor any impersonal symbol could possibly show, Him who is alone worthy of

[6] See Jn. 1:9.

worship. He was not only to *speak* words concerning God, but to *be* the Word spoken of God.

For this sacred career God prepared through other men called to other tasks before him—through priests and prophets, psalmists and apocalyptists. These men were not solely preparing for him. They had their own special places to fill in the life of their people and in the purpose of God. But a part of the meaning of their lives was to prepare for him.

In the fullness of time, God provided for his coming as the child of righteous parents through whom he was richly endowed and by whom he was wisely nurtured in the knowledge, obedience and love of God. Included in this divinely planned endowment was the capacity for that unique filial consciousness of God which we noted earlier.[7]

2. *Faithfulness through Growing Understanding*

We must not suppose that at first Jesus had any notion of this mission to which God called him. He grew from infancy into boyhood and youth, playing with his friends, studying the lessons which every well-reared Jewish boy must learn, doing errands for Mary and helping Joseph in the carpenter shop. As his understanding of God's way with men widened and he was confronted by harder and harder duties, he was remarkably faithful. As God saw how steadfastly he performed the ever more exacting tasks He set before him, His confidence and delight in him increased. What else could be the meaning of that word, "Jesus increased in wisdom . . . and in favor with God . . ."?

Although more learning led to more exacting ideals and duties, this boy of Nazareth eagerly sought to increase his knowledge. When Joseph and the wisest teachers in the local synagogue were unable to answer his questions he stored them up in the hope of having them answered by the teachers in the Temple when he went to Jerusalem with his parents for the annual Passover. Yet after the exciting pleasure of conversation with these wise men of his nation, he returned to Galilee with his parents "and was obedient to them."[8]

Even when grown to maturity he seems not to have taken a prominent place in the synagogue of Nazareth, for when he returned later and read the Scripture there, with comment, his neighbors remembered him only as a local carpenter and were astonished at both the manner and content of his speech. For all the years until he was "about thirty years of age,"[9] he seems probably to have continued his work as a carpenter. But this we do not know with certainty, nor do we know why he did not attempt to teach during this early period of his manhood. Perhaps he had developed deep misgivings about the

[7] See above, p. 246.
[8] Lk. 2:51.
[9] Lk. 3:23.

traditional religion of his people and was thinking long thoughts not yet ready for expression. It may be, too, that the early death of Joseph had thrust upon the eldest son of Mary the heavy responsibilities of family support until his younger brothers could assume them. In any event, he bided his time, seeking to know more of God's will for him and faithfully fulfilling the duties he saw before him.

3. Response to God's Call in Maturity

Finally, there came the day when he joined his fiery relative, John the Baptist, who was preaching to crowds of people and baptizing the repentant in the Jordan River. It would be interesting to know whether John and Jesus had talked together before, as seems highly probable, and to what degree each had directly influenced the other's thought. Unfortunately for our curiosity, the records are silent.

But at the Jordan, culminating all the years of thought, prayer and faithful life, God showed to Jesus his high calling. Awed and perplexed, he went into the wilderness, from which John had emerged with his strong prophetic message. There, for many days of fasting, prayer and thought, he struggled with the problems and temptations which beset such a vocation. He faced there the temptation to seek minor personal advantage from God's favor and the temptation to call on God for a spectacular demonstration, which would give to him immediate, absolute assurance and at the same time public recognition. Then when it was clear to him that either of these courses of action would misrepresent God's way with men and so defeat the very purpose of his life, he confronted the temptation to betray his whole calling and substitute a worldly concern like that of other gifted leaders. All these tests of his devotion he successfully met. He emerged with serene, steadfast courage and the clarion call to pure love and assured faith which he was to sound throughout the land in the decisive months ahead.

4. Identity of Purpose with God

It is not to be supposed that after the wilderness experience Jesus shared the omniscience of God. We have already observed the decisive evidence that his knowledge was subject to quite human limitations. But he did understand and share the spirit and purpose of God's dealings with men. To that spirit and purpose he subordinated all of his own individual interests. Concerning the vast causal order and a great variety of technical truth he shared the knowledge and the limitations of his time. But subjecting his will to the now clearly revealed will of his Father, he valued what God valued, rejected the evils against which God warned and loved even the least and most unlikely persons as God loved them. His moral judgments were in accord with the judgments of God and his spirit conformed to his Father's righteous love.

He did not yet see all his own way clearly and in detail. Of his goal he was confident, but the means were to be found along the way and his faith must be continually renewed. Hence, he faced again and again the necessity of going out alone to think and pray. Probably he often had intimations, after the beheading of John the Baptist, that he, too, was to be put to a violent death. Yet when it confronted him so soon, at what seemed only the beginning of his work, his faith was put to the supreme test. In an agony of struggle, through prayer he was again the conqueror and in this final victory was perfected the fulfillment of his life's calling as Son of God.

In the days of his flesh, Jesus offered up prayers and supplications, with loud cries and tears, to him who was able to save him from death, and he was heard for his godly fear. Although he was a Son, he learned obedience through what he suffered; and being made perfect he became the source of eternal salvation to all who obey him.[10]

5. *The Word Made Flesh*

Because he understood the will of God toward men as no other had ever done and was perfectly faithful in the subjecting of his will to the Father's will, God was able to speak and act in mighty deed through him as through no other. For on the lips of all others the divine Word has been confused with the willful word of man and in the life of every other the image of God has been disfigured by human waywardness. For God to have put upon any such imperfect word and life the unqualified seal of His divine approval would have been to support evil as well as good and to confuse the thoughts of men. But in this one who so "learned obedience" that he was "made perfect," God spoke clearly with word and power and at last put upon him His final seal of authority through the resurrection.

However, there is another way in which the life of Jesus must be viewed. We have been speaking as if for the fulfillment of His purpose in Jesus, God was dependent upon the Galilean's faithful choices. That is true. But it is also true that Jesus was able to learn and know His Father's will only because, step by step, through human teachers and in the silence of long meditations in home, synagogue and wilderness, the Father taught him. Moreover, knowing the Father's will, he was able to do it only by the grace of God, ever-renewed in long hours of prayer. The initiating purpose, illumination, power and achievement of Jesus were all God's as the Master strove constantly to make clear.

[10] Heb. 5:7-8.

Perhaps we can see now and interpret in words of our own day the profound insight into the meaning of Christ which was expressed in the first chapter of John.

The Word or (in the Greek) Logos, of which we read here, conveys a wealth of thought contributed from two sources. In the philosophy of Philo Judaeus, an influential, older Jewish contemporary of Jesus, who drew deeply from Greek thought, the Logos was known as the rational, orderly meaning and structure of the world. But its source and essential being were beyond the world. It was prior to the world's existence an emanation from the eternal One, the mysterious and hidden God. On the other hand, in the ancient Scriptural tradition, the Word was God purposively issuing forth in creative, self-revealing action.

When the Evangelist writes, "In the beginning was the Word, and the Word was with God, and the Word was God," he is telling us that the rationale of all creation, the creative, revealing, purposive order was from the very beginning, not produced by emanation from God, not even eternal emanation, but with Him always. In fact, he is saying, it is of the very nature of God to be purposively creative and self-revealing. He is not a dark, purposeless mystery out of which the light of meaningful purpose comes. There is no distinguishing between His purposive, self-giving and Himself, for His meaningful, creative, self-giving purpose is Himself.

As the great prologue continues, "He was in the beginning with God," we must not be disturbed by the personal pronoun, with its seeming suggestion, in English, of a second personal being with God. For the masculine pronoun follows in the Greek because in that language "word" is a masculine noun. But in English we hesitate to say "It was" because we have just read that the Word *was* God, and we are not now to speak of God as an impersonal substance or abstraction. Yet we should hardly say, "God was in the beginning with God." But if we keep to the nouns in the place of which the pronouns stand, although the style suffers seriously, the meaning is conveyed without this confusing linguistic difficulty. We should then say, "The Word was in the beginning with God; all things were made through the Word, and without the Word was not anything made that was made." That is, all things were made by the meaningful, creative, self-giving, self-revealing purpose of God, and without that purpose nothing was made.

Continuing, we find that in this meaningful, self-giving divine purpose is the life and also the light of men. Of course that is true! For our life, like all existence, has its source in God's creative purpose, and all our quest for truth is, when rightly understood, the effort to discover how everything stands in the meaningful purpose of God.

At last comes the climactic interpretation of the incarnation: "And the Word became flesh and dwelt among us (and we beheld his glory, glory as of the only Son from the Father), full of grace and truth." [11] In Jesus we see what God purposed that man should be. It is such life, in loving, faithful obedience to Him and outgoing sharing with other persons, which was the very goal of creation. The innermost secret of the world's meaning is not to be found in astronomy nor in nuclear physics. All of this vast, complex spatial order of stars and electrons is subordinate to the supreme end of producing such persons as this. There are many truths, but he is "the truth." [12] Moreover, this is the person who is, to the end, in actuality as well as capacity, in God's "own image." In him, as we see the kind of person for whom God made all that was made, we see also all of the outgoing, self-giving attitude and purpose of God that can shine through one human life. Truer than any word of mouth ever spoken about God is this personal Word made flesh, lived in the life of the Galilean.

There is much more to be said, even in this volume, about the work Jesus has done for us, the work which God was doing through him, particularly at Calvary and in the resurrection. But before we leave the present chapter we must consider briefly two subsidiary problems likely to be raised about the Christological account which has been offered here.

6. *The Problem of God's Choosing Him from the Many*

Why, it may be asked, has not God chosen other persons to take the high place to which Jesus was called? Is there not here some unjust favoritism? Why did God wait so long before this supreme revelation? And why has He not called others since that time?

God may, for all we know, have called others before Jesus, others who faltered and failed to fulfill that hard vocation. But even the preparation for his work required the prior calling and response of many others, right down to Joseph and Mary and John the Baptist, in many kinds of specialized functions. It may be that never before had the other tasks been sufficiently well done in preparation so that God had the situation ready for his appearing. For only "when the time had fully come, God sent forth his Son." [13]

After him there could not be another to fulfill his mission. Many are called, it is true, to be "sons of God." [14] But even if someone after him were to be like Jesus in every possible respect, still that one would be unlike him in this all-important respect, that Jesus came first. It was through him that the way was

[11] Jn. 1:14. Though the words of rsv are used here, the Greek order is restored with the parentheses used in asv.

[12] Jn. 14:6.

[13] Gal. 4:4.

[14] Rom. 8:11. Cf. Jn. 1:12.

opened for others to be "heirs of God and fellow heirs with Christ." [15] Many are called to walk in that way, but only he is "*the pioneer* and perfecter of our faith." [16]

As to favoritism, it is an obvious fact that God does differently endow and call to different vocations the various ones of His children. Not everyone is endowed or called to be a Da Vinci or a Bach. Not everyone is equally endowed with Jesus for all-pervasive, filial God-consciousness. But Jesus himself, speaking of the comparative duties before God of those "who knew" and those "who did not know," said, "Every one to whom much is given, of him will much be required." [17] This principle of *noblesse oblige* is the great leveler. Let him who protests of Jesus' special privilege but recall the fastings and awful loneliness, the suffering and sorrow which the Master bore and ask, "Would I really like to take his place?" If so, then across the centuries there comes his voice speaking to the men who wanted to be next to him in glory, "Are you able to drink the cup that I drink?" [18] His privilege was the privilege of humble ministering and his glory the cross. Of crosses there are enough and to spare. But until we learn to *follow* more steadfastly we need not complain of not being "the pioneer."

7. *The Problem of Jesus' Faithful Fulfillment of God's Purpose*

But why, we may ask, was Jesus so faithful in his obedience to God's will as that will was shown to him? When we have so often failed in our much easier task of following him, at much less cost, why did he not fail?

It is answered that it is because God's grace empowered him. That must be true. But God is willing and eager also to empower us for the fulfillment of our vocations. Why did Jesus always respond to the offer, and despite every temptation and agony, persist in prayer until he could say, "Nevertheless, not my will but thine be done?"

Why, indeed, excepting that he chose so to do? Any other answer would make of his faithful obedience a pretense and a show. If he was not truly free and responsible in choosing obedience, then his temptations were no temptations and his perfection was the perfection of an impersonal puppet manipulated by God, not the perfection of a Son.

We rebel inwardly against such a solution. For we have not so faithfully chosen. We have thought we would be true and then we have sinned. We long for some solution of the problem Christ poses for us which would enable us to

[15] Rom. 8:17.
[16] Heb. 12:2.
[17] Lk. 12:48.
[18] Mk. 10:38.

say, "Yes, of course, God kept him true to his vocation, or He kept drawing him close in prayer where his strength was renewed; but I am only an ordinary man and cannot be expected to be perfectly true to my duty as he was true to his." But no such solution can be offered without denying the very honesty of Jesus and even of God.

Our problem is really the personal problem of our own sin. For that there is no theory about Jesus which can be offered as a solution. The only solution is for us to fall at his feet in repentance to God for our sin, acknowledge him as Lord and submit our wills anew to God whose glory we see in Christ.

CHAPTER 31

The Cross

A. CENTRALITY OF THE CROSS IN THE CHRISTIAN FAITH

WHEN the foes of Jesus were having him put to death by that crude and fiendishly cruel instrument of torture, the cross, they would have thought it utterly incredible that it was to become for vast numbers of people the supreme symbol of love, victory and God. Surely this is one of the strangest transmutations in history. For a cross would seem more naturally to represent hate, defeat and devilishness. It is true that the irony of this reversal is matched by the way in which the cross sometimes appears in elaborately carved, costly, glistening gold in churches which have quite forgotten its original offensiveness. But in rough wood or costly metal, the cross is by far the best-known symbol of the Christian faith.

The cross has been likewise a favorite subject of Christian art. Through painting, sculpture, architecture, poetry and music its story has been told, both in stark simplicity and with every conceivable embellishment.

From the earliest sermons of Simon Peter and Paul of Tarsus to the most recent appeals from the world's pulpits, the Cross has also been at the climax of preaching wherever the Christian gospel has gone. In ritual, too, its claims are portrayed, especially when the Mass is celebrated or worshipers bow in Holy Communion.

Not only on thousands of altars but in the very life of the church, the cross is at the center. Why is this so? What is the real significance of the crucifixion? To seek an answer to this question is one of the major tasks confronted by the theologian.

B. THE CROSS IN THE NEW TESTAMENT

1. In the Synoptic Gospels

The crucifixion of Jesus is narrated in all four Gospels and with greater circumstantial detail than is given concerning any other event. Moreover, the advance references to it in the reported predictions by Jesus and the subsequent allusions back to it tend all the more to focus attention upon it. However, in the Synoptic Gospels there is scarcely any teaching concerning what was to be or was accomplished by his passion and death. It is described as fulfillment of prophecy, it is implied at times that it is part of a divine plan which must not be interfered with and it is repeatedly linked closely with the resurrection. But beyond these simple ideas no doctrine is elaborated. Indeed, in one passage Jesus is recorded as referring to his own death simply as the perishing of "a prophet." [1] Jesus himself is described as plunged into deep struggle by the prospect of his death, as condemning the tempting suggestion that it can be avoided and as finally accepting death in obedience to God's will.[2] But if his thought penetrated further into an understanding of the specific way in which his death was to serve God's purpose, the Synoptic Gospels are strangely silent about it.

2. In the Pauline Letters

The earliest recorded explicit interpretations of the good accomplished by the crucifixion of Christ are in Paul's letters. Moreover, Paul concentrates more attention upon the meaning of the cross than does any other New Testament writer, excepting, possibly, the author of the Letter to the Hebrews.

It is apparent that the cross was at first a stumbling block to Paul as he later spoke of its being generally to the Jews.[3] Before Paul's conversion the Christian faith must have seemed to him disgustingly offensive. Here were many Jews so foolish as to think that a wandering prophet, finally crucified, had actually been the Messiah to whose coming they had long looked for the liberation of Israel. Was it not perfectly evident that he had not even tried to free his people and that whatever it was he had attempted had been a failure? After all, his public work had only begun when he had been convicted and crucified. It was evident enough that God's favor was not upon *him*!

This strange foolishness, so obviously contrary to good sense, patriotism and sound religion, would seem easy enough to stamp out. But under persecution the madness grew stronger. Not only did its numbers increase but its adherents showed a remarkable courage and joy which there was no explaining. Persecuting these people, Paul (or "Saul") must have felt strangely futile, and especially at the stoning of Stephen, who seemed to have a lordly and gentle spirit not of earth. For the time being Paul persisted doggedly in his course. Then came the vision on the Damascus road in which the living Jesus appeared in transfigured glory, saying significantly, "Saul, Saul, why do you persecute me?

---

[1] Lk. 13:33. For typical references to the death of Jesus by himself in the Synoptic Gospels, see Mk. 8:31; 10:32–34; 14:8, 21, 27; Mt. 20:17–19; 26:1–2; 26:31–32; Lk. 9:44. Cf. the sermon of Peter in Acts 3:13–21, where salvation by faith in the name of Jesus is preached, but no particular efficacy is attributed to his death, unless as preparation for his resurrection.

[2] See Mk. 8:31 and 14:32–34. [3] I Cor. 1:22–25. Cf. v. 18; also Gal. 5:11.

It is hard on you to kick against goads." [4] That was the end of his persecuting and the beginning of his service to the Master. It was also the beginning of a new mental struggle over the meaning of that strange crucifixion.

The Nazarene was God's chosen one after all. Of that Paul was now thoroughly convinced. But why, then, had God permitted him to be crucified? Plainly this was no mere doing of men. It was part of a divine strategem putting to naught the sinful devices of human wise men. The resurrection showed that men had not been able to defeat Jesus. His death was, then, a mighty portent, a profound revelation, a mysterious work of God. But what had it accomplished?

The solution at which Paul arrived was that Christ had been substituted for sinful men. All sinners, that is all human beings excepting Jesus, had been doomed, under the Law, to suffering and death. But the sinless Christ, sent from God to save His people, suffered and died in their place and so reconciled men with God. Hence, as God raised him from the dead He granted to all who would have faith in him the gift of victorious everlasting life as "heirs of God and fellow heirs with Christ." [5]

Paul does not go further to explain why sin must be expiated in death or why the death of "one man Jesus Christ" [6] should have been an effective substitute for the death of all men. He affirms his conviction "that one has died for all; therefore all have died," [7] but the conclusion hardly follows from the one premise given and he supplies no explanation.

3. In the Letter to the Hebrews

In the Letter to the Hebrews the theme of Christ's death as the expiation of men's sins is taken up again but placed in the setting of the ancient sacrificial system. The author reminds his readers of the many purification rites in which blood has been used. As one example he cites the ceremonies in which Moses "sprinkled with the blood both the tent and all the vessels used in worship." Then he sums up with the statement, "Indeed, under the law almost everything is purified with blood, and without the shedding of blood there is no forgiveness of sins.[8] But Christ has now come to complete and end the whole system of priestly sacrifices by sacrificing himself "once for all." [9] The same conception is implied in the title "Lamb of God," used in the fourth Gospel and in the many references to "the Lamb" and "the blood of the Lamb" in the Revelation.[10]

---

[4] Acts 26:14, with the RSV reading slightly altered. The Greek reads "σκληρόν σοι πρὸς κέντρα λακτίζειν."
[5] Rom. 8:17. Cf. 6:5–8; 3:23–26; 2 Cor. 5:14–15; Gal. 2:19–20.
[6] Rom. 5:17.   [7] 2 Cor. 5:14.   [8] Heb. 9:21–22.
[9] Heb. 8:25–26.   [10] See Jn. 1:29, 36; Rev. 5:6, 8, 12; 7:14; 12:11. Cf. 1 Pet. 1:19.

But nowhere in the New Testament is there any explanation or defense of the assumptions underlying the sacrificial system. To us, reared in radically different traditions, it does not seem at all apparent that blood is a cleansing agent and the very idea of slaughtering animals in a service of worship is repulsive. Hence, the description of Christ as a substitute for the bloody sacrificial offerings of old now seems at best a quaint and alien figure of speech having no real interpretive value, while at worst it seems to imply acceptance of superstitious and unworthy notions. When approached with historical perspective and sympathy, the analogy may be taken to express the idea that sin is an exceedingly grave matter which can be neither tolerated nor overcome without great cost. But other expressions of this important truth would be clearer and more appealing to modern minds.[11]

4. In the Johannine Literature

In the Johannine writings there is even less of a developed theory concerning the cross. The death of Jesus is there represented, in conjunction with his total life, as the supreme expression of God's love and it is taught that by belief in Christ sinners are saved from sin and given eternal life.[12] Jesus is referred to as "the Lamb of God, who takes away the sin of the world," [13] but the idea is not elaborated and no further explanation of the way in which the cross saves men from sin is attempted.

5. Problem for Later Theologians

It is evident that the New Testament writers do not give us a systematic doctrine of atonement. In their various ways they do testify to the experience of the first Christians. That testimony to experience has much more importance for the discovery of the truth concerning the cross than have the partial explanations and analogies which the ancient writers provide. From the beginning, even without a developed theory about the cross, many men accepted the crucified and risen Jesus as the Son of God, supreme revelation of the Father and of the true way of life for men. Having accepted him thus, they experienced a release from the guilt of sin and the fear of death, with a new eruption of love and joy, which changed all of life. The whole New Testament and the existence of the church which produced it are testimonies to this cleansing and creative experience. It was natural that some of the more thoughtful beneficiaries of it should have sought for satisfactory explanations and used their interpre-

[11] For an able effort to defend the sacrificial theory, "freed from all unworthy and pagan associations" (p. 185), as the normative doctrine of the cross and the rightful basis of public worship, see Vincent Taylor, *The Atonement in New Testament Teaching* (2nd ed. London: Epworth Press, 1945).

[12] Jn. 3:14-17. Cf. v. 36; also 17:1-2; 1 Jn. 4:7-12.

[13] Jn. 1:29.

tative accounts to help reproduce in others the faith which had brought new life to themselves. It was also to be expected that later generations of Christians would develop other interpretations. These were needed to deal with questions raised but not answered by the first accounts. They were needed also to place the power of the cross in frames of reference more intelligible and acceptable in later times than the traditional assumptions of Jewish Christians in the first century could possibly be.

C. Types of Theological Interpretation

There have been almost innumerable theories concerning the efficacy of the cross. But they can be fairly well classified as belonging to three types, each characteristic of, though not exclusively dominating, a different period in the Christian era.

1. *Dualistic Doctrines*

After the Apostolic Age, the first kind of theory to develop represented the cross as a means by which God overcame the power of Satan. Such views may be regarded as elaborations of the words attributed to Jesus himself in Mark 10:45: "For the Son of man also came not to be served but to serve, and to give his life as a ransom for many." The Gospel does not suggest to whom such a ransom could be paid. Neither does Paul when he writes, "You are not your own; you were bought with a price." [14] But if the idea of Christ's death as payment of a ransom was to be elaborated into a theological theory, what other answer could have been given than that the recipient of the ransom was Satan? Who else could have been regarded as holding sinful men in bondage and as ready to take delight in the death of the Son of God? This was precisely the view which dominated theological interpretation of the cross from the second to the eleventh centuries.

If it seems a little incongruous to think of the almighty Creator as paying a ransom to one of His creatures, a fallen angel, for the release of His lesser rebellious subjects from bondage, that is not the only difficulty which the theory confronts. For to this implication of divine weakness must be added a further implication of moral compromise. It was obvious to defenders of the ransom theory that the resurrection of Jesus had the effect of canceling and more than canceling the ransom price. Hence, God was regarded as having deceived the great deceiver.[15] When this teaching appeared to bring the character of God into question, it was later claimed that the deception was actually accomplished by Satan himself. But since the work of the cross was still re-

---

[14] 1 Cor. 6:19–20. Cf. 7:23.
[15] This view was developed by Gregory of Nyssa.

garded as within the purpose of God this apologetic device can hardly be considered successful. Even more crude seem the representations of Christ as a fishhook (his divine nature) baited with his mortal human nature which the devil seized upon to his sorrow.[16]

The presuppositions of such views, representing a personal devil as source of all evil and fallen men as having passed from the control of God into his nefarious mastery, to be released only by divine bargaining or deception, are so dualistic and represent such an uncritical and incomplete form of theism as to be clearly dated and worthy only of historical consideration.

Yet there is one idea underlying these crude dualistic theories which does commend itself as true. They do rightly recognize that it is human involvement in sin which is the one real barrier in the way of our reconciliation to God. It is not some unwillingness in God—however plausibly explained—but the hold of sin upon men which needs to be changed. This idea, purged of metaphysically dualistic and demonological representation, must be brought to the fore in any adequate view of the cross or of our salvation.

2. Doctrines of Substitutionary Atonement

The second type of theory concerning the cross is now frequently spoken of as the "classic," traditional or orthodox view, but it was not developed until the eleventh century.[17] It was formulated by Anselm in his famous *Cur Deus Homo.*

According to Anselm's doctrine, the work of the cross has to do solely with the relationship between men and God. Satan has no part in the transaction. Sin, it is said, is a dishonoring of God, and this injury to His honor must somehow be requited. Satisfaction must be provided before men can be reconciled to their Maker. But the gravity of an offense, hence the magnitude of satisfaction required, is proportionate to the rightful honor of the one who has been dishonored. The honor of God is infinite, so the satisfaction must likewise be infinite. Infinite satisfaction is impossible for finite men, so as far as their own powers are concerned they face an endless and inescapable estrangement from God. But God in His infinite love assumed human nature and this God-Man by his death rendered for man the infinite satisfaction required.

Similar ideas of substitutionary atonement have been formulated also in somewhat different frames of reference. Thus, instead of the feudal notion of lordly "honor," the penal theory stressed by most of the early Reformers[18]

---

[16] See Martin Luther, *Works* (Weimar ed.), XX.334–35.

[17] This is one reason why Gustaf Aulén seeks to reserve the title of "classic" to the ancient dualistic view, which, in more refined form, he defends as true. See his *Christus Victor.*

[18] But concerning Luther see G. Aulén, *Christus Victor,* pp. 119–44.

appeals to the idea of abstract, even-handed justice. As seen in this setting, a wrong requires expiation, not necessarily by satisfaction to the person wronged, but by the suffering of an appropriate legal punishment by the wrongdoer. Human sinners could never finish suffering the appropriate penalty for their sin against God. Their plight would be forever hopeless, were it not for the fact that God, by becoming man and dying on the cross, assumed the punishment due to men in order that men might be free to return to Him.

A modification of the penal theory is the *governmental* theory formulated by Hugo Grotius.[19] Setting out to defend the penal doctrine, Grotius actually interpreted it in such a way as to change its ultimate basis. The final appeal of the penal theory, as formerly stated, had been to an abstractly conceived even-handed justice. Grotius, on the other hand, argues that God is primarily concerned with the well-being of all his subjects. He loves them and so desires to forgive them their sins and reconcile all to Himself. But if He simply forgives, they will see that sin is no barrier to a harmonious relationship with Him. Hence, they will think that sin is of little importance. Therefore, God gave His Son to die as a substitutionary recipient of the punishment deserved by sinful men. In this way He gave such an example of the penalty of sin as to impress upon men its awful meaning and consequences. Having set before us this example, He now forgives us without the danger of our accepting the pardon associated with the cross as an easy thing to be presumed upon in further sin.

The governmental theory avoids the ethically indefensible notions implied in appeals to divine honor or an abstract principle of justice really derived from the sub-Christian *lex talionis*. But it shares with the other forms of substitutionary doctrine the idea that it would be just to place upon one innocent person *punishment* regarded as deserved by others. Though it escapes the untenable implication of the Anselmian and penal theories that *guilt* can be assumed by one person for another as a financial debt can be, it is doubtful that the governmental theory succeeds in showing how the death of Christ actually demonstrates the inviolability of the divine moral law. We may well consider the critical questions asked by Knudson:

Does the death of Christ, when viewed as the suffering of an innocent person in place of transgressors, really set the moral law on high? Does it really reveal God's hatred of sin and love for sinners? Does it not, rather, when treated as a mere penal example, "argue a blindness or indifference to moral distinctions which would be a source of terror rather than of confidence"? [20]

[19] See his *Defensio Fidei Catholicae de Satisfactione Christi adversus Faustum Socinium*, published in 1617.

[20] *The Doctrine of Redemption*, p. 368. The words quoted by Knudson are from Borden P. Bowne, *Studies in Christianity*, p. 133.

When, in Charles Dickens' *Tale of Two Cities*, Sidney Carton impersonates his condemned friend and goes to the guillotine in his place, the reader applauds his heroic sacrifice. But such a substitution is possible only when the court and the executioner are blind or indifferent to the real identity of the victim. According to the governmental theory, as in the other substitutionary views, it is God who is regarded as decreeing the punishment and accepting the substitute. Such a view may morally exalt the Christ who died, but it cannot escape the attributing of an unethical personal indifference to the God who decrees the death. For, as Knudson says, "an innocent person may suffer because of the sins of others but he cannot justly be *punished* for their sins." [21]

On the other hand, if the cross be regarded as the expression of a love which bore the suffering inflicted *by* sin in order to show to men both the gravity of sin and the love of God, then the substitutionary theories have been left behind and a form of *moral* theory proposed.

3. Moral Theories

A moral theory was first proposed and elaborated in the thought of Abelard, a younger contemporary of Anselm. Abelard put aside all notions that the cross was either a transaction with Satan or a device for trapping him. Likewise he refused to believe that the crucifixion of Christ was a substitutionary punishment for the sins of men required by the honor or justice of God. The one and only obstacle to men's reconciliation he saw to be human sinfulness. God was eager and free to forgive and receive all His children in love. But their unwilling and disobedient wills prevented their fellowship with Him. If only these rebellious wills could be brought to true repentance so that men could, in gratitude to God, respond to His love, reconciliation would be accomplished, for He is ever eager to receive them.

Abelard, therefore, saw in the suffering and death of Christ the culminating revelation of God's love which illuminated the entire life of the Master. This love, so wonderfully embodied in Jesus' sacrifice, called forth from sinful men an answering love which brought them to repentance, the receiving of the Father's forgiveness and a glad obedience to His will.

One of the dangers always near at hand when the moral theories are accepted has shown itself clearly in the teaching of the Socinians and many other liberals from the sixteenth century onward. This is the reduction of the meaning of the cross to the contagious example of a courageous leader who was so loyal to the lofty faith which he taught as to die by torture rather than be false to it. The cross, on such a view, was not good news of *God*, but only showed *man* at his best. The Socinians did believe that the *Resurrection* of Jesus showed the love

[21] *Ibid.*, p. 369.

of God. But their interpretation of the *cross* would take from it the dimension of divine revelation which has been historically its great source of appeal. Moreover, although every instance of a heroic man's willingness to die in loyalty to his highest convictions is a lofty and inspiring event, there have been vast multitudes of such heroic sacrifices. The Socinian view hardly explains the unique cleansing and creative power which the cross of Christ has exerted.

The basic theme of Abelard's theory is central in the thought of many modern theologians concerning the cross, from Schleiermacher and Ritschl to H. Rashdall, Knudson and Walter M. Horton. It is noteworthy that it is also exceedingly influential as a persuasive component in the teaching of other men who avoid explicit espousal of it or even avow their support of other views usually regarded as contrary to it. Examples are to be found in the work of James Denney,[22] F. W. Dillistone,[23] Vincent Taylor [24] and even Gustaf Aulén.[25]

It is not to be wondered at that this is true. The dualistic and substitutionary doctrines can hardly commend themselves to a modern mind engaged in a critical search for truth and not overawed by tradition. They depend too much on demonological, metaphysical, social and juridical ideas which seemed plausible at some periods in history but will not now bear critical examination. On the other hand, they put too little stress on the specifically personal and ethical categories which are most relevant to a problem of reconciliation. However, if a basically moral view is developed to its full possibilities it will be seen to include a number of the truths and religious values which have been most cherished in the older theories. Here we can only suggest the general outline of such a development.

D. The Cross As Reconciling Men to God

The idea of reconciliation has taken on continually richer connotation in recent times, due to such varied experiences as those of mediation in international and industrial disputes, of marital counseling and of psychiatry. The word "atonement," on the other hand, has tended to be narrowed so that its original meaning of agreement, concord or reconciliation (at-one-ment) has for the most part given way to the idea of reparation for injury. "Atonement" is therefore a better name for Anselm's doctrine than for any other. A view

---

[22] *The Death of Christ, The Atonement and the Modern Mind* and *The Christian Doctrine of Reconciliation*.

[23] *The Significance of the Cross.*

[24] *The Atonement in New Testament Teaching.* See, e.g., pp. 191, 194–96. But cf. p. 204.

[25] *Christus Victor.* Aulén is particularly hostile to the moral or "subjective" theories. Yet in his own reconstruction of the ancient "classic," "dualistic" or "dramatic" (p. 20) view, he adopts the principal "subjective" criticisms both of the Anselmian doctrine and also of the forms in which the dualistic idea was formerly expressed. (See, e.g., p. 175.) Moreover, he insists that the atonement "includes both objective and subjective elements." See *The Faith of the Christian Church,* pp. 240–41.

stressing change in personal attitudes and relations would seem to be better designated as a doctrine of reconciliation. This title has the additional advantage of employing the nearest English equivalent of a New Testament term employed several times in this connection.[26]

1. God's Love Revealed

Christians have rightly seen in the crucifixion of Christ not only a manifestation of human loyalty, courage and loving sacrifice, but also a revelation of God's love. For the acceptance of the cross by Jesus was the climactic expression of his whole life which reflected so marvelously the character and purpose of God Himself. Moreover, God was more immediately involved. This man who was despised, condemned, tortured and killed by sinful men represented the Father's own will as no other had ever done. In condemning Jesus, men were also condemning the purpose of God. How would God respond to this clearest, most unequivocal outburst of human rebellion? It is His own purpose which has guided His faithful Son and brought him into this suffering. Now what will the Father do? Will He send lightning or earthquake to destroy the wretched sinners who have presumed to attack His Son? Not if He is truly the Father who has been faithfully represented by the teaching and life of Jesus. If He is such a Father He may send an ominous darkness over Calvary which men will later recall as the symbol of His withholding the power He possessed to stop or punish them. But He will not contradict the love revealed through Christ by striking down the sinners in wrathful power. He will wait behind the shadows, suffering in such agony as might be guessed at by a human parent who has been compelled to stand by while his child is tortured to death, but such as only the God who is perfect in understanding love and who loves the torturers too can fully know. He will let sin have its way that sinners may know its meaning through to its fulfillment and that they may learn also the love of God.

For many centuries Christians have hesitated to say that God suffered. It was said that His Son suffered and some who held that doctrine asserted that the Son was Himself God. Yet they insisted that in this Son human nature was combined with the divine and it was only the human nature that suffered. To say that God suffered was to defend patripassionism, a dreadful heresy. It would, in truth, be quite intolerable to say that God Himself suffered immediate

---

[26] The noun καταλλαγὴ occurs in Rom. 5:11; 11:15; 2 Cor. 5:18, 19. The verb καταλλάσσω appears in Rom. 5:10; 1 Cor. 7:11; 2 Cor. 5:18, 19, 20. There is no Greek word in the New Testament properly translated by "atonement" or "atone" in the modern sense of those words. Indeed, even in AV, the word "atonement" appears only once, viz. in Rom. 5:11 and then with the marginal reading "reconciliation." In the preceding verse, AV twice reads "reconciled" for the corresponding verb.

physical pain. For "God is a spirit." But we should be truer to the Scriptural conception of God if we affirmed that God does indeed suffer, just as Isaiah wrote, "In all their affliction he was afflicted." [27] For "God is love" and love suffers with the suffering beloved. Indeed, it "bears all things . . . endures all things." [28] To deny that God suffered with Jesus, both in his agony of death and in his anguish of soul for the men who slew him, is to deny that Father and Son actually knew such unity as Jesus reported. It is also to raise unanswerable questions about the real meaning of the saying that God loves.

When we say that God's love was revealed at Calvary and that He suffered with Christ, we are not denying that His love is manifest in any other life nor that He suffers with every sufferer and for every sinner. Rather we are affirming these things. But we learned them from Calvary.

2. God's Power over Death Revealed

An inextricable part of the Biblical story of the cross is the Resurrection. It is also an essential part of Christ's redemptive work.

To achieve a single historical account of the Resurrection consistent with all the narratives seems quite impossible. All the Gospel writers, Paul and other New Testament authors bear witness to it, but many details are divergent. Indeed, it is evident that the earliest accounts were testimonies to experiences which would not fit into the categories of our common life and communication. All agree that Jesus, who had died and whose lifeless body had been placed in a tomb, again confronted the disciples in regnant power and authority. This experience was not an inference or speculation but an immediate perception which swept all their doubts and fears away and gave to them such conviction, joy and courage as nothing could ever dim. Their deeds, as well as their words, bore eloquent witness to all this as long as they lived on earth.

The narratives we have attest to the inescapable reality of the risen Jesus by telling of the empty tomb, his visible body and his audible words. Yet there is an air of indefinable mystery about it all. For closed doors were no barrier to him and although he was clearly seen and heard, standing, walking, sitting and conversing with them, even those who knew him best could not at first recognize him. Having no other experience of a living person so immediate and indubitable excepting the observation of an ordinary man in the flesh, they described him so, yet always with overtones indicating that this was only an analogous and inadequate mode of description. The task of describing an event so unique defied even the best efforts to put it in words. But though beyond all their powers to narrate, these encounters with the living Jesus, victorious even over death, were to the disciples real beyond all doubt.

[27] Is. 63:9.   [28] 1 Cor. 13:7.

The conviction in the lives of those first witnesses has been communicated through their preaching, the writings of the New Testament and the very life of the church itself, with its ever-renewed testimony of the Holy Spirit, to the community of believers down to the present day. Above all else, this Easter faith guarantees to us the power and purpose of God to conquer every obstacle and make us victors over both sin and death.

3. Men Brought to Repentance

The effective barrier to reconciliation is *sin*. It is because of sin that the need for a restored fellowship exists, and only when sin is renounced and annulled is the fellowship possible.[29]

But if sin is to be renounced, repented of and forgiven, two conditions which must be fulfilled are these: the sinner must condemn his sin and he must have hope. He will not renounce his sin if he sees no wrong in it or if he sees insufficient evil in it to counterbalance its attractions. But however much he may loathe it he will not repent unless he has hope of forgiveness and catches the vision of a victorious life.

These conditions are met at the cross. Here great numbers of men have seen as nowhere else the loathsome vileness of sin—just such sin as can be found in their own hearts. In the drama of Calvary they discover the enmity to God of such common human motives as greed, hatred, pride of position, hypocrisy, cowardice and self-centered expediency; for by these the Son of God was done to death.

But sinners find here also the love of God, the sublimity of loyal obedience to Him, and the victory which He gives even in defeat and death. So they are moved to place their hope in the Father, repent with faith and aspire to serve Him in obedient love.

4. The Guilt-sharing God

Dostoevski, in his famous novel, *Crime and Punishment,* portrays a murderer carrying a great burden of guilt which presses him to the very brink of suicidal despair. Yet he is unable to confess to anyone. No one could possibly understand. His anxiety and self-loathing continue to mount until he befriends a poor girl who also has an awful load to bear because her father has sold her into a life of prostitution. But her faith in God has not quite been broken nor her longing for purity corrupted. The wretched murderer is finally convinced that the equally wretched prostitute can understand and sympathize with his frightful predicament. Confessing all to her, he is started on the road to faith, forgiveness and new life.

[29] Vincent Taylor, *op. cit.,* p. 191.

Guilt at its deeper levels must be shared before it can be purged. But one need not be a sinner to invite such sharing, if only to the depths of the soul one is truly the friend of sinners. Indeed, the cure cannot be complete until it is shared with a friend who stands firmly outside the treacherous quagmire of sin and yet is able to share through the most complete self-identification with the sinner. Now the gospel invites the sinner to see Christ on the cross praying for the forgiveness of his foes and beyond him to behold God who already loves all sinners and bears the shame of their guilt with his Son on the cross because they too are His children.

The sinner who becomes acquainted with the guilt-sharing God of Calvary knows that he is not alone. He is not a man whose sins and misery are of no concern to anyone. He knows that the supreme God of righteousness, the Judge of all men, cares for him. He knows that God seeks not to condemn him for his sin but to take from him the burden of his sin.

For God sent the Son into the world, not to condemn the world, but that the world might be saved through him.[30]

This is the heart of the gospel, the good news of God.

At Calvary God has used the very sins of men to reveal to sinners everywhere the despicable evil of sin and at the same time His own glorious love. This is the victory over the power of sin which has often been so crudely portrayed by the teaching that God bargained with or deceptively ensnared the devil. From the first century until now sinful men have experienced this breaking of the power of sin over their lives. Through being offended with their inadequate conceptual explanations and rude figures of speech we must not lose the priceless gem of the real victory to which they have testified.

We can see here also how easy it is to describe this experience as a substitutionary atonement. For as Jesus—and God—enter by deepest, understanding love into the sharing of the sinner's burden of guilt, this suffering of God and of His Son does ease the burden of the sinner and offer to him a way of release. His guilt relieved and his bonds broken, the new man may quite rightly say, but without any notion of a satisfied divine "honor" or legal or governmental requirement, that at Calvary he has seen a substitution made for the suffering and loss which he himself would have had otherwise to bear.

5. An Objective Reconciliation

If anyone should say that what is proposed is a "mere subjective" doctrine, that charge must be vigorously denied.

The term "subjective" suggests that the sinner has only come to *feel* different

[30] Jn. 3:17.

about his sin and his relation to God, so that he no longer *feels* guilty and lost. But that is far removed from the truth as we have interpreted it. The reconciled sinner not only *feels* different; he *is* different. His attitude toward his own sin is new. The dominant purpose of his life is new. Above all, his relationship to God is new. For the initiative of God's love has penetrated the barrier of his rebellious heart, incited him to repentance in faith and through forgiveness brought him into open fellowship with God.

Without all of these changes the sinner's restoration would be incomplete. But when they have occurred, reconciliation is a glorious, objective reality.

CHAPTER 32

The Holy Spirit

A. In the Scriptures

1. *Old Testament Teaching*

THERE is considerable teaching about the "Spirit of God" in the Old Testament which parallels fairly closely the accounts in the New Testament concerning the Holy Spirit. Even the term "Holy Spirit" is not unknown to the ancient Hebrew writers.[1]

In the Old Testament, the Spirit seems to be the power and illumination which God gives as He wills, or God Himself going forth among His people in anger or in mercy.

2. *The Holy Spirit and Jesus*

However, the Christian doctrine of the Holy Spirit developed from certain experiences and teachings specifically related to Jesus Christ. So intimate is this relationship that Paul appears at times to use synonymously the terms "Spirit of God," "mind of Christ," "Spirit of Jesus Christ" and "Christ." [2] The Holy Spirit, according to the New Testament, is continuer of the work of Jesus Christ after his departure from the earth, reminder of Jesus' teaching and sacrifice, guarantor of his authority and gift of power to fulfill his commands. Hence, it is fitting that the part of our study devoted specifically to "Christ and Reconciliation" should include the chapter on "The Holy Spirit."

3. *The Spirit As Personal*

In some passages, the Holy Spirit is clearly spoken of in personal terms. The connotation of personality, it is true, is somewhat exaggerated for readers of the familiar English translations because of the translators' conventional use of the personal pronoun "he" in references to the Holy Spirit. In the original Greek the usage varies. Since the Greek word for "Spirit" (πνεῦμα) is a neuter noun,

---

[1] E.g., see Is. 63:10–11.
[2] See, e.g., 1 Cor. 2:12–16; Eph. 3:14–17; Philip. 1:19. Once Paul says, "Now the Lord is the Spirit" (2 Cor. 3:17).

the grammatical form of pronominal reference to the Spirit is usually neuter also, but at times masculine nouns are used or the writers go out of the way to use masculine pronouns despite the neuter noun.[3] The thought of many references seems unmistakably personal.

It can hardly be denied that personal attributes are being implied when Jesus is recorded as telling his disciples that the Holy Spirit would teach them what to say when they were haled before the authorities.[4] Similarly, the Spirit as Paraclete (Comforter, Counselor, Advocate), promised repeatedly according to the fourth Gospel, is unequivocally represented as a personal agent.[5] Especially interesting is Paul's explicit likening of the divine Spirit to the introspecting spirit of a man.[6] It should be noted too that in this passage the Spirit is absolutely identified with God Himself and that this outright identification cannot be denied without destroying the logic of the argument.

4. The Spirit As Impersonal

Despite the attributions of personality which have been noted, and many others, at times the earliest Christian writers seem to think of the Holy Spirit as impersonal or as a mood or power of personality rather than as a person. Thus various persons are said by Luke to have been "full of the Holy Spirit" or "filled with the Holy Spirit." [7] The Spirit is regarded as something imparted by one person to another by baptism or the laying on of hands or by breathing.[8] In such passages the thought appears to be that the Holy Spirit is a gift of illumination, power or grace from God, rather than God Himself, the giver.[9]

5. Not Theology but Testimony

These apparent contradictions are not due to failing efforts at theological consistency, but result rather from preoccupation with experiential testimony by men innocent of the problems which beset later theologians. When members of the Christian community found themselves divinely gifted with a strange and marvelous personal power, they spoke gratefully of having received the Holy Spirit. But the exact reference of the term varied. Sometimes it referred to the experienced power, sometimes to God who gave this empowering guarantee of His favor. If the attempt is made to weave the words of testimony into a systematic doctrine, confusion and self-contradiction are sure to result. But

[3] See, e.g., Jn. 14:26 and Eph. 1:14.
[4] Lk. 12:11–12. Cf. Mk. 13:11.
[5] See Jn. 14:16–17, 26; 15:26; 16:7–15. Cf. 2 Cor. 1:3–7.
[6] 1 Cor. 2:10–12.
[7] E.g., see Lk. 1:15, 41, 67; 4:1; Acts 2:4; 4:31; 6:3, 5; 9:17.
[8] E.g., see Acts 1:5; 8:14–20; Jn. 20:22.
[9] Cf. 2 Cor. 5:5.

there is no essential disagreement in these passages regarding the reality to which witness was being given. Men and women who were performing wonders of which they had never before been capable and experiencing an unprecedented assurance, joy and fullness of life, gratefully gave the praise to God who had given to them these marvelous experiences. Their using the term "Spirit" to denote now the gift, now the giving and then the Giver does not diminish the importance nor the consistency of the witness to the life-changing reality.

B. SIGNIFICANCE OF BELIEF IN THE HOLY SPIRIT

The doctrine of the Holy Spirit serves in Christendom to conserve and continually reassert a number of exceedingly important truths and religious values.

1. *Warning against Mere Historicism*

Ours is a historical religion. It stresses the acts of God in human history. The loss of this emphasis on history would mean the loss of the Christian faith as a living force.

But if this characteristic emphasis becomes a preoccupation, then, too, the church will lose its relevance and power in an ever-changing world. Against the peril of becoming a mere society for celebrating certain wonderful events of the past, the church's doctrine of the Holy Spirit stands as a perpetual safeguard. By this doctrine the church teaches that God is not only the one who once created the world and who long ago revealed Himself in wonderful ways to certain men and women. He is also our Supreme Contemporary. In the present and in every present He lives, speaks and acts on behalf of His children.

2. *Affirmation of a Growing Revelation*

In the Gospel According to John, Jesus is reported to have said to his disciples, "I have yet many things to say to you, but you cannot bear them now. When the Spirit of truth comes, he will guide you into all the truth." [10] The revelational climax in Jesus Christ was so important to the primitive Christian community that he might conceivably have been regarded not only as the Word of God made flesh but as the last word God would ever speak to men. Actually the dynamic impact of Jesus' life, the shock of his death and the wonder of the resurrection prevented his immediate disciples from adopting any such idea. They could not be true to his memory and live looking backward. But when the first impact of these events had passed, the church was tempted to fall into this or some other form of traditionalism. How real this temptation would soon

[10] Jn. 16:12–13. Cf. 14:25–26.

become is suggested by the announced purpose of Jude "to contend for the faith which was once for all delivered to the saints" [11] and the dire warnings of punishment, at the end of Revelation, to come not only upon anyone who "takes away from the words of the book of this prophecy," but first of all upon anyone who "adds to them." [12] That the peril has never ceased to this day is evident in the fact that many Christians and whole churches are frequently more concerned over guarding the most minute traditions against change than with seeking fresh understanding of God's purpose for them in their own age. Monuments are still raised to past prophets while some convenient stones are laid aside for throwing at anyone who dares to speak a prophetic word in the present.

The doctrine of the Holy Spirit is a guarantee within the ancient Christian tradition itself of every man's right and obligation to look beyond tradition. For there is always "new truth yet to break forth," not only through new study of the Bible, but also through other channels, from the God in whom is all truth and who speaks anew in every age. To close the mind is to deny the Holy Spirit.

In our own time this rejuvenating principle of our faith is especially relevant. We have not yet fully assimilated into our thinking the meaning of the scientific revolutions which have occurred in the last centuries and now a new world-wide social revolution is upon us. It is not enough in such a time to see what ancient men have said. Many ancient words carry the most basic and important implications for our time. But many problems, both theoretical and practical, which are urgent for us were not even confronted, much less solved, by any writers of earlier times. In such a time our hope is that the Holy Spirit will guide humble, truth-seeking men into new understanding and into new realization of the divine purpose.

3. Affirmation of the Divine Presence with Us

Paul was bearing testimony to his experience of the Holy Spirit, as well as arguing, according to his invariable custom, from presuppositions which he held in common with his hearers, when he said in the Areopagus, "Yet he is not far from each one of us, for 'In him we live and move and have our being.'" [13] Unlike Aratus, whom he quoted, he did not believe that we were any part of God. But like the Stoic poet he did believe that God "himself gives to all men life and breath and everything," [14] and he knew from experience that God could and did speak and act presently in and through the freely responsive souls of men.

[11] Jude 3.
[12] Rev. 22:18–19.
[13] Acts 17:28.
[14] Acts 17:25.

C. The Doctrine of the Trinity

It may be thought strange that this topic should be relegated to so subordinate a position as a section of the chapter on the Holy Spirit. But it should be noted that this is still to give a far greater prominence to the doctrine than it has in the Bible, where it is never mentioned. To be sure, the Father, the Son and the Holy Spirit are very frequently spoken of separately, often in pairs and rarely all together. But that is also true elsewhere in the present volume.

The doctrine of the Trinity rightly affirms that God the Father is the ground of all existence, all truth and all hope, that Jesus Christ the Son of God is His Word incarnate, and that the Holy Spirit is our present comforter, guide and enabling power. But the traditional formulas concerning the Trinity have, by making a metaphysical mystery of it, produced a vast amount of needless speculation which is today quite unprofitable to renew. The reader who wishes to pursue this speculation through all its intricacies can turn to the histories of doctrine. There he will see that historically it has been exceedingly important and has turned up much truth and good along the way, as well as no little absurdity and ungodly passion. But here we are concerned with the principal *truths* implied in the experience of the Christian community. The truth concerning the relations of the three "persons" in the Trinity seems far less complicated and difficult of discovery and formulation than most theologians of past centuries have believed.

Since the original root of the doctrine was in the experiences recorded in the New Testament, we must begin with the testimony to be found there.

1. Basis in the New Testament

In Matthew 28:19 occurs "the great commission"; "Go therefore and make disciples of all nations, baptizing them in the name of the Father and of the Son and of the Holy Spirit." Despite the doubts of Eusebius these words have good textual support and probably indicate an early use of a trinitarian baptismal formula. Yet there is nothing here to tell us whether the "three" were each and all God, three and yet one, much less any notion of "hypostases," "persons," "modes," "substance," "procession" or any of the other technically defined concepts which later became tests of trinitarian orthodoxy.

At least equally well known is Paul's benediction at the close of his Second Letter to the Corinthians: "The grace of the Lord Jesus Christ and the love of God and the fellowship of the Holy Spirit be with you all." [15] But these words would hardly be formulated by a self-conscious trinitarian. For if the doctrine of the Trinity were to be strictly represented, the word "Father" would need to

[15] 2 Cor. 13:14.

be substituted for the word "God." The wording actually employed seems to distinguish between God, on the one hand, and Jesus Christ and the Holy Spirit on the other, rather than to accord to each of the three the name "God," as traditional trinitarians have been careful to do. Moreover, "the Lord Jesus Christ," according to developed trinitarian thought, would be thought of as the incarnation of the second person rather than as simply being the second person. Finally, the personification of the Holy Spirit implied in the English translation is not implied in the Greek, for "fellowship" is a translation of the Greek *koinonia* and might mean a *sharing of* or *participation in* the Holy Spirit, instead of fellowship with the Holy Spirit.

There is no more real trinitarian *thought* than this recorded in the New Testament.[16]

This does not imply that there is not in the New Testament any proper ground for the later development of a trinitarian doctrine, much less that because such a doctrine is not explicitly taught in the Scriptures, it should not be believed. But apart from the events recorded in the New Testament there was no reason for altering in this way the austere monotheism of the Jews.

2. Concerns of the Church in Its Formulation

The primitive Christian community presupposed belief in the one true God, the Creator and Lawgiver known to the Hebrews and made known by them to many others throughout the Empire. The lives of the first Christians were so deeply steeped in this ancient faith that every experience of natural wonder, every twinge of personal guilt, every struggle for freedom and justice was a fresh experience of God's living presence. But into their lives had come also the mighty impact of Jesus Christ. His words, his works, his death and his resurrection were to them so all-engrossing and transforming that it seemed at times almost as if they could not have known God at all until they knew Christ. Almost but never quite. The Christian community rejected every move to abandon the Old Testament and the revelations of God recorded there. The God of Moses, the prophets and the sweet singers of old was veritably God. But so, too, was the one who had spoken His decisive, transforming Word in Jesus Christ. The God of the incarnate Word was wonderfully distinct and new, such a one as had never been known before. Yet this new God was the God of old. These two truths, the newness of God in Christ and the identification of that God with the only true God long known as Creator and Judge, must at all costs be preserved.

But this was not all. After the life of Jesus upon earth had become history or a radiant memory, there was found within the church a new life that was

[16] The AV wording of 1 Jn. 5:7 is translated from an indefensible late text.

continuous with his life. This new life was not to be seen in the form of a man teaching here or healing there, but rather in a whole community of men bound together in a new fellowship of teaching, healing and victorious faith. This new life was to them the most real and potent of all realities. It was God speaking and working within them. Yet to say simply that this was God would be to forget the newness of Him and the way in which His work was derived from and always associated, in their experience, with Jesus Christ. The Holy Spirit, as they called this new experience or the God newly known in this experience, was indubitably *new*. Yet God was one. Of that they were sure.

From then until now Christians have expressed two legitimate and immeasurable concerns by their speaking in trinitarian terms. One concern is to preserve the testimony and the reality of the rich, varied and tremendous new powers which have been released from heaven among men and which produced the Christian church. The other concern is to maintain the monotheistic faith. For the Hebrew *Shema* belongs also to the Christians. "The Lord our God, the Lord is one." [17]

3. Some Inacceptable Forms of the Doctrine

Many of the historic formulations of the diversity and unity have been in terms of ancient and medieval metaphysics, giving rise to the teaching that in the Godhead, three hypostases (Greek) or *personae* (Latin) were united in one substance, and so to endless further subtleties. Because many of the metaphysical categories and doctrines which provided the intellectual apparatus for those trinitarian formulations are now not widely familiar, nor vitally related to our most urgent religious problems, nor intellectually acceptable to most contemporary thinkers, the need for restatement is generally recognized.

Moreover, most Christians outside the Eastern Orthodox bodies have received their trinitarian terminology from the Latin usage and hence have been taught to speak and sing of "God in three *persons*." When Tertullian first introduced the Latin word *personae* in this connection, the word was quite ambiguous, having first meant a mask such as was worn by actors in a play, then a dramatic role, and not yet having developed the explicit and precise reference to an individual personality or ego which it came to bear in the Middle Ages, especially under the influence of Boethius. The great change in the meaning of the word has given to the phrase of Tertullian, *"una substantia, tres personae,"* and likewise to our more familiar words, "God in three persons," almost or altogether tritheistic connotation which would once have been regarded as a heretical denial of monotheism. It is for this reason that Karl Barth persuasively insists that we would better avoid misunderstanding by dropping this traditional

[17] Mk. 12:29 and Deut. 6:4.

use of the word "person" altogether and, employing words in their modern connotation, apply the attribute of personality to God in His "unity." [18]

Some contemporary Christian thinkers have accepted the term "person" in its full modern meaning and retained it in the teaching that God is three persons (selves, egos) in a unity more complete than exists in any earthly society, but which is nevertheless a society. This is the pathway of thought marked out by such men as C. F. D'Arcy, Clement C. J. Webb, Leonard Hodgson and Charles W. Lowry.

But such a view must confront many of the intellectual and some of the practical objections to polytheism. Indeed it verges very close upon a tritheistic doctrine in which, however, the name "God" is given to what would generally be called the pantheon of deities. It is true that such careful thinkers as have been named above set up certain safeguards against a polytheistic interpretation. For they would insist that each of the three divine persons is not only a member of the society which is God, but is also Himself God and that there is such an identity of these persons as is impossible for human individuals. Some less sophisticated representatives of this tendency, however, fall quite recklessly into a view hardly distinguishable from tritheism.

Another way of meeting the problems which the older formulas raise for the modern mind is simply to consign all contradictions and difficulties to the realm of mystery. What does it matter if we affirm that God is three individual persons and yet that He is one? Though to our minds this is a contradiction which seems impossible to be true, yet since all things are possible to God, the contradictory affirmations can, it is argued, be held true of Him.

Unfortunately for this line of reasoning, the affirmations are being made by men to other men. Ideas which are so contradictory leave in our minds a confused impression which is hardly illuminating. If the evidences of fact concerning a problem are such that no man has yet succeeded in accounting for them all without contradictory theories, it may be useful to hold such theories tentatively until a more comprehensive and consistent explanation can be found. But there seems to be little to commend such a resort to inconsistency in accounting for the diversity and unity of divine revelation, even though recourse is made to superhuman mystery. There is mystery enough in all the queries we cannot answer, without our introducing more by voluntary self-contradiction. By such introduction we really substitute a false awe before the obfuscation of our own words for a proper awe of silence before the genuine mystery of God.[19]

---

[18] *The Doctrine of the Word of God*, p. 403. Quoted by Donald M. Baillie in his book, *God Was in Christ*, p. 136. Baillie's whole treatment of the subject in ch. VI of the work just named is suggestive.

[19] For a persuasive statement of a diametrically contrary view, see Emil Brunner, *The Mediator*, p. 275.

In the categories of thought developed in modern times, in specific relation to personalities and their relations, there are ready at hand instruments for a more intelligible approach to the task set for us by the church's precious heritage. We can be glad that by one means or another Christian thinkers have maintained both the distinct, rich variety of the divine nature as revealed to us and also the unity of His being. But these values can be maintained more simply and clearly by leaving to history the discussions of hypostases, substances and processions, attributing personality to God in His unity, as Barth has urged, and then employing for further analysis such appropriate personal categories as purpose, will, activity and understanding. In doing this we shall actually be following up a clue which Augustine proposed again and again by personal analogies but which he never carried through to the end and which most of his successors have failed to develop.

4. One God in Three Modes of Revelation

Since the idea of the Trinity arose in certain revelatory experiences, it is those experiences which must be accounted for. As D. M. Baillie says,

the statement that God is three-in-one is virtually meaningless until we go on to indicate the relation of the three to the one concretely on a basis of the Gospel history and the Christian experience out of which the doctrine arose.[20]

But when we do take seriously this method of approach we see that what we have to account for is simply three distinct kinds of historic revelatory experiences of God, through each of which God has given glimpses of a different aspect of His nature.

Returning to the dramatic meaning of *persona*, a meaning still preserved in our adopted Latin phrase, *dramatis personae*, we may then say that on the stage of human experience God has shown Himself in three roles. We have known Him as the eternal Father, the Creator and Judge, in whom all the order and the very being of the world, the moral law and all truth are grounded. We know Him also as the Son, the God who humbles Himself in love for His children, speaking at definite times in history, through specific human beings and supremely in Jesus Christ His transforming Word. We know Him also as the Holy Spirit, the sacred presence within ourselves, binding us to Him and to our fellows with cords of love, opening our eyes to the evidences of God as Creator and Judge, reminding us of His revealing acts in history, summoning us to faith through Jesus Christ and empowering us to obey the divine commands we have heard.

These revelations are not the work of three individuals, however closely united

[20] *God Was in Christ*, p. 122.

in harmonious purpose. They are the work of one God. But He is not in His true nature a being to whom these revelations are foreign and unrepresentative, as the roles of an actor may be. We are convinced that all of them faithfully manifest the richly varied but harmonious purposes and activities of His own eternal will. He does not merely *appear to our understanding* to be Creator, historical self-revealer and self-giving presence. He truly *is* all of these and all these roles are faithful expressions of Himself.[21] We should do well to heed the warnings of Schleiermacher, Ritschl, Barth and many others against allowing the Latin word *persona*, so greatly changed in meaning since Boethius, to carry our thinking away from the experience of the primitive church and away from a thoroughgoing monotheism. Although misunderstanding is always possible, Barth is correct in thinking the danger would be less if we were to set aside the word "person" in our own usage and employ the term "mode" instead.

To the charge of "Sabellianism" we may reply with Schleiermacher by a candid adoption of the title or by an equally candid insistence on deviations from the views of Sabellius. Similarly, when accused of "Modalism" we may, like Barth, emphatically denounce the heresy of that name and insist that it would be a misnomer for a view that regards the three modes of God's revelation as truly representative of His eternal "modes of existence" so that we have not to look for a "hidden Fourth, in order really to enquire about God," [22] or we may simply accept and defend the title. Labels given to whole groups of doctrinal views are likely to mislead the unwary who assume that to accept a label is to be committed in favor of all the views defended by other bearers of it while to reject it is to deny all that they assert. If labels must be used, it would be accurate to say that the view of the Trinity here defended is a modified Sabellianism [23] and a type of Modalism. But labels are not important. If truth is of major concern, then it is the evidence of experience which must be consulted. Increasing numbers of devout scholars are concluding that the evidence points to some form of modalistic view.

[21] Again the view here presented is happily in agreement with Karl Barth. See his *The Doctrine of the Word of God*, especially pp. 438–39. But when Barth writes of the Trinity as a denial of loneliness and an affirmation of love within God, "even apart from the world," he is plainly contradicting his own emphatic repudiation of such social views. See *ibid.*, p. 158.

[22] *Ibid.*, 439.

[23] Note that we are here speaking of the Trinity, as was Schleiermacher when he called his view Sabellian, and not of the Incarnation. Brunner fails to observe this distinction when he criticizes Schleiermacher's adoption of the term. See *The Mediator*, p. 276n.

CHAPTER 33

The Last Judgment

A. Present Uncertainty Concerning the Judgment

1. An Uneasy Conscience

GREAT numbers of Christians have developed an uneasy conscience in relation to the traditional doctrine of the last judgment, but not in the way that its proponents might have expected. For these persons are not stirred by this teaching to more serious thought about their own sinful acts or condition. Instead, they are morally repelled by the notion that they should regard as supremely good a deity who would divide all human beings into two classes and then condemn all in the one class to inescapable and endless torment.

This dissatisfaction has doubtless been much affected by modern changes in ideals of penology, changes influenced, in turn, both by Christian teaching and by technical studies in criminology. It seems far less evident than it once did that every wrong deed ought to be punished by a penalty proportionate to the offense, whether that offense be measured by external effect or responsible intent. The philosophy of penal justice is in a transitional and highly uncertain state at present and this fact is reflected in thought about divine as well as human judgment upon the wrongdoer.

Does justice mean the application of a *lex talionis*? In view of Jesus' emphatic repudiation of that principle in the Sermon on the Mount, a repudiation which has persuaded increasing numbers of thoughtful men in the last generation, it is doubtful whether "an eye for an eye" can again seem right to the more sensitive Christian conscience, whether the penalty is exacted by a human or a divine judgment. Even when the retributive principle is employed in our courts the tendency is to employ it with increasing moderation and mercy. In such a time men are bound to question the justice of a sentence to everlasting torture for any offense committed in a finite time, especially in a life so obviously affected by ignorance, confusion and insecurity.

Traditional doctrines are also called into question for the absolute and indeed infinite division which they would introduce between people whose actual moral differences a careful ethical analysis shows to be far from absolute. Psychological and ethical study shows that human beings simply cannot be divided into two classes, the good and the bad. Making the infinite difference of destiny to depend on the presence or absence of a certain belief or even of a faithful commitment is not likely to allay the objection but may rather render it more acute.

Underneath these changes in penological and ethical thought is the growing influence of the Christian conviction that God is our loving Father. Jesus did not hesitate to argue that since a good human father would be prompted by love to give good gifts in response to his son's petition, God could be the more surely counted on to do likewise. This teaching has often been hidden under a mass of contrary social and theological teaching. But gradually it has gained a central place in the thought of millions concerning God. As its implications come into recognition, the question is bound to arise: will this loving Father consign some of the persons He has created to a torture which will not awaken them to righteous faith but in which they will have no other possible destiny than torment forever?

2. Resulting Denial of the Judgment

Such critical considerations as have just been suggested have led many Christians simply to reject every notion of a divine judgment. It seems to them that either the doctrine of God's love or the doctrine of judgment, with its heaven and hell, must go. Since the belief in His love seems more central in Christian teaching and more tenable in its own right, as well as more comfortable, all notion of the judgment, they think, must be discarded.

This conclusion, however, has troublesome consequences. For one thing, teaching about the judgment is so prominent in the New Testament, especially in the Gospels, that it seems hard to repudiate it without denying the whole teaching of Jesus, as well as of his disciples. It is true that in the earliest of the Gospels there is only one reference to punishment which may be interpreted as implying everlasting, retributive suffering and even there the figures of the "unquenchable fire" and the "Gehenna, where their worm does not die," are cryptic and somewhat uncertain in precise meaning.[1] But there are many references to divine judgment in other forms. In the later Gospels, especially Matthew and John, the teachings are much more explicit and numerous. Moreover, without a doctrine of divine judgment in some form, there would be no point to a belief in divine forgiveness nor repentance to God. In fact, sin in the Biblical sense would be quite impossible, for there can be no such sin without disobedience to divine command and resultant estrangement from God.

The discarding of belief in all divine judgment has further implications of

[1] See Mk. 9:43-49.

immediate, far-reaching and serious consequence. If above all human prefer-
ences and moral opinions there is not a supreme and decisively normative
judgment, then thought can give no coherent account of a genuine moral law.
In a world not under divine judgment there could be *differences* of conduct,
opinion, custom and mores, but no real good and evil, better and worse. We
have seen that there is good evidence of an absolute standard, a divine point
of reference for all moral opinions.[2] But this is implicitly denied when it is
denied that God speaks the decisive word concerning sin and righteousness in
a judgment which is beyond all opinions. We are then left to a morally, religiously and intellectually superficial relativism which threatens our very existence through inviting men to make their own truth by willing it so and backing
their wills with force capable of demolishing opposition.

3. Need for Reformulation

The situation just described calls loudly for a re-examination of the Christian
teaching concerning the judgment. The doctrine must be so formulated as to
concur with the evidence, including the newer evidence, and particularly with
basic Christian conceptions of God. Only then can it command respect and
summon the waning moral forces of the world to the commitment in which
alone is personal and social salvation. A teaching which blows hot and cold,
describing God as love and then as the vindictive everlasting torturer, will, once
men see the contrast as so many now do, produce similarly inconsistent human
lives. In their moral confusion such men will minimize the seriousness of their
own sin because God is loving and can be counted on to forgive all, while
they will resentfully mete out vindictive destruction upon other men in imitation of the supposed judgment of God.

This need for reformulation is recognized by many theologians and philosophers of religion. As evidence we may note the upsurge of interest in conditional immortality—the doctrine that those persons not found prepared for
admission into eternal life with God will simply cease to exist at all. But this
doctrine, too, would place an infinite gulf (annihilation versus infinite length
and value of life) between persons of quite finite (not to say minute) difference.[3]

Another trend is toward belief that all persons are to be saved, a view not now
confined to avowed liberals, but defended by such different theologians as Karl
Barth and Nels Ferré. Yet none of the first-rate thinkers who hold this view
would maintain that it constitutes in itself a doctrine of divine judgment.
Neither Barth nor Ferré, for example, would think of saying that God simply

----

[2] See above, pp. 56–58.
[3] For a brief account of this doctrine, with arguments for and against it, and bibliography, see
my article, "Immortality, conditional," in V. Ferm, *An Encyclopedia of Religion.*

looks on all human beings and their various modes of conduct as equally good or evil and indulgently lets them all into eternal fellowship with him.[4]

The proper reformulation of the Christian doctrine of divine judgment is a major task, and will require the efforts of many scholars in such related fields as ethics, criminology, law and New Testament studies, as well as systematic theology. The barest beginning has been made by anyone.[5] All that can be expected here is the suggesting of some considerations, relative to the judgment, which seem true and which ought to be taken into account in a complete statement yet to be made.

B. SOME TRUTHS REGARDING THE DIVINE JUDGMENT

1. *The Eternal Distinction*

Before God, right is forever right and wrong forever wrong. The ground of all true moral distinctions is in the judgment of God which is at the base of creation itself. Beyond all human judgments is the last judgment of God. Figuratively, this relationship may be represented temporally, the judgment of God coming *after* all human opinions and customs. But the relation is not essentially one of time. The divine judgment is the last judgment in the sense that it is *final*. All others are tentative, conditional, uncertain. God's judgment is absolute, unconditional and truth-determining. For He is the Creator of us all. We have been made and related to our world in ways requiring that for our full self-realization we live according to the principles which He has decreed. Our Creator is Lawgiver and Judge. We have not the power to change the very terms of creation. Hence, we cannot repeal nor modify the moral law to which we are subject. In our efforts to discover it our opinions may differ as we approximate more closely to the truth or fall further into falsehood. But the truth about what we ought to do we cannot change, for that is fixed forever in the creative and final judgment of God.

It is in this way that we ought to accept Jesus' account of the last judgment in Matthew 25:31–46. The Son of man is the embodiment of God's purpose for man. Hence, he is the very incarnation of the judgment. By its relation to him all human conduct is approved or falls into condemnation. There is an element of myth or parable in the account. For most people have sometimes ministered to the hungry, thirsty, unclothed, sick or imprisoned and have sometimes failed

---

[4] What they do say may be found, among other places in Barth, *Die Kirchliche Dogmatik*, II.2, pp. 453–563; and Ferré, *The Christian Understanding of God*, Ch. 9. Concerning Barth's universalism, cf. H. Emil Brunner, "The New Barth," *Scottish Journal of Theology*, Vol. 4 (1951), p. 134.

[5] One of the more significant is in Emil Brunner, *Justice and the Social Order*. Another is Norman L. Robinson, *Christian Justice*.

to do so. Since every such person has actually ministered to more than "one of the least of these" and has also ministered *not* to more than one, if the words are taken literally most persons will have to go both to the "right," entering the heavenly kingdom, and to the "left," condemned to "the eternal fire prepared for the devil and his angels." Apparently Jesus was not here concerned with the judgment as an event to be carefully and precisely described. He was concerned with merciful kindness and said in a colorful and emphatic way that such conduct was under the eternal blessing of the Father and belonged to the kingdom which He had "prepared from the foundation of the world."

2. *Unrepented Sin As Barrier to Communion with God*

The judgment of God is not an abstract or transcendent distinction which does not enter at all into our experience. It is borne to us in many ways of the greatest importance. One way is through the barrier which sin sets up, obstructing man's communion with God. A sin committed and not repented of does not cause God to cease loving and seeking to bring the sinner to Him. But it does make impossible a real communion of the soul with God. For true spiritual communion is a kind of divine-human *koinonia,* an intimate sharing of common purpose, and requires on man's part a deep concern for the doing of God's will and such confident submission to Him as unrepented sin flatly denies.

The gravity of this loss can hardly be exaggerated. Man's most priceless privilege is communion with the Creator who alone is able to fulfill his supreme longings, conquer his darkest fears, and heal the deepest scars of his soul.

3. *Temporal Pains and Sorrows often Divine Judgments*

It is obvious that many of the worst human sufferings result quite obviously and directly from sin. The death and destruction of wars, with all their attendant fear and misery, are clearly caused by the stubborn pride, greed and lust for power of sinful men. Most venereal disease, the vast human losses from crime, corruption, the commercialization of vice and addiction to drugs and alcohol, the suppression and persecution of racial and religious minorities, exploitation of labor, irresponsible fomentation of industrial disputes, tyranny and willful cruelty—all have produced a quantity of human tragedy staggering to the imagination. Someone may insist that the awful consequences of such evils are simply the "natural" results of certain modes of conduct and have nothing to do with a divine judgment. But such a view would introduce, for any theist, an indefensible dichotomy. For it is God who has so created and so orders the world that such conduct does produce such results.

If divine judgment were to be thought of in terms of selective retribution against sinful individuals, it would have to be granted that the tragic temporal results of sin are not accurate in discriminating between the innocent and guilty. The burdens of sin-caused tragedy may fall, in this life, much more heavily on little children than on the proud men responsible for their homeless misery. But if the judgment be regarded as definitive and pedagogic, then it will be seen that by such an ordering of the world God proclaims some kinds of conduct as evil and, at the same time, shows how completely we are members one of another. How essential is this moral ordering of the world to all our conceptions of obligation and right will be readily seen if we ask such a question as this: would anyone suppose that the spirit which we now call unrighteous hate was wrong if that spirit invariably gave rise to beneficent consequences in all the lives concerned? The question cannot be directly answered, for the very *meaning* of that spirit is inextricably bound up with the results expected to flow from it. Since God has so ordered the world, moral law is theonomous to the very core.

4. *Strife and Incoherence Invariable Implications of Sin*

Some sin brings pleasure to the sinner and at times to certain other persons. Yet all sin involves incoherence of intention, both within and between individual persons, but most of all between men and God. Hence, however much the results of sins may differ, it is the very nature of all sin to be disruptive of that harmony which God purposes and which is found only under the reign of His will. The divine judgment upon sin is to be seen, not only in the *effects* of sin but in the internal structure and meaning of sin itself.

Here can be seen the partial truth, but also the superficiality and falseness of the easygoing notion that God judges and condemns sin but never the sinner. Sin is not something external to the person sinning. Just so far as he is a sinner sin is of his very being. God's condemnation of his sin is a condemnation of him. This condemnation is attested in the very fact that the self-contradiction, the incoherence, the internal strife which are of the very nature of sin are in the person of every man who sins. While God thus condemns us in our sin He also loves us while we are yet in sin and seeks to separate us from our sin. But that is to be done only by making us what we are not yet. God's grief over us, reflected in Jesus' anguished cry over Jerusalem, is due precisely to this, that He both condemns and loves us.

5. *God's Judgment after Our Death*

Since God's sovereignty is not confined to this present life but is over all being, His condemnation of sin continues after we die. To believe otherwise is to deny either that He is God the ground of all being or that He is God the ground of all moral integrity and hence steadfast in His own character.

How His judgment will be expressed in our experience after death we cannot know. The forms of that life beyond the grave are hidden from us. This is why the Scriptures speak of them only in figures drawn from our earthly experience, yet always portrayed as transcending our experience—the resurrection of the "body" but a "spiritual body," [6] "streets" but streets of "pure gold," [7] "light" but with need for "no light of lamp or sun." [8]

However, we can be assured that hereafter as now His judgment will be part and parcel of His love. For His judgment is always a defining aspect of His purpose to share His supreme treasures with us. This being true we may speculate that the conditions of our life after death may well be determined by the state of our wills in relation to Him, particularly in relation to God the Son, the eternal Word, His purpose for man shown to us most fully in Jesus Christ. Because even His judgment is an aspect of His love we can be sure that there is no such retributive, inescapable hell of nonredemptive everlasting torture as has been traditionally pictured.[9] God loves us more than any of us love one another. A person who has used well the opportunities he has had here, though they have been meager and in the eyes of men his life may have been a wretched failure, may trust God to open before him a larger freedom than he has known. Yet suffering has its place in His redemptive judgment. To the hardened sinner, especially the proud, self-rightous sinner such as Jesus most sharply warned and condemned, the hell of suffering may well be real and long. Indeed, despite all the eloquent and persuasive words which have been written by such men as Ferré in support of the belief in eventual salvation for all, it is hard to see how we can be sure that all will ever turn in repentant faith to God. While they persist in disobedience men will continue in self-defeat under divine judgment.

And this is the judgment, that the light has come into the world, and men loved darkness rather than light, because their deeds were evil.[10]

As long as he loves darkness rather than light no man can walk in the light. By preferring disobedience to faith men condemn themselves under the terms of God's judgment which is decisive and final. The judgment is irrevocable. But men's relation to it is changed when they are changed from disobedience to faith.

[6] 1 Cor. 15:44.
[7] Rev. 21:21.
[8] Rev. 22:5.
[9] E.g., see Thomas Aquinas, Compendium of Theology, chs. 175–80.
[10] Jn. 3:19.

CHAPTER 34

The New Birth

A. Necessity of the New Birth

1. *Salvation and Our Human Predicament*

THE Christian gospel is good news of salvation. Salvation is the being saved from bondage to sin and entering into the eternal community of love under the reign of God. Salvation thus involves change within the individual, change in his relation to God and change in his relation to other persons.

We have seen how deeply every human person is caught in a network of evil constraints from his very birth. He is not satisfied to live under them and yet he has inadequate power to overcome them so long as he seeks to do so in his own strength. For actually he has not the power to live at all in his own strength and so long as he tries to do so he is basing his conduct on a false construction of his whole situation. From the very root of his being he is dependent on other human persons and absolutely dependent upon God. Every true growth and every victory of his spiritual life must occur in willing acceptance of this relationship to God and to human society.

But his dependence upon his fellows deepens his problem. For human society is deeply infected with sinful motives and customs and many of its institutions are hardened channels of evil. Sometimes, seeing how dependent we are upon the family, church, state, economic order and other institutions, and how potent they are in forming our very souls, we are tempted to think that all would be well if only the institutional forms of our interpersonal relations were set right. Certainly no life can be fully victorious over sin without in some way challenging and combating the institutional evils which cramp and pervert many of our relations with one another. But institutional change alone is shown by experience to be short-lived and futile. The most admirable political constitution can be debased to serve the most unjust and tyrannical purposes. The finest economic organization can be used for the vilest exploitation. Even a church, committed formally to the highest ideals of purity and brotherly love, can be made the cloak for lewd practices or the cruelest racism. Not only the forms of an institution, but also the persons who control it, must be fit if the institution is actually to support justice and right.

2. *"You Must be Born Anew"*

Some theologians have written as if salvation were only a kind of heavenly legal transaction in which God came to treat as righteous persons, sinners who still continued, unchanged, in their sin. It is, indeed, hard to overestimate the importance of divine forgiveness in the work of salvation. But to deny or minimize the real change of life which is brought about here and now in the man who turns to God in faith and is received into His fellowship is to alter almost beyond recognition the teaching of the New Testament and also to deny the witness of a great multitude of men and women, many of whose changed lives can be observed in the present generation. The gospel message does not offer justification in continuing sinfulness, but summons the reader to

be transformed by the renewal of your mind, that you may prove what is that good and acceptable and perfect will of God.[1]

This transformation is essential to life in fellowship with God. God loves and seeks all men. But the riches of His peace can be shared only with those who, being saved from bondage to sin, seek to participate in His purpose. This is not because of some arbitrary requirement of God external to our nature, but because we are created for this obedient participation and can find wholeness of our own spirits on no other terms. Hence, seeing that we have all, in a sinful society, fallen under the power of sin, it is true of every man that "unless one is born anew, he cannot see the kingdom of God."[2]

But what of the person who "grows up in the Christian faith"? If his life from the beginning is nurtured by Christian parents in the knowledge and love of God, must he still undergo a cataclysmic new birth?

In the account of Jesus' warning to Nicodemus about the necessity of the new birth, we are told, Nicodemus was perplexed and Jesus after reaffirming the necessity, added:

Do not marvel that I said to you, "You must be born anew." The wind blows where it wills, and you hear the sound of it, but you do not know whence it comes or whither it goes; so it is with every one who is born of the Spirit.[3]

The spiritual rebirth must come if the life in communion with God is to be entered. *How* it is to come cannot be determined by any formula. We cannot say when or how fast everyone must be reborn. Neither can we say that in everyone the new birth will appear as a radical reversal of direction. The Spirit works in many different ways in different lives.

[1] Rom. 12:2 (RSV marginal reading).
[2] Jn. 3:3.
[3] Jn. 3:5–8.

But let no one say that because the change may occur slowly or in the secrecy of the heart it need not occur at all. For if the soul is to enter into communion with God, there must come sometime somehow the awakening to solemn responsibility before God and the commitment of the soul to side with Him and by His grace to wage unceasing war against evil in the self and in the world.

Nicodemus was not the last man to be puzzled about the meaning of this doctrine of the new birth. It is still a subject of much perplexity and no little controversy. The theologian must make some attempt to find and expound as clearly as possible the truth to be discovered in this teaching. The whole truth that is discoverable will be seen to exceed by far the limits of psychological or of ethical description. Yet the categories of psychology and of ethics do provide useful vehicles for empirical approaches particularly relevant to present thought. We begin with the approach of psychology.

B. Second Birth Psychologically Described

1. *Release from Symptoms of Guilt*

A number of psychologists have described the alleviation or removal of guilt feelings occurring at many conversions.[4] Usually the subjects of such studies have been persons who experienced sudden and dramatic change. This is natural, for the data in such cases are especially conspicuous and easily contrasted. However, the release from consciously felt or long-repressed guilt conflicts is often as great or greater in cases where the changes are slower and less exposed to the public eye.

2. *Change in Capacity for Other-Concern*

A person who was formerly full of fear, anxiety, self-pity and other forms of preoccupation with himself is often observed to have gained confidence and security, through his conversion, and to have turned attention outward in active, sympathetic concern for other persons. By "finding God" many people have been quite observably turned from ingrown self-concern to a genuine interest in the needs of others and to co-operative participation in unselfish benevolence.

3. *Change in Gallery*

We sometimes speak contemptuously of the person who "plays to the gallery" or to "the stands." He prefers the plaudits of the crowd, we think, rather than genuine achievement or qualitative superiority. He seeks the spotlight, the

---

[4] E.g., see William James, *Varieties of Religious Experience*; J. B. Pratt, *The Religious Consciousness*; Edwin D. Starbuck, *The Psychology of Religion*; W. B. Thomas, *Psychology of Conversion*; and Paul E. Johnson, *Psychology of Religion*.

spectacular play, the solo performance. But if we suppose that his fault is in caring for the high valuation by other persons, in contrast to the admirable people who do not care, we are quite mistaken. For every one of us is so completely social in nature that none can avoid a concern for the approval of others. In hours of decision we can all observe our own concern to know how such and such persons would think of us if we made the choice contemplated. We can, however, choose our galleries. The athlete can have a higher regard for the approval of the experts, of his teammates and of his coach than for the applause of superficial and untrained spectators.

Augustine turns, at conversion, from striving to please sophisticated pagans to the effort to please the most thoughtful Christians, especially his mother, but above all to please God. So also the writer of the Letter to the Hebrews calls before the reader one after another of the great heroes of faith and then declares,

Therefore, since we are surrounded by so great a cloud of witnesses, let us lay aside every weight, and sin which clings so closely, and let us run with perseverance the race that is set before us, looking to Jesus, the pioneer and perfecter of our faith. . . .[5]

So Paul reminds the Christians of Thessalonica that they have learned from him how they "ought to live and to please God." [6] The direction of movement in any life depends largely on the secret gallery which he carries within his own soul. So it is a matter of no small import, when a man accepts for his "witnesses" pre-eminent exemplars of Christian virtues, with Jesus Christ at the head, and seeks above all "to please God."

4. Change in Ego-Identification

Everyone carries in his own mind a certain impression of the kind of person he is or means to be. This impression is often far different from the view which his friends and neighbors have of him and it may be far from the reality. But it does profoundly affect what he is becoming.

A youth of seventeen wandered into a city mission one evening looking for food and shelter. He had left his home and school several years earlier and was as aimless a wanderer as one could find. In response to every effort to portray the possibilities of a more meaningful life, he replied that he could not do anything, that he was "no good" or that he had "no will power." He had never received any religious instruction and all he knew about the name "Jesus Christ" was that it was "swear words." Yet after he had been prevailed upon to stay at the mission for a few days some appeal reached him, one evening,

---

[5] Heb. 12:1–2.
[6] 1 Thess. 4:1. Cf. Rom. 8:8; 1 Cor. 7:32–34; Gal. 1:10; 1 Thess. 2:15.

and he went to the altar seeking God. When he arose from his knees that night he had a new conception of himself. From that day he set out quietly and confidently to do the things he had been sure he could not do—quitting strong drink, seeking and achieving reconciliation with his parents, studying conscientiously, obtaining and successfully holding a job. Until that night he had been in his own eyes a bum. Now he was, in his own eyes, a "saved" man, a Christian who could do everything God wanted him to do because God gave him the strength he had not possessed before.[7]

The psychologist, as psychologist, can observe and describe such changes. The description leaves many questions unanswered, particularly questions about the value of the changes and questions about their real *cause*. But when such problems are investigated psychology has been left behind. For example, when we ask whether the changes are for the better or worse and why, we enter the domain of ethics.

C. Second Birth Ethically Described

1. *Narrowing the Gap between Ideals and Conduct*

The youth who first stumbled into the mission dismally condemned himself. His ideals, that is, the types of conduct which he approved, were quite contrary to the mode of life which he daily lived. Yet he was doing nothing to close the gap.

This is precisely the condition of will which is most surely condemned by the ethical theory of many schools. For no matter what criterion of moral judgment may be defended and no matter what the supreme good of life is taken to be, the violation of one's own accepted standards is bound to be self-defeating.

Hence the great increase in self-mastery, enabling the youth to set his direction of development firmly toward his own ideals, was in itself, at least, morally all to the good.

2. *Overcoming of Conflict in Ideals*

Part of the difficulty which the sinner experiences in trying to live up to his ideals is due to the fact that his ideals themselves conflict. For example, if he approves both a sober life of achievement and also an accepted place in a group of irresponsible drifters or when he favors both brotherhood and the making of the most money possible, he is doomed to internal conflict of will. When such a person settles once and for all the question of his supreme allegiance so that

---

[7] This is a factual account of events which I observed.

all else must then be subject to the one organizing principle, that does not resolve for him the countless perplexities and struggles over the means which should be adopted in the various situations of life. But it does resolve the deeper and far more disruptive conflicts over the basic purposes and goals of life.

The student of ethics can observe such integrating organization of ideals in the life of the man who gives himself to God as revealed in Jesus Christ.

3. *Change to More Inclusive Loyalties*

Increased breadth of view is likewise typical of conversion experience. The central principle of organization which brings unity to the ideals of the twice-born requires also a concern as wide as the concern of God is believed to be. Since God, according to Christian teaching, created all men and Christ gave his life for all, this concern is, in principle, universal in scope. The restricting temptations of selfishness and every type of provincialism still confront the converted person. Individuals and whole churches frequently succumb to them. But Christian conversion sets at the heart of the believer an inclusive loyalty which puts all lesser, exclusive devotions on the defensive.

From the standpoint of a rational ethics, this is worthy of approval. The wider the range of perspective taken into account in establishing ideals and determining conduct, the greater the likelihood of eventual subjective and social consistency and harmony.[8]

Specifically, the ideal of what human personality ought to become, as seen in Jesus Christ, gives to the converted person a concrete and superb goal of individual life. Similarly, the ideal of the perfect community taught in his doctrine of the kingdom of heaven and supported by experiences of Christian fellowship, provides an exacting and persuasive norm for the judging and development of all social relationship. Both of these ideals are sufficiently defined in New Testament teaching and narrative and sufficiently concrete in the Christian's experience, to have an appeal which no abstract concept could possess. Yet they also leave adequate scope for creative adaptation to ever-changing circumstances and needs.

But however highly the ethical theorist may approve the ideals and even the moral progress of the convert, he can hardly answer, as ethical theorist, the crucial questions concerning the new birth. For these questions would seek explanation of the power which enables the subject to close the gap between ideals and conduct and the experience because of which God and His kingdom are living realities and not abstract ideals to the transformed person. The raising of such questions, as well as some approached by the psychologist, demand religious or theological description for answer.

[8] Cf. "The Law of the Most Inclusive End" in E. S. Brightman, *Moral Laws*.

D. The New Birth Theologically Described

1. *Repentance*

Near the beginning of the Gospel accounts comes the story of John the Baptist with his warning demand that his hearers repent of their sins. In the Lord's Prayer, no sooner do we ask for the coming of the kingdom, the doing of God's will on earth and the providing of our daily bread than we are reminded of our own unworthiness to receive such blessings. Therefore, we must hasten to add, "Forgive us . . ." Over and over again, in the sermons of the earliest Christian preachers we read the call to repentance:

Repent, and be baptized every one of you in the name of Jesus Christ for the forgiveness of your sins.[9]

Repent therefore, and turn again, that your sins may be blotted out.[10]

The times of ignorance God overlooked, but now he commands all men everywhere to repent.[11]

So near is this to the heart of Paul's message that he describes his work as a declaring to both Jews and Gentiles "that they should repent and turn to God and perform deeds worthy of repentance." [12]

This is the starting point of the decisive transaction between the individual soul and God. God is righteous and true fellowship between Him and the sinner is impossible until the sinner repents.

Yet this is not the first beginning. A man cannot repent until he is moved to be sorry for his transgressions and until he has hope of forgiveness. This sorrow and this hope God has prepared through all His beneficence to the sinner, through every human kindness to him and through the life, death and resurrection of Christ. Through all these instruments the Holy Spirit now moves the heart to repentance. When the burdened heart responds with its plea for forgiveness, the way is opened for the new relationship.

This repentance must be a whole-response of faith. It will not do to select a sin or two, here or there, and ask that these be forgiven. When repentance is genuine it always does include some specific wrongs. But the sinner—anyone—who would enter into life-giving communion with God must ask the forgiveness of any and all mistakes, sins and social involvements which stand as barriers to this communion.

[9] Acts 2:38.
[10] Acts 3:19.
[11] Acts 17:30.
[12] Acts 26:19–20.

2. Forgiveness by God

"If we confess our sins, he is faithful and just, and will forgive our sins and cleanse us from all unrighteousness." [13] God's merciful readiness to forgive us is sure. We can be confident that when we wholeheartedly repent He does forgive.

But there is a pitfall here against which warning must be often repeated. Being sure that when we repent God does forgive, we may then think of our repentance as the important thing. Then the forgiveness is so taken for granted as to be easily forgotten. When that attitude prevails the "repentance" becomes only a subjective self-treatment, losing its character of confession and appeal to the true Father whose forgiveness we need. If the confession is to be genuine it must be truly personal, a prayer to the one who is "faithful and just," but to whom we should therefore all the more look with wonder and gratitude and least of all take lightly for granted.

3. Receiving God's Grace to Do His Will

With God's forgiveness there is given new strength to overcome the old temptations and to do what was previously impossible. Before this, any sinner could testify,

I do not understand my own actions. For I do not do what I want, but I do the very thing I hate. . . . I can will what is right, but I cannot do it. For I do not do the good I want, but the evil I do not want is what I do.[14]

But when God has done His transforming work there is a quite different testimony to make. "For the law of the Spirit of life in Christ Jesus has set me free from the law of sin and death." [15] Those who seek complete and final explanation of this change of life in the psychological forces within the man himself miss both the secret of explanation and the message of hope to be given other burdened spirits. For the change in the self is brought about in an encounter with the one Other who is able to forgive all sin and to set men "free from the law of sin and death."

How God performs this change in us, we do not fully understand. We can see many of the instruments He employs—the psychological and ethical descriptions have suggested some of them—but much we know simply as His work, just as we know that He has created us and not we ourselves, but without our understanding how He creates. This new expansion of our freedom, is, indeed, a new going forth in us of His creative Word.

[13] I Jn. 1:9.
[14] Rom. 7:15, 18–19.   [15] Rom. 8:2–4.

4. *Entering the New Community*

The new influx of spiritual strength does not end with the new birth. For that is but the beginning of a new relationship in which there is ever-renewed communion between God and a man, with God giving the support of His presence and love and with the man responding by an eager seeking of the divine will and by earnest, obedient faithfulness. The man, it is true, remains in the world and many influences press upon him to turn him away from God. But even though he sometimes falls before these temptations, he is quick to seek again the forgiveness of God, renewing the communion by which he lives. The center of power in his life and hence the direction of his development are now controlled by the divine-human relationship.

At the same time he has entered "the communion of saints," the comradeship of the spirit with a host of others who have entered into communion with God. This comradeship includes the "cloud of witnesses" whose work on earth is done. But it includes also the living company of pilgrims of the way. By this company he is sustained and encouraged in his spiritual growth and to it he contributes his own witness of faith and life.

E. FAITH AND WORKS IN SALVATION

The term "salvation" is sometimes used of the single transaction and change which has been here described as the new birth. More properly salvation includes not only the new birth, but the entire process of change and growth from sin to righteous perfection—a process beginning with the first stirrings of spiritual concern, before the new birth has taken place, and continuing on after death.

An old question is the problem of the roles played by faith and works in this process of salvation. There have been those who have denied that works had any place in the process at all. Likewise some, though fewer within the Christian churches, have denied that faith had any place. These denials have often been due in whole or in part to a narrow definition of "works" as formally prescribed ritualistic acts or ascetic practices or a similarly narrow conception of "faith" as a mere assent to a creedal formula. When the opposite denials are based on such definitions they turn out to be strikingly similar in actual meaning, since both are then directed against the notion that God is concerned with our formal compliance with empty, legalistic prescriptions.

In the New Testament both faith and works, more broadly conceived, are given great prominence. In the Synoptic Gospels Jesus' stress seems to be well divided between works of love [16] and an attitude of trusting obedience in relation

[16] E.g., see Mt. 25:31–46; Mk. 10:17–21; Lk. 6:46–49.

to the Father.[17] Since he teaches that God commands love toward Him and one's neighbor, the two strands of emphasis come out practically together. In the Johannine writings faith, with stress on right belief, is given greater emphasis,[18] along with the necessity of a spiritual union with Christ—as of the branches with a vine.[19]

It is, of course, in the letters of Paul and James that the issue is most precisely joined. "For we hold," says Paul, "that a man is justified by faith apart from works of law." [20] James, on the other hand, writes,

What does it profit, my brethren, if a man says he has faith but has not works? Can his faith save him? If a brother or sister is ill-clad and in lack of daily food, and one of you says to them, "Go in peace, be warmed and filled," without giving them the things needed for the body, what does it profit? So faith by itself, if it has no works, is dead.[21]

Now it is apparent that in speaking of "works" Paul has at the center of his thought the formal requirements of the Jewish law. James, on the other hand, is speaking of the deeds which faith, if it is alive, is bound to produce. The central problem and the situation being different, the two writers use different emphasis. But when each comes to a balanced statement of his view, they speak alike. Thus Paul insists that all who have saving faith are bound to obey God,[22] while James declares, "Show me your faith apart from your works, and I by my works will show you my faith." [23]

The faith by which we are brought into a saving relation with God is evidently not a mere intellectual assent to a creed. "Even the demons believe," says James, "—and shudder." [24] We are saved by belief in a Person, not mere belief in a proposition. Such belief in God implies, of course, assent to the doctrine that He is and that He is worthy of our faith. But it includes also the attitude of trust and loyal obedience. It is not mere assent but faithfulness.[25]

When faith is understood, certainly it is by faith that we are saved. It is not by performing a certain number of religious chores, not even by giving to God a large number of acts, however good in themselves, regarded simply as means of purchasing our salvation. For salvation is no more to be purchased than is life itself. God alone can grant to us His saving love. And His love is not given to this or that act, but to whole persons. It is our very selves which must be committed to life with Him if we are to have such life. That whole commitment of ourselves into His hands is faith.

[17] E.g., see Mt. 6:25–34. [18] See, e.g., Jn. 8:24; 1 Jn. 4:2. [19] Jn. 15:1–6.
[20] Rom. 3:28. [21] Jas. 2:14–17. [22] Rom. 6:12–19.
[23] Jas. 2:18. [24] Jas. 2:19.
[25] Cf. Georgia Harkness' contrast between the near-universality of Americans' belief that God exists and the great number of these "believers" who live as if He did not. *The Modern Rival of Christian Faith*, pp. 11–12.

PART SIX

THE KINGDOM AND THE CHURCH

CHAPTER 35

The Kingdom As Present and Growing

THE Christian needs to know what is meant by the kingdom of God. For to him the kingdom is the *summum bonum*, "the pearl of great value" for which everything else ought to be willingly sacrificed.[1]

In the teaching of Jesus the supreme importance of the kingdom could hardly be given greater emphasis. According to the Synoptic Gospels, it was the one theme of his preaching. This is shown both by the examples of his preaching reported to us and also by explicit statement.[2] When the people who followed him from Capernaum "would have kept him from leaving them," he replied, "I must preach the good news of the kingdom of God to the other cities also; for I was sent for this purpose."[3] In the prayer which he taught his disciples, the first petition is "Thy kingdom come." According to his teaching, to have the kingdom is to have also all else that matters. This is to be the supreme object of our life quest, for we must "seek first his kingdom and his righteousness."[4]

A. Definition of the Kingdom

Despite many complications and much controversy concerning some aspects of the kingdom, the essential definition of it is as simple as it is important. The kingdom of God is the reign of God, the realm in which His will is done "as it is in heaven," that is, completely.

The sovereign of the kingdom is God. Its citizens are all those persons whose supreme purpose is that His will be done and so His kingdom fulfilled. His perfect norms are its laws. Its supreme uniting principle is love.

1. Meaning of Love

Problems do begin to arise, however, when we seek to explain what love, in this sense, is. We are assured that "God is love."[5] Paul proclaims that of the three abiding values, "the greatest" is love[6] and hence exhorts his readers,

[1] Mt. 13:45–46.
[2] Mt. 4:23.
[3] Lk. 4:42–43.
[4] Mt. 6:33.
[5] 1 Jn. 4:8, 16.
[6] 1 Cor. 13:13.

"Make love your aim." [7] When Jesus was asked, "Teacher, which is the great commandment in the law?" he replied,

You shall love the Lord your God with all your heart, and with all your soul, and with all your mind. This is the great and first commandment. And a second is like it. You shall love your neighbor as yourself.[8]

But what is the love which is so extolled in the New Testament?

This is not a problem to be solved by linguistic analysis. It is quite appropriate for those who prefer it to use the Greek word *agape* to stand for the special meanings connoted by it in the New Testament. But the New Testament writers occasionally used the unrelated verb *phileo* to signify the same spirit,[9] and they were actually having to convey a new meaning for which the existing Greek was nearly as inadequate as English is today.

2. Misconceptions and Exaggerations

Love, in the special New Testament sense, can hardly mean essentially a spontaneous feeling of admiration or attraction, nor an attitude of reverence, for we are to love our enemies and at the very heart of the gospel is the assurance that God loves sinners. Neither can it mean necessarily a propensity to give with no hope of receiving any good—even spiritual good—unless, with Anders Nygren, we are to minimize "the great and first commandment," the command to love God. For it would be quite unthinkable for me, a dependent creature in need of God's mercy, to approach God in the hope of giving Him some good without hope of any spiritual profit to myself.[10]

The Johannine writings stress that the love which Christians have for one another and for God is the same love which God has bestowed upon them.[11] Although such love could be colored in different ways by its various objects, it obviously could not in itself connote reverence on the one hand nor mercy on the other.

Another problem which narrows the possible interpretation further is set before us when we observe that while Jesus responded to the inquiry about the greatest commandment by giving the commands to love God and neighbor, on another occasion he said to "seek first His kingdom." How many "first" commandments can one observe? Either Jesus was giving contrary instructions

[7] 1 Cor. 14:1.

[8] Mt. 22:36–39. Cf. Mk. 12:29–31.

[9] E.g., in Jn. 5:20, 16:27, 1 Cor. 16:22, Tit. 3:15.

[10] Cf. Nygren's great work, *Agape and Eros*, which everyone concerned with recent scholarship on this problem must know. Despite Nygren's great learning and suggestive thought, he does seem to exaggerate both the self-centeredness of the Platonic *eros* and the exclusiveness of other-concern in the Christian *agape*. Cf. Paul E. Johnson, *Christian Love*.

[11] E.g., see Jn. 15:9, 12; 1 Jn. 4:11–12, 16–17, 19–21.

about the proper first objective of our lives or these commands mean essentially the same thing.

Once again, we must notice that Jesus said, quoting Leviticus 19:18, "You shall love your neighbor *as yourself*." Such a love must be primarily neither a matter of giving nor receiving nor yet of emotional attraction, but must rather have to do with the scope of concern, responsibility and purpose.

3. Love As a Seeking to Share the Divine Riches

All of the New Testament teachings about love fall into harmony if we take the clue to its meaning offered by the spiritual experience of which the whole New Testament bears witness. We have noted that Jesus testified to a new and unique sharing of God's own purpose in intimate communion with the Father. We have seen also how the primitive church was created by a profound experience of the *koinonia*, that new sharing fellowship in which men and women of all classes were drawn together by the Spirit of God.

All the evidence points to the belief that the spirit of this divinely initiated community is precisely what is meant by Christian love. Love is the longing for and delight in that fellowship in which the treasures of God's own life, "the unsearchable riches of Christ," [12] are shared. It was for this that God created us. It was for this that He sought us in our folly and sin. It is in response to His own devotion to this divine-human community that we turn to Him in hope, repentance and gratitude, and then, in the joy of this supreme meaningful "participation in the Spirit," [13] we yearn to share it with others. "We love because He first loved us." [14]

This love is closely related to all true love and friendship in the ordinary sense. In the motivation of true friendship there is neither desire to exploit the friend for the sake of self nor the desire simply to advance the individual well-being of the other alone. There is desire for the transcending of the "I" and "thou" in the "we" of shared experience. Moreover, it occasionally happens that in some hour of extraordinarily rich experience, especially aesthetic or moral, as in seeing a startlingly beautiful scene or a heroic act of bravery, persons who had no thought of seeking one another's company are suddenly forged into a special unit. Some great experiences of value drive us with compelling force to seek someone with whom they may be shared.

Christian love in us, though like these other outbursts of sharing and without doubt psychologically related to them, nevertheless transcends them. It is different in the unlimited and ever-expanding character of the contents shared. It is different in the fact that at the very heart of the contents of Christian sharing is the divine gift of sharing with God Himself. It is different in the

[12] Eph. 3:8.   [13] Phil. 2:1.   [14] 1 Jn. 4:19.

desire to extend this *koinonia* to anyone and everyone. The most unattractive and unlikely neighbor offers to *this* love the spiritual attraction of giving opportunity for the wonderful inclusiveness and grace of the divine love to express itself through us with special clarity and power. And this love is unique in carrying within it the perspective of eternity. It "endures all things" and it "never ends" [15] because it is sustained by God's own Spirit.

This is the love which is the dominant and uniting principle in the kingdom of God. Indeed, the whole community of divine love *is* the kingdom. For the sake of this community, we lose ourselves and in it we find ourselves.

It would be self-contradictory to demand that every person consider himself less than any other person. But it is plain truth that every person is less than the divine-human community and to put that truth into the whole-commitment of faith is to discover what life can be. Even God Himself, in all His power and holiness, so far transcending our imaginations, is yet less than the kingdom which includes Him and also all with whom He is permitted to share His glory. Hence, even He stoops in devotion to the kingdom to which He calls us. How much more should we give ourselves to it!

B. The Kingdom Present

The kingdom is, in some respects and in some human experience, already present.

1. *God Is Present*

God Himself is always perfect in His faithful devotion to that community to which He calls us. In His will the kingdom is already present as perfect love. Whenever He speaks to us or makes us to feel His holy presence, the kingdom is with us.

2. *The Kingdom Present in Judgment*

Even now, "God is not mocked." [16] The kingdom is here in judgment even where it is denied by human sin. We live in a realm of law where sin and folly bring into the community confusion and trouble, while life in accordance with God's will brings healing and harmony. In this way He makes even our refusal of His will to demonstrate His ultimate sovereignty. His law is already in effect. We are judged by it, whether we abide by it or not.

3. *Some Citizens Now*

There are many people who have earnestly committed themselves into God's keeping and who, with the help of His Spirit, are now living in communion with Him. Christian love is their supreme and prevailing motive. Their greatest

---

[15] 1 Cor. 13:7–8.   [16] Gal. 6:7.

concern is to know and do God's will. Although few, if any, are citizens in an ideal sense, many have renounced all contrary loyalties and have begun learning to live as His loyal subjects. They have not completed this training but they have wholeheartedly begun it and God Himself has welcomed them to instruction. They have taken out their first naturalization papers in the divine kingdom.

4. Some Groups Living Cells of the Kingdom

Life under the reign of God is not an individualistic affair. Since love is its dominant principle, it is communal to the very core. This communal life of the kingdom has already begun in some groups and relationships. So far as that love and life are present, the kingdom of God is here.

C. The Kingdom Not Yet

Although the love of God is already a wonderful reality, and in relation to His purpose the kingdom is present in judgment, in personal devotion and in some group life, yet we must continue to look for the kingdom which is to come.

1. Judgment Not Yet Fully Manifest

In the world as we now see it there is much of rank injustice and cruelty. The wicked often prosper while the righteous languish in poverty and suffering. As seen in our earthly experience, every life, however faithful, ends in death. All this is plainly not the last word of divine judgment, the final judgment of God's love. His judgment is present, we see it in many events, and we believe that everywhere it is operative. But it also remains everywhere partially hidden from our eyes. Even as judgment the kingdom is not fully manifest to us.

2. Individual Imperfections and Sin

No one could look around him and suppose that the people of the world were living under the dominion of divine love in their hearts. The individual jealousy, greed, sensuality, pride and hate, the cynicism, unbelief, frustration and sorrow without hope observable everywhere are grim evidence that the kingdom has not come, for God's will is not "done on earth as it is in heaven."

3. Social Evil

Despite all the evident sin and absence of faith in individual lives, the group life of the world is in some respects so much worse that Reinhold Niebuhr could persuasively entitle a brilliant book, *Moral Man and Immoral Society*.

Every nation, as a nation, displays an arrogant pride and thoughtless selfishness which most of its people as individuals would heartily despise. As nations we still live on a level of such anarchical and violent relations with one another as have not prevailed in the affairs of individuals among any people of recorded history.

In our economic institutions we have crystallized the assumptions that everyone will try to get as large a share of wealth for as small a share of work as possible, that materialistic ends are dominant and that individualistic purposes are ultimate. Most of us would deny that these assumptions are true, as Christians we are committed to opposing them, and many do deny them by much generous action in personal relations. Yet when the structure of the economic order is at stake, every deviation from them is resisted as "radical" and "unrealistic."

The family is one institution in which individual ideals are more likely to be operative than in most of the larger groupings. Certainly the life of professing Christians is generally on a far higher level in their family relations than in the economic and political orders. Yet in most families decisions are made with so little consideration of God's will, there is such weak effort to achieve family solidarity in common devotion to the universal community of love, and there is so much of rivalry and jealousy in relation to other families, in addition to whatever tensions exist within the home, that it is evident the kingdom has not yet fully come even in family life.

Nor can the churches find much cause for boasting. They are publicly committed to the purpose of teaching and obeying the will of God and render many magnificent services of love. But they harbor many conditions which are in flagrant contrast to the spirit of the heavenly kingdom. Among these are racial segregation, denominational pride and strife, preoccupation with petty affairs, concern for material wealth and display to the detriment of educational and specifically religious aims, the striving for place and power, moral cowardice and spiritual indolence. Where such evils are present the kingdom of God is not yet fulfilled.

4. Christian Hope, Prayer and Work for the Kingdom

Because the true Christian's supreme devotion is to the kingdom and that kingdom has not yet been realized in its fullness, every Christian is bound to be among those who "through the Spirit, by faith, . . . wait for the hope of righteousness." [17] We believe that there is no problem that is solved rightly until it is solved in God's way and neither peace nor any other long-sought-for

[17] Gal. 5:5.

goal is attainable excepting through the reign of God. All our hope is directed to that reign.

When we pray as true followers of Christ, we always pray, "Thy kingdom come," whether we employ those words which he taught us or not. All other petitions must be subordinated to this, for we are to "seek first His kingdom."

With this same object we must also work, else our prayer and work would be divided. We have many tasks suited to our situations and skills. But any work in which a Christian has a right to be engaged is his calling under God for the sake of the kingdom. Being called of God to his work, he is to do it with the dominant purpose of sharing all the endowment and blessing which God has given him with other persons. If this purpose is to be fulfilled, then his life at work must be lived in the spirit of Christ, an open testimony of gratitude and faith.

But to what kind of coming are the Christian's hope, prayer and work for the kingdom directed? Will God suddenly intervene to establish His reign by one act of divine power? Or will the community of the divine Spirit already known to many grow in purity and in extent until it is here in all its fullness? Does our work express or affect only our own individual relation to the kingdom? Or has our work a place in God's purpose affecting the very realization of the kingdom itself?

These questions have very important implications for the practical moral and religious life. They serve to introduce one of the most controversial problems in recent theological thought, a problem to which our full attention must now be directed.

CHAPTER 36

How the Kingdom Is to Come

A. DIFFICULTY OF DISCOVERING JESUS' OWN EXPECTATION

IT is difficult to determine just how Jesus expected the kingdom of God was to come. There is much evidence to favor either of two irreconcilably contrary interpretations.

There is no question that in Jesus' thought God was the initiator and sovereign of the kingdom. It is by *His* power—however that power is conceived—that the kingdom was believed to be coming. On the other hand, Jesus left no doubt that the kingdom includes the faithful obedience and love of men. But how did he expect God's power to be employed in the coming of His reign? Or how were men to be made perfect in obedience and love?

B. THE TWO STRAINS OF DOCTRINE IN THE GOSPELS

On this problem there are two strains of teaching within the Gospels themselves. In one, the kingdom is expected to be inaugurated by a cataclysmic intervention. After spectacular signs and wonders, the Christ, who has departed into heaven, will return in overwhelming, glorious power to establish the divine rule. Jesus exhorts his hearers to watch for the signs and to be ready at any time for the day of his return.[1] In the other strain of teaching, the kingdom is described as already present. Although it looks small now it is to grow and spread until it becomes great.[2] His hearers are exhorted *not* to watch for signs as sinful people do,[3] for the kingdom is not to come with visible signs. It is, in fact, already in their midst,[4] and will continue to be, for the risen Christ is to remain with them.[5]

There is no textual ground for dismissing either type of teaching as a late addition to the text. In the earliest textual strands we can discover, the two teachings are already present side by side. Moreover, they are not presented as invariable, homogeneous, independent doctrines. Both occur in conjunction with many other ideas and are, from the literary standpoint, inextricably bound up

[1] Mt. 24; Mk. 13; Lk. 21:5–36. Cf. Acts 1:9–11.
[2] Mk. 4:30–32; Mt. 13:33.　　　　[3] Mt. 12:38–39; 16:4.
[4] Lk. 17:20–21.　　　　[5] Mt. 28:20.

with a large common body of narrative and teaching. Both are so clear and emphatic and so thoroughly imbedded in the records that it ill behooves anyone who respects the Gospels or anyone who cares for truth to take his stand with one of the two types of teaching, call it the Biblical view and charge dissenters with being ignorant or willful perverters of the Scripture. If there is to be any hope of finding the truth about Jesus' own view, we must begin by a candid facing of these perplexing and apparently irreconcilable evidences in the New Testament itself.

In our present discussion we shall, for convenience, call the one strain of evidence the *apocalyptic* teaching, but without implying that it is identical with the teaching of other apocalyptic literature. The other strain we shall call the *immanental* teaching, but without meaning, by this term, to identify it with any modern doctrine of divine immanence.

Such contrary evidences can hardly be interpreted by a Christian without the subordination of one strain of teaching to the other. For even if the student of the problem professes to accept both completely, just as they stand, he will find it impossible, in both theory and practice, actually to give both complete authority. How, for example, can he watch for prophetic signs of God's cataclysmic intervention, as he is exhorted to do in the apocalyptic teaching,[6] without falling under the condemnation of the words, "An evil and adulterous generation seeks for a sign"?[7] How is one to believe that "the kingdom of heaven is like leaven which a woman took and hid in three measures of meal, till it was all leavened,"[8] while believing also that, so far from being hidden, rather "as the lightning comes from the east and shines as far as the west, so will be the coming of the Son of man"?[9] Or suppose that we accept as Christ's teaching these words:

But in those days, after that tribulation, the sun will be darkened, and the moon will not give its light, and the stars will be falling from heaven, and the powers in the heavens will be shaken. And then they will see the Son of man coming in clouds with great glory.[10]

We shall then be rejecting as his teaching the most explicit and forthright repudiation of all such notions in the words,

The kingdom of God is not coming with signs to be observed [Gk.: in a manner capable of being watched; visibly]; nor will they say, "Lo, here it is!" or "There!" for behold, the kingdom of God is in the midst of you.[11]

---

[6] Mk. 13:28–30; Mt. 24:32–34; Lk. 21:28–32.
[7] Mt. 12:39; 16:4.
[8] Mt. 13:33.
[9] Mt. 24:27.
[10] Mk. 13:24–26.
[11] Lk. 17:20–21.

C. Possible Methods of Solution

Faced with such dilemmas, there seem to be three logical possibilities open to us. (1) We may suppose that Jesus himself was so confused regarding the manner of coming of the kingdom that he taught flatly contrary views concerning it and sometimes denounced as the work of "an evil and adulterous generation" acts which at other times he commanded. (2) We may think that he was an apocalyptist, expecting the kingdom to come by a spectacular divine intervention but that the contrary teachings are later insertions in the text or in the oral tradition preceding it or that these teachings must be interpreted in such strained fashion as may be necessary to make them conform to the apocalyptic expectation. (3) We may accept the immanental teachings as authentically representing Jesus' own understanding of the kingdom and then account for the apocalyptic passages as reporting Jesus' words inaccurately or out of context or as misunderstood figures of speech.

The first of these alternatives, besides involving a very low view of Jesus' teaching, not to say of his sanity, is intrinsically less plausible than either of the other two possibilities. We know that the teachings of Jesus were transmitted for several decades by word of mouth and various writings before any of our Gospels were written. When confusion and extreme contradiction appear, it is far more probable that they result from misunderstandings, errors of transmission and conflicts of doctrine within the Christian community than that they represent accurately the state of mind of a single man. This *prima facie* probability is strongly supported by the fact that from Paul's letters we know that before any of our Gospels had been written there was already vigorous doctrinal conflict in the churches and the further fact that Jesus' teaching made an impression upon his disciples unlikely to be produced by a man unable to make up his mind about basic matters near the center of his whole message.

Most scholars have actually chosen between the other two alternatives, although among the most conservative this has been done by emphasis, without explicit statement that any type of teaching in the Gospels was being reduced to a subordinate role. On the other hand, among the more radical scholars there are many who defend the second view in interpretation of Jesus' own position while still regarding it as a first-century delusion. It is plainly one thing to believe that Jesus expected the kingdom to come by spectacular divine intervention and quite another thing to believe that it did or will come in that way. Many recent scholars would affirm the historical proposition while declining to accept for themselves the view which they believe Jesus to have held.

Anyone who is inclined forthwith to read all such people out of the Christian community should be given pause by contemplating the heroic discipleship of the best-known among them, Albert Schweitzer. If it is true that "you will know them by their fruits," [12] such a man must be given high place among Christians of the twentieth century. We are fortunately not dependent upon having all of our opinions in proper order to live by the mercy and power of God. Men who have differed extremely on this and other problems of theology have been united in "righteousness and peace and joy in the Holy Spirit; he who thus serves Christ is acceptable to God and approved by men." [13] Paul well advises us, "Then let us no more pass judgment on one another." [14] On the other hand, we must judge ideas with all the critical clarity possible if we are to hope for truth, and in this task we must not be overawed by the personal reputations of those who defend the various views. Truth, like God, is no respecter of persons.

D. Arguments for Emphasis on the Apocalyptic Teachings

Since the writings of William Wrede and Albert Schweitzer on this subject were published in 1901 [15] and especially Schweitzer's *Von Reimarus zu Wrede* in 1906 translated into English and published in 1910 under the title *The Quest of the Historical Jesus,* the tendency among the New Testament scholars has turned strongly in favor of central emphasis on the apocalyptic passages in the interpretation of Jesus' own thought. Despite some noticeable recent reaction against this tendency, the apocalyptic emphasis has dominated New Testament scholarship in the first half of the twentieth century and it continues to be supported by the great learning of such men as Rudolf Bultmann.[16] Of course, this emphasis is based primarily on the apocalyptic passages in the Gospels themselves. However, since it involves, as we have seen, a minimizing of the contrary passages, it requires for its defense arguments for the preference shown to the apocalyptic teachings. Some of the most important of these arguments must now be briefly reviewed.

1. *Prevalence of Apocalyptic Expectations in Jesus' Time*

It is known that in the last two centuries preceding and the first two centuries following the birth of Jesus, the thought of the Jewish people was saturated with apocalyptic expectations. There was a great swelling hope in the hearts of the people, bursting frequently into speech and writing, that God would soon destroy the power of Rome and all others who oppressed His people and that in one final act He would establish His kingdom of righteousness and peace. If Jesus is to be accepted as truly belonging to his age, it is argued, and not as

---

[12] Mt. 7:20.   [13] Rom. 14:17–18.   [14] Rom. 14:13.

[15] Wrede, *Das Messiasgeheimnis in den Evangelien. Zugleich ein Beitrag zum Verständnis des Markusevangeliums*; Schweitzer, *Das Messianitäts- und Leidensgeheimnis. Eine Skizze des Lebens Jesu* (In English: *The Mystery of the Kingdom of God.* 1905).

[16] See especially his *Theology of the New Testament,* Vol. I, Pt. I.

a strange monster neither learning from his people nor intelligible to them, it must be supposed that when he talked of the kingdom he shared in their thought of it, just as his apocalyptic utterances indicate. As Schweitzer puts it,

If Jesus thinks like his contemporaries about the world and what happens in it, then his view of the coming of the Kingdom of God must resemble that of later Judaism.[17]

This argument would be more convincing if there were not so much evidence that Jesus did not "think like his contemporaries" in some matters which the Jewish leaders thought to be of the most vital importance. This is a fact which the accounts of the arrest, trial and crucifixion make abundantly clear. Corroborative evidence is found in the accounts of the disputes with the Pharisees and the frequent complaints of Jesus that even his nearest disciples misconstrued his message.

2. Apocalyptic Expectations of Paul and Other Early Christians

Attention is called also to the undeniable fact that Paul and his Christian contemporaries expected an early divine intervention to establish the kingdom or to make manifest the kingdom already spiritually established by Jesus. Since such belief in a miraculous divine act to end the age and show to all men the decisive power of God was held by Jesus' followers so soon after his ministry and, in the case of Paul, before the Gospels were written, it is said to be highly probable that Jesus had taught some such view.

There is obvious force in this contention. However, it falls short of being decisive for two reasons. First, it is still a fact that the contrary teachings are also in the Gospels. If they do not express the thought of Jesus, they do represent the thought of some authoritative Christian writers and so indicate that some of the early leaders in the church held views of the kingdom opposed to the apocalyptic expectations. Second, it is generally held by such scholars as Schweitzer and Bultmann that Paul's apocalyptic teaching was radically different from that of Jesus. If this view is acceptable it would seem also reasonable to believe that Paul could have differed from Jesus in holding a cataclysmic view of the kingdom's manifestation despite contrary teaching from Jesus.

3. Accounting for the Dramatic Power of the Gospel

The teaching that within a very short time God will miraculously terminate the present age and establish His righteous judgment is an excitingly dramatic teaching. Both the crucifixion of Jesus and the sensational creative power of the

[17] In the Epilogue of E. N. Mozley, *The Theology of Albert Schweitzer* (New York: The Macmillan Co., c.1950), p. 113.

early church show that the teaching and life of Jesus did produce excitement. Is it not reasonable, then, to believe that the passages reporting Jesus as proclaiming the imminent coming of the kingdom do authentically represent the drama of his message?

But if it had been a message of imminent, decisive divine intervention in power which was needed to produce the dramatic birth of the church, then the message of any one of several other apocalyptists might as well have served the purpose. For since the writing of Daniel such proclamations of early deliverance had not been wanting. Moreover, if it was this immediate expectation which was mainly responsible for the creative power of the primitive church, it was founded on an error and its strength should have waned when the error was made evident by events. But actually Christians could expect the immediate return of Christ or reject such expectation without stopping the onward march of the Christian movement. Its main dynamic must have been elsewhere.

4. Explanation of Immanental Passages Proposed

The interpreters of Jesus as an apocalyptist use two principal methods of explaining the presence in the Gospels of passages which we have characterized as immanental or contrary to the apocalyptic teachings.

First, such passages may be referred to rationalizing reinterpretations of Jesus' message after it became evident that his prophecy of the cataclysmic divine ending of the age had not come before the deaths of his disciples.[18] When the kingdom failed to come spectacularly, it is argued, then the Christians of the second generation developed the notion that the inauguration of the kingdom was invisible and spiritual, so that the apocalyptic expectation of a visible heavenly visitation had been a mistake. This rationalization crept into the tradition and record, it is held, so that alongside the authentic apocalyptic teachings are the later denials of them.

Second, some of the passages which seem to imply the present immanence and growth of the kingdom are interpreted to mean nothing of the kind. For example, Bultmann goes so far as to retranslate Luke 17:21, to make it read,

God's reign comes not so that it can be calculated; and none can say, "Lo here or there!" For lo, God's Reign is (all at once) in your midst![19]

If one can change the plain meaning of words in such fashion,[20] it is, of course, not difficult to insist, as does the same author, that the parables of seed

---

[18] See Mt. 24:34; Mk. 13:30; Lk. 21:32; and especially Mt. 16:28. Cf. Mt. 10:23.

[19] Theology of the New Testament. Vol. I, p. 6.

[20] Note that the words quoted are set forth as a translation, not as a theoretical reconstruction.

and of leaven teach nothing of immanence or of growth, but only of miraculous divine action which can inexplicably change the minute into the great.[21]

As for the idea that the immanental teachings were introduced in the second generation, the initial plausibility of the theory must be admitted. Yet it seems questionable that such ideas would have been introduced without any modification of the emphatic passages which they contradicted. For such a device could hardly have relieved the embarrassment which events had created by contradicting teachings attributed to the Master. Indeed, if the device was used, it actually introduced the additional embarrassment of contradicting those same teachings by other words attributed to him.

5. Despair of a Gradual Coming

Some proponents of the apocalyptic interpretation defend it in spite of their own conviction that Jesus was mistaken in holding such a conception of the kingdom.[22] But others maintain that the apocalyptic form of Jesus' hope is shown by events to have been a primary source of strength. The recent history of the world, it is insisted, with the terrible world wars, the new outbreak of cruel tyranny, and the threats of greater disaster, shows clearly that the kingdom is not coming gradually within human affairs, but if it is to come must enter by a breaking in of God to overrule all human actions and institutions by His all-conquering power.

Times of great disaster, when whole nations and civilizations are threatened or destroyed, are times when apocalyptic hopes have special attraction for many persons whose faith can find no other means of support. Such situations were the environment for the original Jewish and Christian apocalypticism and it is natural that the renewal of vast human cruelty and tragedy should revive apocalyptic interests. Moreover, there is in such views the sound idea that any permanent victory must be won in the spirit and power of God. Any notion of "man alone" winning his own peace is as false as the notion that "man alone" can come into existence or sustain his own being. It is to God that we must look for our salvation.

However, it is another thing to say that God will win the victory for us in a unilateral act of sheer power, an act which He will perform at His own good pleasure and an act in which we have no part excepting to be prepared or unprepared as individuals to receive the benefits of His action. It is well that the Christian community early repudiated any such notions as that. It will be a sad day when Christians generally become so disillusioned with the possibilities of God working through human beings that they adopt such a desperate ex-

---

[21] *Ibid.*, pp. 7–8.
[22] E.g., see Schweitzer, in Mozley, *op. cit.*, pp. 114–17.

pedient of faith. For in addition to the passivism it would be bound to induce, such a view would imply the doctrine that God can make all things well whenever He pleases but for the present prefers that men should continue their sinful blundering with all its tragic consequences. In the long run such implications would be sure to bring the downfall of so reckless a faith.

E. ARGUMENTS FOR MAKING IMMANENTAL TEACHINGS NORMATIVE

1. *Apocalyptic Bias to Be Expected in That Time*

As the defenders of the apocalyptic emphasis have pointed out, apocalyptic hopes were very prevalent among the Jews of the first century. That being true, is it not more likely that in their understanding his hearers and later reporters bent his teachings in the direction of apocalypticism rather than against the prevailing trends of thought? It would, indeed, be very remarkable if there were no signs to be found of such intrusions of the dominant thought of the time into the memories, traditions and interpretations recorded in the Gospels.

2. *Oral Report Tends to Substitute the Spectacular for the Spiritual*

The tendency of the prevailing apocalypticism to penetrate the tradition of a spiritual and nonapocalyptic teacher would be strengthened by the almost universal inclination of oral report to minimize morally exacting spiritual teaching and to exaggerate in emphasis and meaning any suggestion of spectacular, sensuous imagery. The popular imagination and memory can be attached more readily to pictures of heavenly figures descending from the clouds than to grim warnings of personal responsibility to bear and extend the testimony of righteous living. Once attached to such images, however they may have been originally introduced, oral reports are likely to elaborate them greatly in a short time.

3. *Jesus' Predictions of National Disaster Misunderstood*

In view of the many abortive uprisings which had occurred in Palestine before and during Jesus' lifetime and the continued nationalistic and materialistic form of the dominant Jewish hope, Jesus may well have predicted, like the earlier prophets, the imminent destruction of Jerusalem and other disasters to the Jewish people. The beginning of the "Little Apocalypse" [23] and also various other sections of it look like parts of precisely such a prophecy. Given the prevalent apocalyptic expectation that there would be new and great tribulations just before the divine intervention from the skies, it would have been natural

[23] Mk. 13; Mt. 24; Lk. 21:5-36.

that such dire prophecies would immediately have been expanded into the familiar formulas of salvation-after-new-disaster. If we may suppose that this is what happened, we may even find evidence that Jesus anticipated and sought to prevent this putting of his prophecy into a mistaken context. For we do have in the midst of the apocalyptic passages repeated admonitions that even after many great disasters his hearers must not suppose that "the end" is at hand and warnings against being misled. On the other hand, if the apocalyptic teachings are taken as literal and authentic teachings of Jesus, it is strange indeed to find these admonitions that even after "wars and rumors of wars . . . the end is not yet," occurring in the same context with insistence that the end is already at hand and will certainly come during the lifetime of the contemporary generation.

4. Some Such Passages Possible Misinterpretations of Other Teachings

The same tendencies to spectacular apocalyptic distortions of his teachings may well have produced misinterpretations of other teachings also and may account for elements in the apocalyptic passages not accounted for by reference to prophecies of national disaster.

For example, in view of Jesus' emphatic teaching of a blessed life after death he may well have assured his disciples that he and they would soon be reunited in the heavenly kingdom and in that sense he would return to them after testings and tribulations soon to come.[24] If Jesus gave such assurance to the repentant thief on Calvary [25] he would be expected the more certainly to give this comfort to his faithful disciples. But in the efforts to organize their memories of his teaching later it would have been easy to place such promises in context with prophecies of other tribulations, namely, those of the nation, and to understand the whole as belonging in the familiar apocalyptic pattern. If it be supposed that Jesus also predicted his resurrection, that prediction might have become similarly misplaced and misunderstood on some occasions.

Again Jesus may have predicted that his message, set forth now as a warning and merciful assurance of ready forgiveness to all true penitents, would return in the harsh form of judgment—as we have seen that the truths of God's law do frequently return within history. In the style of Semitic prophecy such teaching might well have been put figuratively in personal form as a prediction of his own return in vengeful judgment upon the unrighteous.[26] If it be protested that such figurative use of personal identity would have been impossible for him, it must be noted that according to Matthew's Gospel he did say that John the Baptist was Elijah returned to earth.[27]

[24] Cf. Acts 7:56.
[26] Cf. Mt. 24:44-51.

[25] Lk. 23:43.
[27] Mt. 11:14; 17:10-13. Cf. Mal. 4:5.

5. *The Apocalyptic Expectations Were Not Fulfilled*

It is obvious that during the lifetime of the disciples the celestial catastrophes predicted in the apocalyptic passages did not occur and the Son of man did not come "on the clouds of heaven with power and great glory"; nor "send out his angels with a loud trumpet call." Whoever made these predictions was plainly mistaken, even though he was right about the need for placing all hope in God. If Jesus was the genuine source of these passages, then he was mistaken about the very thing which was at the center of his thought and message—the immediate prospect of a spectacular divine intervention to establish the kingdom of God.

This is precisely the view taken by Schweitzer and Bultmann alike. But it raises serious and far-reaching questions about the authority of Jesus and also about the explanation of his actual historical influence. Schweitzer seemed, in *The Quest of the Historical Jesus,* to attribute the authority and power only to certain ideas ("that which is eternal in the words of Jesus"[28]) while the historical figure remained an inexplicable mystery. But in 1950 he took clearer and stronger ground as he wrote,

> Both Johannes Weiss and I have suffered severely through the compulsion which truth laid upon us to put forward something which was bound to offend Christian faith.
> To me, however, Jesus remains what he was. Not for a single moment have I had to struggle for my conviction that in him is the supreme spiritual and religious authority, though his expectation of the speedy advent of a supernatural Kingdom of God was not fulfilled, and we cannot make it our own.[29]

Yet if Jesus believed that the kingdom was to be established by a visible cataclysm, that belief would seem to have important implications concerning the nature of the kingdom itself, implications affecting all thought concerning human responsibility, concerning the spiritual inwardness of God's reign and concerning the other relations between man and God. On these matters Schweitzer is compelled by his own concern for truth and right to adopt views contrary to these implications of apocalypticism. Actually, then, he does not seem in his own spiritual thought and life to accept as authoritative the views which he thinks Jesus as apocalyptist held. Rather he conceives of the kingdom in terms of immanental growth. But since just such a conception appears in the Gospels alongside the others it would be more consistent with Schweitzer's doctrine of Christ's "supreme spiritual and religious authority" to accept the immanental conception as that of Christ himself.

[28] P. 402.   [29] In Mozley, *op. cit.,* p. 113.

With Bultmann the case is different. For he concedes to the Jesus of history no extraordinary authority, apparently regarding him as of no special distinction in either thought or life, excepting that God chose to use his life and death as the occasion for revealing the gospel of which Jesus himself did not know at all.[30] But this view results in a strange dualism of thought. Up to a point there is the most objective, critical effort to reconstruct the history of events and to explain how it is reasonable to think those events transpired. But this explanation leading to a view of a rather ordinary prophetic apocalyptist whose life and teaching could be no explanation of the creative power released in the world through him, this power is then attributed in most uncritical fashion to the mysteries of God. Now if a historian is to account for historical events in this fashion, there seems to be no good reason why he should stop being critical at one point rather than another. If historical explanations are to be given at all, then one thing which the historian ought to take into account is that through the Jesus who actually lived at a particular time a tremendous creative force was released in human society. For such a historical explanation an ordinary apocalyptic prophet with no unusual ideas and without superior character or personality will not suffice.

If such a God as Jesus called "Father" is to reign, then He must reign in willingly obedient, faithful, loving hearts. Such a reign is not a matter of external rule through astronomical displays of awful power, though all power is finally at the disposal of God's will. Love and faithful, willing obedience are not subject to coercion. They are elicited by acts of supreme worthiness to receive them. "We love because He first loved us." We have seen His love in Jesus of Nazareth. So far as we respond to that love by giving our own faithful, obedient love, He reigns within our hearts and lives. That reign is His kingdom, now partial and fragmentary, but destined to grow, by His grace and our response, to its fulfillment.

F. The Kingdom and the World

It must not be supposed for a moment that the immanental view of the kingdom here defended as Jesus' teaching and as truth implies a kingdom limited to this world. To say "the kingdom of God is in the midst of you" is not to say that the kingdom is of this world.[31] The kingdom is God's. It neither began nor will end in the actions or institutions of men on earth. Its citizens are persons whose lives are not limited to the earth. The stuff of the kingdom does not consist of political governments, economic orders nor ecclesiastical organizations. It does consist of a community of persons to which community earthly

[30] *Op. cit.*, pp. 35–37.
[31] See Jn. 18:36.

institutions may be either instrumental or hostile but in which these institutions are never of the essence.

Should the Christian, then, be indifferent to problems of political order and economic justice? Far from it! For the institutions of earth are like the wooden forms within which cement is poured to fashion dens of vice or cathedrals of worship. The forms are but temporary, yet they shape the structure which endures. In the kingdom it is the person and the community of persons under God which will endure. But this community is affirmed or denied by what we do in politics and commerce. By the social evils we tolerate, many a person is embittered, turned against his fellows and blinded so that he cannot see the light of God. On the other hand, a prophetic act which challenges the injustice of the world and defies man's sinful barriers to brotherhood serves to draw many a lonely, hopeless one into the kingdom of love and faith.

The Christian has all the reason anyone has for attacking injustice, war and every other social evil. But he has much more reason than most. For in addition to the evils others deplore, he sees in these evils the denial of God, rebellion against the kingdom and blights upon the priceless, eternal souls of men.

God's kingdom is not of this world. But it is here in our midst that we must now seek that pearl of great value and it is here that we must let God even now reign over us in all that we do and are. It is only as we earnestly work to subject all to His rule that we can honestly pray, "Thy kingdom come, Thy will be done on earth as it is in heaven."

CHAPTER 37

Origin and Purpose of the Church

A. The Spiritual Church

MUCH confused thinking and many false doctrines have arisen from the failure to distinguish between the spiritual church and the organized church. To be sure, the two are often in a most intimate relationship. But, on the other hand, they are unfortunately often far apart. To attribute to the organized church all that belongs to the spiritual church is to make claims which cannot be supported in fact. Such false claims often hide from men's eyes the true glory of the spiritual church. Bad as that is, it is much worse when such claims are made for some mere part of the organized church. For this can be done only in such proud partisanship as to deny the very spirit of Christ by which the spiritual church lives.

1. Not "Invisible"

The spiritual church to which we are now turning attention is not what is often referred to as the invisible church. Strictly speaking, it is not visible to the eye. But neither is it something outside human experience. The spiritual church is not the ideal of what the church ought to be. Neither is it the mere aggregate number of all the individuals known to God as "saved" or destined to salvation.

2. The Koinonia

By the spiritual church is meant that unique and powerful fellowship of sharing created by the power of the Holy Spirit and spoken of hitherto as the *koinonia*. Far from being only an ideal or, on the other hand, a mere aggregation of individuals, it is a living community overreaching all others in extent, surpassing all others in depth of meaning, and richest of all values in the experience of its members. It is, then, closely related to the kingdom of God as already present. For it is the real spiritual fellowship of all those persons who have committed themselves to the reign of God, whose Word was made manifest in Jesus Christ.

3. *The Body of Christ*

Repeatedly Paul speaks of the church as the body of Christ. Thus he says,

For as in one body, we have many members, and all the members do not have the same function, so we, though many, are one body in Christ, and individually members one of another.[1]

But best known is the great passage in which he develops this analogy in detail as he appeals to the Corinthians for love, forbearance and unity. Here he begins by saying,

For just as the body is one and has many members, and all the members of the body, though many, are one body, so it is with Christ. For by one Spirit we were all baptized into one body—Jews or Greeks, slaves or free—and all were made to drink of one Spirit.[2]

In this way he stresses the divine origin of the spiritual church which has enabled it to overcome all human barriers to unity. But he emphasizes also that this God-given fellowship changes the relationships of individuals in a very immediate, experienced, practical way. It is no merely theoretical body in which we might believe without observed evidence. It is so personal and experiential that Paul can write,

If one member suffers, all suffer together; if one member is honored, all rejoice together.

Now you are the body of Christ and individually members of it.[3]

It must be sadly confessed that of no single local congregation, much less of any great association of congregations, can we say unconditionally that these people are constantly, always, a true part of the spiritual church. Although Paul wrote to the Corinthian Christians, "you are the body of Christ," yet it is apparent that this was strictly true only at times. It was not constantly true of those people, in actuality, that when one suffered all suffered together and when one rejoiced all rejoiced together. The sad fact that it was not constantly true provided the very occasion of Paul's writing as he did. He was reminding them that they ought to live continuously under the dominion of Christ, in the exalted spirit of unity and mutual concern which they experienced in their highest hours. They knew well what it was to be the church, but they were not always the church. They were the church, the body of Christ, only when they truly accepted Jesus Christ as head. For "he is the head of the body, the church."[4]

---

[1] Rom. 12:4–5. Cf. Eph. 5:29–30; Col. 1:18; 3:14–15.
[2] 1 Cor. 12:12–13.
[3] 1 Cor. 12:26–27.   [4] Col. 1:18.

Whenever and wherever he is not at the head, that is, when and where a body of men and women have not the communion of the Holy Spirit, hence the true *koinonia,* there is not the body of Christ.

4. *Outside the Church No Salvation*

When we are speaking of the spiritual church, the body of Christ, then, but then only, it is true that "outside the church there is no salvation." This is true because the spiritual church is essential both as means and as meaning of salvation. It is through the love and faith of those who are members of the body that others are won to faith and grafted into the body. Moreover, if anyone belongs to Christ then he will be also in faithful communion with others, on earth and in heaven, who are of the spiritual church. John Wesley spoke truly when he said, "The gospel of Christ knows no religion but social: no holiness but social holiness." [5] The man, woman or child learns to love God through learning to respond to God's love as expressed through the love of a parent, teacher, minister or friend. But as soon as he receives the love of God, responding in faith, he reaches out in love to every brother in Christ. Then, in the strength of this membership in the body of Christ he seeks to share this priceless gift with *every* brother, however wicked or unlovely.

But what has this spiritual church to do with the organized church?

B. ORIGIN OF THE ORGANIZED CHURCH

1. *The Teaching of Jesus*

We do not know how clearly Jesus himself envisioned the organized church. By the time the Gospels were written it was a long established reality. Since the evangelists were churchmen, it is natural to suppose that they were inclined to interpret the traditions in terms of church life. Even more important, the traditions had been for some time transmitted among members of the organized church and so may have been already affected by similar influence. If, therefore, some of the terminology of the church were to have crept into the reports of Jesus' teaching that would be as natural as the translation of his words from Aramaic to Greek.

It is a tribute to the fidelity of the tradition that there is so little actual evidence of such a process. The word "church" (*ekklesia*) does not appear at all in any Gospel excepting Matthew and even there only three times. In contrast,

---

[5] Quoted in R. Newton Flew, *et al., The Nature of the Christian Church according to the Teaching of the Methodists* (London: The Methodist Publishing House, 1937), p. 13, from *Poetical Works of John and Charles Wesley,* I, 22.

the Pauline letters, written before even the earliest of the Gospels, employ the word about forty times. This is not due to a different vocabulary of the *writers,* since Luke uses the word eighteen times in the Acts but not at all in his Gospel. It would look as if there were no occasion to use it in the Gospel because Jesus did not use it.

There is ground for doubt, then, that the three references in Matthew are accurate. This doubt is furthered by comparing the passage on the correction and forgiveness of a brother, in which two of the references occur (Mt. 18:15-18, 21-22) with the instructions on the same subject as reported in Luke 17:3-4.

Jesus spoke continually of the kingdom of God, but it is a question whether he ever spoke of the church. There is no authentic report of instructions by him concerning forms of permanent church organization. He did, however, establish a fellowship of disciples in which the Twelve had pre-eminence. This fellowship appears to have been informal.

2. *Some Organization an Inevitable Expression of Christian Faith*

Although Jesus apparently devoted little attention to planning any organizational structure for the perpetuation and extension of the fellowship for which he gave his life, some such structure was inevitable. That love which belongs to the very essence of the Christian faith implies earnest efforts to share the meaning and experience conveyed by the gospel itself. Such efforts require formal organization. This is necessary in order to provide for the responsible collection, conservation and expenditure of funds,[6] to designate and train qualified leaders, to hold and manage properties needed for education, worship, fellowship and other Christian purposes, indeed to make effective in the world, in every possible way, the message and faith of the spiritual church.

Just as the human individual's body which serves as his means of communication and without which he could not exist in the world frequently tempts him to sin, so the organized church continually threatens to stifle or betray the spiritual church. It does so in ways analogous to the temptings by the physical organism. Social organization sets up its own characteristic forces, just as the body produces its own passions. In both instances the spiritual life must seize and keep the initiative, constantly renew its faithful commitments and ceaselessly pray for divine aid if it is to rule the body. Only when it does rule can the external structure fulfill its own function. There is no sorrier spectacle than an organized church in which pride of office, love of material display and striving for worldly prestige have displaced the fellowship of the Holy Spirit as the governing power. Such a church is not, in fact, a church of Jesus Christ, for Christ is not at its head.

[6] Cf. Acts 11:29-30.

But despite the perils and temptations inherent in organization, the organized church is necessary. To have life in the spiritual church without any concern with its organized, outer expression is almost as difficult as to have a loving heart without employing any material means for loving deeds. Now and then a devout group suddenly awakens to the subtle way in which many people transfer their supreme allegiance from God to some part of the organized church or succumb to other temptations of organization. Occasionally such a group renounces all "denominations" and affirms the pure life of spiritual fellowship without organization. But soon every such group either disappears or takes on many of the institutional forms of other church organizations. For better or worse we are in the world. In the world, life, whether individual or social, requires embodiment in some structural means of nurture and expression.

C. Purpose of the Organized Church

1. Some False Conceptions

a. Solely the Publication of the Gospel

Some Christians suppose that the one and only proper function of the organized church is to declare to sinners the gospel invitation. They hold that the success of any church movement is to be determined solely by the number of its converts. But if the word which is declared approaches even remotely the rich meanings of the New Testament, success in winning converts must lead soon to a broader program. For if converts are to declare the gospel to others, they must be instructed. Teaching requires co-operative effort. It also requires decisions regarding the proper content and materials of instruction. If the guidance of the New Testament is sought in the meeting of these tasks, it will soon be learned that the gospel requires much more than the verbal proclamation itself, however persuasive the proclamation may be.

b. Mainly Social Reform

Some men, on the other hand, are interested in the organized church chiefly or exclusively as a means of bringing about political, economic and cultural change. Now it is undeniable that the organized church has in the past frequently effected such change. Nor should it be doubted that further change is imperatively needed. But an organization formed principally for this purpose would lack the particular kind of power to effect social reform which has been possessed by the church in the hours of its most decisive influence.

c. To Be the Kingdom of God

Some communions have unfortunately identified the spiritual church and even the whole kingdom of God, so far as that kingdom is realized upon earth, with the organized church. The true organized church has been restricted to their own particular organizations. The supreme task of such a church organization has become, then, its own accretion of maximum extent and power.

The Roman Catholic definition of the church is given by Cardinal Bellarmine, as follows:

A body of men united together by the profession of the same Christian Faith, and by participation in the same sacraments, under the governance of lawful pastors, more especially of the Roman Pontiff, the sole vicar of Christ on earth.[7]

Such a conception of the church is indefensible at three points. First, it identifies the spiritual body of men under Christ with the externally formed organization. Second, it identifies the total true church with one particular organization which very obviously has no monopoly on the fruits of the Spirit. Third, by its assignment of supreme authority on earth to this one organization and more specifically to one man, it is guilty of the most arrogant and sinful presumption. No organized church body nor even the total organized church, including all its constituent branches, can rightly arrogate to itself sole claim to be the one channel of God's truth and grace upon earth. God has ordained that men should live in the family, in industry, in the state and in culture as well as in the church. God speaks and acts through all, so far as men submit all to His will. An organized church which asks unconditional submission to its earthly head or makes its own extent and power the supreme earthly goal is teaching idolatry. For we are still to have no other gods but God and we are still to seek first His kingdom, both on earth and in heaven.

This is not to say that all Roman Catholics are idolators. Many are devout worshipers of the one God and always maintain a certain reserve in relation to claims by the officials of their own church. This is true of many priests as well as laymen. As to the intent and the saving faith of other men we must "judge not" that we "be not judged." But this does not absolve us from the necessity of judging between truth and error nor of warning against the mortal peril of some teachings which lead to sin and to monstrous social evils.

d. To Impart Divine Grace by Correct Rites

The spiritual church is, as we have observed, a channel of divine grace. The organized church can be exceedingly useful in the nurture and expression of this divinely given life. But this truth is sometimes distorted into a legalistic

[7] Quoted by G. H. Joyce in article, "The Church," in *The Catholic Encyclopedia.*

and almost magical [8] conception of a divine gift which requires for its transmission a correct adherence to prescribed forms of sacramental ritual and the quite material validity of orders on the part of the celebrants. Unfortunately for such theories, many persons who have received sacraments in "irregular" fashion from persons laying no claim to any outward apostolic succession, or who, like many of the Friends, have never received any of the prescribed sacraments at all, still show such fruits of the Spirit as to put most of us to shame.

Apparently, however neatly men define the channels through which the Spirit must pass, Jesus' word still remains true, that the Spirit moves, like the wind, with force and direction which we are unable either to predict or to define with any degree of exactness. It would also seem true that God is still more concerned with "clean hands and a pure heart" [9] than with outward conformity to prescriptions of any law, new or old. He who condemned the love of broad phylacteries, long fringes and "being called rabbi by men" [10] would probably have little patience with those elaborate prescriptions of proper vestments and of exclusive orders so dear to the hearts of some churchmen today.

The sacraments, however, have a very important and rightful place in the church's life. That rightful place will be discussed in a later chapter.

2. *True Purposes of the Organized Church*

The purposes which the organized church ought to serve are those implied by its relationship to the spiritual church.

a. Nurture and Expression of Christian Love

Foremost is the cultivation and expression of the sacred *koinonia* itself. In all the relations of the various officers and members of the organized church they are to pursue the "more excellent way" of love.[11] For only in this way can the outward church organization truly incarnate that other body, the body of Christ, the spiritual church. The first duty of the church is to *be* the church, the outward embodiment of the divine Word still living in the world "full of grace and truth." So far as it fails in this it must fail also in the various tasks which arise from this, its rightful nature. Paul speaks to every church when he writes to Corinth, "Let all that you do be done in love." [12]

---

[8] Probably never altogether magical in the thought of responsible churchmen. The Roman Catholic doctrine, as defined by the Council of Trent, that the efficacy of the sacrament is *ex opere operato*, but only for "those who put no obstacle" in the way, is a case in point. The tendency of Roman Catholic writers is to interpret even the lack of various active intentions on the part of the recipient as an "obstacle," and hence to keep in view positive spiritual requirements for the recipient, even though not for the minister. Yet the doctrine makes the distinction between spiritual sacrament and mere magic dangerously thin.

[9] Ps. 24:4.

[10] Mt. 23:5-7.

[11] I Cor. 12:27-13:13.

[12] I Cor. 16:13.

b. Instruction and Exhortation

Without the gospel there is no church. In every new generation the church must seek afresh to know the truth which God has long sought so wonderfully to disclose and must make it known to all its members. There will be in this truth much that is familiar to the Christian community. But the Holy Spirit is still at work and much that needs to be taught in any age will be new. If the church is to perform its teaching function aright it must be constantly faithful to its truth-seeking task also. Every teacher must be first and always a learner, with open eyes and heart.

But if the people are to be "doers of the word, and not hearers only," [13] they must not only be taught but also exhorted and persuaded to act upon the truth disclosed. This, as well as teaching, is a task for every preacher. But it is also a task for all members of the church, for all need encouragement and incitement to good from all. "Therefore," says the apostle, "encourage one another and build one another up," [14] and also, "admonish the idle, encourage the fainthearted, help the weak, be patient with them all." [15]

c. Maintaining Communal Worship and Prayer

The people who are of the body of Christ need not only to commune with God but to do so together. The organized church has the task of providing the necessary place, media of communication, staff and helpful symbols to encourage and extend this practice and to see that "all things" are "done decently and in order." [16]

d. Corporate Acts in the World

Every Christian is impelled by the Spirit of God to perform various acts of kindness and useful generosity through many institutional channels and in direct personal relations with his neighbors. But wherever the spiritual church is strong within the organized church there is also a strong impulse to act together as a Christian body in relations with the world. Hence, the organized church properly establishes hospitals and supports the training of doctors and nurses for healing, supports agencies for the relief of poverty, establishes schools and colleges to raise the level of both intelligence and character and in many other ways ministers to multitudes outside its own membership and often in distant lands. These things must be done if the church is truly to live in loyalty to the Master, who said,

---

[13] Jas. 1:22.
[15] I Thess. 5:14.

[14] I Thess. 5:11.
[16] I Cor. 14:40.

. . . whoever would be great among you must be your servant, and whoever would be first among you must be slave of all. For the Son of man also came not to be served but to serve. . . .[17]

More than this the church must do. It must unceasingly proclaim, by word and deed combined, the good news of salvation. So long as its people possess the true riches of the kingdom within their own fellowship they are bound to seek the sharing of them with others. A church that is not a missionary church and an evangelistic church shows that either it has no life which it prizes or that it has not enough love to care about extending that life to others. In either case it condemns itself as lacking the *koinonia,* the true spiritual church, within its gates. In short, whatever its admirable qualities may be, it is not in truth a church.

Yet that is not all the church must do in its outreach into the world beyond its own borders. It would not show true compassion to minister to those who are bruised and broken by injustice or war and yet not to raise a hand in defense of the multitudes who are being prepared for fresh injuries. To sit by while one man injures his brother, however promptly we may minister to the wounded one, shows little love for either wrongdoer or victim. Rather the church must incessantly raise its voice in prophetic warning against the social evils in all the institutions of the day. The church must not try to *be* a state or an economic order, but remaining in its own role as conserver and voice of the spiritual life within, it must continually speak to the state and the economic order. In all its judgments it must avoid even the appearance of being one organization competing for power and prestige among other organizations. Its peculiar power lies not in self-seeking but in searching for truth and justice and peace for all, in the spirit of Jesus Christ. For this, too, is part of being "first" by being "slave of all."

[17] Mk. 10:43-45.

CHAPTER 38

Division, Unity and Authority of the Church

A. DIVISION

1. *The Present Disunity*

CHRISTIANS throughout the world are increasingly concerned with their separation from one another. The barriers introduced between them by political strife and all its interference with fellowship and even with factual communication must bring sorrow to everyone who prays for the coming kingdom of love. But in some ways it is even more humiliating and tragic that we are separated by loyalties and convictions arising within the organized church. For barriers enforced by external powers can be surmounted at least by spiritual intent. On the other hand, the willingness, and often the determination, of Christians to exclude other Christians from their own organized expression of faith strikes at the very heart of the spiritual church itself.

Where in all the present organizational division and confusion is the one body of Christ to be found? The Roman Catholic apologists say, of course, that it is only with them. But by their exclusive claims they only demonstrate that their church is one of the most narrowly sectarian and schismatic of all. For few other church organizations would deny that the body of Christ included many outside their own bounds. Few others would so dogmatically assert the part for the whole. But why should *any* Christians separate themselves from one another?

2. *Shame and Burden*

Even though the members of one organization freely grant that others, outside their group, are within the true spiritual church of Christ, the separateness of organization is an exceedingly serious matter. Even though the Methodists and Presbyterians in a community agree on mutual recognition in Christian fellowship—as they generally do in transfer of membership—so long as they maintain separate church organizations they do not often, in actual fact, worship together or share in common Christian concern and work. Some of them are united in lodge and political party and even work side by side in factory or office all through the week. Their families may be socially intimate. Yet when

Sunday comes, just when Christians should be drawn closest together, and when all associations should be exalted by being taken before God in common worship, these good friends part and go their separate ways to the churches of their choice or of their traditional family loyalty. Here is one reason why so many Christians remain secular in their associations with one another. Their faith, instead of providing a common sacred basis for all that unites them, becomes the occasion which divides them.

The churches are continually speaking to the world about the need for understanding, peace and brotherhood among all classes and nations. Yet their testimony is immeasurably weakened by the fact that they themselves are unable to unite as they ask the world to do. Moreover, as H. Richard Niebuhr has so convincingly pointed out,[1] much of their division follows the very lines of race, nationality and social and economic status which divide the world.

These deep and all-pervasive compromises of the Christian fellowship and message are not the only burdens placed upon us by our divisions. We must add the waste of effort and funds in overlapping work, resources which could be used to meet some of humanity's appalling needs. Further, the dingy inadequacy of many struggling, competing churches, unable to provide trained leadership or appropriate buildings, testify to the world how shameful a price Christians are willing to pay to keep themselves apart.

Differences of temperament and experience which prepare various Christians for divergent types of worship and other religious expression explain some of the divisions, but hardly justify them. Radically different religious observances can be provided within a single fellowship if there is the will to serve one another's needs. Even the doctrinal differences seem not to explain most of the denominational cleavages. Between laymen and even between ministers of the same church there are usually greater theological differences to be found than between the main doctrinal emphasis of that church and the central emphasis of some other churches. Moreover, we do not usually regard the theological divergence from truth of neighboring churches as so serious that we cannot recognize their pastors and people as Christians. Why, then, do we not agree to differ and yet unite in worship and service? The very fact of our organizational separation compels us to confess that Niebuhr is right when he says,

We accept the correction, limitation and complementation of one by the other unwillingly and, rather than remain in the community of forgiveness and truly common faith, we separate from each other by withdrawal or excommunication.[2]

---

[1] See his *Social Sources of Denominationalism in America.*

[2] H. Richard Niebuhr, "The Disorder of Man in the Church of God" in "The Amsterdam Assembly Series" entitled *Man's Disorder and God's Design* (N.Y.: Harper & Brothers, 1949), Vol. I, p. 83. The entire series constitutes a valuable source work on recent ecumenical thought.

B. Unity

1. *In God's Love and Purpose*

The one point at which the division of the church is wholly transcended is in the love and purpose of God Himself. To men and women of many churches alike He has given assurance of His love and the fruits of His grace. The Holy Spirit shows no regard for denominational lines.

2. *In the Loyalty of Many Christians*

Great and increasing numbers of people in the churches unhesitatingly place their loyalty to organized Christendom as a whole above their allegiance to any of its particular branches. Indeed, many devout and faithful church workers care so little for denominational differences that they willingly place their wholehearted membership in any one of a dozen churches which in a given local community seems to offer best opportunity for helpful association and useful service.

3. *In the Spiritual Church*

The external division is, as we have observed, evidence of grave spiritual disunity. However, despite the serious existing limitations of fellowship, members of the churches do frequently share their Christian experience across all the barriers of organization. Not only does such fellowship cross the lines which separate different churches in the same great traditions, but frequently brings together in mutual inspiration and grateful exchange of Christian witness members of the most diverse communions. Such experiences of sharing are only partial and often individually short-lived. But collectively they do link together the broken fragments of the church in a priceless network of spiritual brotherhood.

4. *The Quest for Organizational Unity*

Efforts to heal the divisions of the church have increased rapidly in the middle of the twentieth century and have become the most distinctive characteristic of churchmanship in this period. Besides the cultivation of personal fellowship many more formal movements are under way. Local churches arrange increasing numbers of united services of worship and co-operative community service. Carefully organized councils of churches are at work from local communities to the ecumenical World Council and their functions are steadily increasing. Several churches have formed complete organic unions and others are negotiating toward similar ends.

Meanwhile, many local churches have wearied of waiting for union of their parent organizations and have locally united or federated. Some of the local unions to form community churches have tended to narrow rather than broaden the extent of fellowship since they have lost participation in denominational missionary programs and narrowed the geographical perspective of their people more than they have widened their vision by breaking local barriers to fellowship. Nevertheless, they are encouraging and warning testimonies that many people in the local churches believe organic church union to be an urgent need and are impatient with the slow progress of their leaders toward that end.

C. The Ecumenical Dilemma

In all efforts to attain complete ecumenical unity of the organized church a hard dilemma is confronted. On the one hand are the sins of present division. On the other is the temptation to even greater sins of false unity.

1. *The Sins of Division*

Certainly the present division of the church involves all Christians who at any level consent to it in material sin. God's will is that the church should be one. We know that Christ's prayer for the unity of his disciples, in John's Gospel,[3] must be echoed by the prayer of every true follower in his way. Yet as we promote the strength of our denominations we perpetuate the denial of our prayers. We may not see any way to avoid it without falling into greater evil and so we may not be guilty of formal sin. But we are confident that God does know a better way. We are not living in accord with His will as we perpetuate the division of the organized church and through that division the disunity also of the spiritual church itself, the body of Christ.

Moreover, we must candidly face the mixed motives and social evils which have so important a part in perpetuating the division. When we see them we know that the formal sins of selfishness and of personal, racial, national, social and economic pride are all aspects of our present divisions. There are few, indeed, who are wholly free from such motives.

Hence, so long as we remain divided we must pray that God will forgive us for all the blindness and sin which keep us from full Christian unity with all our Christian brothers.

2. *The Sins of False Unity*

In the desire to overcome the sins of division we are tempted to fall into other sins of false unity. Some of these are so obvious that they could be omitted from serious consideration if they were not bewitching so many Christian

[3] Jn. 17.

people. For example, there is the easy solution proposed by the Roman Catholic Church and by several small churches, the sin of arrogantly supposing that other people only are responsible for the division, hence those others should repent and come into the one true church. Then there is the sin of indifferent "tolerance." Many who fancy themselves broad-minded and spiritually superior to the people working in the churches are actually so far from the attainment of a wider Christian fellowship as to have none at all of sustained depth and fruitfulness. They may even be described as little denominations of one member each!

But there is a more serious temptation. This is that the official representatives of two or more churches may, in their haste to bring unity, work out a compromised plan of union which will represent only a least common denominator of faith or may be so ambiguous as to mean different things to the different uniting groups. The factions of a political party often patch up their differences in party platforms which express the real convictions of no one but likewise offend no one. This procedure may successfully hold a political party together for the winning of an election. But such a strategy would strike at the very heart of the church. For the church cannot live by words but only by the Word and the Word is known only in hearts that care more for God's truth than for any expedient device.

3. Unity Dependent on Both Love and Truth

If true unity of the organized church is to be approached, then at every step the churches involved must come nearer to representing faithfully the true spiritual church which is the body of Christ. Any step away from that goal, however skillfully executed and however many organizations it may bring together, is a step away from Christian unity. This is true as surely as that any compromise by which two disagreeing scientists might formulate a "solution" of their disagreement would be a step away from real scientific agreement if it drew them further from the truth they sought as scientists.

The heart of the spiritual church is Christian love. If the churches are to be drawn into greater Christian unity there must be more of that love. When the experience of the "unsearchable riches of Christ" is wide and deep enough and the desire to share this experience is earnest enough, most of the present barriers to unity will be dispelled like morning mists before the sun. Doctrinal agreement is not necessary where the presence of God is shared and love abounds. For there the very tension of difference and the agonizing over opposition become means of grateful growth in both the knowledge and service of God.

But *some* doctrinal differences do make organic union impossible. When some persons sincerely believe that their own church organization is the one divinely instituted church, its creeds infallible and its present rightful authority upon earth absolute and that accepting those propositions is necessary to membership in that church, then no union is possible with other churches whose members sincerely believe those propositions to be false. That is, union is impossible *so long as the beliefs remain unchanged.*

This extreme instance, which represents others of less extreme character, shows that the unity of the church requires growth in the knowledge of God's truth as well as growth in Christian love. Truth is one and when we know enough of truth the doctrinal barriers to unity which now appear insuperable will be reduced and finally surmounted.

To the common task of search for more love and more truth all Christians are called by the illuminating and creative Word of God Himself.

D. Authority of Organized Churches

When we raise the question of the authority of the churches we mean by authority what was meant in the earlier question about the authority of the Bible. By authority is again meant "rightful claim to be believed."

1. *None Infallible*

Roman Catholics maintain that God's love implies that He would not have left Himself without an infallible interpreter of His Word to men. But this a priori reasoning would require that such an infallible interpreter must have been known to all men in all ages. For this abstract argument no more proves that such an authority is provided for some men in the twentieth century A.D. than for all men in the twentieth century B.C. The specific arguments intended to prove the pope at Rome to be that infallible authority are even more unconvincing. The "proof" most stressed, based on Matthew 16:17-19, confronts good ground for doubt at every stage. First, the passage is, as we have seen, of doubtful authenticity as recording actual words of Jesus, let alone absolute truth. Second, it is doubtful, to say the least, whether it was meant to imply an infallible authority of Simon Peter in all matters of faith and morals. Third, there is not the remotest suggestion that such authority as was to be assigned to Peter would be transferable to any successor, let alone a long line of such successors. Finally, there is little or no evidence that Peter ever took a step to make any such transfer or that the peculiar and variable processes which have been used to select the various popes have actually provided divinely appointed successors to the authority alleged to have been assigned to Peter.

On the other hand, there is abundant evidence that the popes have not been infallible. According to Matthew's Gospel, it was precisely concerning the authority of men who profess to speak in God's name that Jesus said, "Thus you will know them by their fruits." [4] If that test is applied, then some of the men who have occupied the papal throne have not been worthy of a very respectful hearing.[5] Further, even many of the most solemn pronouncements of the popes have shown so much sign of inconsistency, of the partisan human influences affecting their thought and of political strategy in the ambitious efforts of power-hungry men that their altogether human and fallible character has been clearly evident.

The fact that the leaders of other churches do not make similarly fantastic claims is not, as Roman Catholic writers sometimes allege, a sign of their actually inferior position. The words of Jesus are relevant:

You know that the rulers of the Gentiles lord it over them, and their great men exercise authority over them. It shall not be so among you; but whoever would be great among you must be your servant.[6]

2. No Usurpation of Divine Judgment

The equivocal Roman Catholic doctrine of the "keys" is commonly, though not precisely, interpreted to mean that a person's entrance into heaven is dependent upon the fiat of the priesthood. The common acceptance of this belief by Roman Catholic laymen has given to the hierarchy a great power to coerce their thoughts and actions and has led to innumerable abuses of political control and personal exploitation. Yet the doctrine so outrages the moral sensibilities of men that when it is attacked, apologists are accustomed to emphasizing the ambiguous conditions and safeguards by which it has been surrounded.

The notion that the judgments of God are bound or invariably expressed by the decisions of any man or group of men is so outrageous as to make it seem incredible that any devout believer should ever accept it. Every man is himself subject to emotional distortions of perspective and sometimes to sinful motives. No man knows the whole range of God's holy law. No man knows the secret motives nor intentions of any other man nor the actual limits of his moral freedom. We can and must judge the material conformity of men's actions to what we understand to be the will of God. Without such judgment we could not intelligently engage in political action, carry on the work of the courts, choose our children's associates nor select the rightful persons for the various offices in church or business. But as for judging the moral responsibilities of other persons or setting a limit to God's mercy, it is utter folly for any man or body of men to consider such presumption. "Judge not, that you be not

[4] Mt. 7:15-20.
[5] E.g., see the article on Alexander VI in *The Catholic Encyclopedia*.
[6] Mt. 20:25-26.

judged"[7] is a word for men banded together in organized churches as well as for others.

3. Factors Determining the Rightful Authority of Churches

The authority to be properly attributed to any particular organized church is determined by a number of relevant considerations.

a. Quality of Corporate and Personal Life

"Thus you will know them by their fruits."[8] A church which meets this test well produces in superior measure "the fruit of the Spirit," such as "love, joy, peace, patience, kindness, goodness, faithfulness, gentleness, self-control."[9] It displays a minimum of "the works of the flesh," such as

immorality, impurity, licentiousness, idolatry, sorcery, enmity, strife, jealousy, anger, selfishness, dissension, party spirit, envy, drunkenness, carousing, and the like.[10]

Such a church must not be building its life wholly on falsehood. The teachings which it most emphasizes are *prima facie* worthy of a respectful hearing. They are not to be accepted without further thought. Churches of radically varying doctrines are sometimes strikingly similar in "good works." Fortunately, God does not wait until all our opinions are in correct order before giving to us His mercy and empowering us with His grace, else who could hope to be saved? Yet a sustained high level of personal and corporate life is one sign favorable to a church's rightful authority. "Are grapes gathered from thorns, or figs from thistles?"[11]

b. Numbers and Age

It has frequently occurred that one man with a new idea has been right while the rest of the world has been wrong. The lonely figure of Christ himself warns us that truth is not always on the side of numbers. However, for every instance in which a new idea of one man has been right there are a thousand instances of the opposite kind. Most of them are never widely heard about. But most of us have had experiences with men and women with new and—they think— revolutionary religious ideas. Some such persons claim to have had miraculous visions. Others think they have found new truth hidden away in the Scriptures. Yet others have thought out some novel philosophy. Such claims are especially common among people who have lived too much alone, with insufficient cross-fertilization and social criticism of their thought.

---

[7] Mt. 7:1.   [8] Mt. 7:15–20.
[9] Gal. 5:22–23.   [10] Gal. 5:19–21.
[11] Mt. 7:16.

In the struggle for survival in the minds of men, the mortality rate of new ideas is exceedingly high. Most of them deservedly fall quickly by the wayside. The history of human thought is the story of a long series of testings in which ideas have been tried in the crucible of criticism and practical application. Most new ideas which finally commend themselves as true are deeply rooted in history, as the Hebrew prophets and Jesus rooted their teachings in the best of their nation's past. Doctrines which can have no pride of ancestry usually have little hope of posterity and deservedly so.

Hence, doctrines which have been held by churches aggregating many members for a long period of time have a limited but legitimate *prima facie* claim to respectful consideration for acceptance.

c. Freedom from External Coercion

In some churches the members' minds are trained from childhood to submit to dictation from certain officials or are subject to threats of punishment for deviation from prescribed doctrines. Such minds do not usually enter significantly into the great trials by thought through which error is commonly eliminated and truth sustained, both inside and outside the churches. As a result, in applying the last preceding consideration, the great numbers of members who in consenting to their churches' doctrines simply yield an unthinking and often only external conformity to official coercion must be discounted.

d. Knowledge and Earnest Search

It is not true, as commonly alleged, that "one man's opinion is as good as another's." The person who has mastered the available information relevant to a problem and who has made long and disciplined effort to interpret this information with a single eye to discovering the truth, should be conceded more authority regarding that problem than others who have not paid the price.

Somewhat offsetting this obvious truth is the fact that some kinds of intellectual training may unfit the mind for the reception and recognition of some kinds of truth. A narrowly trained specialist, for example, may be so limited in perspective that in dealing with problems outside his field he may be unable or unwilling to adopt methods suitable to the subject in hand.

Moreover, the pride of learning or of position may keep a man from that spiritual humility which alone, through repentance and the commitments of faith, will open a life to the most significant data for the seeker of theological truth. A truth seeker in any field needs to know the most significant data in that field. The most important data bearing on the truth about the Christian gospel occur in religious experience. Any intellectual or official pride which keeps a man from the depths of such experience keeps him from the knowledge sometimes possessed by persons who in the eyes of the world are unlearned. God has "hidden these things from the wise and understanding and revealed them to babes." [12]

4. *Proper Acknowledgment of a Church's Authority*

If a particular branch of the organized church does present impressive marks of authority, how should that authority be acknowledged by the individual Christian?

Since no organized church is infallible, the pronouncements even of an authoritative church are not to be simply accepted without his critical thought. In general, however, he should view its solemn teachings with initial sympathy and respect. He should then critically examine these teachings, in co-operation with other persons, especially those who defend or reject them with trained minds and humble, prayerful hearts. He should be careful to relate these doctrines to the testimony of Scripture and to his own experience. He should then hold fast to such teachings as he is convinced are probably true.

Moreover, some church of which the main teachings and works thus gain his critical approval should have his full support and, if it will accept him with his sincere convictions as they are, his membership. Other churches which similarly qualify for his general approval merit all the co-operative aid he can give, including effort to draw his own church into closer fellowship and eventual organic unity with them. For ecumenical unity is a task in which all Christians, by the very nature of their faith, are called to participate.

[12] Mt. 11:25.

CHAPTER 39

The Sacraments

A. DEFINITION AND ENUMERATION

1. *Definition*

ALTHOUGH any rite, indeed any act or outward event, which conveys unusual spiritual meaning may by poetic extension be called a sacrament, this is not the intent of the term as usually employed in the church. The traditional meaning is stated in the Anglican Catechism as

an outward and visible sign of an inward and spiritual grace given unto us, ordained by Christ himself; as a means whereby we receive this grace, and a pledge to assure us thereof.

Many Christian thinkers would find the true meaning of the Christian sacraments between these two definitions, rejecting some one or more of the specifications in the Anglican Catechism and yet restricting the denotation of the term to two or more of the traditional rites of the church.

For the present discussion a sacrament is defined as a rite symbolizing human faith and divine grace and, according to the New Testament, invested with special solemnity by Jesus Christ.[1] What further meanings a sacrament may have it will be a part of our problem to discover.

2. *The Number of the Sacraments*

a. Variability in Church History

The New Testament defines no list of sacraments and the teaching of the church concerning them remained for a long while quite flexible. Bernard called the washing of feet a sacrament and other leaders of the church employed the term occasionally in a broad sense. Hugo of St. Victor, in the twelfth century, published a work entitled *On the Sacraments*, in which he described six

---

[1] Cf. W. M. Clow: "Sacraments are those rites or ordinances which have been instituted to symbolise the truths of the spirit evident to the soul, by the things of nature evident to the senses." *The Church and the Sacraments*, p. 11.

sacraments. Of these he thought two especially important, namely, baptism and the Eucharist, for they alone, he believed, were necessary to salvation. The other four were confirmation, penance, last unction and matrimony. He thought there must be a seventh because there were seven sins, but it remained for Peter Lombard to designate it as ordination.

b. The Seven Sacraments of Catholicism

The Eastern Orthodox and Roman Catholic bodies, and likewise many Anglo-Catholics (in contradiction to the Twenty-fifth Article of the Church of England), recognize seven sacraments. According to the Roman church they are as follows:

Baptism is a rite to be performed by a priest unless impossible, either by immersion, pouring or aspersion (sprinkling) but usually by aspersion, believed to cleanse the recipient from original sin, effecting an actual change in character, and admitting him into the church.

Confirmation, normally performed by a bishop, through the laying on of hands and anointing with chrism (consecrated oil), is to confer upon a person already baptized the power of the Holy Spirit for lay participation in the responsibilities of the church.

Penance is the performance of some act specified by the priest after he has heard the confession of sin. The act was formerly regarded as punishment and is widely so regarded now, but in theological instruction is generally represented rather as an expression of earnest supplication for forgiveness. Penance is the condition of receiving absolution in which the priest judicially declares God's forgiveness of sin and restores the sinner to fellowship in the church.

The Holy Eucharist is the partaking of bread (by laymen and priests) and wine (by priests only) of which it is believed that by a prayer of consecration the substance has been miraculously changed into the substance of the living body and blood of Jesus, with his full human and divine nature. Through this sacrament the church offers the one acceptable sacrifice to God and the soul is thought to be renewed in spiritual strength and united with God.

Extreme Unction is a sacrament of anointing with oil a baptized person believed to be dying. This is done by a priest. It is believed to bring about the remission of sins and fortification of the soul.

The sacrament of Holy Orders is the laying of hands by a bishop upon the head of a baptized man, with appropriate words, conferring power to exercise all the functions of the priesthood.

Matrimony is the uniting of a baptized man and woman in marriage. The marriage is effected by the words of the two persons marrying and the priest blesses the union thus formed.

c. The Two Sacraments of the Protestant Churches

Some Protestants believe in no sacraments, some regard the number as properly flexible and relative to varying religious sensibilities and others plead for the acceptance of three or more of the seven recognized by Rome. But most Protestant churches acknowledge two sacraments and two only. These are baptism and Holy Communion or the Lord's Supper. This limitation is based upon three principal considerations. Baptism and Holy Communion are the only ones of the traditional rites which, according to the New Testament, Jesus instituted or in which he directly participated either as ministrant or recipient. Historically, these two are much older than the others and have often been regarded as the most important even when others have been recognized. Each of these two represents the essential message of the gospel as no other does.

B. Dangers in the Use of Sacraments

The use of any such prescribed forms as we find in the sacraments is fraught with certain perils to true religion. Against the evils to which formal rites have often led, the ancient Hebrew prophets uttered many a warning cry and thundering condemnation. Jesus denounced the false religion of outward forms and pleaded for the inwardness of secret prayer and the unseen faith of the heart. In a day when many Protestant churchmen are showing revived interest in a greater emphasis upon the sacraments and there are evident tendencies toward a more elaborate formal development of ritual, the dangers which attend all formal rites, as well as the values they offer, should be carefully considered.

There is the peril of drawing such attention to material objects and precise forms of words that the minds of worshipers are actually distracted from God Himself. There is also the danger that worship will lapse into superstition. When stress is laid upon the benefits to be received through certain outward rites it is only a step to the supposition that men may surely bring about predictable results, not through the offering of themselves to God, but through the operation of a kind of supernatural, quasi-material causal order. Not only is the tendency to such ideas intellectually, morally and religiously corrupt in itself but it leads to further abuses. Especially does it encourage the substitution of external rites for the inner disciplines of mind and will, a ritualistic law for faith and obedient love. At the same time it gives to the clergy who are thought necessary to such rites an unwholesome power, based on office and not on character and spiritual discernment. This, in turn, tempts the ministers to pride of power and position, while it reduces the laymen to a degrading place of secondary responsibility and often a mediated religion by proxy rather than a personal communion with God.

It is no accident, then, that ritualistic, priestly religions have so often been found in history to be morally sterile shells, encrusting and protecting injustice and tyranny, while the prophets of true faith and righteousness have cried out against them.[2]

C. The Propriety and Usefulness of Sacraments

Despite the evident perils, there are cogent reasons why sacraments should be employed, with care to preserve the centrality of the Word of God as contrasted with any specific forms in which that Word may be presented, and to provide sound instruction concerning their meanings and limitations.

1. Material Symbolism a Necessity

We are in the body and all of our communication with other human beings usually and perhaps always takes place with the aid of some form of bodily expression. If, therefore, our religious life is to be shared in any sort of group experience of worship there must be some bodily means of communication. Group worship is made imperative by the very nature of the Christian faith, which, as we have seen, is social to its very depths. Where the spiritual church exists, the *koinonia* is, then, bound to be expressed in group worship making use of material symbolism in one form or another.

Many kinds of symbolism are actually employed in the Christian churches. The gathering together of a group in a particular place designated for worship is itself a simple mode of religious symbolism. Preaching, hymn singing, the reading of Scripture, audible prayer, all are material symbols. So are the plain meeting room and the discipline of silence in a meeting of Friends. When any material symbols have proper place in the church service at all, they represent invisible spiritual transactions between men and God, shared in a community of worship.

2. Importance of Verbal Symbolism

Since some kind of material symbolism is inevitable in the worship of God by the church, the only question concerns the kinds to be used. The spoken word ought always to be given special emphasis. It has an adaptability to timely needs, a range of precise meaningfulness, a directness of personal expression and an antiquity of use in the Judeo-Christian tradition unmatched by any other symbolic act. Churches which stress the open Bible and the responsibility of intelligent faith, expressed relevantly in godly living, have made the reading of the Scripture and the sermon central in most services of public worship. There is ample reason why they should keep them in this position.

[2] E.g., Amos 5:21-24.

3. Need for Other Modes of Representation

But there is good reason also why speech alone should not be made the exclusive medium of expression. Man is not only a creature that speaks and hears. He also customarily carries on communication through sight, touch and action. The gospel may well be shared through these other modes of expression.

Moreover, if the symbolism of worship is to express the community of believers, as well as communion with God, it should have dimensions far transcending the here-and-now of the particular congregation. The sacred *koinonia* extends to the faithful of all churches and of all generations. A proper sign of this universal Christian communion must be one deeply steeped in the tradition of the ages, so that a Christian who now participates in it can have the sense of spanning the centuries and participating with the Christians of distant lands and ancient times.

4. Sacraments As God's Word

But more than that is needed. While worship does unite the Christian with other Christians, at the center of that union is his union with God. Hence, the fullest and deepest expression must be one in which God Himself can be regarded as participating. Indeed, since God is the author of the whole spiritual church, the expression would be particularly meaningful if it could be looked upon as having been itself instituted by Him as part of His saving Word to man. We have such expressions in many passages of Scripture through which God speaks to the congregation His warnings and His assurances. But for concentration of varied symbolism, including words, sight, touch, action and, in the Lord's Supper, taste, there are no modes of worship which so epitomize the gospel as do the sacraments of Baptism and the Lord's Supper. Each of these two sacraments might well be described in the words Emil Brunner used to characterize the Lord's Supper, as an "illustrated Word of God." [3] Both belonging to the life of Jesus himself, both are part of the incarnate Word God gave to us in him. At the same time they represent that Word as a whole and the unity of the Christian church as a whole. They are God's Word spoken long ago and spoken anew to us in our own active present participation.

They should by all means, then, be used, with all the solemn dignity and joy which befit the proclamation of the gospel through us. At the same time, by careful instruction and due attention to strengthening every part of the service, the perils into which sacramental enthusiasts sometimes fall can and should be guarded against.

Much of what has been said in favor of baptism and the Lord's Supper can-

[3] *Our Faith*, p. 135.

not, however, be said for the other rites employed as sacraments in some branches of the church. For they are all much later in origin, none evidently sanctioned by the institution or participation of Christ and none has both the breadth and universality of meaning which characterize the two. Some have, as sacraments, connotations which are either oblique to the gospel or threaten the very denial of it. On the last-mentioned ground, Protestants have particularly good reason to reject as sacraments the rites of penance, holy orders and extreme unction. Confirmation echoes baptism and tends to detract from its meaning as Protestants understand it.

Matrimony is properly regarded by all Christians as a solemn and sacred rite. Indeed, it has higher place for Protestant than for Roman Catholic thought, for with us marriage is not regarded as a "second-best" state inferior to religious celibacy. But we have no record of Jesus participating in any way in matrimonial rites—though he spoke highly of marriage and was reputed to have attended wedding festivities at Cana and to have performed a miracle there. Moreover, this is not a rite in which all members of the church are called to participate. Hence, it cannot be an expression of the total Christian community and has been wisely placed among rites of a different class from the sacraments, both in the ancient church and among Protestants.

CHAPTER 40

Baptism

A. ORIGIN

1. Precursors

BAPTISM in various forms has been used as a rite of cleansing in many religions. It was familiar to the Jews before John began baptizing in the Jordan. They had already been employing baptism by immersion in the ceremonial admission of proselytes into the Jewish nation. Joseph Klausner believes that the symbolism represented both cleansing and rebirth.[1] Immersion was also used in a dramatic climax of the initiation rites in some of the contemporary mystery cults. What influence the Mysteries had upon Christian baptism in the primitive church is problematic. The similarity of interpretations is striking, but the Jewish usage seems to offer sufficient background.

In any event, the baptism practiced by John was familiar enough to be quickly understood without much explanation. Yet its precise purpose was new. For this was not a cleansing of pagans for admission into the Jewish nation, but a "baptism of repentance for the forgiveness of sins," [2] to prepare for participation in the kingdom of God which John announced as "at hand." [3] John called upon the people to accept baptism, not because they were not Jews, for many, presumably most, of them were,[4] but because they were sinners and hence not ready for God's reign.

2. Place in Teaching and Example of Jesus

The precise use made of baptism by Jesus is problematical. All three Synoptic Gospels tell of his being baptized.[5] John does not report Jesus' being baptized, but is alone among the Gospels in reporting the use of baptism in his own ministry.[6] There is a somewhat puzzling reference to baptism in the conversation with Nicodemus.[7] There is no other mention of literal baptism in the

---

[1] See Joseph Klausner, From Jesus to Paul, pp. 508–9.
[2] Mk. 1:4.
[3] Mt. 3:2.
[4] Cf. Lk. 3:8.
[5] Mk. 1:9–10; Lk. 3:21; Mt. 3:13–16.
[6] Jn. 4:1–3. Cf. also 3:22.
[7] Jn. 3:5.

teaching of Jesus until we come to the accounts of his postresurrection appearances. Jesus did, however, speak of the baptism of suffering and death which he was to undergo, and which his disciples were called upon to share.[8] In Mark 16:16 is written as a teaching of the risen Lord, "He who believes and is baptized will be saved." But this is in a passage which is textually highly doubtful. On the other hand, there is no textual ground for doubting the postresurrection command reported in Matthew:

All authority in heaven and on earth has been given to me. Go therefore and make disciples of all nations, baptizing them in the name of the Father and of the Son and of the Holy Spirit.[9]

Many scholars question the authenticity of these words as belonging to Jesus himself, both because they are reported after the resurrection and also because the trinitarian formula would appear to belong to a later doctrinal and ritualistic development.

3. In the Primitive Church

Among all the reports of baptism in the Acts and the letters of Paul there is no instance of a trinitarian formula. Rather, the people were baptized "in the name of Jesus Christ." [10] In one passage the statement that some people in Samaria had not received the Holy Spirit, "but they had only been baptized in the name of the Lord Jesus," seems to imply clearly that the baptism had not been in the name of the Holy Spirit, an impression strengthened by the words that immediately follow.[11] On the other hand, Paul wrote to the Corinthians, "But you were washed, you were sanctified, you were justified in the name of the Lord Jesus Christ and in the Spirit of our God." [12] As Hugh Thompson Kerr points out, this is "a near approach to the trinitarian formula found in Matthew." [13]

In any event, the New Testament bears abundant testimony that baptism was used in the primitive church as the initiatory rite for new converts. We have additional confirming evidence, which also shows an early adoption of a trinitarian formula. For in the *Didache* (first half of second century) we read,

Concerning baptism, thus baptize ye: having spoken beforehand of these things, baptize into the name of the Father and of the Son and of the Holy Ghost in living water.[14]

[8] Mk. 10:38–39. [9] Mt. 27:18–19.
[10] Acts 2:38. Cf. Acts 8:16; 19:5; Rom. 6:3; Gal. 3:27.
[11] Acts 8:14–17. [12] 1 Cor. 6:11.
[13] *The Christian Sacraments*, p. 47. The whole book is excellent, presenting concisely an abundance of references to source materials, for which I am indebted, and many thoughtful suggestions particularly useful for pastors.
[14] Ch. 7.

B. Symbolism

1. Cleansing

Water having always been a means of cleansing, its use in the baptismal rite is bound to symbolize a cleansing. In the baptism of adults it represents the repentance which is required and the forgiveness which God gives to all who truly repent. In the baptism of infants it is the symbol of God's prevenient grace already asked by the parents or guardians, but also by the church and assured by God's love. This grace is to surround and infuse the life of the growing child, with its cleansing influence, through Christian home and church.

2. Reception into the True Church

Since a similar rite had been in use as a symbol of admission into the Jewish nation, the idea of admission into a community, with its privileges and responsibilities, was already associated with baptism. Hence, it became easily the symbol of admission into the profound fellowship of sharing which was so treasured in the Christian Church. To baptize a person "in the name of Jesus Christ" or in the name of the Trinity is to welcome him into "the body of Christ," the community of faith.

3. New Birth

Especially evident in the rite by immersion is the symbolism of death to the old and resurrection in the new life. Paul states this meaning clearly.[15] There are overtones of immortality in Paul's interpretation, for being raised to new life in Christ we are assured of deathless life.[16] But he is not speaking of something which will happen to us some day, when we die. He is speaking of the new birth which we have now when our lives are committed without reservation into His keeping.

C. Mode

There is good evidence that the baptisms by John and by the earliest disciples of Christ were by immersion. The Greek word, *baptizo*, usually implies immersion, though not with necessity.[17] John's choice of the Jordan River as the place of baptism for "the people of Jerusalem," [18] as well as for other Judeans, suggests the need for considerable water. The Greek of this passage is most naturally

---

[15] Rom. 6:3–4. Cf. Col. 2:12–13.
[16] See Rom. 6:5, 8–9.
[17] Cf. Mk. 7:3–4 and the relation between Heb. 9:10 and 5:19.
[18] Mk. 1:5.

understood to mean "*in* the Jordan." In John's Gospel we read that John was, at one time, "baptizing at Aenon near Salim, because there was much water there." [19] Pouring or sprinkling would hardly require "much water." After Jesus' baptism, it is reported, "he came up out of the water." [20]

There is good reason to agree with John Calvin that "baptism" in the New Testament implies immersion but also to agree with his teaching that the mode is "of no importance." [21] Christ and his disciples were determined to set men free from bondage to prescribed external forms. They would not have cared to see their examples made the occasion for forging new bonds of similar character.

The ancient church was quick to develop a flexible adaptability in the mode of baptism. We know this from the pictures in the catacombs and even more specifically from the instructions in the *Didache*. Here, after the general formula we have already cited, the Christians of the second century were told,

> But if thou hast not living water, then Baptize in any other water; and if thou art not able in cold, in warm. But if thou hast neither, pour water upon the head thrice in the name of the Father and of the Son and of the Holy Spirit.[22]

The most serious argument of contenders for the exclusive use of immersion is that it alone clearly symbolizes death and resurrection, one of the meanings which Paul explicitly attached to baptism. Certainly it is true that immersion most vividly portrays this idea. Nevertheless, here, too, we have a right to our hard-won freedom from the Law. Symbols mean what instruction, usage and association make them mean. To many Christians, long accustomed to the associations of churches not insisting upon immersion, a plunge beneath the water would carry less of any spiritual connotation, whether of rebirth or any other change, than would a less dramatic and preoccupying rite. The means must not divert attention from the end, nor the symbol from the reality. In freedom we may all here practice what is most meaningful to us in our various traditions.

D. INFANT BAPTISM

At the beginning Christian baptism was apparently administered to persons who repented in faith and sought admission to the church. How, then, does it happen that from at least the third century most churches have baptized infants who have not sinned, could not yet repent if they had sinned and are quite incapable of seeking admission to the church? Is infant baptism justifiable?

[19] Jn. 3:23.   [20] Mk. 1:10.
[21] *Institutes*, IV.xv.19.   [22] Ch. 7.

1. *New Testament Practice*

There is no statement in the New Testament reporting explicitly that any infant was baptized. At Pentecost Peter said, "Repent, and be baptized every one of you in the name of Jesus Christ for the forgiveness of your sins," and we are told that "those who received his word were baptized." [23] Here and in many other instances baptism is presented as a rite following upon repentance and reception of the gospel.

However, not always in the New Testament record is the benefit of baptism given only to those who themselves believe. Before any of the Gospels had been written, Paul wrote his plea for belief in immortality and in the midst of it said,

Otherwise, what do people mean by being baptized on behalf of the dead? If the dead are not raised at all, why are people baptized on their behalf? [24]

The baptism of living persons for the benefit of the dead was evidently a common practice. Happily, nothing more was said of it and it seems to have been soon dropped. However, Paul's interpretation of baptism was not of a kind requiring his condemnation of the practice to which he here appealed in *ad hominem* argument. More directly to the point, there are several accounts of whole households or families being baptized. Lydia of Thyatira, after her heart was opened "to give heed to what was said by Paul . . . was baptized, with her household." [25] In Philippi the jailer "was baptized at once, with all his family." [26] It is not likely that in none of such instances were there any infants or small children.

2. *Other Considerations*

There is no doubt that much use of infant baptism has been and is now based upon the belief that all human beings are born under the guilt of original sin and that baptism removes that guilt, even when the recipient is not able to repent. Few Protestants who participate in infant baptism would care to defend either such a doctrine of original sin or such a quasi-magical conception of baptism.

However, there are sounder doctrines which support the desirability of continuing this ancient practice.

Jesus expressed with beauty and tenderness the doctrine that children are not to be put somewhere outside the community of God's love but to be welcomed

[23] Acts 2:38, 41.
[25] Acts 16:14–15.

[24] I Cor. 15:29.
[26] Acts 16:33.

within it.[27] But if it is true that "to such belongs the kingdom of God," then the church may rightly testify to this fact in the established manner by which is affirmed its faith that a person has been accepted by God as a member of that kingdom. To be sure, if he is to continue in it he must eventually make his own decision of faith. But before he is able to return his love to God the church properly gives its love to the child and witnesses to its faith that God Himself likewise receives and blesses him as Jesus did long ago.

Moreover, in infant baptism the church acknowledges the unity of the family in the sight of God. We have in our day learned such an extreme individualism that it is hard for us to understand how deeply social is the conception of man in the New Testament. It was perfectly natural for the ancient disciples to receive whole households into the church on the faith of one man or woman, just as it was natural to describe various persons as healed by the faith of others.[28] Actually life is like that. Every individual must bear his own share of responsibility, but these responsibilities interpenetrate in countless ways. Especially in the family our attitudes and destinies are closely, even though never absolutely, bound together. The simple fact, which our excessive individualism obscures, is that the question whether the child here before the church will live in faith or not is a question to be answered principally, though not finally, by the parents. Some of the remaining responsibility rests upon the church itself. The rite of infant baptism is a recognition of these facts in the solemn consecration of the child by parents and church, while the primary responsibilities of Christian nurture are laid upon the home.

[27] Mk. 10:13-16.
[28] See, e.g., Mk. 2:1-5; 9:17-27; Lk. 8:40-41, 50.

CHAPTER 41

The Lord's Supper

A. ORIGIN

THE Lord's Supper was the center of worship in the primitive church. About its observance were clustered and held together the precious memories of the Master and all the priceless love and faith which he had engendered. There was abundant reason for the place which this rite held. Besides the rich and mysterious suggestiveness of its symbolism, it was based upon the last meal which Christ had eaten with his disciples before his crucifixion, and the instructions which he had given at that time.

Of that supper and the rite which Jesus there began, all three Synoptic Gospels report and there is a yet earlier written account in Paul's First Letter to the Corinthians.[1] Some scholars have questioned Jesus' own institution of the rite, but the testimony is so abundant and the textual authority so clear that there seems little ground for doubts excepting in presupposed reconstructions of doctrinal development which would contradict the records.[2]

At the beginning, the Lord's Supper was observed in the form of a meal, no doubt literally a supper. For Paul complained that the Corinthians ate and drank so greedily that they denied the very spirit of Christ and so profaned "the body and blood of the Lord." [3] But when Justin wrote his *Apology,* in the middle of the second century, the observance of which he spoke was not a meal but a ceremonial rite.[4]

B. REALISTIC DOCTRINES

Unable to be content with the metaphorical language of Christ and Paul, many theologians have endeavored to defend theories of the Lord's Supper which assign a realistic meaning to the words, "This is my body" and "This is my blood." Indeed, some churches have adopted such teachings as official doctrines.

---

[1] 11:23–26. Cf. Mt. 26:26–29; Mk. 14:22–25; Lk. 22:14–19. See also Jn. 13:1–35 and 6:48–58.
[2] E.g., see Rudolf Bultmann, *Theology of the New Testament*, Vol. I, ch. 3, par. 13.
[3] 1 Cor. 11:17–28.
[4] Ch. 67.

1. *Transubstantiation*

From at least as early as the time of Cyprian, in the third century, doctrines have been taught in Christendom which took almost or altogether literally the sayings that in the Lord's Supper, or Eucharist, the bread and wine actually were the body and blood of Christ. A number of influences effected this tendency. One was simply the heightened doctrinal interest in the words of the Gospels which tended to make metaphysical formulas of poetic figures. The increasing Greek influence encouraged this interest. Another was the inclination, present everywhere, to find material wonders and miracles in religious experience. This inclination is doubtless a perversion of the proper recognition that God's ways far exceed our understanding and of the legitimate hunger to find some extraordinary sign of God's reality and favor. A third influence was the rapidly developing sacerdotal conception of a priesthood with prerogatives and powers exceeding all those possessed or understood by laymen. Many priests were, of course, not at all adverse to such conceptions. In fairness it should be said that the resulting increments to their own authority not only must have pleased their secret vanity but also helped them to maintain difficult moral and religious discipline in the church against the constant and heavy pressures of paganism. Analogous ideas in the mystery cults were doubtless a fourth influence. All of these influences save the last have continued to operate in the development and maintenance of the Roman Catholic doctrine of transubstantiation,[5] and others, too, have become important—from the use of religious discipline for increasing political power to the dramatic religious values in the ideas of the Real Presence and the repeated sacrifice.

This doctrine leans heavily on the metaphysical conceptions of Thomistic Aristotelianism and would be impossible to state in terms of any modern metaphysics. It involves some notions which contradict the most basic Aristotelian conceptions, too, particularly the idea of the accidents of a substance (the color, texture, taste, size, etc., of the bread and wine) remaining in full being and influence when the substance itself has ceased to be at all. But this, of course, is simply left to the mystery of divine miracle. Fortunately, there is no evidence in Scripture or in experience to require acceptance of such a metaphysical contradiction in terms.

Its great religious appeal, apart from the attraction of the sensational and miraculous in general, is in the conviction it fosters that at the Mass the worshiper is in the Real Presence of Jesus Christ himself, that is to say, of God. The latent pseudo-materialism of the whole position here shows itself. It can

---

[5] See *The Catechism of the Council of Trent* (tr. by J. Donovan. Baltimore: Lucas Bros., n.d.), p. 156.

be sympathetically understood, but it cannot be accepted by one who truly and fully believes in the God who "is spirit" so that He is not to be found and worshiped in some unique presence "on this mountain nor in Jerusalem," but rather anywhere so long as it be "in spirit and truth." [6]

God is present and His power is effective wherever He is called upon and obeyed in faith. To seek Him in any miracle of substance-changing by a specially empowered priesthood is to retreat from the spiritual teaching of the New Testament.

With the doctrine of transubstantiation there falls to the ground also the idea that every Mass is a repetition of the one perfect sacrifice of Jesus Christ, a sacrifice wrought through the priestly miracle. As disciples of Christ we are called upon, indeed, to be ready to drink the cup of suffering which he drank and to take up the cross in following him. But this is not to be done by our making Christ to repeat *his* sacrifice on ten thousand altars. Paul speaks to us of one offering, but one only which we are called upon to make at all times as he writes of "the sacrificial offering of your faith." [7] This we must do even if such an offering leads us, as Paul then expected it would lead him, to a martyr's death.

2. *Other Realistic Doctrines*

In other ways also, the symbolism of the Lord's Supper has been interpreted as literal or nearly so. The Eastern Orthodox bodies maintain nearly the same teaching as Rome, but are more mystical and flexible in the teaching of it.

Martin Luther held that in the Eucharist the body and blood of Christ, coexist, together with the bread and wine. At times he seemed to mean "body" and "blood" quite literally, but sometimes he explained by similes which clearly implied a figurative usage. He was concerned to stress that God acts in the Eucharist, through the giving of Christ's pardoning love anew to faithful recipients. Even when he seemed most literal in interpretation he rejected the notion of a privileged priesthood for the conception of the ministering congregation and he denied that it is a repeated sacrifice.[8]

C. Symbolism

In the sacrament of the Lord's Supper, many meanings, reaching through the whole range of the gospel, are presented. Even a casual study of the rituals used in our churches will show that to be true. Here we can only discuss a few of

---

[6] Jn. 4:21-24.

[7] Phil. 2:17.

[8] See the brief but excellent article by T. Almar Kantonen, "Lutheran Doctrine of the Lord's Supper," in V. Ferm, *An Encyclopedia of Religion*. See also *The Augsburg Confession* and Gustaf Aulén, *The Faith of the Christian Church*, pp. 385-400.

the most important ideas in this sacrament which is indeed the Word of God illustrated in object, word and act.

1. *The Crucified Christ*

The circumstances of Jesus' last meal with his disciples, and the figures which he used when he passed the bread and wine to his disciples, alike remind us of him who was crucified for our redemption. As we participate in this service we remember "that the Lord Jesus on the night when he was betrayed took bread." [9] The bread reminds us of his "body which is broken" [10] and the wine of his "blood of the covenant, which is poured out for many." [11] Anyone who knows of the events in that upper room and on Calvary next day would find it difficult, indeed, to participate in the sacrament without being reminded of them and so obeying that command of his: "Do this in remembrance of me." [12]

2. *The Living Christ*

Although we memorialize the Christ who died long ago, we do not think of him as a dead Christ. The ritual speaks again and again of "life" and of his presence with us. It is his table at which we gather and he presides over it. For he who once died lives now in the glory of his Father.

It is not only Thursday night and Good Friday that we remember at the Lord's table. It is also Easter Sunday. The first Christians were not content to celebrate the resurrection once a year. Every week they gathered on the first day of the week to recall the victory of Christ over death. So it happened that the Lord's Supper came to be observed in the weekly celebration of Easter Sunday! No wonder they called it the Eucharist—the giving of thanks! They entered, it is true, into the depths of sorrow with him and faced the death which was often for them very immediately and vividly near the darkened rooms and caves where they sought refuge from their persecutors. But they were also lifted in victory and joy with him. So too are we when we share their heroic obedience and their faith that Christ has both died for us and "been raised from the dead, the first fruits of those who have fallen asleep." [13]

3. *The Committed Believer*

Out of all the world's striving for place and position we come to the Lord's table. There we hear again the words which Jesus spoke to the sons of Zebedee when with their mother's aid they sought places of privilege and honor in the kingdom soon to be:

[9] 1 Cor. 11:23.　　　　　　　　　　　[10] 1 Cor. 11:24.
[11] Mk. 14:24.　　　　　　　　　　　　[12] 1 Cor. 11:24.
[13] 1 Cor. 15:20.

You do not know what you are asking. Are you able to drink the cup that I am to drink? . . . You know that the rulers of the Gentiles lord it over them, . . . but whoever would be great among you must be your servant.[14]

Here the world's values are turned upside down. Greatness here is not in "such boastings as the Gentiles use"[15] but in humility. Wealth here is not in getting and keeping but in giving. Freedom here is not in doing what we please but in being slave for the service of all. Power here is not in the force to kill but in the grace to die.

When we eat the bread and drink the wine of the sacrament, we commit ourselves by faith to this reversal of values. Christ asks us, "Are you able to drink the cup that I am to drink?" In humble reliance on the help of God we answer, "We are able" and add, "To the death we follow Thee."[16]

4. The Fellowship of Faith

The cup of blessing which we bless, is it not a participation [Gk.: *koinonia*] in the blood of Christ? The bread which we break, is it not a participation in the body of Christ? Because there is one loaf, we who are many are one body, for we all partake of the same loaf.[17]

No amount of theological diversity, nor even the tragic refusal of many Christians on grounds of conscience to share fully in the sacrament as administered by those of different understanding, can obscure the clear *meaning* of fellowship and unity in the sacrament itself. For by this rite the people of many churches participate in the life of the one spiritual church, the body of Christ. If some of our brethren, in their own supreme loyalty to the Word of God as they have received and understood that Word, separate themselves from the mode or the ministry which we accept, or, like the Quakers, renounce all *material* sacraments, nevertheless we express our unity with them too. For the true *koinonia,* the spiritual participation in the body of Christ, is theirs with us.

The Christians of all the ages are here at the Lord's table with us. The apostles of the upper room in Jerusalem, the members of Caesar's own household slipping away to a sacred meal in the Roman catacombs, the medieval mystics illuminating the world with divine radiance, the Reformers heroically calling the church from sacerdotal captivity to the priesthood of all believers, dusky slaves enabled to sing under their heavy loads, recent martyrs of eastern Europe and China, Christian scholars, statesmen, mothers, farmers—all are here, seen and unseen, in the company at the table of the Lord. Here the *koinonia* is both represented and made real to all who have the faith to seize it.

[14] Mt. 20:22, 25–28.
[15] Kipling, *Recessional.*
[16] Mt. 20:22; Earl B. Marlatt's hymn, *Are Ye Able?*
[17] I Cor. 10:16–17.

5. *Other Meanings*

Many other ideas and affections crowd the mind of the thoughtful believer who returns again and again to receive the great sacrament. Only a few will be briefly suggested before we leave this subject.

In the presence of perfect faithfulness and sacrifice exemplified in the life and death of Christ, we must all bow in shamed repentance for our wayward love of selfish ease. We are constrained to go beyond the words of the ritual in expressing sorrow for our sin, and take our specific wrongs to God for forgiveness and cure.

We are reminded that we cannot truly "live by bread alone." [18] As surely as our bodies require food and drink, our souls require the food of the spirit which God alone can provide. Humbly and gratefully we seek this nourishment from Him in order that we may grow in grace, learn more of His will and better do the work to which He calls every one of His children.

Here we learn anew the sacredness of common things and of everyday life. Jesus spoke of a lost coin and every household search became a parable of the kingdom. He watched a widow's tiny offering in the temple and transfigured every sacrificial gift of the poor. He laid tender hands on little children, to destroy infanticide, inspire new ideals of education and create a new vision of what families could be. He gave thanks for bread and wine in an otherwise unknown upper room and brought millions of people into the presence of God. In the light of his radiance nothing which God has made and no task which serves a human need is common. Everything belongs to God and is too sacred for any purpose but His.

Seeing how Christ changed the cross, instrument of cruelty, humiliation and hopeless sorrow into the world's best symbol of love, victory and indomitable joy, all discouraged and grief-stricken men and women find here new hope. Many a bereaved person, trying vainly to crush his sorrow with sheer strength of will, has come dry-eyed to the Lord's Supper and suddenly found his wound laid bare, cleansed and healed by the touch of God Himself. So powerfully does the "illustrated Word" of the sacrament stir human faith to receive the divine Spirit.

[18] Mt. 4:4.

CHAPTER 42

Prayer

THE very heart and soul of religion is prayer. The highest privilege any created being can enjoy is communion with God, the One who is supreme in goodness, power and glory. That privilege is grasped in prayer. God is the source of our being and of every renewal of our being. It is in prayer that our spirits are refreshed by His Spirit. Without prayer, religion becomes an empty form, an ugly dogmatism, or, at best, an idealistic human association. With prayer it becomes the gateway to heaven.

A. Kinds of Prayer

Although various classifications may be made, five types of prayer may be most clearly and simply distinguished. In practice two or more are and should be usually joined. Frequently all are blended together in a single symphony of the divine and human spirits. Indeed all must be at least implicit in every true prayer.

1. Petition

First among them is the prayer of petition. It is mentioned first here because it is most widely known and for many constitutes the gateway to the practice and interpretation of prayer.

Many persons turn attention to God only on occasions when a personal need is urgently felt, and they see no ordinary, earthly prospect of satisfying it. "Foxhole religion," it is sometimes contemptuously called. To be sure, a prayer life which has never gone beyond being used as a temporary means for meeting a temporary emergency is very immature. Yet if this can serve for a beginning, as it often does, the prayer which starts here may go far.

Moreover, petitionary prayers are not always isolated, spasmodic efforts to call God to aid when ominous dangers have appeared on a road taken without thought of Him. Petitionary prayer may be the regularly offered word, "Give us this day our daily bread." It then takes on an almost sacramental character, discovering in the common means of life the constant provision of the Father.

Likewise, prayer may so cleanse and elevate the desires of the one who prays that he asks not only that bread be given, but also and first of all, "Thy kingdom come, Thy will be done, on earth as it is in Heaven." Not often does prayer rise higher than that.

There are several problems concerning prayers of petition which have stirred in many minds sincere doubts about the propriety and effectiveness of this kind of prayer. They will be given consideration after we have introduced the other four types.

2. Repentance

Genuine prayer to the holy God requires repentance. A man or woman, being a sinner, may yet say words suitable for prayer without repenting. But if the prayer, rather than being mere words, is truly *prayer,* so that communication actually takes place between God and man, then there must soon be felt a deep unworthiness to stand before Him.

Probably there is no other cause for failure to find comfort and help in prayer so common and important as failure in repentance. Too often we want *God's* help to accomplish *our* purposes. If we are to expect His help our purposes need first to be cleansed by our repentance and His forgiveness.

If prayers for forgiveness are genuine they will be specific, concrete and personal. Pastoral prayers of repentance in behalf of an entire congregation must of necessity be broad and inclusive, though they need not be as abstract and pointless as they often are. But their effectiveness depends upon the willingness of individuals to provide the specifications in the silence of their own hearts. Where this fails, individual members may pattern their private prayers after the experience of the sanctuary and habitually hide their own particular vices behind a misty curtain of generalities.

Genuine repentance also implies earnest effort to separate oneself as far as possible from the sins for which forgiveness is asked. Prayers of repentance therefore include pleas for God's help in overcoming temptation. Here again the Lord's Prayer shows us the way. For immediately after saying, "And forgive us our trespasses, as we forgive those who trespass against us," we continue, "And lead us not into temptation, but deliver us from evil."

3. Praise and Thanksgiving

Ingratitude, in personal relations of any kind, is one of the most blighting and confining of all attitudes. Gratitude, on the other hand, opens the doors of the soul to the sunlight of both human and divine love. He who would open his soul to God in prayer must open it with praise and thanksgiving.

If we would know God at all we must acknowledge Him as He is. Since He is perfect goodness and the source of every good, to know Him is to praise and adore Him. If there is anyone we love or anything in which we take delight then our thanks are due to Him who has made every good and has given to us the power to desire, to know and to enjoy. But above every earthly good we praise His own sublime being and love.

The prayer which Jesus taught us begins with adoration and praise. We are reminded, as we start to pray, that the one whom we address is He who is "in heaven," that is, high above all that we know on earth, in goodness, power and glory. As soon as we are reminded of this we say in adoration, "Hallowed be Thy name." Again, after completing the prayer which Jesus taught, the church learned long ago to add in a final paean of praise, "For Thine is the kingdom and the power and the glory forever."

4. *Self-dedication*

Every earthly life is yielded to something or to many things. Life is time and time cannot be kept. Indeed, this yielding of life to some cause, whether sublime or trivial, godly or devilish, is unfailingly absolute and final. Death sees to that.

In the prayer of self-dedication the one who prays yields his purpose, his will, his very life into the hands of God, to be used of Him. Here we find the one cure for all that worrisome, self-dividing life of compromise which saps our joy and wastes our power. Here is that losing of life by which life is found.

We cannot pray, "Thy kingdom come, Thy will be done," and mean it, without yielding our wills to His.

5. *Communion*

The culminating height of prayer is communion with God. Far above every gift God can bestow upon us is Himself. Above every love is He who is love and who first loved us, making possible all other love. God Himself is the object in prayers of communion, not only as the one addressed but also as the one desired, sought and enjoyed.

There are many kinds of communion. Most common and yet priceless in possession is the sense that He is near and that He cares for the person who is aware of His presence. From that kind of experience to the mystic's ecstasy which transports him out of his whole ordinary frame of association and leaves him enraptured with the love of God, there are many stages and variations.

It is often assumed that the raptures of mystical union with God are higher and more to be desired than any other experience of communion. Perhaps they are. Those who have enjoyed them say that there is nothing to be compared with them. Some of these witnesses have shown in life such convincing fruits of patience, wisdom and selfless love that their testimony is exceedingly impressive.

On the other hand, Jesus himself did not speak in terms of such rapture. In prayer he found peace in the midst of agony and illumination when the way seemed dark and uncertain. In prayer he found also a task which so overwhelmed him with its burden that it drove him into many days of temptation in the wilderness. In prayer he found the cross before him and also the strength to die upon it. Most of all, he found such a consciousness of the Father's presence and favor as made all his life radiant with the serene assurance of His love. Yet never, in our records, do we have a report of his talking about sweet raptures nor about being transported out of himself in ecstatic union with the Father.

Paul told of a man who had a wonderful experience of being "caught up into Paradise," and Paul was willing to rejoice with him. But as for himself he gloried only in his "weakness," the suffering and perils he had borne in obedience to God's will.[1] It would be a reckless judgment which would say, in the light of Paul's total life and ministry, that the man who reported having been transported to Paradise was closer to God than was the missionary campaigner who could tell of no such experience.

God apparently has different plans for various men. And so He equips us with diverse capacities, prepares us with dissimilar experiences and calls us to different tasks. He must intend that some should be the poets of prayer and so He fills them with that rapturous sense of intimate communion with Him of which they sing for the enchantment and encouragement of others. But this is not the vocation of all. We are all called to be members of one body, but not all are called to see in this life the most luminous visions of God. What is supremely important is not that we experience rapture or do not experience rapture, but that we do His will in love.

Historically, the more extreme forms of mystical communion have shown a marked tendency to encourage pantheistic ideas concerning the relation between God and man. This tendency has been most marked in Hindu practice and thought, but has been frequently observed also in Christendom. This inclination is a natural one. For when a life is given over to the quest for a closer and ever closer union with God, the final goal suggested is the closest union conceivable, which is complete identity. Moreover, after an ecstatic rapture of communion, the mystic returns to his human associations with an overwhelming urge to report the most wonderful of all experiences but finds himself unable adequately to describe it, because of its incomparable character. As he struggles to tell of the communion of spirit he has enjoyed, in which no spatial

[1] 2 Cor. 12:1-10.

distance intervened, no clash of purpose interfered and all his consciousness was filled with the glory of God, he may use terms of description which belong to complete identity, much as Paul in a very different sense was impelled to say, "For me to live is Christ." [2] Since to the mystic these experiences constitute the norm for the understanding of all life, he may be led on to assert that all men are always one with God, but that this identity is only occasionally perceived.

Any such views must be firmly rejected.[3] God is always the Other, however near.

But if our being is not included within His, then is our knowledge of Him always a knowledge by mediated inference? Do we only find, at times, some elements within our own consciousness which we interpret as signs of Him?

There is a middle course between assuming a point of monistic overlapping where the "I" and "Thou" are metaphysically identical, and assuming that we can never have more than an indirect acquaintance with God, mediated by inference from elements in our consciousness which are taken to be signs of Him. That middle course is simple and obvious, but may nevertheless be true. It is to say that although God and I are never at any point the same being, there is not any third being interposed between us. On occasion He makes us immediately aware of Him, not as we are aware of some part of ourselves, which bears witness of Him, but as we are directly conscious of Him, the Other immediately at hand. This consciousness of Him is not discursive knowledge. Later on, we may think of the *encounter* with Him, interpret *it* and so make of *it* a mediating datum by which to infer something *about* Him. Then we shall have some more or less true discursive knowledge about Him, a knowledge altogether dualistic in form. But the encounter itself, it is being contended, was not an encounter between the "I" and some part of itself or some abstract concept, but quite directly and simply an encounter with Him.

As all our powers are dependent upon His sustaining action, so if we are sometimes enabled to be as immediately aware of Him as ever of our own imaginings, while yet He is other than ourselves, that too is because He so empowers us. And though the perception be immediate for all who truly commune with Him—and immediacy cannot be more or less—yet the clarity of this vision and its purity from the diversion of awareness of other objects would be expected to vary greatly, as it does.

The likelihood of such communion and the clarity of our vision of God are heightened by purity of life and faithful devotion to Him. But in all probability they are dependent even more upon God's own will for us in our various vocations, of which none is higher and none a cause for boasting.

[2] Phil. 1:21.
[3] See ch. 15, above.

B. Some Problems Concerning Petitionary Prayer

1. Why Does Not God Always Answer Prayer?

Jesus said, "Ask, and it will be given you." [4] He compared God with human fathers who are responsive to their children's requests, and said,

If you, then, who are evil, know how to give good gifts to your children, how much more will your Father who is in heaven give good things to those who ask him? [5]

But, as everyone knows, we do frequently pray long and fervently, only to see our worst fears realized and our fondest hopes dashed to earth. Why?

The ways of God are not fully known to us. But all that has been defended in this work as our reasonable faith makes reply.

Sometimes our prayers are not answered because they are not prayers. They are not the reverent petitions of an often wayward creature to the holy Creator. They may be petulant demands or faithless complaints or attempts to use a prescribed formula of magic. But they lack the reverence, repentance and self-dedication which must accompany all true prayer to God.

On the other hand, they may be true prayers, and if they are we may be sure that they are answered with the good gifts promised by God's love. He knows more of what the good truly is than does any man. There may be suffering in it. There may be failure of our cherished and noble plans. There may be a cross in His gift to us. But, in a world where there is much of sin, He answers our prayers with the best of gifts to be given in the total situation before Him. It is not assured that we shall enjoy more of pleasure, longer life nor better health because we pray. Jesus experienced great hardship, short life and deepest agony of body, not in spite of prayer but because of it. Yet because of prayer he became also the Savior of men and the victor over death. [6] The cup which he prayed God to take from him was not removed but an eternal crown was added.

2. Why Should He Respond to Our Petitions?

If God knows better than we what is best in the total situation, and if He will do what is best in any case—as He must if He is the good Father—then why should He ever change His course in any way because of our prayers? Is He to turn sometimes from the best that is known to Him in order to give the second-best which is the highest we know, just because we ask it? Surely not. But if not, then why should we ever offer prayers of petition?

[4] Mt. 7:7. Cf. Jn. 14:13.
[5] Mt. 7:11.   [6] Cf. Heb. 5:7-10.

These questions, which seem so stunningly decisive to many, presuppose an idea which is surely false and without it fall of their own weight. That idea is the notion that the best for a specific time and place is a fixed quantity, altogether independent of attending circumstances. It is the assumption that the best food for the diabetic patient is the best for the healthy toiler. It is the assumption that the best book for the kindergartner is best for the college graduate. Shall we suppose that what is best for all in a situation where no one prays is always best also when someone does pray?

3. How Can He Answer in a World of Law?

The sciences have taught us to look upon our world as a realm of regular, predictable sequence, where everything happens according to an established, permanent order—in short a world of causal law. When we present our petitions to God, are we asking Him to set aside the laws of the universe while He answers our prayers?

Even if causal law were the rigid, confining machine which the questions assume, we should still have to offer prayers of petition in order to pray at all. For we do sometimes have desires which possess our very souls. Not to present them to God would be not to go before Him in truth, as we are, and not to subject our purposes to the purification of His presence.

But actually we have found earlier that such a conception of a God confined and helpless in His own world is quite unreasonable. Even we creatures are able to exert our wills in the world and make some things different. Surely God is not more helpless than we! [7]

4. Does Intercessory Prayer Ever Affect Another?

Granting that God can and does do for me after I pray what He would not have believed best for me while I refrained from prayer, does my petition ever affect His treatment of another person? Shall I believe in and practice intercessory prayer? Will He not treat each man according to his own individual need?

If I share in the faith of Christ I am bound to pray for other persons, however I may think about the doctrinal basis of such prayer. I will pray for them because I love them with the love which was in Christ and which is particularly renewed in me as I come before God's throne. I cannot pray as a member of the body of Christ *without* praying for my brother.

When I think it cannot affect my brother, is that not because I am again victim of that individualistic way of viewing life which we have seen so contrary to experience and to the Biblical conceptions of man? God sees us as

---

[7] See also above, ch. 16, A.

deeply interdependent with our fellows and His supreme purpose is that we shall be drawn into the kingdom in which all of us know that we are "members one of another." [8] Do I not, then, advance His purpose for me and also for my brother when I pray for the brother? Is not the best possible for both of us, as presented before God here and now, heightened as one of us intercedes for the other? The ways and means He employs I cannot predict, but I know that it is He whose love impels me to offer intercessory prayer. His love will not let it fall back in vain.[9]

C. How God Speaks

A young boy of seven, closing his evening prayer and still on his knees, looked up to his father and said earnestly, "Why doesn't God ever talk to me? I talk to Him every night. But He never says anything to me." This eager, wistful protest has been made by many people, not all of them children, who have rightly expected prayer to be a conversation and not a monologue. God does speak, not only in answer to our prayer, but rather before we think of saying anything to Him.

He speaks in creation.

> The heavens are telling the glory of God;
> and the firmament proclaims his handiwork.
> Day to day pours forth speech,
> and night to night declares knowledge.[10]

In all the beauty, orderliness, power, beneficence and mystery of the natural world He speaks to us of His love, orderly and steadfast purpose, and greatness far exceeding all our powers of imagination.

He speaks in the voice of conscience. The secret warning and the warm approval within the heart, though often muffled by our willful desires, distorted by minds badly trained, and heard confusedly among the clamorings of the world, nevertheless are His beneficent, guiding words given for our assistance.

He speaks in the events of our personal lives in which we are able to see the workings of His providential care. Sometimes in answer to our prayer, sometimes when we have forgotten to pray, He has led us in ways we neither planned nor deserved but for which we ought to give thanks.

---

[8] Eph. 4:25.

[9] See also Edwyn Bevan's thoughtful essay, "Petition: Some Theoretical Difficulties," in Harold Anson, et al., Concerning Prayer. The whole collection of essays constitutes a valuable resource. Cf. the helpful discussion of these problems by Karl Barth in his little book, Prayer according to the Catechisms of the Reformation.

[10] Ps. 19:1–2. Cf. Rom. 1:20.

He speaks by the lives of other persons devoted to Him and serving as channels of His grace. Who is there reading the words of this book who cannot say that God came to him in the person of a parent, minister, teacher or friend—indeed in several or in many—to lead him upward?

He speaks in the midst of prayer His word of comforting presence, guiding light or sustaining love. Sometimes He speaks to us first in these ways and sends us to our knees before Him. Often He speaks so quietly and serenely that it all seems quite natural and not at all strange. At other times He comes with such unexpected rebuke or in such radiant light that, even though we were seeking Him in prayer and expecting Him, His coming is all surprise and novelty, like the first sight into the Grand Canyon by a tourist who thought himself well prepared, or the splitting of a giant pine by lightning, right beside the road, when many signs have announced that a thunderstorm was near. God is full of surprises. We cannot chart His coming nor secure an advance copy of the word He will address to us.

He speaks also in the historic community of the Word. Indeed, this is the sustained and normative speech which He addresses to us. It is in relation to the testimony and the thought and the ongoing community of the Spirit declared by the prophets and founded by Jesus Christ that we must test the other voices to see if they be of God. For He does not speak to us as individuals alone. He speaks to us most of all together, "where two or three are gathered" in the spirit of Jesus Christ.[11]

This is the answer to those who sometimes point to Jesus' words about praying in secret and not "at the street corners" to "be seen by men," [12] as proof that we should not meet for public prayer. To be sure, we are not to pray in order to be seen and praised by men. Indeed, we could not possibly do so, for any words spoken with such a motive would not be prayer. But we must pray together with others, in family, church and other groups, in order that we may teach our children and youth to pray by "good example," and also in order that we may be heard together and our hearts knit together in the sacred bonds which only God can fashion in His presence. For this is His will for us. Only thus can we learn to say "*Our* Father" both in prayer and by all of our common life together.

[11] Mt. 18:20.
[12] Mt. 6:5–6.

CHAPTER 43

Knowledge, Mystery and Faith

WE began this study with the observation that in all reasoning there is some ground for doubt and hence the necessity of faith in order to live—or die. It is fitting that we should close by observing again the human limitations of our knowledge.

There is reasonable ground for committing ourselves wholly in belief and service to God the Father of our Lord Jesus Christ. This commitment is Christian faith. When we have made it we then begin to be given other evidences confirming our faith, but also correcting and maturing it.

It is right that we should seek to learn the answers to a host of other questions. Some have important relevance to the practical decisions we must make as we try to live our faith in the contemporary changing world. Others are of less importance for present practice but do confront the man who seeks seriously to love God with all the mind.

Yet when we have learned all that God's revealing purpose and our wandering minds permit us to know for the present, an ocean of mystery still lies before us. In view of all the vast unknown and the uncertainty of much we think we know, dogmatic arrogance, intolerance and intellectual impatience are utter folly.

The student of theology, however wise he may be, can see very near at hand the limits of his knowledge. But his situation is much like that of a pilot flying a sky route that is new to him. Occasionally signals, sometimes very dim, sometimes clear and strong, encourage him to believe he is on course. But his vision is limited by the horizon which looms like a great wall around him.

If he is wise he will not mistake the horizon of his knowledge for the limits of his world. God and truth and human destiny are not bounded by the horizons of our ignorance. Yet by faith we can claim them all as the God-given heritage of our everlasting careers.

BIBLIOGRAPHY

of Some Representative Theological Literature

A. General

1. BIBLIOGRAPHIES

Princeton Theological Seminary Library, *A Bibliography of Systematic Theology for Theological Students*. Princeton, 1949.

Theologische Literaturzeitung. Leipzig: C. H. Hinrichs, 1876—. (Biweekly survey of theological books and articles in many languages.)

Die Theologische Literatur des Jahres, 1922—. Leipzig: C. H. Hinrichs, 1922—. (Annual listing with no reviews.)

2. WORKS OF REFERENCE

Ferm, Vergilius (ed.), *An Encyclopedia of Religion.* New York: The Philosophical Library, 1945.

Gunkel, Hermann, and Leopold Zscharnack, *Die Religion in Geschichte und Gegenwart.* 5 vols. and index. Tübingen: J. C. B. Mohr, 1927.

Hastings, James (ed.), *Encyclopedia of Religion and Ethics.* 12 vols. and index vol. New York: Charles Scribner's Sons, 1908.

Hebermann, Charles G., *et al.* (ed.), *The Catholic Encyclopedia.* 15 vols. and index vol. New York: Robert Appleton Co., c. 1907–12.

Schaff, Philip (ed.), *New Schaff-Herzog Encyclopedia of Religious Knowledge.* 12 vols. and index vol. New York: Funk, 1908–12. (Reprinted, Grand Rapids, Mich.: Baker Book House, 1949–50.)

3. JOURNALS (with publishing addresses)

The Ecumenical Review. World Council of Churches, Geneva, Switzerland. (American subscriptions received by World Council of Churches, 156 Fifth Ave., New York 10, N. Y.)

Esprit. 27, Rue Jacob, Paris, France.

Evangelische Theologie. Christian Kaiser, Munich, Germany.

Franciscan Studies. The Franciscan Institute, St. Bonaventure, N. Y.

Hibbert Journal. George Allen and Unwin Ltd., London, England (American subscriptions received by Leroy Phillips, 569 Boylston St., Boston 16, Mass.

The Journal of Religion. Uni. of Chicago Press, 5750 Ellis Ave., Chicago 37, Ill.

The London Quarterly and Holborn Review. The Epworth Press, 25–35 City Road, London, E. C. 1, England.

Religion in Life. 810 Broadway, Nashville 2, Tenn.

Scottish Journal of Theology. Tweeddale Court, Edinburgh 1, Scotland.

Theologische Rundschau. (Reviews only.) J. C. B. Mohr, Tübingen, Germany.

Theology Today. P.O. Box 29, Princeton, N. J.

The Thomist. The Thomist Press, 20 Hopkins Place, Baltimore 1, Md.

Zeitschrift für Systematische Theologie. A. Topelman, Berlin W 35.

Zeitschrift für Theologie und Kirche. J. C. B. Mohr, Tübingen, Germany.

4. Introductions to Theology for Laymen

Ferré, Nels F. S., *Pillars of Faith.* New York: Harper & Brothers, 1948.

Harkness, Georgia, *Understanding the Christian Faith.* New York and Nashville: Abingdon-Cokesbury Press, 1947.

Horton, Walter M., *Our Christian Faith.* Boston: The Pilgrim Press, 1945.

Kerr, Hugh Thomson, *A Manual of Faith and Life.* Philadelphia: Westminster Press.

5. Systematic Theologies

Althaus, Paul, *Die Christliche Wahrheit.* Gütersloh: Verlag Bertelsmann, 1949.

Aulén, Gustaf, *The Faith of the Christian Church.* Tr. by Eric H. Wahlstrom and G. Everett Arden from the 4th ed. Philadelphia: The Muhlenberg Press, c. 1948.

Barth, Karl, *Dogmatics in Outline.* London: Student Christian Movement Press, 1949.

——, *Die Kirchliche Dogmatik.* Multivolume work in process of writing and publication. Munich: Chr. Kaiser Verlag, 1932——. Vol. I tr. under title, *The Doctrine of the Word of God,* by G. T. Thomson. New York: Charles Scribner's Sons, 1936.

Berkhof, Louis, *Systematic Theology.* Grand Rapids, Mich.: Wm. B. Eerdmans Publishing Co., 1941.

Brunner, H. Emil, *The Theology of Crisis.* New York: Charles Scribner's Sons, 1929.

——, *Dogmatik.* Multivolume work in process of writing and publication. Zürich: Zwingli Verlag, 1946——. Vol. I tr. under title, *The Christian Doctrine of God,* by Olive Wyon. London: Lutterworth Press, 1949.

Church of England: Commission on Christian Doctrine, *Doctrine in the Church of England.* London: SPCK, 1938.

Farrell, Walter, *A Companion to the Summa.* 4 vols. London: Sheed and Ward, 1938–42.

Headlam, Arthur C., *Christian Theology.* London: Oxford University Press, 1934.

Knudson, Albert C., *The Doctrine of God* and *The Doctrine of Redemption.* New York and Nashville: Abingdon-Cokesbury Press, 1930 and 1933.

Rall, Harris Franklin, *Christianity: an Inquiry into Its Nature and Truth.* New York: Charles Scribner's Sons, 1940.

Tillich, Paul, *Systematic Theology.* Vol. I. Chicago: University of Chicago Press, 1951.

Wiley, H. Orton, *Christian Theology.* 3 vols. Kansas City, Mo.: Nazarene Publishing House, 1940–43.

6. HISTORY OF DOCTRINE

(1) GENERAL HISTORIES OF DOCTRINE

Fisher, George P., *History of Christian Doctrine.* New York: Charles Scribner's Sons, 1923.

Harnack, Adolf von, *History of Dogma.* 7 vols. Tr. from the German by N. Buchanan, *et al.* London: Williams and Norgate, 1894–99.

——, *Outlines of the History of Dogma.* Tr. by Edwin Knox Mitchell. New York: Funk and Wagnalls Co., 1893.

McGiffert, Arthur Cushman, *A History of Christian Thought.* New York: Charles Scribner's Sons, 1932–33.

Neve, J. L. and O. W. Heick, *A History of Christian Thought.* 2 vols. Philadelphia: The Muhlenberg Press, 1946.

(2) GENERAL INTRODUCTIONS TO RECENT THEOLOGY

Aubrey, Edwin E., *Present Theological Tendencies.* New York: Harper & Brothers, 1936.

Ferm, Vergilius, *Contemporary American Theology; Theological Autobiographies.* Series I and II. New York: Round Table Press, 1932, 1933.

Horton, Walter Marshall, *Contemporary Continental Theology; an Interpretation for Anglo-Saxons.* New York: Harper & Brothers, 1938.

Kepler, Thomas S. (compiler), *Contemporary Religious Thought, an Anthology.* New York and Nashville: Abingdon-Cokesbury Press, c. 1941.

Mackintosh, Hugh Ross, *Types of Modern Theology; Schleiermacher to Barth.* New York: Charles Scribner's Sons, 1937.

(3) SOME THEOLOGICAL CLASSICS (TO 1900)

The Shepherd of Hermas (c. 100).

Ignatius, *Letters* (c. 115).

The Didache (c. 150).

Justin, *Apologies* (c. 150).

Irenaeus, *Against Heresies* (c. 180).

Tertullian, *Apology* (197).

Clement of Alexandria, *The Instructor* (c. 200).

Origen, *Against Celsus* (c. 248); *On First Principles.*

Augustine, *On Free Will* (395); *Confessions* (397); *On the Trinity* (397); *On Nature and Grace; The City of God* (426); *Retractations* (428).

John of Damascus, *The Orthodox Faith* (c. 740).

Anselm, *Monologium*; *Proslogium*; *Cur Deus Homo* (1098).

Peter Abelard, *Sic et Non* (1122–23).

Peter Lombard, *Four Books of Sentences* (1145–52).

Thomas Aquinas, *Summa Contra Gentiles* (c. 1260); *Summa Theologica* (1256–72); *Compendium of Theology* (1273).

Martin Luther, *On Christian Liberty* (1520).

Melanchthon, *Augsburg Confession* (1530).

John Calvin, *Institutes of the Christian Religion* (1535–59).

Jacobus Arminius, *Declaration of Sentiments* (1608).

The Westminster Confession (1647).

Robert Barclay, *Apology for the True Christian Divinity* (1676).

Joseph Butler, *The Analogy of Religion to the Constitution and Course of Nature* (1736).

Jonathan Edwards, *Freedom of the Will* (1754).

John Wesley, *A Plain Account of Christian Perfection* (1777).

William Ellery Channing, *The Evidences of Revealed Religion* (1821).

Friedrich Schleiermacher, *The Christian Faith* (1821, 1830).

Albrecht Ritschl, *Justification and Reconciliation* (1870–88).

Adolf von Harnack, *What Is Christianity?* (1900).

7. BIBLICAL THEOLOGIES

Bultmann, Rudolf, *Theology of the New Testament.* Vol. I. Tr. by Kendrick Grobel. New York: Charles Scribner's Sons, 1951.

Burrows, Millar, *An Outline of Biblical Theology.* Philadelphia: Westminster Press, 1946.

Davidson, Andrew Bruce, *The Theology of the Old Testament.* New York: Charles Scribner's Sons, 1904.

Knudson, Albert C., *The Religious Teaching of the Old Testament.* New York: Abingdon Press, c. 1918.

Minear, Paul S., *The Kingdom and the Power.* Philadelphia: Westminster Press, 1950.

Scott, Ernest F., *The Varieties of New Testament Religion.* New York: Charles Scribner's Sons, 1943.

Sheldon, Henry C., *New Testament Theology.* New York: The Macmillan Co., 1911.

B. On Particular Subjects

(*Arranged according to the Six Parts of This Book*)

1. PRESUPPOSITIONS OF CHRISTIAN THEOLOGY

(1) REASON, REVELATION AND FAITH

Baillie, John, *Our Knowledge of God.* New York: Charles Scribner's Sons, 1939.

Barth, Karl, *The Doctrine of the Word of God.* Tr. by G. T. Thomson. Edinburgh: T. and T. Clark, 1936.

Brunner, H. Emil, *Revelation and Reason*. Tr. by Olive Wyon. Philadelphia: Westminster Press, 1946.

Buber, Martin, *Two Types of Faith*. London: Routledge and Kegan Paul Ltd., 1951.

Cotton, James Harry, *Christian Knowledge of God*. New York: The Macmillan Co., 1951.

DeWolf, L. Harold, *The Religious Revolt against Reason*. New York: Harper & Brothers, 1949.

Ferré, Nels F. S., *Faith and Reason*. New York: Harper & Brothers, 1946.

Gilson, Etienne, *God and Philosophy*. New Haven: Yale University Press, 1941.

Hazelton, Roger, *On Proving God*. New York: Harper & Brothers, 1952.

———, *Renewing the Mind*. New York: The Macmillan Co., 1949.

Hodgson, Leonard, *Towards a Christian Philosophy*. London: Nisbet and Co., 1943.

Macintosh, Douglas C., *The Problem of Religious Knowledge*. New York: Harper & Brothers, c. 1940.

Niebuhr, H. Richard, *The Meaning of Revelation*. New York: The Macmillan Co., 1941.

Ramsdell, Edward T., *The Christian Perspective*. New York and Nashville: Abingdon-Cokesbury Press, 1950.

(2) PHILOSOPHICAL THEISM

Bertocci, Peter A., *The Empirical Argument for God in Late British Thought*. Cambridge: Harvard University Press, 1938.

Brightman, Edgar S., *A Philosophy of Religion*. New York: Prentice-Hall, 1940.

Hocking, William Ernest, *The Meaning of God in Human Experience*. New Haven: Yale University Press, 1912.

Seth Pringle-Pattison, Andrew, *The Idea of God in the Light of Recent Philosophy*. 2nd ed. rev. New York: Oxford University Press, 1920.

Sorley, William R., *Moral Values and the Idea of God*. New York: The Macmillan Co., 1924.

Taylor, Alfred E., *The Faith of a Moralist*. London: Macmillan and Co., 1930.

Tennant, Frederick R., *Philosophical Theology*. Cambridge (Eng.): The University Press, 1928–30.

Whitehead, Alfred North, *Process and Reality*. New York: The Macmillan Co., 1929.

Wieman, Henry Nelson, *The Source of Human Good*. Chicago: University of Chicago Press, 1946.

2. THE BIBLE

Carnell, Edward J., *An Introduction to Christian Apologetics*. Grand Rapids: W. B. Eerdmans Publishing Co., 1948.

Dodd, Charles H., *The Authority of the Bible*. New York: Harper & Brothers, 1929.

Knox, John, *Criticism and Faith*. New York and Nashville: Abingdon-Cokesbury Press, 1952.

Richardson, Alan, and Wolfgang Schweitzer (eds.), *Biblical Authority for Today*. London: Student Christian Movement Press, 1951.

Warfield, Benjamin B., *The Inspiration and Authority of the Bible*. Introduction by Cornelius Van Til. Philadelphia: Presbyterian and Reformed Publishing Co., 1948. (A new edition of an old book.)

3. GOD AND THE WORLD (see also above, "Philosophical Theism")

Bett, Henry, *The Reality of the Religious Life; a Study of Miracle, Providence and Prayer*. New York: The Macmillan Co., 1949.

Brightman, Edgar S., *The Problem of God*. New York: The Abingdon Press, c. 1930.

D'Arcy, Martin C., *The Pain of This World and the Providence of God*. London: Longmans Green and Co., 1935.

Ferré, Nels F. S., *The Christian Understanding of God*. New York: Harper & Brothers, 1951.

———, *Evil and the Christian Faith*. New York: Harper & Brothers, 1947.

Jones, E. Stanley, *Christ and Human Suffering*. New York: Abingdon Press, 1933.

Knudson, Albert C., *The Doctrine of God*. New York: Abingdon Press, 1930.

Lewis, Clive S., *Problem of Pain*. London: Centenary Press, 1940.

Lewis, Edwin, *The Creator and the Adversary*. New York and Nashville: Abingdon-Cokesbury Press, 1948.

Robinson, Henry M., *Suffering, Human and Divine*. New York: The Macmillan Co., 1939.

Tsanoff, Radoslav A., *The Nature of Evil*. New York: The Macmillan Co., 1931.

Weatherhead, Leslie D., *Why Do Men Suffer?* New York: Abingdon Press, 1936.

4. MAN

Baillie, John, *And the Life Everlasting*. New York: Charles Scribner's Sons, 1933.

Barth, Karl, *The Resurrection of the Dead*. Tr. by H. J. Stenning. London: Hodder and Stoughton, 1933.

Berdiaev, Nikolai A., *The Destiny of Man*. Tr. by Natalie Duddington. London: The Centenary Press, 1945.

Bergson, Henri, *Time and Free Will*. New York: The Macmillan Co., 1913.

Brunner, H. Emil, *Man in Revolt; a Christian Anthropology*. Tr. by Olive Wyon. London: Lutterworth Press, 1939.

Hocking, William Ernest, *Human Nature and Its Remaking*. New Haven: Yale University Press, 1923.

Holmes, John Haynes, *The Affirmation of Immortality*. New York: The Macmillan Co., 1947.

Knudson, Albert C., *The Principles of Christian Ethics*. New York and Nashville: Abingdon-Cokesbury Press, 1943.

Lewis, Hywel David, *Morals and the New Theology*. New York: Harper & Brothers, 1948.

———, *Morals and Revelation*. London: Allen and Unwin, 1951.

Machen, J. Gresham, *The Christian View of Man*. New York: The Macmillan Co., 1937.

Niebuhr, Reinhold, *The Nature and Destiny of Man*. 2 vols. New York: Charles Scribner's Sons, 1941, 1943.

Robinson, Henry Wheeler, *The Christian Doctrine of Man*. Edinburgh: T. and T. Clark, 1911.

Rowley, H. H., *The Biblical Doctrine of Election*. London: Lutterworth Press, 1950.

Streeter, B. H., *et al. Immortality; an Essay in Discovery, Co-ordinating Scientific, and Biblical Research*. New York: The Macmillan Co., 1917.

5. CHRIST AND RECONCILIATION

Adam, Karl, *The Son of God*. Tr. by Phillip Hereford. London: Sheed and Ward, 1934.

Aulén, Gustaf, *Christus Victor*. Tr. by A. G. Hebert. London: S.P.C.K., 1931.

Baillie, Donald M., *God Was in Christ*. New York: Charles Scribner's Sons, 1948.

Brunner, H. Emil, *The Mediator*. Tr. by Olive Wyon. London: Lutterworth Press, 1934.

Cadbury, Henry J., *The Peril of Modernizing Jesus*. New York: The Macmillan Co., 1937.

Case, Shirley Jackson, *Jesus through the Centuries*. Chicago: University of Chicago Press, 1932.

Dillistone, Frederick W., *The Holy Spirit in the Life of Today*. Philadelphia: Westminster Press, 1947.

Forsyth, Peter T., *The Work of Christ*. London: Hodder and Stoughton, 1910. Reprinted, London: Independent Press, 1946.

Gore, Charles, *Belief in Christ*. London: J. Murray, 1922.

Hodgson, Leonard, *Doctrine of the Trinity*. London: James Nisbet and Co., Ltd., 1943.

Mackintosh, Hugh R., *The Doctrine of the Person of Christ*. New York: Charles Scribner's Sons, 1916.

Paterson, William P., *Conversion*. New York: Charles Scribner's Sons, 1940.

Pittenger, William Norman, *Christ and the Christian Faith*. New York: Round Table Press, 1941.

Rawlinson, Alfred E., *The New Testament Doctrine of the Christ*. New York: Longmans, Green & Co., 1949.

Schweitzer, Albert, *The Quest of the Historical Jesus, a Critical Study of Its Progress from Reimarus to Wrede*. Tr. by W. Montgomery. London: A. and C. Black, 1910.

Scott, Ernest F., *The Spirit in the New Testament*. London: Hodder and Stoughton, 1923.

Streeter, B. H. (ed.), *The Spirit; the Relation of God and Man, Considered from the Standpoint of Recent Philosophy and Science*. New York: The Macmillan Co., 1919.

Taylor, Vincent, *The Atonement in New Testament Teaching*. London: Epworth Press, 1940.

6. The Kingdom and the Church

(1) LOVE AND THE KINGDOM OF GOD

Johnson, Paul E., *Christian Love*. New York and Nashville: Abingdon-Cokesbury Press, 1951.

Manson, William, *Christ's View of the Kingdom of God*. London: James Clarke and Co., 1918.

Moffatt, James, *Love in the New Testament*. New York: Harper & Brothers, 1930.

Niebuhr, Reinhold, *An Interpretation of Christian Ethics*. New York: Harper & Brothers, 1935.

Nygren, Anders, *Agape and Eros; a Study of the Christian Idea of Love*. Tr. by A. G. Hebert. 3 vols. New York: The Macmillan Co., 1932–38.

Ramsey, Paul, *Basic Christian Ethics*. New York: Charles Scribner's Sons, 1950.

Schweitzer, Albert, *The Mystery of the Kingdom of God; the Secret of Jesus' Messiahship and Passion*. Tr. by Walter Lowrie. New York: Dodd, Mead and Co., 1914.

Wilder, Amos N., *Eschatology and Ethics in the Teaching of Jesus*. New York: Harper & Brothers, 1939.

(2) THE CHURCH AND THE SACRAMENTS

Clow, W. M., *The Church and the Sacraments*. London: James Clarke and Co., 1923.

Cullmann, Oscar, *Baptism in the New Testament*. London: Student Christian Movement Press, 1952.

Ferré, Nels F. S., *Christian Fellowship*. New York: Harper & Brothers, 1940.

Flew, Robert Newton, *Jesus and His Church*. London: Epworth Press, 1938.

Kerr, Hugh Thomson, *The Christian Sacraments. A Source Book for Ministers*. Philadelphia: The Westminster Press, 1944.

Kirk, Kenneth E. (ed.), *Apostolic Ministry; Essays on the History and the Doctrine of Episcopacy*. London: Hodder and Stoughton, 1946.

Lilley, A. L., *Sacraments*. New York: The Macmillan Co., 1929.

Niebuhr, H. Richard, *The Kingdom of God in America*. New York: Harper & Brothers, 1937.

———, *The Social Sources of Denominationalism*. New York: Henry Holt and Co., c. 1929.

Pittenger, W. Norman, *His Body the Church*. New York: Morehouse-Gorman Co., 1945.

Streeter, B. H., *The Primitive Church, Studied with Special Reference to the Origins of the Christian Ministry*. New York: The Macmillan Co., 1929.

Tillich, Paul, *The Protestant Era*. Chicago: University of Chicago Press, 1948.

(3) PRAYER

Anson, Harold, *et al.*, *Concerning Prayer. Its Nature, Its Difficulties and Its Value*. London: Macmillan and Co., 1917.

Barth, Karl, *Prayer according to the Catechisms of the Reformation*. Tr. by Sarah F. Terrien. Philadelphia: Westminster Press, 1952.

Buttrick, George A., *Prayer*. New York and Nashville: Abingdon-Cokesbury Press, 1942.

Harkness, Georgia, *Prayer and the Common Life*. New York and Nashville: Abingdon-Cokesbury Press, 1948.

Heiler, Friedrich, *Prayer. A Study in the History and Psychology of Religion*. New York: Oxford University Press, 1932.

Hügel, Friedrich von, *The Mystical Element in Religion as Studied in Saint Catherine of Genoa and Her Friends*. New York: E. P. Dutton and Co., 1923.

Kepler, Thomas S. (compiler), *The Fellowship of Saints. An Anthology of Christian Devotional Literature*. New York and Nashville: Abingdon-Cokesbury Press, 1948.

Poulain, Augustin F., *The Graces of Interior Prayer. A Treatise on Mystical Theology*. London: Routledge and Kegan Paul, Ltd., 1951.

Steere, Douglas V., *On Beginning from Within*. New York: Harper & Brothers, 1943.

INDEX OF NAMES AND SUBJECTS

[*See also Table of Contents, Bibliography and Index of Biblical Passages.*]

INDEX OF BIBLICAL PASSAGES

[Prepared by Dean Hosken and Wilhelm Linss]

Set in Linotype Granjon
Format by Edwin H. Kaplin
Manufactured by The Haddon Craftsmen, Inc.
Published by HARPER & BROTHERS, *New York*